# ★ SOLDIER BOY ★

Letters and History
of an Illinois Union Soldier
Who Left His Family and Farm
and Fought in Sherman's Destructive
Army from Tennessee through
Atlanta to the Carolinas

*Betty E. More*

HERITAGE BOOKS
2012

# HERITAGE BOOKS
*AN IMPRINT OF HERITAGE BOOKS, INC.*

Books, CDs, and more—Worldwide

For our listing of thousands of titles see our website
at
www.HeritageBooks.com

Published 2012 by
HERITAGE BOOKS, INC.
Publishing Division
100 Railroad Ave. #104
Westminster, Maryland 21157

Copyright © 2000 Betty E. More

All rights reserved. No part of this book may be reproduced or transmitted in any form or by any means, electronic or mechanical, including photocopying, recording or by any information storage and retrieval system without written permission from the author, except for the inclusion of brief quotations in a review.

International Standard Book Numbers
Paperbound: 978-0-7884-1551-7
Clothbound: 978-0-7884-9465-9

SOLDIER BOY

# SOLDIER BOY

Letters and history of an
Illinois Union soldier
who left his family and farm
and fought in
Sherman's destructive army
from Tennessee through Atlanta
to the Carolinas

Betty E. More

Includes letters written by:

Eugene McBride Swaggart
Henry Holt
Henry Lego
Elvira Van Alstine/Swaggart
Amanda Ludisky Van Alstine/Swaggart
Jennie Van Alstine
Anna Swaggart
Mary Ann Miller
S. Whitman Dodge
Maria Van Alstine
Mary Crosit

IN MEMORY OF

Nellie Eugenia Swaggart Briggs
my Grandmother
who was born during the war


LeOla Äline Briggs Meredith
my Mother
who knew them when she was a child


John Lee Meredith, Jr.
my Brother
who wanted to see this written

## TABLE OF CONTENTS

| | | |
|---|---|---|
| Illustrations | | ix |
| Acknowledgments | | xiii |
| Preface | | xv |
| Chapter One | At Home In Salem | 1 |
| Chapter Two | Camp Fuller | 25 |
| Chapter Three | Through the Holidays in 1862 | 39 |
| Chapter Four | Guarding Kentucky | 69 |
| Chapter Five | En Route to Tennessee | 93 |
| Chapter Six | In Camp at Nashville | 101 |
| Chapter Seven | Franklin, Tennessee | 119 |
| Chapter Eight | The Hospitals, Triune & Nashville | 155 |
| Chapter Nine | The Crossing | 173 |
| Chapter Ten | On to Chickamauga | 183 |
| Chapter Eleven | Guarding the River & the Railroad | 195 |
| Chapter Twelve | Operations in North Alabama | 211 |
| Chapter Thirteen | Georgia - Skirmishing & Picketing | 229 |
| Chapter Fourteen | On To Atlanta | 255 |

| | | |
|---|---|---|
| Chapter Fifteen | Atlanta is Ours | 281 |
| Chapter Sixteen | In Pursuit of Hood | 293 |
| Chapter Seventeen | March to the Sea - Savannah | 303 |
| Chapter Eighteen | The Carolina Mud March | 317 |
| Chapter Nineteen | The War Is Over | 331 |
| Bibliography | | 347 |
| Glossary | | 351 |
| Index of People | | 367 |
| Index | | 387 |

Family history of some people mentioned in the book   a-h
(following Index)

# ILLUSTRATIONS

| | |
|---|---|
| Flag logo of 92$^{nd}$ Illinois Volunteers | Cover |
| Eugene McBride Swaggart - Soldier | i |
| George Swaggart & Sarah Whiteside/Swaggart | 1 |
| Eugene McBride Swaggart - Young man | 3 |
| Marriage License of Eugene McBride Swaggart & Elvira Van Alstine | 10 |
| Letter dated 2/28/62 to Eugene Swaggart from Henry Holt - written at Fort Donelson, Tennessee | 11 |
| Lincoln Stationary Letterhead | 18 |
| Washington Stationery Letterhead | 24 |
| Elvira Van Alstine Swaggart & Jennie Van Alstine | 27 |
| Envelope depicting Fort Sumter | 38 |
| Anna Swaggart | 57 |
| Letter dated 12/20/1862 to Anna Swaggart from Eugene Swaggart - written at Danville, Kentucky | 59 |
| Elvira Van Alstine Swaggart | 67 |
| Letter dated 1/12/63 to Eugene Swaggart from Henry Lego - written at Murfreesboro, Tennessee | 78 |
| Envelope depicting the American Flag | 91 |

Letter dated 2/5/63 to Elvira from Eugene Swaggart - written at Fort Donelson, Tennessee    96

Preamble and Resolutions of General Baird's Division    114

Envelope depicting Star Spangled Banner    118

Letter dated 4/16/63 to Elvira from Eugene Swaggart - written at Franklin, Tennessee    134

American Express Company Receipt dated 5/4/63    137

A Rainy Day In Camp booklet cover    158

Letter dated 8/28/63 to Elvira from Eugene Swaggart - written at Chattanooga, Tennessee    180

Letter dated 10/22/63 to Elvira from Eugene Swaggart - written at Brownsboro, Alabama    197

Letter dated 12/25/63 to Elvira from Eugene Swaggart - written at Huntsville, Alabama    208

Charles W. Reynolds    234

Letter dated 5/1/64 to Jennie Swaggart from Eugene Swaggart - written at Ringgold, Georgia    236

Letter dated 5/15/64 to Elvira from Eugene Swaggart - written on the battlefield, South Dalton    243

Letter dated 5/26/64 to Elvira from Eugene Swaggart - written at Adairsville, Georgia    249

Letter dated 6/10/64 to Elvira from Eugene Swaggart - written at Kingston, Georgia    258

Letter dated 6/15/64 to Elvira from Eugene Swaggart
   - written at Kingston, Georgia                          262

Letter dated 9/12/64 to Elvira from Eugene Swaggart
   - written just after the siege of Atlanta             289

Letter dated 1/20/65 to Elvira from Eugene Swaggart
   - written at Savannah, Georgia                        313

Letter dated 4/22/65 to Elvira from Eugene Swaggart
   - written at Chapel Hill, North Carolina            329

Discharge papers of Eugene M. Swaggart         341

# ACKNOWLEDGMENTS

THANK YOUS are due to several people who helped me find material for the book.

Alvin Dixon Stokes, an avid supporter of the South, filled his suitcase with material every time he traveled down to the Republic of Panama. His interest and enthusiasm inspired me to keep going when I felt the task of researching material for this book was insurmountable from a pueblo in the interior of Panama where there are no libraries.

In Carroll County, there were several who helped me in various ways. Arthur Robbe mailed the booklet for the *Rededication Ceremony of the Carroll County Civil War Soldiers and Sailors Monument* that he and Richard Hinton compiled from information found in local records. It brought the young men mentioned in the letters to life for me. Kathy Bruner and the Savannah Library staff helped me immensely in locating background material using the *History of Carroll County*. A young lady at the Carrollton Inn drew wonderful maps showing me the way to the cemetery on State Street and Salem township and the local caretaker of the cemetery spent over an hour helping me to locate the graves of George and Sarah Swaggart.

Dr. Frank J. Welcher sent me the *Records of Events* from the *Illinois (Union) Troops, $92^{nd}$ Illinois Infantry* and a very encouraging letter. His books *The Union Army, Volume I & II*, were always right beside me when I needed to look up a point.

My brother, Jack, who was in the last months of his life fighting his own losing battle to cancer, spent as much time as he could on the computer looking up various points for me and emailing them to me along with words of encouragement.

Some of the Van Alstine family background came from Van Alstine Family History written by Lester Van Alstine and sent to me by his daughter, Beverly Seitz, from Salem, Wisconsin.

A great stroke of luck came when I found Lucille Bigelow, a distant cousin who is the great granddaughter of Nelson Swaggart, a half brother of Eugene McBride Swaggart. She sent information she had compiled and the address of Tom Swaggart in California, great grandson of Moses who put me in touch with Lynda and Richard Swaggart in Oklahoma. Richard Swaggart is also a great grandson of Moses, brother of Eugene McBride Swaggart. Input from all of us, information we had individually and photos with identifications helped us all to identify the members of the family.

Lucille also encouraged me to write to William R. Whiteside who along with William Boulineau and Dr. Larry Griffin, gave me a complete understanding of the Whiteside family.

Online, I found Jerry Harris who had compiled a lot of information concerning the Dodge family. He gave me a good identification of the family who were discussed in the letter of 1853 from Kenosha, Wisconsin.

Last of all, but not least, I want to thank my husband who took over my other tasks when I needed to work and my sons and their families who gave me a workspace in their homes when I visited the states.

## Preface

In my childhood days, my grandmother, Nellie Eugenia Swaggart/Briggs lived with our family. I was younger than my brother by nine plus years and I spent a lot of afternoons and summers with her alone. While she sewed and made beautiful rugs and bedspreads, she told me stories. Many were about her childhood, and her parents, one who was of German/Irish descent and one who was Dutch/English. She spoke a little German herself, a few words, that she learned from her mother and father who spoke German and Dutch occasionally to the older family members. However, the primary language in her family was English.

While going through the contents of my great-grandfather's home years after the death of a family member, many letters were discovered that covered a period from 1858 to 1930. In one box was a pack of letters written during the Civil War, as well as other items such as a comb, a razor and strap, a belt, insignia of the Civil War, handmade tools, and a newspaper with the article about Lincoln's assassination.

As years passed, memories of the stories told about the family began to surface, especially when I read the letters several times. At the time I heard the stories, I lived in Texas, surrounded by members of my father's family. They were a weekly part of my life. Some of my mother's family lived in the same state, but we did not see them as often. My father's family was southern in the strictest sense. My great-grandfather, Lewis Poe Jones, fought for the South along with his brothers and cousins. I grew up in the light of the Confederate cause and always thought of myself as an avid supporter, although I really do not know why. I never did understand why one person would want to own another. However, many members of my father's family did own slaves in the South, but as far as I know, Lewis Poe Jones' family did not. They moved to Texas from Tennessee and I have never seen proof that they owned slaves, yet he and two of his brothers fought avidly for the South.

It was stated often in our immediate family that if Lewis Poe Jones had known his grandson married a girl whose grandfather fought for the North, he would have never spoken to him again. Since Lewis Poe Jones died six years prior to the marriage of my father and mother, the issue never surfaced. To my knowledge, not too many in my father's family were aware that my mother had a Union soldier as a grandfather because Mother was born in Palestine, Texas and grew up in Oklahoma and Texas.

Out of curiosity, I began to research both of my great-grandfathers and found a lot of similarities. Both were farm boys known to be good horsemen and good shots, as many farm boys were in those years. Lewis Poe Jones served with the $10^{th}$ Texas Cavalry, Company I, in General John B. Hood's Army. They dismounted later in the war. Eugene McBride Swaggart served with the $92^{nd}$ Illinois Infantry, Company I, that became the $92^{nd}$ Illinois Mounted Infantry, Company I. He served in the armies of General Absolom Baird, General Gordon Granger and General William Tecumseh Sherman riding with the cavalries of Colonel John T. Wilder of Indiana and General Judson Kilpatrick. Eugene McBride Swaggart was twenty years of age when he joined up and Louis Poe Jones was twenty-one. Both served as privates, were educated in country schools, could read and write, loved to play the fiddle, came from families well known in their communities and their families owned several properties.

Eugene McBride Swaggart married before entering the service, but Lewis Poe Jones married after the war. Both suffered with illnesses during the war, but neither was wounded nor killed. Strangely enough, both suffered income losses due to the war, their properties and financial outlook diminished, but recovered in later years. It is a general assumption in the South that only southern families suffered from the war, but from the letters, it would appear that families in the North, whose husbands or sons fought in the war, also struggled to make ends meet as payrolls went unpaid for months at a time.

Eugene McBride Swaggart and Lewis Poe Jones fought against one another in several battles, including the battles of Chicamauga, Kenesaw Mountain, and Atlanta. It is possible they came face to face in combat during the war, perhaps near Jonesboro when the $92^{nd}$ circled Atlanta with General Kilpatrick and fought General Hood's army. We know Lewis Poe Jones was there as well as Eugene McBride Swaggart because of a story told about him returning under heavy fire to retrieve his hat as he was retreating south of Atlanta because "he would rather be dead, than without a hat in Georgia, in the summertime."

Soldier Boy contains compiled material from many sources including letters Eugene McBride Swaggart and his family members and friends wrote during the Civil War. As I read the letters and remembered stories I had heard as a child from my mother and grandmother, I began to develop a personality picture of him and his family that I interjected into the book. To the best of my knowledge and interpretation, the personality profiles are very close to factual.

All battles, skirmishes and other war information are from books listed in the bibliography and information concerning the $92^{nd}$ Illinois Infantry. I am not a historian and would not consider entering war material that was not from a historical source.

The title Soldier Boy was a choice made as I read the letters written by Eugene McBride Swaggart and others. A picture came to mind of a young man, who in reality must have been like many others, who went off to war because he felt it would be a wonderful thing—to wear a uniform, carry a gun and march in parades amidst cheers. Later, in the dirt, sickness, cold, and reality of war, he began to wonder why he was there.

Brothers fought against brothers and families against families. Young men fought against other young men so like themselves, except for geography. The officers received the glory, while the soldiers who fought beside them were only pawns in a game.

In the Civil War, disease, due to bad water and food, lack of supplies, and poor sanitation seemed to play a larger part in the condition and loss of soldiers than all of the skirmishes and battles. Many of the young men who fought for the North and the South were boys when they joined up. Those who lived came out as men, but many were bitter for the rest of their lives.

Eugene McBride Swaggart was a young soldier in age and experience when he left his family for the war. In the beginning, he was shocked at the destruction that went on in a war but as time passed, he hardened until he became one of General Judson Kilpatrick's "bummers" who picketed and foraged for the Army, burning and pillaging as they rode. Principals and eagerness to serve turned into skepticism.

This story is about Eugene McBride Swaggart because I had so much material to use concerning his life. Besides the letters seen in this publication, there were many more written until he died.

A lot has been written about the officers and what they thought about the war, but very little about the enlisted man. My intention in compiling and writing this book is to tell the stories of many soldiers mentioned in the letters and through them, to represent the lives of many young soldiers, in the North and the South, who fought in the Civil War. It is a tribute to them and to their families who lost so much and gained so little—the Soldier Boys.

## Chapter One
## At Home in Salem

Carroll County, located in the Northwest portion of Illinois, at one time included the communities of Mount Carroll, Salem, Rock Creek, Fair Haven, Savannah, Freedom, Cherry Grove, Arnold's Grove, Woodland, York, Lima, and Washington. It was a pretty place with prairie, rolling hills, and vast woods. Eugene McBride Swaggart was born in Carroll County, son of George Swaggart, one of the original settlers in the area.

Many of the settlers of Carroll County were soldiers who served during the Blackhawk Indian Wars and returned there following the war. George Swaggart, a veteran of the War of 1812[1] and the Blackhawk Indian Wars[2], moved to Cherry Grove just after the Blackhawk Indian Wars, as most of the early

George Swaggart

Sarah Whiteside Swaggart

---

[1] Index to War of 1812 Pension Application Files & Bounty Land - State Historical Library in Springfield, Illinois.
[2] Official rolls on file in the War Department, Washington, D. C. via Lucille Bigalow, great, great granddaughter of George Swaggart.

settlers did. His fourth wife, who died in 1834, was the first person buried in Cherry Grove where George ran a tavern.[3]

George took as his fifth wife, Sarah Whiteside[4] who had been previously married to John Miller and had one son also named John Miller.

In 1837, George Swaggart, along with David Christian, Samuel H. Hitt and Nathaniel Swingley, arranged to form a mill but never completed it. Purchased in 1841, it became the mill of Emmert, Halderman & Company. They sold the land and the rights for $3,000. [5]

Sometime between the years of 1837 and 1840, George Swaggart built an "extensive log home" in Salem Township, where several German families resided. In 1839, he was appointed a grand juror for the first court session of the county and his son, Nelson, a petit juror.[6]

George and Sarah had sons named Moses, born in 1838, Eugene McBride Swaggart, born on October 22, 1842, and a daughter, Anna M. Swaggart, born in 1845. John Miller, Sarah's son, lived with them as well as a handyman named William Eaton.[7]

Eugene McBride Swaggart was the fourth son of Sarah Whiteside Swaggart and the fourth known son of George Swaggart. The family and his friends called him Mack.

Eugene's childhood was one of a farm boy. He worked long hours on the farm and learned to ride and shoot at an early age, as most young men did who lived in that era. Hunting was necessary. The boys and George killed turkeys and quail for fresh meat and deer for curing. They also raised on the farm hogs and chickens for meat and cows for milk.

John Miller was older than Moses by four years and Eugene by eight and was usually in trouble with the family for his escapades. Moses was the dependable, steady one of the three.

---

[3] *History of Carroll County, Illinois,* Published by H. F. Kett & Co., Chicago, IL. 1878 and Unigraphic, Inc., Evansville, IN 1976., p. 251
[4] Information concerning Sarah Whiteside came from Lucille Bigelow, great granddaughter of Nelson Swaggart, and from William R. Whiteside.
[5] *The History of Carroll County,* pp. 163-164
[6] Ibid., pp. 236 & 719
[7] Census Records of 1850.

He had developed asthma and weak lungs as a young man. He worked hard, but tired quickly.

Eugene was the most adventuresome of the three.

Eugene McBride Swaggart

He had many companions including George Wait Downs, Henry Lego, Henry Holt, William Reynolds and Charles

Reynolds who he considered to be his good friends. Physically strong and intelligent, but restless and inquiring, he often did not agree with the others in the family. He farmed, but always said he wanted to be an engineer.

Anna was the youngest, the baby of the family and very spoiled.

On November 18, 1857, George Swaggart died[8] and a long lawsuit started over the disbursement of his property. It involved Nelson, his son by Elizabeth Brown, Sarah, his wife, and Moses, Eugene and Anna from his wife, Sarah. Nelson had previously left Carroll County and moved to Oregon with his wife, Mary Adeline and children, George, Ann, and Alice and mother-in-law, Louisiana (Higgins) Harper to follow his father-in-law, George Washington Harper because of his disagreement with the family.[9]

In the same era, a family moved into Kenosha, Wisconsin from New York whose family eventually became very important to the Swaggart family through double marriages.

Emaline Dodge Van Alstine lost her husband, Alonzo Van Alstine when he was only thirty-six years of age.[10] Emaline who was in poor health, had five living children to care for. Her parents, John and Sarah Serepto Dodge, lived in Kenosha, Wisconsin and Emaline hoped they could help her with the children. However, due to poor health and advanced age, they were not able to take care of Emaline and the children, so the family placed the children, except for the eldest, Maria, in other homes. Her mother kept Maria to help her until her demise.

In 1858, just after Emaline's death, Whitman Dodge wrote to his niece, Amanda Ludisky Van Alstine. Amanda was a teacher in Salem Township, Carroll County. She moved there at the age of seventeen in 1856 just after the Oakville School in the township of Salem, built by John Mackay in 1846, was replaced with a new brick schoolhouse. The school hired the best

---

[8] Death records of Carroll County

[9] Information concerning the lawsuit is Carroll County records and his disagreement with the family and move to Oregon was presented by his great-granddaughter, Lucille Bigelow.

[10] Lester Van Alstine, *Van Alstyne-Van Alstine Family History, Volume 3,* Publisher J. Grant Stevenson, Provo, Utah, pp. 250-251

teachers they could find. Among those was Amanda.[11] Amanda was engaged to Moses Swaggart when she received the letter.

*Kenosha, June 9th 1858*
  *Dear Niece*
*Hopeing you will receive the undersigned I venture to write. The years have elapsed, yet I recollect my little niece Ludisky. I am at sister Pamila's. Maria is sitting in the room with me and talking of your kind Mother, my dear sister, Emaline. My dear niece I only know you as the sweet little child that I left 18 years ago, but the fond recollection of you embraces the endearing ties of that loved one, your Mother, when I take a retrospective view of the past. I am filled with sadness and remorse that I have so long estranged myself from those I loved. Well, those years have flown and now, Ludisky, hope with me that ere long we may meet to enjoy the Society of each other, and too, with all our folks in Kenosha as I think of visiting this place often in future. And if you come, come here. I will visit you when that may be. I shall return to New York about the first of July. Try and come before I leave. Your Aunt Martha, my wife, is here with me. So is your Aunt Lizzie, Lyman's Wife. Do now come if you can as we canna call on you this time. I am going to see your Uncles Edward & Philaman, Leaur for dinner with John at 12 AM today. Will write you again soon.*
*I want you to write to me as soon as you get this. Tell me all about yourself. I want your likeness.*

---

[11] *History of Carroll County, Illinois*, Published by H. F. Kett & Co., Chicago, IL, 1878, and Unigraphic, Inc., Evansville, IN, 1976, p. 232 and a letter dated 1858 stating Amanda's name as Ludisky. I feel certain Amanda was the same person as Ludisky because of the references of Elvira and Jennie to Amanda as sister, an invitation to Amanda L. Van Alstine, and Amanda's nickname, Dickey, which was more likely to have come from Ludisky than from Amanda.

*Will send you mine and by Mrs. Jabcase send your Mother's likeness down for I am very anxious to get one taken from it. Send it and yours and I will send mine and your Aunt Marthas. Tell H. Graton to write immediately if not sooner. Maria will finish this so for now, good by.*
*I am, my dear niece*
*Your affectionate Uncle*
*S. W. Dodge*

Enclosed in the letter was a letter from Maria, Amanda Ludisky Van Alstine's sister.

*Dear Sister,*
*Uncle Whitman has been wrighting to you and invites me to finish it. I like to. I will do with plasure and hope to do so often hereafter. Oh My dear sister, I am so lonely here without my Mother. You know very little about living as I have lived in world. Oh, how many times I have wished that Mother had given me away as she did you, but as she used to say, perhaps it is all for the better.*
*I received a letter from Elvira a few days since. She was better but Jenny was not and I do not think she ever will be again. Poor Jane*[12]*, she has not been herself since Mother died. It was a hard blow for us all, but our loss was her gain for there was very little comfort for her in this world. But, if ever a person went to heaven, she was won.*
*Oh my Dear sister, I feel very sad to day. It seems as though their was nothing in Kenosha that I cared for. I wish that I was with you to day but there is no use of nothing. It is now raining very hard and has*

---

[12] Jenny and Jane are the same person and she is referred to using both names in other letters.

*been raining for the last two months. It is very dreary hear.*
*Oh, I hope you will come before they go home - <u>do come dont miss of it</u>. We are all well at presant. I cannot think of any thing more to wright and good by. Give my to Mer and Mrs. Grafton after receiving a large share for yourself and write to your loving sister. Maria E. Van Alstine*
*When you write direct to care of A. Leslie*

After receiving the letter from her sister, Maria, Amanda Ludisky Van Alstine wrote to Maria asking her to visit in Carroll County. Shortly after Amanda and Moses were married in Whiteside County on July 4, 1858,[13] Maria traveled to Carroll County to meet her new brother-in-law. While visiting her sister, Maria met Andrew J. Guyon and they were consequently married on October 15, 1858 in Carroll County.[14]

John Miller married, also, and he and his wife, Mary Ann, who was a Mount Carroll girl, moved to Winnebago, Faribault, Minnesota where John farmed. [15]

Eugene was close to Moses and Amanda. He was comfortable in their home and visited often in the years that followed. Within a year or two after his father's death, Eugene settled on a portion of his father's farm and built a small home. The family land was close in proximity. His Mother, Sarah, and, his sister, Anna, stayed in the large log structure that George had erected. When it was time to cultivate, plant, or gather the crops, the entire family, including the handyman, communed from one farm to another until they finished the work.[16]

For several years, there had been talk about the legality of owning slaves. Most northern states were against slavery. However, southern states, which depended on slave labor to

---

[13] Marriage records of Illinois
[14] Marriage records show the marriage in Carroll County, Illinois but they probably left shortly after their marriage as no mention was made of them in the letters afterward.
[15] Letter from Mary Ann to Elvira.
[16] Family letters

work their large plantations, definitely wanted to keep the slave market going. Eugene's family did not own slaves. He did not really have much of an opinion about slavery, but the talk of a possible conflict on the horizon stirred his blood, as it did many young men in those years.

In December of 1860, South Carolina voted to secede from the union and preparations for war began in the South. On January 6, 1861, "Florida troops seized the Federal arsenal at Apalachicola" and on January 9, 1861, the "Star of the West", on the way to the Federal Fort Sumter retreated due to an unfriendly attack. Over the next few months, one state after another voted to secede until April 12, 1861 when the Civil War began with a battle at Fort Sumter.[17] On April 17, Carroll County held the first war meeting and the York township boys poured forth to enlist. The Fifteenth Illinois Infantry Regiment formed on May 24 followed by the Thirty-fourth Illinois Volunteer Infantry on September 7, 1861.[18]

It is unknown why Eugene did not go to war in 1861. Perhaps the farm kept him home. Most people felt the war would not last over a few months so did not bother to enlist.

In 1860, Amanda Ludisky's sister, Elvira, traveled to Carroll County for a visit. Elvira was there to attend the birth of Frankie, second child of Amanda and Moses and to care for Jennie, the first born. Elvira, called Vira by the family, was a little older than Amanda. Jennie Jane and Sylvester, their partially blind brother who the family often called Vet[19], were the remaining siblings in the family.

While she was visiting with Amanda and Moses, Elvira met Eugene. Elvira was five feet two inches tall, with dark brown hair and brown eyes. Her waistline was small, drawn smaller by the tight corsets she wore. Her dresses were fashionable due to

---

[17] World Almanac Publication, *The Civil War Almanac,* Intro. by Henry Steele Commager, A Bison Book, New York, NY, 1983, pp. 41-42, 50
[18] Arthur Robbe and Richard Hinton, Booklet from *Rededication Ceremony of the Carroll County Civil War Soldiers and Sailors Monument.* The information concerning the meetings and formation of troops was taken from *History of Carroll County.*
[19] Lester, *Van Alstyne - Van Alstine Family History, Volume 3,* Publisher J. Grant Stevenson, Provo, Utah, and several family letters - Fact that Sylvester was blind.

her talent for sewing and copying fashions out of newspapers.[20] Elvira loved farming and her personality was not like other girls Eugene knew. Next to Eugene's five feet ten inch height, she seemed diminutive, but she could work as hard in the garden as anyone he knew. Elvira had a mysterious side that kept everyone guessing. Eugene learned from Amanda about her ability to use herbs which she gathered or grew herself.[21] In time, Eugene fell in love with the girl who was unlike any he had known before, although she was five years older than he was. She "swept him off his feet."[22] He did not let the question of age come between them. He had his own farm and had the respect of his family and friends. He did his own work and could ride and shoot better than most. With his height, dark hair and mustache, along with hazel eyes, he looked older than nineteen and certainly felt as old as the young woman he admired.[23] His girlfriend, Josephine Reynolds, was a local girl he had known all his life, whose brothers, William and Charles were his good friends. However, she was no match for Elvira in Eugene's mind. Elvira, nearing spinsterhood for that era, was delighted when Eugene asked for her hand in marriage.

In 1861, snow fell early in Illinois and the sleigh, brought out of the barn, cleaned and prepared for the winter. Sleigh rides were a delight of the winter season, especially with a loved one. Many things went on under the blankets and Eugene and Elvira were no exception.[24] As their courtship grew into love, the sleigh rides were frequent. They talked about everything. Elvira told Eugene of her love of farming and gardening while Eugene spoke about his desire to be an engineer. Elvira was a good listener, even if she did hope he would return and want to farm as she did. On December 25, 1861, a Christmas wedding took place in Mount Carroll, with B. L. Patch presiding.[25]

---

[20] Pictures and family history
[21] Letters and family history
[22] Letter to Josephine Reynolds Woodin who became his second wife two years after the death of Elvira.
[23] Pictures, War Department Reports, and remarks made about my Grandmother, who was 4'9" being 5" shorter than her Mother.
[24] Letters and family history
[25] Marriage certificate

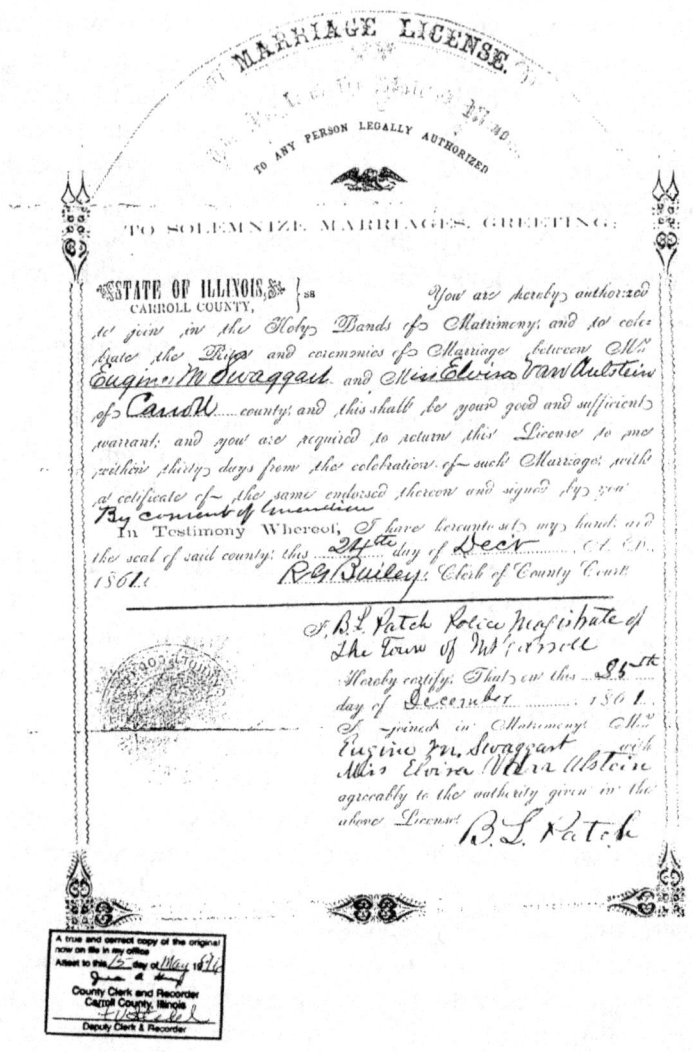

The first month of their married life together was wonderful. They set up the household together, took long sleigh rides to the homes of friends and family where they sang and played music with Anna or Amanda on the piano and Eugene or Sylvester on the fiddle. Sylvester, who visited Mt. Carroll to meet his sister's new husband, impressed Eugene with his musical talent on the fiddle.

Reality set back in with a letter to Eugene from his friend Henry Holt. Henry was in Tennessee at Fort Donelson. He had left Mount Carroll in May of 1861 with the Fifteenth Illinois Infantry, Company K. Eugene read in the Mt. Carroll Mirror that the Fifteenth Illinois Infantry arrived at Fort Donelson in time to take part in the surrender of the Fort on February 16.[26]

*Fort Donelson, Tenn. Feb 28$^{th}$, 1862*
*Friend Mack,*

---

[26] World Almanac Publication, *Civil War Almanac,* Intro. by Henry Steele Commager, A Bison Book, New York, NY 1983, pp. 85-86 and Arthur Robbe and Richard Hinton, *Rededication Ceremony of the Carroll County Civil War Soldiers and Sailors Monument* booklet, p. 5

I think it is about time for me to open our corispondence again and not having any duty to do this afternoon, I thought that I would sit down and drop you a few lines and let you know what is going on down here in the land of Dixie. First, it is the dullest place that we have ever been in. There is no news, no money, and worst of all, there is no women. I have not seen ten since I landed here. I wake up every morning with a hard on and there is no way to get it off. I wish you would inform me how to do it.

We arrived here on the $16^{th}$, only about five hours after the rebels surrendered the fort, just in time to miss all the fun. Our boat landed, but we were not allowed to go ashore untill next morning. Four hundred of the prisoners were sent on board and your humble servant had the pleasure of helping to gard the gentlemen during the night. I had some interesting conversation with them concerning the war, the cause, and the principle for which they were fighting. Many of them said that they had been forced to join the Army or leave their country. They said they never wanted to fight against the government and that they would die before they would again if they could get away. Many of them seemed to feel bad, saying that they had been missled by their leaders. And this, I judge to be true, for I think the majority of them are such damned fools that they do not know what they are fighting for. But, I must leave off politics.

Morning came. We went ashore and pitched our tents on a high hill overlooking the fort, and but a few rodds back from the river. As soon as matters could be aranged, we prepared our regular grub, as we call it dinner, and then lazed ourselves down to rest, feeling just as if we did not care whether the school kept or not. In the afternoon, visited the battlefield, a place which I had often wished to see. On arriving, the things that met my eye was guns, knapsacks, blankets and all manner of clothing, which the enemie had thrown away while retreating. The next was dead men. I had walked about 40 rodds and I had counted eighty and all but a few of them were our men. By this time, I had got tired of counting the poor fellows and concluded that it was enough to see them, without trying to remember their number. Still, I could see them lying on all sides as I passed along. Besides this mournful sight, I saw several nice horses which had shared the same fate. I passed on over the field and still the looks of distruction was plain to be seen on all sides. There was hardly a tree or bush, but what bore evidence of terrible struggle.

Well, Mack, I will not try to give you a further discription of the Battle, for my pen would fail in the attempt. But, it be remembered by all, that altho it was a glorious Victory, it was dierly won. So far as war is concerned, I can say but little, for what is going on in other parts, we know nothing about. We can get no papers with no news of any kind. All we know is what our Commander tells us. They say that the Union troops are careing everything before them, that we have done here, but whether it is so in other parts of the Union, I cant say. We hope such is the case, but can see no reason why it should not. We certainly have men and means enough to close this war insid of six months, if properly managed. There is now a stong Union element in the South and all this being in our favor. Why cant we subdue them. I am well convinced, from the information that I obtained from some of the Prisoners taken here, that their Army is but a hand full compaired with that of the North. It is believed by many here that the war will end in three months and to this, let us all say, God send.

The weather here now is warm and nice. The birds are singing in the groves. The grass has begun to grow, the budds to swell. In fact, all nature seems to have once more awakened from her long and dreary slumber. The country around our camp is quite rolling and the tented villages of our troops are to be seen on every hill, and besides this, can be seen the glorious old stars and stripes floating in the balmy brezes of the sunny south, where but a few days ago, floated the damnable rebel rag.

It is now almost sundown and I shall have to be brief or I will have to finish by candlelight. So here goes. Everything goes on after the old sort in camp. We have plenty of hard crackers and old boar yet and as long as that lasts, we intend to fight secish. We have plenty of fun, and but little work, and you know that suits a soldier. One of my branch mates has just fryed a nice lot of cakes and he wants me to help him eat them, an invitation which is always accepted by one. You will please excuse me one moment. Well now, Ill proceed. The cakes were really nice and reminded me of Holts Spree, no, not the Spree, but mother Holts very nice and long remembered cakes.

While I write, several of the boys are in front of me pitching quarters. Two are beside me writing letters to som distant friend, while several more are at the camp fire frying more of those nice cakes I just told you about.

Mack, you can see that we are not a set of deadheads. We are perfectly indipendent. We have sold ourselves to Uncle Sam and we get our pay every two months, according to contract. We were *mustered today for our pay and we expect to get it next week.*

*Company K is all right with but few exceptions. Some of the boys are unwell, but none very sick. Five or six have gone home on furloughs and two or three have just returned from home. Three of our men were discharged in Md., but we consider these deadheads. They were never no use to the company. This is all the news that I can think of now and I presume I have already written more than will interest you so I will close by requesting you to give my respects to all that love the Union and my love to the girls. Keep a share for you and your wife and the rest give to Annie.*

*From your friend, HH*
*Direct Via Cairo*

    When Eugene received the letter from Henry Holt, who was one of his best friends at the time and an admirer of Anna's, he could hardly contain himself. He wanted an adventure. Elvira was naturally against it, so Eugene waited a little longer. He reasoned that if he waited to get the crops in the ground in the spring, it would be easy for Elvira, with the help of Sylvester, Moses and William Eaton, to harvest. Eugene and Sylvester had a few talks and Sylvester promised him to take over the farming if Eugene wanted to go to war. Elvira, however, put the thought out of her head and hoped that no new regiments formed from Carroll County soon.

    Letters from relatives arrived. There was one from her sister, Jennie Jane Van Alstine. She was in Kenosha, Wisconsin, living with their cousins, the Crosit family. David Crosit was a blacksmith and carriage maker and the family decided to open a boarding house. Jennie, known to be a very level headed young woman and a hard worker, was a big help to them. On March 27, Jennie wrote to her dearest sister, Elvira.

*Kenosha March 27th, 1862*
*My Dear Sister-*
*Youre kind letter remainet in this offise a long time. It come at last however and was gladly recived. I asure you the news it brought was not unexpected to me.*
*Sylvester spoke very high of your husband when he was here. He said he was one of the best and noble hearted men in the world. I wish I could see you both. You must give my love and a kiss to him and tell him I hope to be better acquainted sometime. Our friends here seem very glad of your good fortune. Aunt Nehsuh send her love to you.*
*Mary has just returned from Milwaukee where she has been taking lessons in Grecian paintings and she has learned to paint beautiful.*
*I shall stay here all summer for any thing I new of. We think some of taking in all the boarders we can accumudate. It will last well fur me, then we shall have a girl.*
*The Regiment of the First Wisconsin Cavelry left for Suaint Louis last Monday. James Vled and Charly Wright are there. Twelve hundred soldiers and two thousand citizens were at the depot when they went away. It was quite a sight-to-see, so many at once.*
*I hope that Sylvester will cume and see me this summer. Give my love to sisters family and Sylvester and keep a share fur youself. You must read these papers to Jennie. Write as soon as you receive this . See you by.*
*from your sister*
*Jennie Van*
*I cant believe you can read this.*

    Enclosed in the same letter was a note from their cousin, Mary Crosit.

*Dear Cosin, Jennie has left a spase for me. She says and that I must write, so I will say a few words to you and my new cosin. We are all well and often think of you.*

*MaryTrims has been at Kenusha about six weeks and is just fine here. She is quite a large girl. I do not gain very much. I am almost as little as ever. I had a very nice present a short time ago. Father gave me a very nice piano. I practice every day. I guess that I play better than I did when you left here, or at least I hope so.*

*Well, how do you like marrid life. He He. When you answer Jennies letters, dont forget to tell me. I guess I must come to a slipe if he is good looking. Give him a kiss for me if not. Tell him I send my best respects. Please give my love to Ledrieu and family keeping a share for your self and family. Good by.*
*from your cousin*
*Mary Crosit*

Anna Swaggart took a position as a teacher in Rock Springs, Illinois to teach the summer session. She turned sixteen and graduated from school. It was an exciting experience, living away from home and earning her own money. She decided to write her new sister-in-law, Elvira.

The letterhead she used when she mailed her letter home had a picture of Abraham Lincoln, published by Mumford & Co., Cincinnati. It contained the following words: *" Let no man into whose hands my letters may fall, believe for a moment I will ever desert the STARS AND STRIPES. They may hang me, rob and burn my possessions, be you assured. Let not their lying, treacherous tongues rob me of my good name.* W.G. BROWNLOW."

Let no man into whose hands my letters may fall, believe for a moment I will ever desert the STARS AND STRIPES. They may hang me, rob and burn my possessions, be you assured. Let not their lying, treachrous tongues rob me of my good name.           W. G. BROWNLOW.

*Schoolroom**Apr 10th, 1862*
*Thursday morn.*

*Dearest sister[27]*
*According to my promise I am seated to pen a few lines to you and all. I have not been the least bit homesick yet (well not much). I think of you all very often but Mr. Shores folks are so good to me and they are such nice people, in every respect, that I cant help but enjoy myself here. Mr. Shores is a great musician. He plays everything you can think of, from the mandolin down to the jurs harp. You could not help but like them both. If you was acquainted with them and I hope you will come*

---

[27] The term "sister and/or brother" was used by this family to address the wife or husband of the spouse as well as a sister or brother by blood.

*down and spend the afternoon with her and with me also. She is very fond of company.*

*I like teaching but I had twenty five scholars the first day, twenty five the next and yesterday, twenty four. They are mostly large scholars.*

*I would like to see you all, but I would not like to go home this week. I am better contented here than I thought I would be. I am very glad of it. I should like to come home about week after next. You and Mc come after me, will you not?*

*Give my love to Mother and kiss little Jennie and Frankie for me.*

She referred her niece and nephew, the children of Moses and Amanda Ludisky Van Alstine Swaggart.

*Tell Mc to be shure and get me a watch. I cannot barely get along with-out one. You must excuse my writing. I have not built a fire yet and my hand is numb with cold. I must close and sweep, make a fire and call School.*

*Good by. Your sister till death.         Annie*

Eugene and Elvira were busy during those months. The crops were planted early as planned. A letter arrived from Mary Ann Miller, the wife of Eugene's half-brother, John Miller. They were living in Winnebago, Faribault, Minnesota.[28]

*Dear Sister*

*We received yours and Macks letter dated 25th of June & 16th of July, but all in the same envelope. We are not very well. The children have got the Whooping Cough. Genie & the baby are the worst*

---

[28] Although this letter was not dated and the date on the envelope was impossible to read, I believe it was written in this period of times because of the discussion of Tommy's death which was also mentioned in the letter Anna wrote to the family. It is believed the Tommy is Thomas Emmest, a friend of the family. Arthur Robbe and Richard Hinton, Booklet from *Rededication Ceremony of the Carroll County Civil War Soldiers and Sailors Monument.*

now. I am very much afraid the baby wont live through it.

Oh, Vira, you better believe I miss you & Jennie now. Everybody is afraid to come here that has any children, so I am left alone, all but Mary. I guess she would come if we had the small pox. She says she wont forsake me because we have the Whooping cough.

Thomas Emmest, a friend of the family was in the 8$^{th}$ Illinois Cavalry, Company G. He was killed in Alexandria, Virginia.[29]

We was very much shocked to hear of Tommys death. I feel sorry for the family, but how uncertain is life. It may be our turn next but, oh, if we are prepared, it will only be a happy change.

You certainly are having a wet time down there. I dont wonder you get home sick. We have had a delightful summer here, so fer, crops look fine.

Vira, I tell you Mack left in the wrong time. Your farm near Winnebago cant be bought for $1000 now. John has offered his farm for sale. He has been offered $1200, but I dont want him to sell. If he sells, he thinks he will go farther north. We like a homestead, I suppose.

You would like to hear how your neighbors were prospering. Well, Mrs. John Aldrich has a young daughter, also Mrs. Bermers. Old man Merston is still confined to his bed. Mr. Bucks folks come back & stayed a short time & then he sold his place & have moved up where her brother lived. All the rest are doing well. As for us, I know I must close for the school teacher is waiting to take this to town. Give my love to Dickey & family. I would write to her but, dear me, I have so much to do. I have not

---

[29] Arthur Robbe and Richard Hinton, Booklet from *Rededication Ceremony of the Carroll County Civil War Soldiers and Sailors Monument*.

written to Delia since you left. I suppose you have heard she was married.
Well goodbye. Love to all. Write soon for I dont know when I can write again but not till the baby is better.
I remain your sister
Mary Ann[30]
John is so busy haying he cant write now.

Eugene enjoyed his time with Elvira, but he wanted to go to war. He felt he owed his time and loyalty to his country. The "War Between the States" was the opportunity of a lifetime, fighting in a battle as his father had and having something to talk about to friends from that day forward.

Eugene and Sylvester made the final arrangements for Sylvester to take over the farm. In spite of his poor eyesight, Sylvester felt he could take care of it properly. Eugene wanted to get everything done before enlisting. He wanted to leave the farm in good condition so it would not be too difficult for Elvira and Sylvester when he left. Everyone knew the war could not last many months.

Twice there were trips to Rockford, where Elvira and Eugene, along with their friends William and Elizabeth Reynolds, went to check on enlistment possibilities coming up. Elvira and Elizabeth called Lib by friends and family, shopped while Eugene and William (called Bill) investigated the enlistment possibilities. Elvira had to admit the trips were fun and exciting.

Anna wrote to Eugene and Elvira, wanting them to come after her, but it is possible the letter arrived while they were gone. By the time Elvira and Eugene returned, it was too late to go. Anna, who was very spoiled by the family, let her anger show when no one showed up.

---

[30] The one uncertainty I have about the people involved is Mary Ann. In her letters she referred to Elvira as sister and always asked about Jennie and Amanda (Dickey) as though they were also sisters. However, no reference could be found in the letter concerning Emaline's death for Mary Ann, or in any other documents, tying her to the Van Alstine or Swaggart families other than through marriage to John Miller, a half-brother of Eugene and Moses Swaggart.

Mr. Shores    April 26th, 1862
Saturday
Dear Parent, Brother and Sister Vira
If you could only imagine how very homesick I am today, you could not wrest confidential, I am sure, and it is all your fault, Master. We first expected you after me and you disappointed me. I only wish I had a cord around your body. I will be willing to try to pull you here until I could give you a piece of my tongue and then let you go.. I did not write home because I thought, of course, you would be here. Mrs. Shores waited patiently for you half an hour and come here to play. I would expect you for you told me you would come and why did you not write and tell me the reason. I have a mind not to write home any more this summer. Ill write this once for a fighte.
My clothes are all most all dirty and I have no chance to wash them. Mrs. Shores has three men boarders, besides myself, and a very small house, so you can imagine my chances for washing.
Oh, you little Scampes. Why did you not come after me. Why did you not all three come see me. I looked last night until my eyes were almost sore but was doomed to disapointment.
I received a letter from Viola last night but I have no thanks to you for it but it seemed to me you might have wrote this week.
You knew you were not coming and you knew I would expect the letter if you did not come. Indeed I am I am allmost mad with you. I imagine you will laugh at me when you read this but it is no laughing matter. If I was around and you laughed it would not be good for you I assure you. I cannot help but write as I do. I would not write atal but you see I cannot help it.

Referring once again to Thomas Emmest.
*Viola said Thomas was killed and I pity Desiree.*
*The baby is clinging to me so I can hardly write. Perhaps you cannot read it. I do not care though. You do not deserve a good letter so I will not send you what you do not deserve. I want or would like to see you.*
*How do you get along? Is Mother well? I do wish you would write. Has Mr. got me a wach yet? I would like one, first rate. It would come in very handy.*
*I have thirty five scholars down on my schedule - five young ladies, one older than myself. There are no young folks here hardly. Bill Trake is the only young man I have seen yet and he is a old batchelor. Martie Duerke is mad at me, I supose, for she said that she wishes these upstarts of teachers, that are not fit to teach any more than a ten year old, would find something else to do besides lower the image of good TEACHERS. The directors offered her twenty before they hired me, but she would not take it. But, the best of all is, she had to take up with 18 and board herself.*
*I will have to close and get ready to go. I am going to Millgeville today. I remain your sister. Write soon.*
Annie Swaggart

Once Eugene made up his mind to enlist, he was anxious to leave. He promised Elvira to enlist for only nine months, but the only enlistments available were for three years. The explanation given to him was that troops would be mustered out earlier if the war ended sooner, an abundance of soldiers unnecessary if there was no war. In 1863, the Enrollment Act went into effect and all soldiers had to enroll for a minimum period of three years. However, at the time Eugene enrolled, that was not the case. He knew, however, the war could not last for more than a few months, so he decided to take the enlistment and say nothing to Elvira. Why upset her if it was unnecessary!

By the end of the summer of 1862, many changes had come to the lives of the family. John and Mary Ann Miller returned to Mount Carroll and Eugene left for war.

Stationery letterhead used by Anna Swaggart during the Civil War

## Chapter Two
## Camp Fuller

Colonel Smith D. Atkins, a lawyer from Freeport, Illinois[31] was responsible for the formation of the Ninety-second Illinois Infantry. He had been in the military with the 11$^{th}$ Illinois Volunteers, but had to resign due to illness. After a two-month recuperation on the seacoast, he returned to Illinois to raise the Ninety-second Illinois. There were five companies from Ogle County, three from Stephenson County and two from Carroll County.[32] Each company contained approximately eighty-to-ninety men.[33]

August 2, 1862 dawned. Eugene arose early. Excited and anxious, he reported to the Courthouse where transportation awaited to Camp Fuller in Rockford, Illinois.[34] Elvira did not accompany him to Camp Fuller. Other wives and families accompanied the troops to Rockford, but she did not. This was his day—a day he had been looking forward to for some time. The trip to Rockford was uneventful and long on the train. Arrival in camp was late.

The morning of August 3 came early. The first day at camp was busy, with soldiers trying to discover their duties in camp. Soldiers were arriving at all times of the day and night - some early and some very late. The soldiers who arrived early thought they were marching immediately to Lexington, Kentucky - rumored to be their destination. There, they would fight and put an end to the war.

Eugene was twenty years old when he enlisted. He was a man physically, but a boy in Army affairs, as many soldiers

---

[31] Glenn Tucker, *Chickamauga, Bloody Battle in the West,* Konecky & Konecky, New York, NY, 1961, p. 17

[32] Thomas M. Eddy, *The Patriotism of Illinois, A Record of the Civil and Military History of the State,* Chapter XXII, Regimental Sketches, Ninety-second Illinois Infantry, 1865, p. 369

[33] *Illinois Troops (Union) – Infantry Records of Events, Volume 13, Record of Events for the Ninety-second Illinois Infantry, September 1862- June 1865,* from all reports of the companies.

[34] War Department Pension Records and Company Muster Rolls

were. Their idea of the Army was enlistment followed immediately by conflict. Eugene had only his father's experiences in the Blackhawk Wars and the War of 1812 to base his expectations on and he was not the only one. Many young men had the same idea. Training and discipline was not something they considered to be necessary. Eugene's marksmanship was good and he knew the woods—what more did he need?

Elvira told Eugene she was going to ask her cousin, Jennie, to come live with her while he was away.

Eugene decided to write a letter to Elvira and Jennie before the troops pulled out. He was totally unaware that he would be in camp for a long time before leaving for war.

> *Camp Fuller*　　　　　　　　　　*August 3rd, 1862*
> *Dear Wife and Sister*
> *I arived safe in camp last night at 12 o'clock. We will march just as soon as we get our rations cooked and get our money. I guess we will go to Louisville, Ky and from there, the Lord knows, we dont. I am going in the kitchen next week, if we camp anywhere. If not, we will not want any cook, you know. Mrs. Reynolds came up with us. She said that you ought to been with her, as you was with her both times before. I will quit for this time.*
> *Well, Vira, since I was writing I went to the picture man and had myself taken for you and another taken with for Sister Annie. We are getting nap packs this afternoon. They are large for a mule to carry. We are not drilling today. The boys are in a big way marking their things and geting ready for a march, all but myself. It does not trouble me much.*
> *I am ready when the ress are . I will send my pictures home by Wm Graham with this. My likeness is very good, all but my ears. They dont show in the picture at all. I am sorry abut it.*
> *I will not write again next week unless we march!*

*Yours with Affection Vira and Jennie, Mack*

Left - Elvira Van Alstine Swaggart, wife of Eugene
Right - Jenny (Jane) Van Alstine - sister of Elvira

The next few weeks were fun for Eugene. He had many companions to talk with and all were as excited as he. They were all volunteers and ready to fight for their country to put the rebellion to rest. They drilled and learned how to set up and tear down camp. They practiced packing knapsacks. Meals needed preparing and Eugene was the cook! Somehow the days passed but the muster did not take place.

> *Camp Fuller Aug 29th, 1862*
> *Dear Wife*
> *It is with pleasure that I write you a fiew lines. I am well and all the rest of the boys. Our camp is the prettiest place I ever saw in my life. It is situated 1 mile East of Rockford on the banks of Rock River. We have very near 3,000 men here. It looks to me like a late fare. The boys elected all the officers in Mt. Carroll Patch and some more of the court house click, so I am the companys cook.*
> *They pay me $20.00 extra a month and my $18.00 per month makes $38.00 every month. It is hard work, but any man must work to earn that. Vira, I would like to see you and I will before long. We will be musterd into service next Monday. There, we will get our cloths. I had to buy me a shirt and pants to work in. I have three men detached every 2 days to help me and I am boss. I am exempt for duty, but have to drill a little, once in a great while. Need not then, not if I dont want to. I will write Sonday, a big sheet full. I have hard work to keep my blankets. Goodby. Here is a kiss.*
> *Your loving Husband, Mc*

Elvira was certain a baby was on the way. She thought she was pregnant before Eugene left but did not want to say anything to him so she just told him she would be asking Jennie to live with her. Sylvester, her brother, was there with her, but she knew she needed Jennie's midwife skills and would enjoy the companionship. Jennie answered her on Sunday.

*Sunday evening, Aug 31st, 1862*
*My Dear Sister*
*I received a letter from leundt. of you saturday, with an invitation to come down and live with you. I shall be very happy to come and all that for Vira.*
*I am sorry, Dear sister, that young Husband has gone to the war, but you must hope and pray for the best and that will give you comfort. Were it not for hope, the heart would break. This terrible war leaves sadness in many homes. When will it end. May it be soon.*
*Jaxson Judge has enlisted. They feel very bad.*
*John Fosters wife is very sick. She has been confined to the bed eight months. She has a little boy seven weeks old, but she has got the Consumtium, and she cannot live very long. The baby is sick, too, but a little better.*
*Aunt Nehsuh sayes that she does not know what to do, or how to get along without me, but my duty is with you, if you want me, in time of sickness and trouble. I am glad Sylvester is with you. We shall all be together. I can come sooner if you want me to. Write and tell me, for they want me to stay here as long as I can, but I will come now if you want me. They all send love and sympathy to you. Give my love to sister and family, Sylvester and yourself. Write soon. I remain your loving sister Jennie Van*

Eugene was concerned about Elvira and wanted to be sure Jennie was going to be with her. He was not too worried, however. He had written to her a week before, but forgot to mail it, as he was busy cooking for the camp and learning to be a soldier.

*Camp Fuller Sept 1st 1862*
*Dear Wife*
*I wrote to you last Friday and it was not mailed, I guess, so I thought I would write again.*
*We have preaching today in our barricks at 3 o'clock.*
*I only get 2 meals today. We are going to, for our dinner and supper, boiled beef and beans, tomatoes, bakers bread, coffee and sugar. We have milk twice a day. We draw 10 lbs. of coffee for one days rations and only use 6, so we can sell the other 4 for milk at 5 cts, a quart.*
*We have good times here. The fifes and drums are going all the time. A fellow cant hardly hear himself think.*
*One of our boys is very sick. We thought he would die last week. His name is Bashaw. He is out to a farm house.*
*Vira, I will be home as soon as we are musterd in and we draw our cloths. I am geting pretty dirty. I have one clean shirt yet and I am keeping that to wear home.*
*Write to whether you heard from Sister Jane or not and what she is going to do. Give her my address and tell her to write me a fiew lines and I will answer them.*
*There is not much news in camp, now, to write. Now, I will write this week again. I have all the boys picking over beans while I write. I cook 25 pounds of meat to one meal. Well, Vira, my pots are boiling over, so goodby for this time.*
*Your Husband,  Mack*


On September 3, 1862, the Ninety-second Illinois Infantry mustered into service. Colonel Smith D. Atkins said in his report, "The regiment was mustered into the service at Camp

Fuller, Rockford, Illinois. It is armed with Enfield rifles, there being about eight men in each company not yet furnished with guns and equipment. Its drills and efficiency for the short time it has been organized is excellent. Many of the officers have been before in service in the old regiments. We are under orders from Governor Yates to report to General Julius White at Cincinnati as soon as paid our bounty".[35]

Eugene did not get a furlough home right away. The next time the wives went into Rockford, Elvira traveled with them and took her husband a new gold pen. Eugene was delighted to see her. He missed her so much, when he had to time to think about it.

Elvira traveled to Kenosha to see family and friends and Jennie went back with her to Carroll County, Illinois. After Elvira arrived home, she wrote Eugene all the news, some he was not happy about hearing. John Miller and Mary Ann had returned from Winnebago, Minnesota. Anna was back in Carroll County after teaching her summer session and she and John were fighting. Eugene left his buggy and permission for John to use it if necessary, but John took advantage of Sylvester and used it everyday, often leaving Elvira and Anna without transportation.

Amanda Ludisky and Anna had words also. Amanda, always thinking as a big sister, tried to solve the problem between John Miller and Anna, but both were perturbed with her. For a while, they avoided one another rather than fight. However, Amanda and Anna made up and were on good terms again.

*Camp Fuller          September 23rd. 1862*
*Dear Wife*
*I received your very kind letter writen last Sunday, just now, with the greatest of pleasure. I was glad to here that you arrived home safe and also, that Jennie is there with you and I am glad to here that Annie & Dicky is on good terms. That is the one*

---

[35] *Illinois Troops (Union) Infantry, Records of Events, Volume 13, Records of Events for the 92$^{nd}$ Illinois Infantry, September 1862 - June 1865,* pp. 494-495

*good thing that troubled me, to think that my own folks were not on good terms enough to speak, but I hope it is all over with.*

*Vira, this is the second time I have written you since you were here, but I like to write to you withe my new gold pen. You say you would like to see me, but I am afraid that cant be possible. I suppose we will leave for the Dixieland soon, but if we do stay here this week, I guess Downs and myself will be home Friday night, if we can get a pass out of the lines.*

*John and Annies quareling is no more than I expected. I know both of them well. As for John useing my buggy, just tell him for me that I told Annie before I left home that he could use the bugy in cases when it was necessary, but as for running it all the time, I dont want Sylvester to let him do it, and if you cant take care of it, sell it for anything you can get. You say you will take lots of comfort with your sister. I know you will take lots of comfort in knowing that there is a friend there with you. I will be at home at the middle of winter to take comfort with you. You say that Ned is going to the fair. Write to me and tell me all about the fair and all that is going on in general. Well, my letter is about as long as yours and I guess I must close. I was down to Rockford today and bought me a whole kit of writing papers and Portfolio ink stand so I prepared to write you all the letters. I am get redy. The long roll is beatting, so goodby for this time.*

*I remain your loving Husband*
*Eugene Mc                  Care of Capt. Becker*
*Swaggart*

Captain Becker was a few years older than many of the soldiers, approximately twelve years older than Eugene.[36] He was often a big brother figure to most of the soldiers throughout the war. He grew up in Salem and was a close friend of the family.

Eugene had a picture taken for Amanda and wanted her to know it was coming.

*P. S. Tell Dicky to look for my likeness this week.*
*Give my love to all enquiring friends.*

Several of the soldiers were sick. The medicine the Army issued was terrible, as Eugene knew. He took one dose and vowed never to try it again.

Letters were slow going back and forth and sometimes did not arrive at all. Eugene worried because of the lack of mail.

Several soldiers slipped out at night and returned home for a visit. He and George Wait Downs discussed doing whatever they had to in order to get home for a visit before they left the state. However, the possibility of a furlough was unrealistic and he did not want Elvira waiting hopefully for his arrival.

*Camp Fuller Sep 28$^{th}$ 1862 Sunday Morning*
*Dear Wife,*
*I seat myself to write you a fiew lines. I wrote home last week, but received no letter, as yet. I have watched ever since Monday for some word from home but it was all of no use. I am well at presant but with the exceptions of being somewhat homesick. I could be cured by receiving a letter once a week. We have been here now nearly 5 weeks and I have had 3 letters and wrote about 12 or 15. I cant solve this problem. It is becaus they do not reach their place of destination, I guess, but that is all right. I will write once a week as I promised.*

---

[36] 1850 Census records for Carroll County.

*The 74<sup>th</sup> Reg. leaves this morning. They are having a big time of it. All the rest of the camp escorts them down to the depot. I guess that there will be no more fulough. We will leave next week, so our Capt. says. Wait and myself intended to come home Friday but we could not get a pass out of the lines to go to town, but old Marsh is gone now and we have a damd site worse man in his stead.*

*Vira, you and Jennie both write. You do know I want to hear from you. There is som of the Carroll folk out here now and I guess I will send this by some of them.*

*There is 5 of our boys down sick, some of them are in the hospital. I would not go there if I was sure of dying. Their medicine itself would kill a fellow, even if he was not sick. I took one dose and that will do me for about 3 years, I think.*

*Vira, dont look for me home now, be caus it is impossible for me to get another furlough at presant.*

*Well, I must soon close. I must get ready for inspection drill. I guess you dont know what that is, do you. Well, I will tell you. In the first place, we must put on our best clothes - clean shirts, black our shoes, clean our guns. Our guns must be kept as bright as a new dollar. If they are found to be dirty, we are reported to the Colonel and the third offense, we get in the house, where we dont like to go very well. We had George Gotshell in the guard hous the other day, just be caus he missed roll call. Goodby, Vira Dear. Be sure and write immediately. From*
    *Mack*

For two days, Eugene thought about a furlough. Several others left without one and nothing happened to them. Elvira went to Kenosha to get Jennie and the two of them did not even bother to stop for a visit on their way back. Eugene felt a need to get home to see what was going on without him. He thought more and more about taking off without a furlough.

He received a letter from Elvira concerning a revolver belonging to John Miller and he knew it would come in handy in the war. Besides, it looked good with uniforms. He wrote to Elvira to tell her to give the revolver to Captain Becker to deliver to him as he was going to Carroll County on furlough. He wanted John Miller to take the corn from the farm in payment.

*Camp Fuller Sept. 20$^{th}$, 1862*
*Dear Wife*
*As I do not drill today, I will write you a fiew lines. We are all well. I was on guard last night and I am pretty sleepy, but not so sleepy but what I can write you. The 92$^{nd}$ Reg is going to the fair today, but I dont like the fair well enough to go and stand in ranks 5 hours with out mooving. Beckers girls are here and the old Captain. If you had stoped, you could have went home with them, but it is just as well, I suppose. I guess you are not quite so lonsome now as you was, since Sister Jennie arived. Dear Vira, I know I am as happy as you are to have her there.*
*There is some talk of our reg. moving next week for Dixieland. Our army is doing good work down there, so the news is this morning. The Mt. Carroll boys got in Camp last night after being home all week without a furlough. Nothing was said to them about staying. If we stay here another week, I think I will try a french furlough, as the boys call it.*
*Vira, you and sister Jennie have your likeness taken right of immediately, for fear I dont get them. Be sure and send both on seperate plates. I can get cases here for them.*

*Tell John, that Colts revolver is all the go here, and if his was one, I could take for it any time I wanted it. Tell him I will send over by Capt. Becker, when he comes home. Keep your blankets and let John have the corn, if he wants it, and if not, he will have to wait until I can pay him the money.*

*Thear is more visitors here, now, than you can shake a stick at. Well, I must bring my sheet to a close and go to the washer woman and get my clean shirt for sabath. We have to attend church twice tomorrow fore noon, prayr meeting in the evening. Some folks say the army is a rough place, and if you here anybody say different, let them try it on once. That is all I have to write at presant.*

*My love to Mother, John and Johns folks, Moses and Dicky and sisters*

Your Husband<br>Mc Swaggart

*Vira his wife*
*Direct in care of our Captain*
*$92^{nd}$ Reg., Co. I, Ill. Vol.*
*Via Rockford Illinois*

That very night, Eugene woke up feeling sick and decided he had to get home. He slipped out in the middle of the night.[37] Some of the young men covered for him. He intended to return in a day or two. When he arrived home, he really was sick. Captain Becker dropped by to pick up the gun and found him there. Perturbed with Eugene for leaving without permission, he nonetheless passed the word that Eugene was sick and would return when he could.

On October 10, the Ninety-second Illinois Infantry left for Kentucky without Eugene. He knew he had to return but he was not sure what his status would be when he arrived. However, his biggest problem was finding his regiment in

---

[37] War Department Records said he was "at home sick without leave."

Kentucky. After inquiring at Camp Fuller, his orders were to report to Chicago, Illinois where transportation awaited for his return to his unit.

Just after Eugene left home to return to the ranks, Anna received a letter from her friend, Emma Miller who lived in Rock Creek. They both thought of going back to school. Emma had part of her money saved up, but not enough to enroll. Emma wrote to Anna to inquire about her status.

> *October 29<sup>th</sup>, 1862*
> *Dear Friend*
> *Cheerfully do I now seat my self to communicate to you this pleasent eve. How I would like to have a good social chat with you, but that is impossible, so I will try and see what use I can make of my poor pen. Should have written before, but have been very busy indeed! This week we have "thrashers"[38] and we have to work.*
> *I arrived home safe a week ago last Monday. Went to meeting that we had a very pleasent time. I went to Lanark, yesterday, and a visiting in the afternoon and in the evening, also. I was down to the Grove last week one day. We went after some apples.*
> *Has Mc gone back yet. Suppose he went last Monday. How bad you must all feel. How I would like to see him and Jennie and the rest of your folks. Give my best regards to them.*
> *Today we had company. Ev Thompson was up. Eula went home with him to stay all night. Justin was in a wedding in Carroll. You know him. Liz Couple went out with him. Was married at the Raines' house. Had a gay old time.*
> *Well, Anna, do you think you will go to school any this year. Ma thinks we had better go 4 weeks from now, but I dont expect we can get the sum before*

---

[38] Thresher – separates seed from wheat or rye

January, but wish we could. Have you been out to see about the room. I guess our folks can cut the wood. I have got $38.50 of my money. Dont know wether or not I can draw any more this fall. Hope so.

I have not written half I was to but Pa is going up to town and I want to send this letter to the office now. Write soon. Do you think we could get the sum about the first of Dec. I wish we could now. Write me soon as you get this and let me know all of the news. Sara is going up to Janesville in a week or two. I am going to send and get me a clock. Dont you want to send.

The girls send their love to you and yours

With much love, Emma

Excuse mistakes and writing for I am in a hurry[39]

---

[39] Written by Emma Miller who later married Phil Gelwix - stated in letter by Amanda Ludisky Swaggart to Elvira and Jennie Jane on February 3, 1867.

## Chapter Three
## Through the Holidays in 1862

    While Eugene was absent, the Ninety-second Illinois moved to Kentucky, under orders, and joined the Army of Kentucky with General Gordon Granger, who was in need of reinforcements. They were attached to the Department of Ohio, Army of Kentucky, Second Brigade, Third Division.[40] There was a lot of action expected from guerilla rebels and troops were needed to guard the supply depots. On October 10, 1862, the Ninety-second Illinois Infantry began their trip to Kentucky. They arrived at Mount Sterling, Kentucky on October 31 after marching over one hundred forty-five miles.[41] On November 14, they marched to Johnson's Farm looking for better water.

    When Eugene arrived in Lexington, Kentucky, he and his travel companions, who were also "absent without leave", were arrested immediately and taken into custody. The following morning, the Provost Marshall gave them their papers to return to their regiment. Many young volunteers were needed to fight so the Army was lenient with them. Eugene arrived in camp just in time to march toward Lexington, Kentucky under orders from Brigadier General Absalom Baird to join the division at Nicholasville, Kentucky. They camped for the night on Mr. Skinner's farm after a fourteen-mile march.[42]

    Eugene was still immature as a soldier, hardened to farm life, but not to discipline and certainly not to marching all day. He was prone to do stupid things. He had a lot to learn before he would make a good soldier.

    He wrote to Elvira to tell her of his trip and the days that followed.

---

[40] Frederick H. Dyer, *A Compendium of the War of the Rebellion, Illinois Regimental Histories, Ninety-second Regiment Infantry*, Des Moines, 1908, p. 1085
[41] Mileage came from *Illinois Troops (Union) Infantry, Records of Events, Volume 13, Records of Events for the Ninety-second Illinois Infantry, September 1862 – June 1865*, p. 493
[42] Ibid

Kentucky          Nov 16$^{th}$, 1862
Dear Wife

I now pen you a fiew lines to inform you that I arived safe into camp I will give you my jorney. We got into Chicago the next morning after I left home, about 5 o'clock A.M. and laid over all day, got our transportations to our regiment and started at 7 P.M. for Cincinnati. We got there the next day, Friday, at 8 A.M. We then went from there to Covington, that is just across the river from Cin. O, and there we got transportations for Lexington, Ky. at wich place we arived on Friday night, at 9 P.M., where the guards arested us, and took us to an old secesh hall for us to sleep in the dirt, 3 inches deep, on the floor. We were, then, taken to the Provest Marshels. He then gave us our papers and, then, we were at liberty once more. We then went to the sale stable and hired us a team to take us to Mount Stearling, for which they only charged us $39.00 for to take 4 of us 35 miles on the nicest turnpike that ever was built. Well, we got here, at last, on saterday night about 11 P.M. and on this morning, we were ordered to march at 8 o'clock.

Well, we started. The Col. told us if we were not able to cary our knapsacks, we should stop at the hospital, so I was the only one that sholdered it among the sick. I marched six miles and throwed away my gun and marched about 3 miles farther and then throwed down my knapsack and when we got here, I was just about gone up, but not so bad but what I can write.

The reason we are marching back to where they came from is this. Every niger that comes to our lines, they confiscats and Gen. Bird is a Ky. He has ordered us back to his brigade. We expect a little fight tomorrow with 2 reg. of cavelry because Col.

*Atkins wont give up the Contre bands. They are encamped in the winchester, where we have to go through and they say they are going to have their negroes or whip us. I will not see the fun, as I will be left withe the train to ride.*

*Dear Vira, I know you must be very lonesome now, but our Col. says he will bet $1000 against $100, that we will be at home in 6 months. He says we are going into Ten. to fight. He says this thing of playing off is all played out.*

*Capt. Becker jumped about 4 feet high when he see me coming into camp. Wait was glad to see me. You better believe I was glad to get here.*

*The long roll is beating now and I must close. We march in the morning at 7 o'clock.*

*Wait is out on picket duty tonight. He went out about 4 miles from camp. My love to all. Tell Sister Jennie she must write me a fiew lines. At presant no more.           Loving Husband    Mack*

*P. S. Nigers are plenty, 30 in camp now.*

*Direct Via Cin, Ohio, Care Capt. Becker, 92$^{nd}$ Reg. Co. I*

The Ninety-second Illinois Infantry traveled an additional forty-eight miles over the next three-day period. They arrived in Nicholasville on the evening of the November 19. They took shorter, more frequent marches because the weather was bad and rainy.[43]

Many Africans were entering camp and the Ninety-second Illinois Infantry became known as the "Abolition Regiment."[44] Colonel Smith D. Atkins and some of his officers had made them into personal servants. Colonel Cochran of Kentucky

---

[43] *Illinois Troops (Union) Infantry, Records of Events, Volume 13, Records of Events for the Ninety-second Illinois Infantry, September 1862-June 1865,* p. 493
[44], Thomas M. Eddy, *The Patriotism of Illinois, A Record of the Civil and Military History of the State, Chapter XXII, Regimental Sketches, Ninety-second Illinois Infantry,* 1865, p. 370

expressed outrage because the Africans were slaves of many of his fellow statesmen. Colonel Atkins refused his demand to return them to their former owners. The Kentucky Grand Jury indicted Colonel Atkins for "stealing men chattels", but as long as he was in camp, their jurisdiction was meaningless.

Thanksgiving came and there was no turkey, just baked beans. Many men were sick including his friend George Wait Downs, but Eugene was better. The officers were feeling very good—at least they were the night before Thanksgiving when they had a little party.

> *Camp near Nicholasville, Ky Nov 18$^{th}$ 1862*
> *Dear Wife*
> *I now take my pen to write you a fiew lines. I am well and am geting fat. I like it much better here than I did at Camp Fuller. We expect to be paid off this week and then, I guess, we will take up our march again for Dixieland. This will be the fourth letter I written, 3 to you & 1 to sister Ann. I will not expect any answers untill the last of this week.*
> *This is Thanksgiving here. We had about a peck of baked beans for dinner. I hope you had something good and eat some for me. We will all be at hom in a little while, so our Col. tells us. I would like to be at home mighty well, although, I am not homesick.*
> *Our major[45] & Col.[46] & Liut. Col.[47] were all on a drunk last night. We never had so much fun before in the reg. They got out on the parad ground, after we got nicely to bed, and began to gass and talk untill the whole battalion were out of bed and we got them to runing foot races and jumping. I think we were in a pretty plight for to be in a reble land.*

---

[45] Major John H. Bohn
[46] Col. Smith D. Atkins
[47] Lt. Col. Benjamin F. Sheets

*Well, I guess they felt good over the paymaster coming to give us a few green backs.*
*I would like to send you a few dollars today, but you will have to wate a little while longer.*
*My writing desk is geting me awfull tired. I am laying on the ground and writing. We have 19 boys sick now at Mt. Stearling Our company is getting down fast. We discharged 2 men, Mr. H. Hobert and Warren Aldrich are both discharged and gone home.*

Mark H. Hobart transferred to another hospital because records show that he was discharged in June of 1863. Warren Aldrich died at Mount Sterling hospital on February 18, 1863.

November 18 continued

*Well, it is drill and must stop for this time.*
*Now, I will finish my letter. We had a good drill. Our Brigadier[48] was out to see us. He says the 92d Reg I, V., is at the head of the Div.. That is something for the Ill. boys. Wait Downs is on guard today, He is not very well. He has a stiff neck. I rather think Wait would just as leave be at home as not. He says not, though. Well, enough of that. I would like to hear from you and see you better.*

Referring to Sylvester and his brooms.

*I guess Vet is about done making brooms. Brooms are worth $3.50 per Doz. here. Tell him to send them to Dixie if he wants a good price for them. The darn boys make so much noise that I will have to quit. Write often and give my love to all. Jennie, you must remember me to all our Wis. friends.*
*Direct to 92$^{nd}$ Reg., Co. I. Care of old Eg Via Covington, Ky*
*No more. I remain your Husband    Mack*

---

[48] Brig. Gen. Absalom Baird, Army of the Kentucky, Third Division.

When Colonel Atkins and the Ninety-second Illinois moved from camp to march to Lexington, Kentucky on November 19, Lexington citizens formed an angry mob and met them to take the slaves by force. One woman went into the ranks and attempted to drag her manservant from the ranks. The servant refused and she called out for help from her neighbors. Colonel Atkins ordered his troops to fix bayonets and the neighbors backed down. They marched through town without incident. Colonel B. F. Sheets, from the head of the command, ordered the troops to sing "Kingdom Come" and the troops joined in with a zeal for the anti-slavery movement.[49]

On the night of November 19, Eugene wrote to Elvira. He was under the assumption that they would be marching again the next day. However, they camped for a while.

*Ky November 19$^{th}$, 1862 Camp near Nicholasvill*
*Dear Wife*
*I receaved a letter from you last night dated Oct 6$^{th}$, but it was all disappointment that I did not get any news. Well, Vira, I wrote to you last night but do not wait for an answer. You can guess how it is to write here, 18 boys in one little tent. A fellow dont know whar he is writing half the time.*
*We are on the march now and dont know when we'll get done. We left Mt. Stearling the next morning after I got there and are now on our way south and the general supposition is that we are going to Nashvill, Ten. Our Col. told us that we were going to find some game and if that is the case, we go to some other place than this.*
*Ky. is a hard place. We have to use water out of frog ponds. I have not seen a bit of running water*

---

[49] Thomas M. Eddy, *The Patriotism of Illinois, A Record of the Civil and Military History of the State*, Chapter XXII, Regimental Sketches, Ninety-second Illinois Infantry, 1865, p. 371 and Arthur Robbe and Richard Hinton, Booklet from *Rededication Ceremony of the Carroll County Civil War Soldiers and Sailors Monument*, p. 13

in the state. When the water is boiled, the green scum raises to the top of it. Well, enough of that.
I stand the marching first rate & have not had any knapsack carried but one day. I have a severe cold. My throat is a little sore, but I guess it will come around right.

Regarding the incident that occurred with the Lexington citizens.

Oh! we had an awfull fight. We came within about ½ mile of the town and we were ordered to halt and fix bayonets and load. We then started again for the town. We marched right throug and there was not the first word said. That ended our fight.
I would like to know when we get our pay, but I dont know. Well, I guess I will close for this time. It is raining now like everything. I guess we will have better water. I hope so. Good night.
Well, I guess I will finish my letter. We are laying still today for to wash and cook. The boys are having a big time of it. The darkies are washing for the boys. I had to sell my boots. I could not get them on this morning and I sold them for $7.00. That is a small price for boots here. Wait Downs is cleaning his gun. He is having a hard time of it. Our Brigadier came into camp this morning. His name is Baird. He looks like a 40 pounder. Well, I guess I am done for this time. Write often wether you get my letters or not. Give my love to Jennie, Vet & all the folks at the other place.
Yours with love Vira,    Eugene Mc Swaggart
P.S. Write soon. I know you will.

The Regiments had two important inspections in the next few days. On November 21, the officers ordered the troops out for inspection and General Henry Moses Judah inspected them. On

November 24, General Absalom Baird also reviewed the Regiment.[50]

On November 26, General Baird issued orders for the Ninety-second Illinois Infantry to proceed to Danville, Kentucky. The first day, they marched ten miles, camping near the Kentucky River. The second day, they pushed for sixteen miles and arrived in Danville, Kentucky on November 28.[51] Their campground was the local fairground.

In the record of events, Colonel Smith D. Atkins reported, "The discipline of the regiment is considered very good, whether on the march or in camp", but the truth was that the sick were piling up. Water was scarce. When water was available, it was bad. Eugene related the problems to his brother, Moses, in a letter.

> *Camp near Danvill, Ky Nov. 28$^{th}$, 1862*
> *Dear Brother*
> *I now seat myself to pen you a fiew lines to let you know I get along in Dixie. I am well, at presant, but that is not the case with some of our boys. We have about 25 in the Hospital. They are scatered all along the road betwen here and Mt. Stearling.*
> *We are now in camp in the fairgrounds. It is the nicest place I ever see in Ky. We are allowed to go out of lines here at leasure, so we dont go to town, we are all right. We are within 7 miles of the battle grounds at Perryvill.*
> *Our Col. says we will stay here some time to guard some reble property which Gen. Buel took from them.*

Brigadier General Don Carlos Buell, Commander of the Army of Ohio, was ordered to Louisville and then to Perryville where he challenged General Braxton Bragg of the Army of the Tennessee. Neither won a clear victory. General Bragg was

---

[50] *Illinois Troops (Union) Infantry, Records of Events, Volume 13, Records of Events for the Ninety-second Illinois Infantry, September 1862 - June 1865*, p 495
[51] Ibid. p. 528

able to escape and General Buell did not pursue him. He was removed from his command for his failure to overtake General Bragg.[52] However, General Bragg's army left a lot of supplies behind when he fled.

November 28 continued

> There is 1000 stand of arms, 16 pieces of canon and 5 or 600 bbls. of pork which must be guarded.
> We are within 20 miles of a rebel camp of cavelry, but they are retreating south. We have camped there on Old Biggs camp grounds. We could see lots of places where they burnt strings of fences for 3 and 4 miles. They have raised the very devil in this part of the country.
> Well, I must stop. There is an Ordelys call, what is it for, I will tell you as soon as he comes back. It is for us to be ready to move at 12 o'clock, so you see how it goes. We came here last night and we thought we would stay, but now we will move somewhere - the lord knows, I dont.
> Give love to all. Tell Vira I have writen 3 letters to her and one to Annie.
> Yours with affection.    Mack

The move the Ninety-second Illinois made was not too far—it was only across town in search of better water.

Elvira wrote to Eugene that Aunt Davis was coming for a visit. She also told him that Anna was having trouble finding enough money to pay for her room at school.

Eugene hoped the troops would receive some pay soon. He wanted to use it to help at home, but none was in sight so far.

Pickets went out to no avail, as they could not find General Bragg in the area. The 96$^{th}$ Illinois Volunteers joined them and with them was a friend, Ed Shipton.

---

[52] World Almanac Publications, *The Civil War Almanac*, Intro. by Henry Steele Commager, A Bison Book, New York, NY 1983, pp. 116-117

All of the Ninety-second Illinois were still in Danville with the exception of Company A, who was guarding a bridge.[53]

The weather was worse and it was difficult staying warm. Eugene stole a blanket, possibly from a nearby house or farm to help keep him warm at night.

> *Camp near Danvill, Ky              Nov 29th, 1862*
> *Dear Wife*
> *I received your letter last night, and if there was ever a thankful heart, it was mine. It was dated Nov. 22d. It came in good notice.*
> *Well, we are camped on Old Bragg campground. I wrote to Moses yesterday. I told him that we were going to march. We did, from the fair ground to the other side of the town.*
> *Our G.Q. has ordered stoves for us, so I think by that, we will winter here. The rebles are in 25 miles of us now. The citizens say the rebles are all around us now. We have between 60 & 80 men out of our regiment on picket everyday.*
> *The 96 Ill are here now. I saw Ed Shipton last night, he looks well. Our company is prety well at presant.*
> *There are only 25 sick in bed, Oh, I mean 25 in the hospitals along the road from Mt. Stearling. Here and there is about as many more withe us that is unfit for duty, so it brings the boys on duty every other day. In regard to my health, it never was better with the exception of a bad cold I caught one night on guard when it rained and froze. The folks up north think it is warm in the sunny south, but let them come down here and try it. It snowed last night like everything. We marched one day in snow 6 inches deep, that was very nice.*

---

[53] *Illinois Troops (Union) Infantry, Records of Events, Volume 13, Records of Events for the Ninety-second Illinois Infantry September 1862 - June 1865*, p. 496

*Dear Vira, I know you must need some money, but we are not paid off yet. We expect to be soon. Then, you will get it.*

*You know I am glad to hear that Aunt Davis is going to make you a visit. I would like to be at home, but as it is I cant be now, not exactly. We have got a little work to do here first, then all is right, thats whats the matter, and it will soon be done, I guess.*

*I am glad that we can corispond with each other in 10 days time. That is better than I expected.*

*We are living better here than we did in Rockford. We have everything, nearly, that the country affords, but good water. That is miserable stuff, but we can live on it a little while.*

*Wait was on guard last night as usual. He is on every other night, regular. He is snoozin away, by my side, as I write. I am looking for a mirror everyday nearly. We cant get a paper here unless it is one sent to some of the boys. You say Annie is getting in trouble with her board bill.*

*Write to me and give me the particulars and all the news in general.*

*I have got me a blanket, but I did not draw it. I pressed it in to service my own self. That is alright.*

*Well, I guess I have writen enough already so good by.      I remain your loving Husband*
*Eugene McBride Swaggart*
*This is the 4$^{th}$ letter to you.*

It was cold in Kentucky and many nights the soldiers could not stay warm. In the tents, the soldiers huddled against one another, trying to use body heat to stay off the cold. The campfires, always lit, had soldiers huddled around them at night, talking about going home when the war was over. Eugene thought the war could not last much longer, with all the troops in action while the Ninety-second Illinois was inactive. He could not understand why they were not fighting while so many others were carrying the burden of the war. He thought it had to be because the war was almost over. It was December 6, 1862, and the Ninety-second Illinois, still in Danville, bored quickly with the service. Company B was detached to Camp Dick Robinson to guard and secure some public stores, but Company I was still in camp.[54]

News from home concerned John Russell who had come to stay with Elvira and Sylvester. He was the new handyman who took the place of the family handyman, William Eaton. William Eaton followed Elvira, making advances toward her so much that she and Sylvester asked him to leave. She needed help, but, with Eugene away, it was better to have someone a little younger for a handyman. Eugene understood the problem and wanted to assure Elvira that he approved of the change.

> *Camp Baird near Danvill, Ky         Dec 6$^{th}$, 1862*
> *Dear Wife*
> *I have just read a letter from you, bearing date of Nov 27$^{th}$, withe the greatest of pleasure to hear such good news from home. I am glad to hear that you have John Russel living with you and, also, that Silvester is good to you. I think that you will get along fine for 5 or 6 months. By that time, I will be there myself.*
> *I just mailed a letter to you. I told you I expected a letter from you and sure enough it came, so I am answering it so soon. I gave you all the news at present in the one before this, so I guess I will not trouble you with much this time. You said something about four dollars. I could not make out what you meant by it. Please explain it to me. I thought it was what you was to have from the county.*

---

[54] *Illinois Troops (Union) Infantry, Records of Events, Volume 13, Records of Events for the Ninety-second Illinois Infantry, September 1862 - June 1865,* p. 496.

*Send me some papers quick, wont you. I want to see something from home.*
*Wait is sitting here by the fire smoking his old pipe. It is cold as jehue. It snowed here yesterday pretty hard. It makes us fellows spoon up close. We have a large fireplace in one end of our tent and we bought us a sheet iron stove, which we have in the other end. Our G.Q. sent for stoves, but we could not wait for them to come. There is 15 of us in our tent, that makes us pretty thick. The negroes bring fresh pork into camp - sausage, milk and most every thing but mersys, it is so cold that they would freeze. Oh, I cant think of anything to write.*
*I guess I will come home and tell you all the news in general, so goodby. Give my love to all.*
*I remain your loving Husband, Mack*

Ten thousand in troops gathered in Danville and the soldiers were a little bored. They were wishing something would happen soon.

*Camp Baird Danville, Ky      Dec 16$^{th}$ 62*
*Dear Wife     I received your letter about one week ago and have neglected writing untill the present time, for want of postage stamps. They cannot be had at all times. I have wrote to you twice and could not mail them, but I will mail this one.*
*I am well and all ways ready for my hard crackers and frog coffee. Your last letter stated you was not very well. I hope that you may be blessed with good health, if nothing more.*
*Well, we have not had that fight, yet, with old Morgan, but expect him every night, let him come, we are ready for him. We have 14 large guns and about Ten Thousand Troops of Infantry here.*

Colonel John Hunt Morgan, of the Confederate 2$^{nd}$ Kentucky Cavalry, was famous for raids into Kentucky, Tennessee, Mississippi, Indiana, and Ohio where he struck quickly with great destruction, taking many prisoners and supplies, thus lowering the morale of many Northerners.

December 16, 1862 continued.

*Gen. Burnside is giving them fits on the Potomic. He is going to whip them out, I guess. You get more news than we can get here.*

Rumors flew concerning General Ambrose Burnside. In December, he attacked Fredericksburg with approximately one hundred and six thousand troops. General Stonewall Jackson defended Fredericksburg with seventy-two thousand Confederate soldiers. The truth was that the Union took a big hit in mid-December with approximately twelve thousand, seven hundred dead or wounded while the Confederates reported a smaller loss with more or less five thousand, three hundred dead or wounded. General Burnside took full responsibility for the failure.[55]

December 16, 1862 continued.

*We buried one of our boys last Saturday. His name was Henry Thomas.[56] He was from York. He died with the measels and quick consumption and was buried in military form. There is from 1 to 2 buried everyday out of the Brigade.*

*I was sorry to hear from Jennies plant being killed. It was a peticular favorite of mine, but we will have another, one of those days, that you will have to turn your attention to. Dont tell anybody, ha ha. Ill*

---

[55] World Almanac Publications, *The Civil War Almanac*, Intro. by Henry Steele Commager, A Bison Book, New York, NY 1983, pp. 122-123

[56] Henry Thomas, Mount Carroll, 92$^{nd}$ Illinois Infantry, Company I, died at Nashville on 12-10-62. Arthur Robbe and Richard Hinton, Booklet from *Rededication Ceremony of the Carroll County Civil War Soldiers & Sailors Monument.*

*be gay and happy still, and more so, when I am there to help see to that plant, I tell you what.*
Referring to replacing William Eaton with John Russell.

*I am glad you have (so good a boy) to live with you in Bills stead. He was a perfict neusance for to be there without old Mc, is not that so.*

*Well, Vira, I got one a pair of new pants today, a new coat and shoes, but we cant get any socks till next month. I done a very foolish thing when I left mine at home, but a soldier would die if it were not for disappointments, but we will not be so very long anymore. Our time is half out, our Col. says.*

*Wait is out on picket and it is cold and snowing like the deuce. Like as not, tomorrow it will be warm and nice. It is very changeable here and that acounts for so many bad colds.*

*I expect a letter from you or Annie tonight, so I will close for tonight with happy dreams to you all, good night.*

*Well, good morning. No letter here this time and I will try and finish. It is pretty cold today and I am detailed on guard. We have been put under strict orders and cannot sleep nor have any fire. It is just the thing we want. Some boys will go to sleep on their posts and you know that it will never do for us to sleep when our punishment is death. They are now more strict in everything than they ever was before. I guess something will be done. Brigadier Gen. Baird says it will be settled before long. He says it cannot run much farther . Well, I guess I will have to stop for this time. It will be the last one until I can get some more stamps. They cannot be had for money here, but that need not stop you from writing to me. I have not had a letter since the $8^{th}$ of this month. Give my love to all.*

*I remain your loving Husband and Mc*

Back home in Salem, Carroll County, Elvira was not doing well. She was sick and problems on the farm mounted up. The corn crop was a failure, yielding just enough corn for feed for the cows, the pigs slaughtered and eaten. Food supplies were running low. Money was scarce with little arriving from Eugene.

The good news concerned John and Mary Ann Miller's new baby. John decided to try trapping to earn a living. He, Eugene and Moses trapped some in their youth, but John had a new partner to go with him.

*Camp Baird Danvill, Ky    Dec. 20$^{th}$, 1862*
*Saturday morning*
*Dear Wife*
*It is with pleasure that I seat my old self to answer your kind letter which came to hand last night Dated the 16$^{th}$. It was the firs one in two weeks and the stamps which came are very exceptable. As I have told you before, we cant get them. I mailed you a letter yesterday and gave 5 cents in sutter checks for one stamp.*

The army sutlers followed the troops, selling them clothing, liquor, tobacco and other supplies. When the soldiers paid the sutlers, they received change in sutler checks that could be used at a later time.

December 20, 1862 continued.

*I am feeling a great deal better now than when I wrote last. I am glad that you are so well as you are. I am afraid that you will not be able to write much to me but Jennie will, wont you Jane. You say Jennie is sick. You must be carfull and not let her run down to the old place and trapes around when it is not necessary, for she can not stand it.*

*Oh! if I was there, I would let you know a thing or two. You must not take any pride in what I say in this epistle. Thats so.*

*Vira, your crop of corn was a big los, but it was better than nothing if you kept enough for your cows. Your pigs are gone up. That is one good thing. You will not have them for to bother you.*

*Wait Downs recd. a letter from Westley Rowley last night and one from home. Wes is in Nashville, Tenn. He says they have awfull hard times there in Ten. I am glad we are not ther, but I dont know but we will be there soon, but hope not. He says they have hard crackers and in every mouth full there is a big flour worm. They do not draw any sugar, no beans, nor potatoes. We could not live without our sugar to put in our coffee, for that is the main stand by. Potatoes, we get twice a week. We get rice or beans every other day, just which we want.*

*We are to have soft bread now. Our Col. ordered the quarter master to take posescion of the bakery in Danvill and detail men out of the regiment to run it and he has done so. He will commence next Monday to make our bread. If I was a baker, I could get a nice situation. The quarter master offered $1.50 cents to any man that would take charge of the concern, but I am not posted enough.*

*I will give you a list of what my clothes cost me. So far, we are allowed $42.00 a year for our cloths. You can see for yourself that I can not keep myself in cloths with $42.00 a year.*

| | |
|---|---|
| *Cap, I had $ Cents None but they cost* | *$6.00* |
| *Pants, 2 pair, $3.03 per pr.* | *6.06* |
| *Dress Coat, one* | *6.71* |
| *blouse coat, one* | *2.63* |
| *shirts, 3 at 88 cts a piece* | *2.54* |
| *drawers, 2 pair 50 cts a pr.* | *1.00* |

| | |
|---|---|
| shoes, 2 pair $1.95 per pair | 3.90 |
| socks, 2 pair 26 cents per pair | .52 |
| over coat, one | 7.20 |
| wool blanket | 5.90 |
| rubber blanket | 4.00 |
| Total | $40.46 |

*I have been here 4 months and have drawn $40.00 already. Our hap sack and haver sack and canteen, we dont have to pay for unless we loose them, and if we loose them, we are to pay for the hap sack, $3.50, haver sack, 48 cts, canteen, 48 cts and you see, it keeps a soldier on the look out all the time or when pay day comes he will not draw very much. The will steel the acorns away from a blind pig.*

*I think John will do well trapping, but his croany is a big specimen, but everyone to their own fancy, as the boy said when he kissed the cow. Well, I guess I will close for this time as I must answer Annies letter which came with yours. You must tell Moses to answer the letter which I wrote to him. Give my love to mother, Jennie, Vet, Dicky, Mary, Anna and John. Tell John to write to me. Kiss baby for me. Goodby.                 Your affectionate, Mack*

*You will heer from me soon and often. P.S. Send me a paper by next mail. P.S. Do not forget that receipt for it is the best thing in the U. S. Army.*

In camp, Eugene and others were sick with diarrhea caused by the bad water in Kentucky. Elvira made a big batch of her medicine from her recipe and sent it with Eugene when he left the first time. However, he had used a lot himself and given even more away to other soldiers. Elvira sent the recipe that consisted of 2 cups of molasses, 1 cup of butter, 2/3 cup water, 1/2 teaspoon of soda, 3 tablespoons of vinegar, and ginger.[57]

---

[57] The recipe - called a receipt by Eugene - was found with the letters and looked as if it had been carried for a long time.

Eugene received a letter from Anna who was away at school and still needed money. She hoped her brother could help her by sending money to pay for her room and board.

Anna was very special to Eugene before Elvira came along. She was closest in age to him and he had always given her whatever she wanted that he could afford.

Anna Swaggart

She was the pretty one and the baby of the family, the only girl. All of his friends were hoping to be the one in her life. It was very difficult for Anna when Eugene married. He wanted to help Anna, but he could not come up with enough money to send home to Elvira at the time.

*Camp Baird   Danville, Ky.     Dec. 20$^{th}$, 1862*
*My Dear Sister*
*I received a letter from you last night with pleasure to hear from you. It was a good while coming, but better late than never.*
*I am well and hope this will find you the same. I was well pleased to hear that you are going to school and like your school so well. You must study hard and try and come out No. 1 next spring. You are now at an age that you can see the need of learning and I have no doubt but you will take hold of your studies harder than ever, but, I dont know as you want me to give you a lecture on it. It is drill time and must stop.*
*Well, we had a bully drill. It is fine exercise this cold weather. Annie, I wish you and Vira could see us out on battalion drill. We can make a better appearance, now, than we did at Rockford. That is so, so it is we have a Silver band belongs to our regiment. I tell you what, the 92$^{nd}$ Ill. Vol cuts quite a dash in Old Kentuck. Our Col. is a regular ladies man. They are flocking around him everywhere we go, but thats no matter. Beauty is only skin deep. There is not a clear white woman in the darned place, hardly.*
*You wished me to direct my epistles to you more than I do. This will make 3 I have written to you and recd one. If you write to me I will answer them, you can bet on that, if I can get stamps.*

Camp Baird Danville Ky. Dec 30th 1862

My Dear Sister

I received a letter from you last night with pleasure to hear from you it was a good while coming but better late than never. I am well and hope this will find you the same. I am well pleased to hear that you are going to school and like your school so well you must study hard and try and come out No 1st next spring you are now at an age that you can see the need of learning and I have no doubt but you will take hold of your studies harder than ever. But I dont know as you want me to give you a lecture on it, it is drill time and must stop

We in had a bully drill it is fine exercise this cold weather Annie I wish you and Vira could see us out on battalion drill we can make a better appearance now than we did at Rockford that is so so it is we have a Silver band belongs to our regiment I tell you what the 92 Ill. Vol. cuts quite a dash in Old Kentuck Our Col. is a regular Ladies man they are flocking around him

Annie, I would like to send you your money but I dont know how or when we will get our pay. You need it but you must try and get along without it if you can. About the law suit, I guess they will have a good time settling it. I think if Mose was in his right mind, he might have it set off.

Eugene referred to the lawsuit involving Eugene, Moses, Anna and Sarah Swaggart as well as Nelson, George's son by Elizabeth Brown Swaggart and Leticia Lundy, George's granddaughter. They were trying to get clear title to all of George Swaggart's homesteaded land. Moses handled most of the details in Eugene's absence. Moses was stubborn at times and did not want to go along with all of the family.

December 20, 1862 continued.

*Your Unity recd a letter from you not long since, which he answered. He sends his regards to you and Emma. Give my respects to Emma and all enquiring friends. I wish I was at home to spend Christmas & New Years with you but I suppose we will not spend a very happy one this year but I think we will make up for this one next year. I hope so. Good by Dear sister.*
*Your brother                                      Mack*
*Tell Emma, Frank recd her letter last night.*

Christmas in Danville, Kentucky in the Union Army camp was not like Christmas at home in Salem, where the family gathered together with all of the women cooking their favorite dishes to compliment the wild turkey. Sleighs or buggies proceeded to Sarah's home where there was laughter, carols, and stories told around the fireplace while the children ate their goodies.

The food in camp was plentiful, but Eugene's diarrhea bothered him and he was homesick and miserable. He needed more medicine desperately but the medicine the Army supplied did not work nearly as well as that made by Elvira. He was angry with himself for leaving and joining up with the cause when he was needed at home so badly, much more so than in Kentucky. The glamour gone, all that remained was the cold, the sickness, and a few threats from the Confederate rebels.

Camp Baird     Danville, Ky     Christmas
Dear Wife

I wish you all a Merry Christmas. I am not spending mine very happy but that is accountable for, I suppose. I am pretty well at presant with the exception of the diarrhea. My medicine is about gone. I have given a good deal of it to the other boys. You must send me the receipt for making it, for it is worth more than anything else we can get.

Well, Vira, I will tell you how we are spending our Christmas. We have cooked four cans of fresh Oysters and eat them and we have 5 chickens in the kettles boiling for our dinner. We are not on drill today.

The Col is trying to make it as pleasant for us as possible. There is 15 of us in our mess so that when we get anything we dont have to share with an hundred men so that our 5 old hens is for 15 of us.

One year ago today, Dear Vira, I did not think of being so far away from you today, but we will only hope to be together next year this time, I hope before this time. It makes me feel mad at my fool self for getting in to this abomanable humbug. Well, there is one thing. I have got my eye teeth cut plum into the gooms. Never mind thoug . We will come out right yet.

Our boys are playing poker for sutter check, some are playing ball and some doing as I am, writing a homesick letter. That is the way it goes here all the time. Oh! Dear, I am lonesome today.

Tomorrow, I am to go out on picket. Our Engineers were drove in yesterday by a squad of rebels and we have to put out a double picket.

The people hear say that old Kirby Smith will be here before long.

The local civilians told the soldiers that General Edmund Kirby Smith, who served with General Braxton Bragg, was nearby. Kirby Smith, a fighter, would later become disillusioned with General Bragg because of his lack of aggression in his "hit and run" philosophy of fighting.[58] However, on Christmas Day, rumors that circled saying both were nearby could not be ignored. The Union Army placed double pickets on the outskirts.

Dec. 25$^{th}$ cont.

*Let him come. We want something to wake us up a little. We are spoiling for fear of a fight. The 92$^{nd}$ Ill. is geting to be a regular set of dead heads laying round so much, but it is all for the Union. Well, our chickens are pretty near done and I am to, for I am not in a very good writing mood. Downs is bothering me so I cant half write, so goodby. Write soon and give me all the news you can.*
*Give my love to your folks and Mother and the folks down there.*
*I remain your loving Husband*
*Eugene Mc Swaggart*
*P S Butter is worth 50 cents per lb.*

On December 21, General John H. Morgan went into Kentucky and raided the railroads, destroying communications between General William S. Rosecrans and Louisville. He struck the Louisville and Nashville Railroad north of Munfordville first, followed by Elizabethtown and Muldraugh Hill.[59] On December 25, Morgan's Raiders clashed "with Union troops near Bear Wallow in Kentucky".[60]

---

[58] World Almanac Publication, *The Civil War Almanac*, Intro. by Henry Steele Commager, A Bison Book, New York, NY 1983, p. 379
[59] Frank J. Welcher, *The Union Army, 1861-1865, Organization & Operations, Volume II, The Western Theater,* Indiana University Press, Bloomington & Indianapolic, 1993, p. 808
[60] *The Civil War Almanac,* p. 124

> *Camp Baird, Danville, Ky Dec 28$^{th}$*
> *Dear Wife   I will try and write you once more. I am well at present and hope this will find you the same.*
> *Well, Vira, since I wrote to you before we have been on a forced march for 2 days. The way it hapened, old Morgan started to make an attack on us and, Christmas, we were ordered to pack napsacks and cook 2 days rations,*

Christmas evening, the Ninety-second Illinois Infantry received orders to take up arms in pursuit of General Morgan as they were within fifty miles of the raiders. They were to reinforce Lebanon, Kentucky, threatened by General Morgan, but after a fifteen-mile march, they returned to Danville, under orders.[61]

December 28, 1862 continued.

> *so the next day we started and it began to rain . It rained all day, hard, and we marched about 18 miles and camped in an old muddy cornfield. It rained so hard that we could not keep the water out of our tents, but we bore it all manfully, for it was all for the Union.*
> *Well, we stayed there all night and at 1 o'clock in the morning, we were called out for to take up march again. We were ordered to take 20 rounds of extra catradges and leave our napsacks, tents and take it double quick to Lebanon. That was 14 miles, but about the time we were ready, there came another order for us to go back to bed and be ready for march at 8 o'clock back to Danville, so we are back home again, all but home. We are under a Ky. General*[62] *and he is bound to keep us here for to guard their infernal state.*

---

[61] *Illinois Troops (Union) Infantry, Records of Events, Volume 13, Records of Events for the Ninety-second Illinois Infantry, September 1862 - June 1865*, p. 496
[62] Brigadier General Absalom Baird

*Dear Vira, I never was tired in all my life, it was last night when I got back from our march, but I feel better now. The boys have put me in cook again, so I have no duty to do atall. I dont have to drill unless I want to. I get a little pay extra, enough for to buy my papers with. We would have got our pay if we had not marched, but when we left, the Pay Master skedadled. He was afraid to stay here.*

*Luit. York is pretty sick. We lef a lot of our boys in the hospital that were playing of sick, so the doctor gave them each a dose caster oil and cussed them and then, that if they were not better, he would repeat the dose, so next morning every boy was all right and mighty glad to get with us again. Shirks are treated pretty hard here in the army. If a man goes to the hospital and the Seargeons thinks he is not very sick, they will put him to carrying water or sawing wood. That is the way we are treated, as a general thing. They will never get me to there holes unless I am carried there, but I hope that that time will never come.*

*Well, Vira, I must close so good by. Write soon. Give my love to Mother and all the folks. I remain yours as ever.         Eugene Swaggart*

*Tell Moses that I wrote to him sometime ago. If he dont get it, let me no. I received a letter from you on Christmas that you wrote to me on the 12 of this month and mailed the 22 so I think Moses must have mailed it.*

*He always carys a letter a week or two before he mails it. The envelop was worn out a both ends.*

There was one last stand that year in Danville. The Ninety-second Illinois Infantry, called out along with the others, to pursue General Morgan on December 31, 1862, hoped to intercept him on the Louisville and Nashville railroads.

Company A left the previous day to guard a bridge over the Kentucky River with Major John H. Bohn in command and had not returned.⁶³. However, after being called to arms, the rest of the troops were dismissed, to their disappointment. News came that Morgan left the state.

Measles was rampant in the camp. Many men, transported to the hospital in Lexington, Kentucky, died. Others decidedly were unfit for duty and discharged. Among them were several from the Ninety-second Illinois Infantry.

After the Emancipation Proclamation was signed on January 1, 1863, freed slaves poured into the Union camp thinking they would be allowed to fight. Eugene was not familiar with Africans. He knew them only as servants of the officers. He overheard their conversations and knew they were angry and wanted to fight, but he thought they would need a lot of training before they were ready to take on an army.

> *Camp Baird, Danville      Dec 31$^{st}$ 1862*
> *Dear Wife      Through the kind blessings of the ever smiling heavens, I will try and write you a fiew lines to inform you that I am still well and hope this will find you the same.*
> *Well, Vira, we have not had that fight, yet, with old Morgan, but came very near it this morning. We were ordered to arms this morning and sood in line of battle about an hour. We then heard that Morgan had left the state, so that was a good joke on us, but there is rebels around here at this presant time and if they dont look prety sharp, they will get snubed up, one of these cold nights. The weather is very wet and cold here now, but will not remain so long, I hope.*
> *Co. I. is in a prety bad standing now. We have 3 of our boys in camp with the measles. They are all*

---

⁶³ *Illinois Troops (Union) Infantry, Records of Events, Volume 13, Records of Events for the Ninety-second Illinois Infantry, September 1862 - June 1865,* p. 497

*very low, and there is about 8 or 10 in the hospital at this place, and there are others at, of the company, at Lexington, sick, that will be discharged from the service.*

*Well, Vira, I commenced this yesterday and did not finish for I expected a letter from you, but was disappointed, so I will finish on New Years Day 1863. I will wish you all a happy New Years, although I am not going to spend my New Years as happy as I did Christmas, but next years, we will make it all up I hope, that is, if we all live long enough for to see that time.*

*I have got a sore throat but it is better than it was. I have not had a letter from you since Christmas, and that was an old one, and papers I received, one the Kanosha paper. I have not seen but one Mirror since I have been here. I dont know whether old Mount Carroll is there yet or not, but I hope so. I intend to visit it in less than a year.*

*You must tell Sylvester Brookens not to work to hard and hurt himself untill I get back. We are going to stay here, for protect the state, untill we cant stay any longer, then we will come home. The darkies are in Camp from every direction. After this time, now, there is no more slavery in the U. S. and as soon as the niggas can be, they will all be armed. Then you will hear of some fighting done. It will take all of the whites for to make the nigers fight well.*

*I guess I have writen all you will care about reading. Write and tell me all about yourself and give my love to All. Dear Vira, I wish I could be at home with you a little while, but that cannot be, so you will have to beare with troubles that I cant help any. Oh! Vira, vowed to God I had never left you in the time I did. If it was not for that, I could stand it*

Elvira Van Alstine Swaggart

*first rate, but we must trust in him who is ever watchfull and kind to us and he will do the right thing by us. Goodby. I remain your loving Husband    E. M. Swaggart*

*Give my love to Mother and Annie and all the res*

## Chapter Four
## Guarding Kentucky

The first three weeks of January were quiet in Camp Baird in Danville, Kentucky. Except for pickets and guard duty, nothing much concerning the war happened to the Ninety-second Illinois Infantry. However, many young soldiers fell sick to measles, fever, and diarrhea during that period.

Company A of the Ninety-second Illinois returned to camp on January 3 from their assignment guarding Hickman's Bridge over the Kentucky River.[64]

*Camp Baird,    Danville    Ja 3$^{rd}$, 1863*
*My Dear Wife*
*With plasure that pen cannot express, I seat myself to ans. a long letter I received from you, together with one from my big sis. It was the first I had in over a week. I am pretty well at present and hope these few lines may find you the same. I am glad to hear that you are as well as you are.*
*Well Vira, the prospect of a fight now is poor, more so than I wish it was. We came here for that purpose and we wish to do something that will aid in puting down this rebelion, but instead of that, we are kept here to guard a one horse secesh hole of a Town, but it may be all right for what I know. We keep Morgan out so he cannot get his suplies so easy. Danville was his headquarters.*
*We received news last night that Gen. Rosecrans was fighting Old Bragg in Ten. and that he was wounded and was still in the field and was giving him pefect fits. I hope he will whip them out there, for that is the main reble force.*

---

[64] *Illinois Troops (Union) Infantry, Records of Events, Volume 13, Records of Events for the Ninety-second Illinois Infantry, September 1862–June 1865,* p. 496.

On December 31, 1862, the battle of Stone's River in Murfreesboro, Tennessee began, involving the Union Army of the Cumberland commanded by General William Starkie Rosecrans and the Confederate Army of Tennessee, commanded by General Braxton Bragg. It was a bloody battle where neither Army could take a clear victory. However, General Rosecrans claimed victory when General Bragg pulled out on January 3, although Bragg's troops retained control of essential positions. Rosecrans, after two days of burying the dead and caring for the wounded, took possession of Murfreesboro on January 5, 1863.[65] There were many fatalities, but neither of the Generals were injured or killed. General Bragg received criticism for his decision to pull out of Murfreesboro.

January 3' 1863 continued.

*Our men have taken all of Morgan's Artilery and all of his provision train. If that is so, he is gone up. New Years Eve, Col. Atkins made us a short speech, and he said there was no show for keeping this fight up more than 6 months longer, but he dont know much more about it than you do. It is hard to think how hard Burnsides fought and gained nothing, but I guess he is good for them yet. We hope so.*

*You stated that you will get your county pay. It will be very good for you indeed, for if it were not for it, I dont know what you would do. I dont know as we will get any money for sometime yet.*

*Dear, you must enjoy yourself, as well as you can, and do not fret about me. I know we have to endure a great many hardships, but I knew that before I came here and must put up with what comes. And when it comes to hard for us to stand, why there is another place where we can find rest. You wished me to tell you whether I would come home inside of three years or not. Cap. Becker said I should have*

---

[65] World Almanac Publications, *The Civil War Almanac*, Intro. by Henry Steele Commager, A Bison Book, New York, NY 1983, pp. 125-126

a furlough next winter if we were in the service that long, if such a thing can be had.

Vira, I would like to have been with you at Eds very much. Vira, I have wrote to Ed twice and I guess he dont care enough about a poor soldier to answer my letters.

Vira, indeed I know how to appreciate a home. A home is a home, however poor it may be. Instead of a bed, we have a little pile of straw, and our grub we eat any way we can catch it, but it is all for the Union. If we can only restore it again, we can feel proud that we did what we do, but if not, we can know who to blame.

And Vet has been trading horses again. That takes me, but if he cheated Bill Small, he will do to trade with anybody. I wish I could have been at home to have seen Bill. What did he think about me going to war. I know about what he thought.

I am glad to hear of Vet getting along so well with his making brooms. Tell Jennie to give my love to Aunt Davis folks. You say that you have writen letters to me. I have received most all of them, but the papers never come. I guess you might as well not try to send them. It is postage paid for nothing.

You say you wrote to me Christmas, but it has not come yet. I wrote to you on that day and one sonday and one New Years and today. I guess I average 2 letters a week to you.

Dear Vira, I guess I do recolect our ride and the big comforter. I dont forget such times so easy. If ever we can be permited to enjoy ourselves that well together, I will be satisfied, wont you. Vira, if it were not for your letters, I should give up in dispair and I am thankful mine affords you as much pleasure as yours does me. I am sory that Moses is so poorly and Dicky in the condition that she is. I

guess they miss Mack and Vira there this winter. Tell Jennie I am coming home as soon as the kind lord will enable me to come to see my little plant when it comes to hand.
Well, Vira, I guess I will close. Give my love Jennie and Mother. I remain your loving,     Mack

    The letter Elvira had written to Eugene on Christmas Day arrived, but Eugene was in the hospital with a bad case of diarrhea. The medicine they gave him was not as good as that of Elvira, but it was better than nothing. There were two other soldiers in the hospital with him.
    False rumors were still flying around camp concerning General Braxton Bragg and General John Hunt Morgan. This time, the rumors were false when they told of their deaths.

              Danville    Ky     Jan 6$^{th}$, 1863
Dear Wife
I will try and write to you and ans. the letter you wrote on Christmas day. It came to hand 3 days ago, but was not able to ans. it before . I had a severe attack of the Billous Fever but I am geting better. I will go into camp, tomorrow, if I still gain. Co. I. has a hospital of its own. There is 3 of us in it now. Plat Willis & Tom McKracin, they are both very low with the fever. Dear Vira, I cant write much to you this time. I wrote to you, Annie and Mother the day I was taken sick and gave you about all the news. Our forces are giving it to the rebles everywhere in the westrn Armey. We heard that Old Bragg was killed and his men all taken prisoners. If things (go) as they are going now, we will all be home in 3 or 4 months and hope it will.
Give my love to all. Excuse this short letter. I will write again this week. Good by Dear
I remain your Sincere Husband         Mack

Eugene had good news when he wrote to Elvira - a little money was on its way. He knew Elvira needed the money badly with the baby coming, but sending money was a problem because rebel forces intercepted letters while raiding the railroads.

> Camp Baird, KY                         Jan $8^{th}$ 1863
> Dear Wife
> I will try and ans. your kind and welcome letter which came to hand the $4^{th}$, but I delayed writing for the reason that we expected to be paid and we were happily disappointed, for they made out to pay us for one month and 15 days. I am pretty well at presant, with the exceptions of a very sore breast where I was blistered, but it will be well enough in a fiew days.
> Vira, we have been having good news, for, a fiew days back, we heard that Vicksburgh was taken, but tonights news has contradicted it.
> The news is that Gen. Sherman had to give it up again, but I hope he will flog them out.

General William Tecumseh Sherman attacked Vicksburg on December 29, 1862. He failed in his attack and in his own words, said, " I reached Vicksburgh at the time appointed, landed, assaulted, and failed."[66]

January 8, 1863 continued.

> I expect we will march south now, as we have got our pay, they will move us on forward. Well, that is just what we want. We propose to do something or let us go home and I guess we will have enough of it to do yet and we are going to do it in a hurry. Captain Edg is reading the latest news wile I am writing on his mess chest. Cap is not very well at

---

[66] World Almanac Publications, *The Civil War Almanac*, Intro. by Henry Steele Commager, A Bison Book, New York, NY 1983, p. 125

*preasant, but is so as to be around all the time. He is one of the best men in the old 92d, thats so.*

*Company I was made to feel sad over the loss of another of our brave comrades, Robert Pitman.*[67] *He was from White Side Co. His parents are living there. He died with the quick consumption, that always takes a great many at this time of year. We have another that is not expected to live. He has the measles.*

*I was very glad to get that receipt and am thankfull to you for sending it. You spoke about sending me some socks, but I fear we will leave here before it reaches us, but, if I get them, I shall be very happy for I have bare one pair and they are pretty dirty, but can get along without any for you know is in vain for a Soldier to complain. However, they will a little. The general complaint is they want to go home. I, for one, would like very much to be at home a fiew days, but, it is as it is. We are here and we must put up with it, the best way we can. I intend to keep up as good cheer as a poor soldier can.*

*I think you very noble and kind for such good advice. I shall profit by it surely, but My Dear, it is for you that causes me all my trouble, left all alone, almost, and nobody to look to for help, in time of need. I know I could not be of much good to you, but still, I could show my good will, you know. Well, be it as it may, I pray that you will get along nice. I will enclose $10.00 to you, and if you get it, I will send you some more. It is geting pretty late and they are all wanting to go to bed, so I will have to*

---

[67] Robert Pitman, Wysox, Ninety-second Illinois Infantry, Co. I. – Died at Danville on 1-6-63. Arthur Robbe and Richard Hinton, Booklet from *Rededication Ceremony of the Carroll County Civil War Soldiers & Sailors Monument.*

*close. Oh, you wanted to know whether we are 9 months men or not. There was some such talk, but it (is true) we are 3 years (men).*
*Give my love to all. Remember me to Mother. I remain your loving Husband,*
*Eugene M. Swaggart, Esq*

In Kentucky, the days passed slowly. Rumors were about as usual, but morale was down. So many were sick that it was better to set aside drills for a while.

Officers encouraged the men to live off the land when they could so nothing was said when they brought in food that was much better than that supplied by the Army. Eugene's frame of mind was a little better perhaps because of the nice ham dinners provided by raids on smokehouses nearby. His thoughts returned to the good times he and Elvira had together and he wished they could be together once more so he could reinforce his feelings for her. He was thinking of the baby and hoping it would be a son.

*Camp Baird, Danville, KY    Jan 10$^{th}$ 1863*
*Dear Wife*
*After waiting a long time for a letter I got one last night. It was a pretty old one but I was glad to hear from home.*
*I am well at presant and hope this will find you the same. We are all well as could be expected.*
*The weather is so bad. It rains every other day, regular, and makes it very muddy and bad, you know, for our kind of houses. Plat Willis is very sick and Martin Lower will surely die if he does not get a discharge.    Actias Gaylord got a discharge yesterday and Old James Walker. They will start home in about 2 weeks. Mary Adams man got a discharge and Rily Stoddard, also.*
*Dear Vira, it is not my luck to get one yet, nor do I want one, unless I am useless to Uncle Sam. I want*

to go home as bad as anybody, but we are going to put down this rebelion first. Then we can return thinking that our duty had been preformed.

We are having very good times at presant. We have not drilled any, since well, in two weeks and very seldom that we have dress parde, but I think it will soon be over, for we expect marching orders everyday, but let them come. It is just what we want.

Ed Shipton is sick here in the hospital. He has not been well since he has been in Kentucky. I guess he will get a discharge.

We live pretty well now. One of our boys went out to chop wood and went to a house to buy some butter and the folks not being at home, he tore open the smokehouse and took four nice hams. I tell you what, they are good. They taste old fashioned. We eat the last today for dinner, but I would like some of those big sheep nose apples. I paid 10 cents in town yesterday, but they are to much for the money to buy many of them, dont you think so.

Orderly English is sick. I dont know what is the matter with him.

Well, I dont know hardly anything to write that would be interesting to you. Laying still so long in one place, there is nothing happens of much importance. I think I was at home, I might tell you a thing or two, which I cannot write. Although, I cannot tell as much yet as I can after I get out of the war, that is, if ever I see that happy day. I can only hope to see it ere long as the boys tells me. I want to see my young volinteer. Oh! that I could only be there, but it is no use talking about it, for when I get home, I will be there.

I guess Gen. Sherman is still waiting for reinforcements in front of Vicksburgh. I guess he *will pich in before long. Gen Rosecrans is still after Bragg and taking prisoners every day like everything.*

General Sherman pulled out of Vicksburg and General Rosecrans was criticized for his lack of aggression in the pursuit of General Bragg. The soldiers never seemed to know the truth, possibly because the news arrived slowly and through many sources. As in gossip, the stories grew as they passed from one to another. It is also probable that the War Department deliberately sent false reports in an effort to raise the morale of the troops.

January 10, 1863 continued.

*I hear that you have nice weather, there, this winter. Some of the boys got a letter and they said that the people were plowing there yet, but I think it a little mixed.*

*Vira, I sent you ten dollars by mail. If you get it, I will send you some more. Well, give my love to all. Remember me to Jennie and Mother. Good by.*

*I remain your*
*Mack*

Several of Eugene's friends were in the Stone River battle at Murfreesboro. One was Henry Lego.

*Jan the 12$^{th}$ 1863*
*Camp near Murfreesboro, Tenn*
*Friend Mack*
*It is with pleasure that I write to you and let you know that I am well at preasent and hope these few lines will find you the same. I received your kind and welcome letter a few days ago and was glad to here from you. We have had a hard Battle at Murfreesboro. It commensed the 30$^{th}$ day of Dec. 1862, Wednesday morning. Our Division was supprised and driven back about 2 miles with a*

Jan the 12th 1863
Camp near Murfreesboro Tenn

Friend Mack
it is with pleasure that I write to you and let you know that I am well at present and hope those afew lines will find you the same I received your kind and welcome letter afew days ago and was glad to here from you we have had a hard battle at Murfreesboro it coinmesed the 30 day of Dec. 1862 wednesday morning our Division was suppised and driven back about 3 miles with a heavy loss we succeed in driving the rebbles back aways and held our position

heavy loss. We succeed in driving the rebbles back aways and held our position until they evacuated. Our loss in the company is sixteen in wounded, killed and missing.
I now will give you a list of the boys that is wounded and killed.

> *John Phillip Gelwicks is wounded; Hiram H. Maynard, Joseph Teeter, Joseph Sawer, George Robins, Caleb Ramsome, Levi Lower, Jesse N. Burlin, Philipe Quickbrener, Peter Farel, Christian Boughman - they are all wounded men. I will tell you who was taken prisoner: Frederick Ikerman, Alfred Ward, Adam Lauver. The rebbles took those three last to Vicksburgh for safe keeping.*

John Phillip Gelwich was wounded but returned to war. He was discharged on May 9, 1864 for wounds. Hiram H. Maynard and Joseph Sawer died from wounds immediately. George Robbins died in the hospital at Nashville on March 9, 1863 from wounds received in the battle. Caleb Ransome was discharged with a bad eye, Phillip Quickbranner with a wounded thumb, and Peter Farrell was discharged for wounds on April 21, 1863. A sharpshooter near Dallas, Georgia killed Jesse Berlin on June 24, 1864. Joseph Teeter was shot through the body at Stone's River but served his entire enlistment. All of the others returned to duty and mustered out at the end of their enlistment.[68]

January 12, 1863 continued.

> *I was not in the fight myself. I had bin detailed the Sunday before to go with the Division teames to Nashville to guard men. We started from the Division. They was camped on the Nolinsville Pike, but the next morning, they moved over to the Murfreesboro Pike. We went to Nashville and got our loads and started back. We went within about 2 miles of where we was camped when we started away. We then found out that our Divisions had moved. We then turned off on a mud road that went to the other pike. Went on that road about 3 miles from the pike, we then camped for the night. We had not been in camp a half hour until there was 5 cavalry men come in, all mud, and said that the*

---

[68] Arthur Robbe and Richard Hinton, Booklet from *Rededication Ceremony of the Carroll County Civil War Soldiers and Sailors Monument.*

*rebbles was after them. We only had twenty guards with 48 wagons. We throwed out a picket and expect to be attacked, but they did not come where we was. The next morning we had to turn back, for we could not get through for the mud. We got back as far as Nolinsville. We seen where the rebbles had burned 6 wagons the night before and took 109 prisoners and paroled them. They was hunting after us, but could not find us. We went back to Nashville. The rebbles had burned 104 wagons on the Murfreesboro pike the same night. When we got to Nashville, we staid there 2 days longer and when we got to our Division on the battlefield, they had nothing to eat but corn for two days. They was very hungry. I tell you that the boys seen hard times at this battle.*

*I guess I have said enough about the battle. I presum you know more than I can tel you about it, by this time.*

On January 3, 1863, General Braxton Bragg retreated to Manchester[69] leaving General Rosecrans as the victor.

January 12, 1863 continued.

*Willis Ray, Larntine Johnson, Charles Brace has joined the fourth regular cavalry. They are Rosecrans bodyguard. I see Willis the other day. He was well.*

*Give my best respects to the boys. Excuse bad spelling and writing. Write soon. Nothing more from your old friend.*

*Henry Lego*

*Direct to company I 34 Regiment Ill. Vol, Via Nashville, Tennessee*

---

[69] Robert E. Denney, *The Civil War Years, A Day-by-Day Chronicle of the Life of a Nation*, Foreword by Gregory J. W. Urwin, Sterling Publishing Co., Inc., NY, p. 253

The Ninety-second Illinois Infantry moved again to seek better water in Kentucky and he wanted Elvira to know. After writing to Elvira and begging her for medicine, she tried to mail a large amount to him. It did not arrive, but Eugene was already worrying about how to carry it when it did.

*Camp Baird, Danville, Ky    Jan 13$^{th}$ 1863*
*Dear Wife*
*I receive a good long letter from you last night with pleasure. I only wish I could write you as good a one in return. I am quite well at presant.*
*We changed our camp to the opposite side of the town for the purpose of getting better water. We have a very nice place here. I think that it will be healthier.*
*The boys spilled my ink and I will have to write with a pencil for the first time. The box which you spoke about has not come yet, but we are geting very anxious for to receive something from home, although we did not come here with the expectations of geting much from home. We came here to live on uncle sams grub and wear his cloths and we are going to do it, for all it is hard, but it cant last a great while longer, can it, Dear.*
*I was in town today on a pass from our Col. It was the first time I have felt anything like being free in a long time. You have no idea how strict we are kept here. We are in a worse condition than ever slaves were, but we are geting so that we dont mind it so much. That is what made one so homesick when I first came to Kentucky, but I am geting so that, let what will come, I am satisfied.*
*I saw Shipton today. He looks very bad. He has applied for a discharge and I do hope he will get it for the poor fellow will bleach his bones in this reble land if he dont get one.*

*Dress parade now and I must stop for this time.*
*Dear Vira, I will now try and finish my letter. You say you hope that we will never get into a fight. I think that there is not much danger of having a fight as long as we stay under Gen. Baird. He is a good man, but he is like the rest of our generals, he wants to make his pockets heavy before he does much fighting. That pleases me well enough, if it would bring the war to a close.*

Elvira wrote that the medicine was one its way. However, it did not arrive before Eugene wrote to her.

*I am sorry you sent so much medicine. My napsack is very heavy, and it will be pretty heavy for me to toat. You know, if a man cant carry his napsack, he is left behind, so we must carry everything that we have or leave it. I have, in my napsack, 1 pr of shirts, 1 pr of drawers, 1 pr of pants, dress coat and over coat, 1 ruber blanket, 1 woolen blanket and portfolio, besides, haversack, canteen and 40 rounds of catradges and rifle. It makes a good load for a fellow, again might, when he carries it all day.*
*Dear, I am as carefull of myself as I can be. A fellow cant be to carefull here. I find that so. You wanted to know if I was as thin as I was when I left home. Before I was sick, I weighed 182 pounds. I guess that wil do, wont it, but I am not so fat now. My weight is, at presant, 174. I will be a man by the time I get home.*
*Vira, there is no danger here standing picket. You must not let that trouble you.*
*Cooking is hard work here. Everything is so unhandy. We have to carry our water over a mile, chop our own wood and take care of everything on the march besides my own things. I guess I will not cook more than one month.*

*We have not had any news from the Tenesee Army in sometime, but I hope things are progressing finely.*
*I am glad that you are geting along so well at home. It makes me feel happy. Dear Vira, I would like to be at home for the next fiew weeks as well as you would like to have me but, as you say, one must try and brave it through and look forward for happier days. I would like to see little Frank very much. I guess he will hardly know me when I get home. I am glad that Mother is better. Give her my love. Tell Jennie I would like some of her sausage very much, but would like to be at home to eat it. Thats so. I hope you will have a good sleigh ride on that old plank. Well goodby. Give my love to all.*
*I remain your        Mack.*

It was extremely cold in Kentucky when the Ninety-second Illinois moved camp. The snow started to fall shortly after they moved until there was almost five inches on the ground and straw was difficult to find so the men suffered once more. The Regiment that started out with nine hundred men was down to five hundred and Company I was down from ninety-five men to thirty without fighting a single battle.

*Camp Baird  Danville, Ky Jan 18$^{th}$ 1863*
*Dear Wife*
*It is with great pleasure that I write you once more. I am quite well at presant, and hope this will find you all enjoying the same great blessing. Dear Vira, I have not had a letter since the 11$^{th}$, but the reason, I suppose, is because the cars cannot run between here and Covington on account of the snow and ice. On the track, it has snowed and rained and froze all this week. We had a hard time of it on account of moving our camp. We had no straw and*

*could not get any. The snow is about 5 inches deep here now. The citizens here say it is the worst storm they ever see, but I guess it will not last long. The sun is shining quite warm today.*

*Vira, Co I is having very bad luck. We buried another one of our boys yesterday. His name is James O'Neal[70] from Milledgeville and another one died this morning by the name of Benjamin F. Eshleman,[71] both with Tifoid Fever. That makes four with in 6 weeks and there is 2 or 3 not expected to live, but your Mack is all right yet. Actias Gaylord[72] will start home in about a week and I guess that I will write and send one by him, and will all so send my likeness to Mother. I expect 4 or 5 letters when the mail gets in.*

*We got a firkin of butter last night from Mt. Carroll. You better think there was some cheering done for old Carroll. The box has not come yet, but there is no danger but what we will get it, I guess.*

*As for old Morgan, he has left the country for good. We have not heard anything from him in a good while, but I am thinking that we will be kept here a good while.*

*Our Col has left us. He has been promoted to brigadier Gen, and our little agitant is Agitant Gen, so our Lieut Col will be Col. of the 92d. He is a splendid man. He is very pious. Col. B. F. Sheets is his name.*

---

[70] James O'Neal, Wysox, Ninety-second Illinois Infantry, Co. I, died at Danville, Kentucky on 1-17-63 - Arthur Robbe and Richard Hinton, Booklet for *Rededication Ceremony of the Carroll County Civil War Soldiers and Sailors Monument.*

[71] Benjamin F. Eshelmon, Mt. Carroll, Ninety-second Illinois Infantry, Co. I., died at Danville, Kentucky on 1-19-63 - Ibid. Robbe and Hinton, Booklet for *Rededication Ceremony*

[72] Actias Gaylord, Rock Creek, 34th Illinois Infantry, Co. I., discharged for wounds on 2-3-63. - Ibid. Arthur Robbe and Richard Hinton, Booklet for *Rededication Ceremony of the Carroll County Civil War Soldiers and Sailors Monument.*

None of the promotions took place until much later.
January 18, 1863 continued.
*You would hardly know the 92d reg now. We muster only about 500 men now and when we came here, we could muster over 900. They are most of them sick, only what fiew have discharged. Co I. have 30 men fit for duty and 65 unfit for duty and details on other duty, so it brings the boys on every other day, thats whats the matter. You must excuse poor writing for I had to hurry so that I could mail it today. Give my love to all. Remember me to the little folks. Goodby. I remain you*
*Affectionate Husband.*
*Mack Swaggart*
*Give my love to Bill Small and John Miller. Tell them to write if they have time.*

By the campfire at night, Eugene was thinking about the wonderful sleigh rides he and Elvira took and he decided to write to her.

*Jan 20$^{th}$ 1863     Camp Baird,     Danville, KY*
*Dear Wife*
*After waiting a long time for a letter I got one last night. It was a pretty old one but I was glad to hear from home. I am well at present and hope this will find you the same.*
*It is raining like everything, and is taking all our snow from us and the sooner, the better. I suppose you have nice sleighing now. I would like to have one more good old ride with you like some we had last winter. Dear Vira, them old times are not forgoten yet. It does one good to sit and think of good times past and times that are to come, if I am permited to live to see them, which I hope I will and that soon.*

> *We heard last night that Burnside is advancing into Fredericksburgh. He intends to give them all that he has got in his shop, for this will be the third time, so guess he will whip them out this time.*

Indiana's General Ambrose E. Burnside, with his army of the Potomac, made preparations to take Fredericksburg in the second half of January, but it was raining so hard, his march became known as the "mud march". Frustration caused him to pull back and accept failure again. President Abraham Lincoln consequently removed him from his position and he later assumed leadership in the Western Theater.[73]

January 20, 1863 continued.

> *We have not heard anything from Gen. Shermans army in sometime, but I guess he will come out all right in a fiew months, but we cannot tell. We may get through in three months, and we may not in three years, but we are determined to whip them and we cant do it unless we fight . I do not desire to get in a fight, for you know that I all ways a coward, but I would like very well to have revenge for coming here and enduring the hardships that we have to, and the only way to get it is to kill about 2 dozen of the darned butternuts, and I will, if ever I get chance, for I am dread full savage nowadays. You would think so if you could see me, I bet.*
>
> *Vira, you wished to know who I sleep with. It is young Downs, son of the old man Downs. He is a very good bunky, but not so good as I have had in my life. We take turns in making our bed. He makes it one night and me the next. As for me cooking any longer, I would not do it for 20 dollars a month. It is to hard for one to cook all the time. There is so much bad weather. Standing guard here*

---

[73] World Almanac Publications, *The Civil War Almanac*, Intro. by Henry Steele Commager, A Bison Book, New York, NY 1983, pp. 127-128, 319

*now is not very hard, for Gen. Baird lets the pickets do about as they please. If they stand near a house, why they go in to it and stay all night and you see that a house is better to stay in than an old tent.*
*You must give my respects to Mrs. Emmert. I am glad that you have so good a neighbor and so close by you. I will write to Mother every little while. You see I cant find anything to write to at one place, that would be interesting. I wrote to little Jennie and will write to all in time. Tell Wm Small I should be very glad to rec. a letter from him.*
*I am glad you got your pay from the county. It will help you very much indeed.*
*Well, goodby. Give my love to Jennie and Vet.*
*I remain your,                Mack*
*Tell Dicky I would like to hear from her and Moses very much. I have writen twice to Mose withe out an answer.*

Eugene was sending Henry Lego's letter to Elvira and had some comments to make about it. He was particularly upset about Phillip Queckbranner who was going home with a wounded thumb. Thumbs were lost often in plowing and farm duties, but a farmer could work easily with a missing thumb and there were so many men dying with high fevers and diseases that could not get discharges.

Eugene had just written a letter to his friend, James Masters and then received the news of his death. The Captain of the Ninety-second Illinois, Company C died of an illness and he was feeling the misery of the Captain's wife and all of the families back home who were receiving news of their loved ones. Anger had begun to surface in Eugene. The war was hitting home more so than it had before. A lot of thought was going into living and dying and Eugene wondered which was better. The only thing he was sure of, was his desire to be with Elvira and hold her in his arms.

In Salem, Moses and Amanda Ludisky were still sick and the farm suffered. Elvira was doing all she could but she was seven months pregnant and she needed the little food that was available to them for Jennie, Sylvester and John Russell. Sylvester's eyes were worse and he decided to seek help with a local woman known for her ability to cure ailments and tell fortunes.

The Army was four months behind in pay and no one knew when it was coming, but hoped it would be soon.

On January 22, when Eugene wrote to Elvira, he was preparing to move out. No one knew where they were going or why, but a lot of talk passed through the camp.

> *Camp Baird, Danville, KY, Jan 22$^{nd}$ 1863*
> *Dear Wife*
> *I had the pleasure of reading a long letter from you last night, to hear that you were all well. I am well with the exception of a cold, but that is nothing to complain of here in the army. I wrote to Annie yesterday and to you the day before. I had just writen to James Masters, but I guess he will hardly get it, poor fellow. His folks will take it very hard, but he is better off than if he had been spared to live in the army three years. I suppose you do not think as I do, but a man had better be dead, at once, than to enlist and die by inches. We cannot expect to ever come out sound men. There is no such thing in the book, but we must do the best we can, you know, get through all right, if we can. If we dont, all right, for we had no business here, thats whats the matter. Our boys that are sick now are getting better. Mrs. Stouffer has a sad journey to take the body of her dead husband home with her. The regt. has to escort the corps[74] to the express office this*

---

[74] The corpse of Capt. William Stouffer, Mt. Carroll, Ninety-second Illinois Infantry, Co. I, died 1-21-63 from illness - Arthur Robbe and Richard Hinton,

afternoon. There, she will be alone with it. It is hard, but cant be helped. The high must fall as well as the low.

There is some talk of us marching, but I dont know as we will. They all think we are to go to Vicksburgh, Ten.. I hope not, dont you.

Oh! how I would like to see my little Wife and____ but I must only look forward to that day when I will stop on the old place. I bet I will jump ten feet. That will be a big jump for me, wouldent it. I be glad to be coming in on the 9 o'clock train some nice morning. Oh, it is so good to think about, but will wait with great patience till that time comes.

I feel very sorry for Moses & Dicky. They are having hard times of it. Dear Vira, I think you very kind to help them all you can, but you must not rob yourself and Jennie. I guess that we will be paid off soon. There is four month pay back yet. I will send you some more. You will need more by the time I can send it.

Our box has not come yet. I dont know what keeps it so long on the road. I cannot get any stamps here. I am glad you remember me so well with a fiew every letter, for it is all the comfort I take to write to you, although I cannot write much.

I am glad that Henry Lego come out all right. I am in hopes I will get to see him if we march south. I bet there would be some shaking hands done bout that time. Yes, I can all most imagine what is going to transpire. I can see how everything looks there plain as day, but I cant see one thing.

I do hope that Sylvester will get his eyes cured. It will a wonderfull thing, indeed.

---

Arthur Robbe and Richard Hinton, Booklet from *Rededication Ceremony of the Carroll County Civil War Soldiers and Sailors Monument*.

*Tell David if he enlists to come to the 92$^{nd}$ Co. I, we need him here and 10 or 12 more good men just like him.*

*Well, Dear Vira, I guess I have writen all I can for this time, and I expect you will hear of me geting my thomb shot off so I can come home like all the rest.*

*Give my love to sister Jennie and Dicky and Mary and Mother*

*Well everybody. Good by*

*I remain your      Swaggart*

On January 20, 1863, a new division formed in Louisville under General Gordon Granger, which he took to Nashville, Tennessee in the Department of the Cumberland. Fort Henry and Fort Donelson transferred from the Department of the Tennessee to the Department of the Cumberland[75] and the Ninety-second Illinois Infantry became part of that division.

The long awaited marching orders came. The Ninety-second Illinois left Camp Baird in Danville, Kentucky on January 26, 1863. Their loss in soldiers due to illness, discharge and death was nearing two hundred.[76]

*Camp Baird,    Danville, Ky     Jan 24$^{th}$ 1863*

*Dear Wife*

*As we are about to march, I will write you a fiew lines. We are going to reinforce Rosecrans so we will have something else to do besides standing guard. Tomorrow is sunday and I guess we will start. I wrote you yesterday, but if I get on the march, you know I cant write very well untill we stop.*

---

[75] Frank J. Welcher, *The Union Army, 1861-1865, Organization & Operations, Volume II, Western Theater,* Indiana University Press, Bloomington & Indianapolis, 1993, pp. 129-130

[76] Thomas M. Eddy, *The Patriotism of Illinois, A Record of the Military History of the State, Chapter XXII, Regimental Sketches,Ninety-second Illinois Infantry, 1865,* p. 370

Dear Vira, I hope that we are going now to do something so that we can get home sometime. I suppose that we will take the cars from Lebonon to Louisville and from there we will go on the river. I guess we will have a good time going. I hope so anyway.

Vira, I have got me a new pen. It dont write very good yet. I paid two dollars for it. Dont you think me extravigant, but I had so much writing to do that I could not do it with a steel pen. Vira, you can write to me the same for the mail will follow us up everyday. I am afraid we will have to leave without our box. It has not come yet. Goodby, Dear. I will write as often as I can.

*Mack*

## Chapter Five
## En Route to Tennessee

On January 26, 1863, the Records of Events of the Ninety-second Illinois Infantry said, "Struck tents before daylight and commenced our march. We marched from Danville (Kentucky) sixteen miles, and camped for the night five miles north of Hamsling." The following four days, they marched eighteen miles, twenty miles, twenty miles and fourteen and one-half miles consecutively. The second day they camped near Lawrenceburg and the last day within two and one-half miles of Louisville, Kentucky.[77]

On the way to Louisville, Eugene wrote to Elvira.

*January 25th Ky. 1863*
*Dear Wife*
*I will write you a fiew lines to let you know how we get along in our march. I stand the march first rate. We are within 35 miles of Louisville. We have marched 3 days and expect to get through to Louisville in 2 days more. From there I dont know where we will go.*
*It is very hard weather for us. It has rained and snowed all the time since we left Danvill. Tonight we had to shovel the snow away so we could put up our tent but that is nothing. We will not have it as hard as the old 34th regt. did when they were in that last battle. I had a letter from Henry Lego. He said he was not in the fight. He that he was after provisions but did not get to the regiment till after the fight was over. He said that they were with out rations 2 days and lived on raw corn all the time.*
*I had a letter from you a short time before we left Danville and answered it. I have not had time to*

---

[77] *Illinois Troops (Union) – Infantry, Records of Events, Volume 13, Records of Events for the Ninety-second Illinois Infantry, September 1862 - June 1865*, p. 496

*write much but think I will write a gain when we get to Louisville.*
*I hope you are well as I am. I like marching better than laying still. We have not carried our napsacks on this march and get our bitter twice a day.*
*Write via Louisvill Ky.*
*Give my love to all. I remain your*
*Eugene Swaggart.*
*I will send you Henrys letter*

    The dawning of morning on January 31 found the Ninety-second Illinois marching once again until they arrived at the port where they boarded the transports, Tempest and Antonio, in readiness to sail the following morning. The trip took five days, but it was February 8 before they disembarked. The packet boats, turned into transports, went down the Ohio River and up the Cumberland River into Nashville, Tennessee. The total distance they traveled was five hundred forty miles.[78]

    Eugene hated the trip. He sailed on the Packet Tempest where man and beast crowded body to body. Eugene had never sailed before and he tired quickly. There was no room to move, but he wrote to Elvira on his first day out.

*Louisville, Ky. Feb 1$^{st}$ 1863*
*Dear Wife*
*I will try and write you a fiew lines to let you know how I am getting along. By this time we are on the boat, now, and it is almost impossible for to write. There is 500 of us on our boat, on lower deck among the mules, so you see, it makes us pretty thick. I am well, but am rather sore and tired after our march. I wrote to you while we were on the march.*

---

[78] *Illinois Troops (Union) - Infantry, Record of Events, Volume 13, Records of Events for the Ninety-second Illinois Infantry*, September 1862 - June 1865, p. 496

*We arived here Jan 30th and that evening, I was made happy with a letter from you. I never, in all my life, see such times. We comenced going on board yesterday morning and they kept it up all day, loading wagons, mules and horses and military stores of every description. I expect we will leave for Nashvill tonight sometime.*

*Oh, I cant write now, hardly, but I will try and write something. I heard that that Mrs. Butler tells fortunes. I wish you could have her tell yours and see what becomes of poor me. I hope she will cure Vets eyes. It would be a great thing, indeed.*

*Dear Vira, I am looking everyday for news of great importance. I am allmost afraid of hearing bad news, but I hope and pray that God will take it in his care. Of course, he will.*

*We are on board the Packet Tempest. She is a new boat, has never made but one trip, but I guess she will carry us throug all right.*

*Tell John Miller I will write him as soon as I get a better place to write. Give my love to all. Remember me to Jennie.*

*Good by Dear Wife. From your loving      Mack*
*Excuse this for it is the best I can do this time.*

Aboard the Packet Tempest, the soldiers heard all of the news and received reports of what others had seen. Eugene wrote to Elvira about the battle reports he had heard.

*Fort Donaldson, Tennessee          Feb 5th 1863*
*Dear Wife*
*I will try and write yu a fiew lines to let you know that I am yet well. We arived here yesterday, just one day to late for to have a hand in the fight. Our men were atacted by about 5,000 reble Cavelry and we only had one regiment here. They would have*

Tennessee

Fort Donaldson Feb. 5th 1863
Dear Wife
I will try and write you a fiew lines to let you know that I am yet well we arived here yesterday just one day to late for to have a hand in the fight. our men were attacted by about 5.000 reble Cavelry, and we only had one regiment here they would have whiped our men had it not been for our gun boats that was escorting our division up the river but they opened on them just in time they killed about Two Hundred of the buternuts and we lost about 13. killed the boys went out on the battle ground to see them bury the rebles they say. that they were the worst looking beings they ever looked at our side was under Col. Hardee from

whiped our men, had it not been for our gun boats that was escorting our Division up the river, but they opened on them just in time. They killed about two hundred of the buternuts and we lost about 13 killed.

Confederate General Nathan Bedford Forest and Brigadier General Joseph Wheeler, commanders of the rebel forces, attacked Fort Donelson on February 3, 1863. Colonel Chester Harding from Missouri was in command at the fort. Troops garrisoned at the fort under Colonel Harding fought back. The gunboats escorting the Union troops arrived in time to help by opening fire on the Confederate troops. Reports from the Union forces listed twelve killed with thirty injured. "Southern reports listed one-hundred killed, four-hundred wounded and three-hundred taken as prisoners."[79]

February 5, 1863 continued.

*The boys went out on the battleground to see them bury the rebles. They say that they were the worst looking beings they ever looked at. Our side was under Col. Hardee from Illinois.*

*I have not heard from you, Dear Vira, since we were on the march from Danville and cant tell when I will. I dont know where we will go yet. We are on the old stinken boat yet, but hope to get off soon. We have had a hard time of it. Our grub has been hard crackers and raw fat pork, but we are cooking now. The boat is tied up for that purpose. It has been very cold on this trip untill last night. It moderated and snowed all night.*

*Dear, I dont know what to do. I want to hear from you so bad and cant, but I will write as often as I can. It is a very hard place for to write. Direct your letters by the way of Louisville, Ky. Give my love to all, to Jennie & Mother from Mack.*

After disembarking from the packet boat, Tempest, the Ninety-second Illinois "marched out on the Franklin Pike and

---

[79] World Almanac Publications, *The Civil War Almanac*, Intro. by Henry Steele Commager, A Bison Book, New York, NY 1983, p. 130

made camp three miles South of Nashville".[80] On February 9, 1863, they marched into camp and saw a lot of the aftermath f the battle. Eugene, after some thought, decided to get a look at the prisoners, but saw a sight much worse.

Eugene was thinking a lot about Elvira and the baby that was on its way. He wondered just when it would arrive. Without mail from home, he just did not know.

*Nashville Ten. Feb 9<sup>th</sup> 1863*
*Dear Wife*
*I am going to write you a fiew lines to let you know that your Mc is yet well, after our long march. We arived here at Nashville last Saterday, but did not get into camp untill today. It seems good to get in camp after being on board of that boat so long.*
*Dear Vira, I have not writen as often to you as I would like to have done, for the reason that I could not write on the boat. I wrote to you while we were at Fort Donaldson. They had a nice little fight at that place. It was one of the greatest victories ever won by our army. The rebles say that they lost between 500 & 800, killed and missing, while we only lost 13 men. I thought, when we landed, that I would not go out on the battleground for I thought I would get a chance to see all the dead rebles some other time, that I wanted to, but the next day, I concluded to go up and see the prisoners. They were bad enoug to look at, but while I was out, here come a wagon load of dead rebles, so I got a sight of them. Oh! horror, I never saw such looking beings in my life. They were some that the rebles tried to take of with them, but the gun boats hussled them off to fast, so they had to leave them. They were buried, all in one hole, just like covering up so*

---

[80] *Illinois Troops (Union) Infantry, Records of Events, Volume 13, Records of Events for the 92<sup>nd</sup> Illinois Infantry, September 1862 -June 1865*, p. 497

many dead hogs to get them out of sight. Dead horses lay in great heaps. I saw in one place, ten horses, all killed at one shot from a big siege gun as they were making charge on it.

So, we were passing through the town of Nashville, Wait Downs Cousin came to see him. He was wounded in the right thigh. He says that Henry Lego is well. Their regt. is about twenty miles from here, but I guess I will not get to see the little man. Wait was glad to meet with him.

It was Caleb Ransome. He says that they have got 16 men in their Co. fit for duty. That is geting down pretty fast.

Dear Vira, I have not had a letter from you in a good while. I am looking for one tonight. It is about time for me to look for them. I heard that our mail matters would not come through by the Ky. railroad anymore. They are in some kind of a mess with Uncle Sam, so it will come by water and, consequently, will not be so regular, for at times, the Cumberland is blockaded by the rebles. One fleet was fired in too, but they see the old dirty gun boats and got back. We stoped and skirmished a little, but did not do anything worth note. Our forces just now passed us with 28 prisoners. They are fighting a little south of us everyday. The citizens say that the rebles are deserting like fun.

Vira, I would like to see you and my little _____. I dreamed that it was all over with and all well.

Well, my Dear, I hope you will not get to feeling to bad because you do not hear of oftener, but I will write as often as I can.

Give my love to all. Tell Jennie, she will have to get that gound ready for me. Good by my Dear Wife. I remain yours as ever.

Eugene Swaggart

## Chapter Six
## In Camp at Nashville

When the Ninety-second Illinois Infantry arrived in Nashville, they heard the news that they were to be reserve troops. Tempers were short when they thought they would be sitting and waiting while other troops did most of the fighting.

Eugene and his bunkie, George Wait Downs, had been inseparable for five months, living in crowded quarters that were too close to suit either one of them. A fight broke out that Captain Becker had to break up. He had known both Eugene and Wait since they were young boys. He understood what they were going through being away from home and their families. If they could not fight the war, they would fight each other. He knew Eugene had been sick with diarrhea for sometime and his temper was short, so he broke up the fight and did no more.

The package with the diarrhea medicine and socks still did not arrive. Now the chances were poor that it would come.

*Camp near Nashville Tenn    Feb 12$^{th}$ 1863*
*Dear beloved Wife*
*I received two long letters from you last night, one date Jan. 27, with two sheets in it. The other was Feb. 3$^{rd}$. They found me well, with the exception of a Diarrhea which I have had for near 2 months. It grows worse. I did not get the medicine you send and guess I never will since we have got so far away from Danvill. I expected to hear of some great disaster, but did not.*
*We have nice weather hear now. It is clear and warm one day, the next is cold and rainy, and I suppose such weather will continue all spring. It generally does, so I am told, in this country, but I am still in hopes that we will not be long here in this C.S.A.*

*Dear Vira, the first letter I read of yours last night, gave me good news. That was that Vet was going to live there and farm and all of you live togather, but the other contradicted it, saying that you were going to split up. I was in hopes that you would live there untill I got home, but if you cant, Dear, you must do the best you can.*

*I thought I could send you some more money by this time, but on our march down here, we were so near starved that it took very near all I had to carry me through. While on the river, we could not get anything but hard crackers and coffee. That was pretty tough. I dont know as I ever told you. Our route down hear, we marched from Danville to Louisville, Ky. There we took boats, went down the Ohio to Smithland. There, we went up the Cumberland to Nashville, where we are yet.*

*There is another of Co. I. dead. It is Thompson Shore[81], one of Dickys old Scholars. He died at Danville. Since we left there, that makes five that is better off than if they were in the service of U. S. We dont get any news here now atall, so we dont know where or what is going on, but there is some talk of having another big fight at Mrfreesboro. I dont know how true it is. We are in the 1st brigade, 3d Division of the Army of the Cumberland, so we are the reserves. We are in the rear, so we dont have any guard duty at all, or scarcely any drill. Our Co. is pretty good health. Mart Lower is very sick. He is the only one, I believe.*

*I received 5 letters last night but guess I will hardly ans. all of them this time - 2 from you, 1 from Mose, 1 from Mother, 1 from Annie.*

---

[81] Thompson M. Shore, York, 92nd Illinois Infantry, Co. I, died at Danville, Ky on 2-26-63 - Arthur Robbe and Richard Hinton, Booklet for *Rededication Ceremony of the Carroll County Civil War Soldiers and Sailors Monument.*

*Wait and me are not on very good terms at presant. He called me a damd liar and that I could not take from any person and was going to thrash the gent, but the Capt. stoped the mess. He has not spoken to me since. I have spoke to him but he never answers me, but I guess he will come to after while.*
*Well, I guess I will close for this time. Give my love to Jennie and all of the rest. I remain your loving Husband*
*E M Swaggart*
*I guess we will get our pay soon.*
*Direct Via Cairo, Ill.*

The weather was raining and cold, not good conditions for those who were sick. Nashville had a large hospital where the Army placed the wounded and sick. It was so wet that some of the soldiers, who were in Nashville, because of wounds or sickness, could not return to their troops.

Eugene really enjoyed music. When the infantry band played, he always admired the musicians. He played the fiddle and sometimes, on lonely nights, he played with some of the members of the band. One of the men who played in the band in Danville, Kentucky was dead. His name was Henry Browning and Eugene knew he would miss him a lot.

George Wait Downs and Eugene had distanced themselves from each other at Captain Becker's request. Things were better between them and they each had new bunkies to share their quarters.

Back home, Moses was still dragging his feet with the lawsuit concerning the land and Eugene was getting a little irritated. He had confidence that Moses knew what to do; he was just reluctant to push on, possibly because of the pressure John Miller was putting on their mother, Sarah. John had lived with the Swaggart family for years and thought he should have a portion of the settlement. John wanted to be sure Sarah received a portion he would be able to use.

Nelson was also a factor in the lawsuit and he lived in Oregon where it took a lot of time to send paperwork for signatures.

*Camp near Nashville Tenn.      Feb 14<sup>th</sup> 63*
*Dear Wife*
*As I am doing nothing at presant, I will pass away an hour or two with you. I am about the same as I was when I wrote you before. We are having very wet weather now. It makes one feel lonesome and bad when they are sick.*
*Caleb Ransome is here with us today. He came out with Wait yesterday and could not get back to town on account of the rain. I like him very much. We had a good long talk concerning the fight. There is but 16 left in their Co. fit for duty. He says Henry Lego would like to be at home, but makes a bully soldier. Jake & Fred Hedling are both well. Peter Zimer is well, and all of the boys from there except poor James Masters*[82]*, but I suppose he is better of now than he was before, for they tell that all soldiers go to heaven when they die, but I am afraid that a good many never see that land to rest. Well, I dont want to preach to you now for when I get home, I will tend to all such things as that, you know.*
*We heard that Henry Browning*[83] *was dead. We left him at Danville. It will be awfull heard blow on his Mother. He was one of our band. It makes a vacancy there, for he was good musician.*
*Charly Reynolds is not very well. I guess he will get over it. I sleep with him, or in other words, he is my bunky. I feel, sometimes, as though I had of better never traded off my old bed fellow, but I will change back sometime, I hope, if the lord is willing, wont I,*

---

[82] Corp. James Masters, Mt. Carroll, 34<sup>th</sup> Illinois Infantry, Co. I, Killed at Stone's River 12-31-62 - Arthur Robbe and Richard Hinton, Booklet of *Rededication Ceremony of the Carroll County Civil War Soldiers & Sailors Monument.*
[83] Henry Browning, 92<sup>nd</sup> Illinois Infantry, Co. I – died at Danville, Ky - Only information is from the letter.

*dear old gal. If I had hold of you, I would give you the hardest old Hugg Ever you had, I bet.*
*I expect Actias Gaylord has got home by this time. I have not heard yet. Geo. Fomlinson has applied for his discharge and I guess he will get it, for he is no account here, for nothing, but let him go. He never come for to fight, but probably, if I should get mine, you would say the same by me.*
*I guess there is no danger. I hope not, dont you. I am anxious to hear from you. I got 5 letters the other night, but they were all old ones. I expect one or two in tonights mail.*
*Vira, I did not say anything to Mose in regard to the law suite, but will the next time I write. I will give him fits if he dont do something towards settleing it. I should think he would try and do some more than he does about it. He knows the condition of affairs better than I can tell him, if he would only act, but I guess it will all come right.*
*Dear Vira, I am writing this for a Valentine, as it is the 14$^{th}$. It is the best I can do, so you will have to excuse me and guess who it came from. That hard to do. From..*
*You know who sent it*
*To my old Gal Vira.*

On the sixteenth of February, Eugene wrote to Elvira once again.

*Camp near Nashville Tenn    Feb 16$^{th}$. 1863*
*Dear Wife - I with pleasure will seat my self to ans. your more than wellcome letter which I received last night bearing date of Feb 10$^{th}$. I am so anxious to hear form you. In every letter I look for great news. As for my health, it is not very good. I expect to have the ganders. I have simtoms of them.*

I was never so pleased in my life as I was to hear that you were going to stay at home. Oh! you have no idea how bad I felt to hear of Sylvester not farming. It seemed to me as though you would all be split up and you would not have proper care but your last letter settles all.

Dear Vira, you want me to come home I know but not much more than I would like to be there. But it is as you say, hope is the stamp of life. We must have patience and trust in god for my restoration. I know that he doeth all things well. You say if you only knew when to look for me home it would be a great comfort to you. Dear Vira, if I could tell I would but I dont see much farther than I did at first. But Dear beare with your troubles and I will with mine and when the time comes we will be more than paid for our suspence. I think you a little hero and more yet a true and noble hearted wife.

You told me in your other letter that you walked down to Mothers and back. I dont see what in the world you are made off for to tumble round as you do but I would rather see you that way than to see you like Dicky or Flora, so awfull cross X.

My dirrhoea is very bad. It runs me night and day. I am afraid it will run in the cronic but hope not. I am doctrin with Dr. Stevenson but he dont help me much yet.

Vira, in regard to my likeness, I did not have an opportunity of getting it before Gaylord went home but will get it as soon as I can.

I have got quite a mostach. You ought to see it but am getting poor. I have lost 15 lbs. since we left Danvill in about 8 weeks.

I am really sory that you spilled your ink but I did not know you had a carpit. I am glad you have one.

> *I rather think you get a long at home better than if I were there, dont you.*
>
> *Oh yes about that garden. I dont know as I will be there in time to help you make it but I want you to have a good one and plenty of potatoes for you know soldiers in Tenesee dont get many of them so when I come I can have some. I would give more for a peck of potatoes than any thing else in the earthe line but no use talking.*

Concerning the baby.

> *You say I could tend to my little plant but I am a very poor hand you know. I have heard what Madame Butler said but I rather think she is flatering you but hope not.*
>
> *Give my love to all. Tell Jennie I might make a small rack and send it to you in a letter but it might not get through the post office safe. I love you as ever,*
>
> > *your Mack.*
>
> *Be sure and direct by Louisville. I told you by Cairo but it is rong.*

Troops were pulling out, but the Ninety-second Illinois was still waiting. The current rumor was that many of the troops were going to Vicksburg. Eugene was hoping they were not a part of that movement as he would have to get on a boat again and his one experience was enough for him.

Reports of more deaths came in and some of his friends, dismissed from the hospital, complained that they had poor treatment. They said doctors were eating soft bread sent for the patients, while the patients just had hard crackers. Eugene knew Elvira participated in the Soldier's Aid Society, rolling bandages and giving provisions when she could. He wanted her to know exactly what was happening to those supplies. He was still waiting to hear about the birth of the baby, but no news arrived announcing the birth. He was happy, however, to hear that Elvira was all right.

*Washington's Birthday, 1863*
*Camp Near Nashville, Tennesee*
*Dear Wife*
*I will ans. your welcome letter which came today while I was out choping wood (Sonday). It gave me pleasure to hear that you was well, but I was expecting different news from what I got, being I had no letter for so long.*
*Well, Vira, my health is better than when I wrote last. I guess I will come out all right after while.*
*The troops are all leaving here. Some are going to Vicksburgh, Mississippi, and some are going to Murfreesboro. We dont know but we will go to Vicksburgh also, but hope not, would rather not take anymore boat rides in the Military line.*
*Our boys are well as usual. Martin I. Lower[84] is dead. He died on his way to Louisville from here. I guess he was buried at Fort Donolson. He is the 7$^{th}$ out of our Co. He ought to been discharged but our efforts never done anything for him in trying to get him discharged.*
*I had a letter from Henry Lego. He is well and says the other boys are, now. We cant get any news here of any importance, so we are just living, living in hopes, merely, and that is about all. We are looking for a fight at Murfreesboro, or in that vacinity, but dont know whether they will make a stand or not. Sam Hall is here from York. He came after Geo.*

---

[84] Martin L. Lower, Salem, 92$^{nd}$ Illinois Infantry, Co. I, died at Nashville on 2-20-63 - Arthur Robbe and Richard Hinton, Booklet of *Rededication Ceremony of the Carroll County Civil War Soldiers & Sailors Monument.*

Robbins[85]. *I have not seen him yet. Robbins is wounded in the knee. He is a brother-in-law to Hamilton Starns.*

*Dear, Vira, you must be carefull and not get to feeling bad if you should not hapen to get my letter regular, for we are among so many, and such large mails, that a great many letters are miss carried, but I hope you will get all of them. I guess Mary Christian's all right now her man is at home safe and sound, by this time, with the exception of one thomb, that is not much to what some of us will loose, I am afraid. Still, I think we will all see our home, that lives, by next fall. They cant keep this thing a going any longer without foreign aid, but of all things, keep out of that soldiers aid society, as they call it. It is the biggest humbug ever was practiced in. They may mean well enough, but instead of aiding poor sick soldiers, it goes to the hospitals and the damnable sholder straps reap the benefit of it. I know it. I see it in our own regt., where soft bread was furnished for the sick, and the doctor and waiters and clerks would eat it and give the sick hard crackers, that is the way it goes, but god, I trust, will bring all such things to account in the future time. Give my love to all. Remember me to Jennie and Mother. Excuse my pencil as my ink was spilled.*

*Goodby from your*
*Eugene*

Life was not going as Eugene had planned. When he left home, he thought Sylvester was going to farm his land for him,

---

[85] George Robbins, 34${}^{th}$ Illinois Infantry, Co. I – died at Nashville on 3-9-63 of wounds - Ibid. Arthur Robbe and Richard Hinton, Booklet of *Rededication Ceremony of the Carroll County Civil War Soldiers and Sailors Monument.*

but Sylvester decided to try making brooms. John Russell left and Sylvester could not farm alone, not with his poor eyesight.

Elvira gave the medicine for diarrhea to the family of Lieutenant David Colehour to be mailed with other supplies. The box arrived filled with cakes and sausages but no medicine, so Eugene was disappointed.

> Camp Nashville Tenn   Feb 27$^{th}$ 1863
> Dear Wife
> I had the exquisite pleasure of reading your kind letter dated Feb. 21$^{st}$ which I received just now. I am about the same old thing. I am not any worse nor any better as I knows on as the boy said.
> That long looked for box came at last. We opened and found every thing but my medicine. My socks were done up very nice and came through in good order. I can allmost define the reason of it not coming. You know in the first place the box was got up for Luit. Colehour and when they come to pack the box it would not hold the bottles so the med was cast out. They packed the box full of cakes and minse pies and sausages and were on the road so long that they were all rotten when they opened the box. I was really glad when I see the game they were playing. I suppose you could find the bottle at town but if you do you need not try to send it to me.
> Oh! what a nice day it has been. It is as warm to day as June weather and yesterday it was cold and rainy. We have good weather about one third of the time.
> I am writing on a wood pile in front of our tent House. I hope we will not have to use the kind much longer.
> Dear Vira, it is the greatest wonderment I ever heard of for you to toddle around as long as you

*have. I expect to hear of it every day. You will have some one write immediately wont you.*

*So Sylvester has made up his mind at last not to farm. Oh it is awfull for me to bear. Had it not been for him, I would not have enlisted for you know our bargains as well as I can tell you. But, if Mose does what you say, I think it will be a great deal better than for you to move down to his place dont you.*

*Vira we have news that there is to be a call of from 6 to 800,000 more men called out as soon as the Conscript law passes Congress. I think that there will be some kicking and squirming among those copperheads of Traitors you have up North. It will be time for them to talk about peace compromise and all these sort of things. No old fools down here are not dead yet and they will hear from us in your county paper ere long about what the soldiers oppinions of mothers and things.*

*Death has found its way in our Co. again and taken 2 more of our boys. Edgar Bennitt[86] from Fair Haven. Warren Aldrich[87] from Lanark which makes 9 and dont know how soon it may call on some more of us.*

*John F. Smith[88] is not expected to live. He is a relation of Mr. Emmerts. We left him at Danville, Ky. I guess he will never raise. Herr Browning has deserted instead of dieing. We think the later far superior.*

---

[86] Edger Bennett, Fair Haven, 92nd Illinois Infantry, Co. I – died at Lexington, Ky. 2-19-63 - Arthur Robbe and Richard Hinton, Booklet of *Rededication Ceremony of the Carroll County Civil War Soldiers & Sailors Monument.*

[87] Warren Aldrich, Mt. Carroll, 92nd Illinois Infantry, Co. I – died at Mt. Sterling, Ky. hospital on 2-18-63 - Ibid. Robbe and Hinton, Booklet of *Rededication Ceremony*

[88] John F. Smith, Mt. Carroll, 92nd Illinois Infantry, Co. I – died at Danville, Ky. on 2-26-63 - Ibid. Robbe and Hinton, Booklet of *Rededication Ceremony*

*You say Russel has left. Where did he go? I made great calculations on him. I thought he would raise a good crop this year for us.*
*Give my love to Mother and Jennie and all the folks and reserve a portion for your Dear self and oblige a loving Husband.*
*Eugene*

Problems were mounting up for Eugene. His health was bad and he was troubled. He knew he had to get help soon and planned to make a trip into Nashville for medicine.

More than his illness was getting him down. Eugene was a farmer, even if his dream was to be an engineer. He learned to appreciate the beauty of the land, and the destruction, created by the Union troops, worried him. He knew it had to be, but wished he did not have to see it.

*Camp near Nashville Tenn      Mar 2$^{nd}$ 1863*
*Dear Wife*
*I received your letter No. 2 yesterday, with pleasure, to hear that you are all well.*

Referring to his little niece, Jennie, daughter of Moses and Amanda Ludisky.

*I am sory to hear that little Jennie is sick, but I hope she is not bad.*
*My health is about the same. I am still fit for duty and that is about all. I am going to Nashville to get some medicine tomorrow, if nothing happens to prevent me from going.*
*The weather is nice. Today, it looks as if I ought to be plowing, or sowing grain, but that is played out for a while, I guess.*
*Contrabands are coming in everyday, lots of them. Last night, there was a family of 13 of them came into our lines. They were all small, barefooted and naked & starved, almost. The planters here, most of*

*them, are getting so reduced, that they have to drive their negroes off, or let them starve.*

Freed Africans were pouring into camp. After Abraham Lincoln signed the Emancipation Proclamation, many left their homes immediately. Plantation owners who could no longer afford to feed them forced many others out.

*This country is the worst looking place ever any person had to live. I know the houses are all tore down, the fences are all burned, nice large orchards burned out for Uncle Sams boys to camp on. Turnpikes are completely worn out, railroads torn up. There never was such distruction on gods earth before, I dont believe.*

*We mustered for pay Feb. 28$^{th}$, but I guess we wont get it untill about the 15$^{th}$ of this mo. We got news yesterday that they had got their canal nearly done there, before Vicksburgh, and that the rebles suplies were cut of and they were in a starving condition all most, but I dont know how true it is.*

*Rosecrans army are all quiet but expect to move as soon as the weather will permit. There is a force of 60 to 70 thousand within 60 miles of us. They are at Chatanooga in this state. I guess we will have to clean them out there. Vira, I think that you are doing the best you can by staying where you are. You will not have to stand back and be nosed around by others. You will be on your own place. I am writing with washing fluid, but I guess it will not rub of till you get to read it.*

*I had one or two letters from you with stamps in, but they did not come Via Cairo. Them, I have not recd yet. Direct Via Louisville. Give my love to all. This little ring is for little Jennie. It is not very nice but will please her just as well. Goodby.*

*Your husband,                    Mack*
*Give my love to Mother, Jennie and Annie*

The soldiers serving under General Absalom Baird's division were getting discouraged and the officers knew they had to come up with something to prepare them mentally for action. The officers composed and presented a Preamble and Resolutions to the soldiers who had a chance to adopt it in an effort to renew patriotism and a fighting spirit.

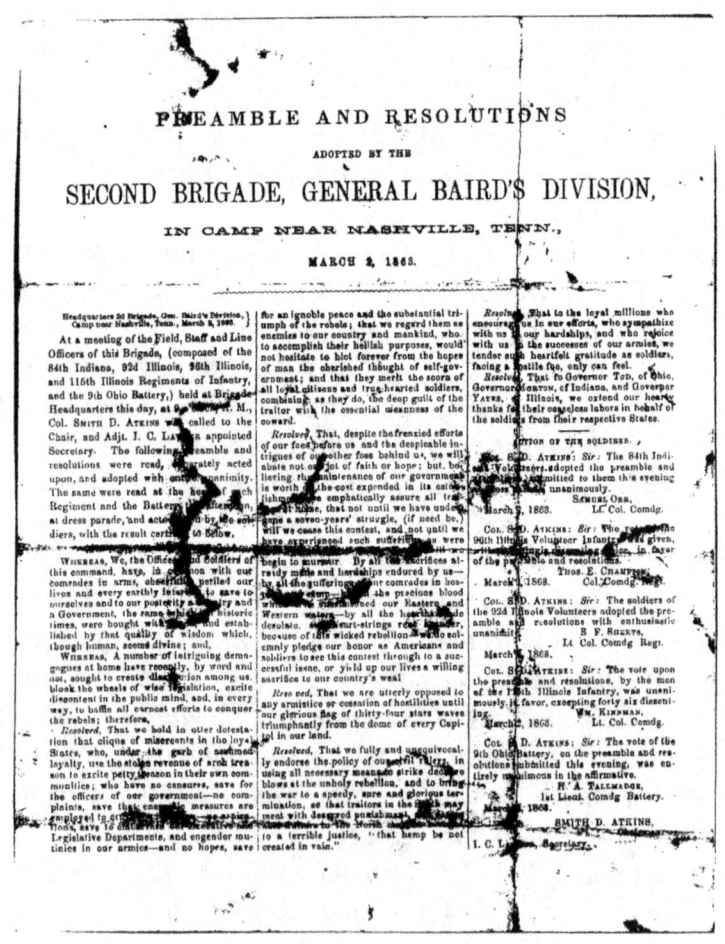

## Preamble & Resolutions
### March 2, 1863

## PREAMBLE AND RESOLUTIONS

## ADOPTED BY THE
## SECOND BRIGADE, GENERAL BAIRD'S DIVISION

## IN CAMP NEAR NASHVILLE, TENN.

## MARCH 2, 1863

Headquarters 2d Brigade, Gen. Baird's Division
Camp near Nashville, Tenn, March 2, 1863

At a meeting of the Field, Staff and Line Officers of this Brigade, (composed of the 34th Indiana, 92nd Illinois, 96th Illinois, and 115th Illinois Regiments of Infantry, and the 9th Ohio Battery,) held at Brigade Headquarters this day, at 9 o'clock A.M.

Col. SMITH D. ATKINS, was called to the Chair, and Adjt. I. C. LAWYER, appointed Secretary. The following preamble and resolutions were read, separately acted upon and adopted with entire unanimity . The same were read at the heads of each Regiment and the Battery, this afternoon at dress parade, and acted up by the soldiers, with the result certified to below:

WHEREAS, We, the Officers and Soldiers of this command, have, in common with our comrades in arms, cheerfully periled our lives and every earthly interest, to save to ourselves and to our posterity a Country and a Government, the same which is historic times were bought with blood and established by that quality of wisdom which, though human, seems divine; and

WHEREAS, A number of intriguing demagogues at home have recently, by word and not, sought to create disaffection among us, block the wheels of wise legislation, excite discontent in the public mind, and, in every way, to baffle all earnest efforts to conquer the rebels; therefore

Resolved, That we hold in utter detestation that clique of miscreants in the loyal States, who, under the garb of assumed loyalty, use the stolen revenue of arch treason to excite petty treason in their own communities; who have no censures, save for the officers of our government - no complaints, save that energetic measures are employed to crush the rebellion - no inspirations, save to embarrass our Legislative Departments, and engender mutinies in our armies - and no hopes, save for an ignoble peace and the substantial triumph of the rebels; that we regard them as enemies to our country and mankind, who, to accomplish their hellish purposes, would not hesitate to blot forever from the hopes of man the cherished thought of self-government, and that they merit the scorn of all loyal citizens and true-hearted soldiers, combining as they do, the deep guilt of the traitor with the essential meanness of the coward.

Resolved, That, despite the frenzied efforts of our foes before us and the despicable intrigues of our other foes behind us, we will abate not one jot of faith or hope, but, believing the maintenance of our government is worth all the cost expended in its establishment, we emphatically assure all traitors at home that not until we have undergone a seven years struggle, (if need be) will we cease this contest, and not until we have experienced such sufferings as were bravely endured at Valley Forge, will we begin to murmur. By all the sacrifices already made and hardships endured by us - by all the sufferings of our comrades in hospital and camp - by all the precious blood which has crimsoned our Eastern and Western waters - by all the hearths made desolate and heart strings rent asunder, because of this wicked rebellion - we do solemnly pledge our honor as Americans and soldiers to see this contest through to a successful issue, or yield up our lives a willing sacrifice to our country's weal.

Resolved, That we are utterly opposed to any armistice or cessation of hostilities until our glorious flag of thirty-four stars waves triumphantly from the dome of every Capitol in our land.

Resolved, That we fully and unequivocally endorse the policy of our civil rulers in using all necessary means to strike decisive blows at the unholy rebellion, and to bring the war to a speedy, sure and glorious termination, so that traitors in the South may meet with deserved punishment, and damnable traitors in the North may be brought to a terrible justice, "that hemp be not created in vain".

Resolved, That to the loyal millions who encourage us in our efforts, who sympathize with us in our hardships, and who rejoice with us in the successes of our armies, we tender our heartfelt gratitude as soldiers, facing a hostile foe, only can feel.

Resolved, That to Governor TOD, of Ohio, Governor MORTON, of Indiana, and Governor YATES, of Illinois, we extend our heartfelt thanks for the ceaseless labors in behalf of the soldiers from their respective States.

ACTION OF THE SOLDIERS

Col. S. D. ATKINS, Sir. The 84$^{th}$ Indiana Volunteers adopted the preamble and resolutions submitted to them this evening at dress parade unanimously.

SAMUEL ORB      Lt. Col. Comdg.

March 2, 1863

Col. S. D. ATKINS, Sir: The vote of the 96$^{th}$ Illinois Volunteer Infantry was given without a single dissenting voice, in favor of the preamble and resolutions.

THOS. E. CHAMPION      Col. Comdg. Regt.

March 2, 1863

Col. S. D. ATKINS, Sir: The soldiers of the 92$^{nd}$ Illinois Volunteers adopted the preamble and resolutions with enthusiastic unanimity,

B. F. SHEETS      Lt. Col. Comdg. Regt.

March 2, 1863

Col. S. D. ATKINS, Sir: The vote upon the preamble and resolutions, by the men of the 115$^{th}$ Illinois Infantry, was unanimously in favor excepting 46 dissenting.

WM. KINNMAN      Lt. Col. Comdg.

March 2, 1863

Col. S. D. ATKINS, Sir: The vote of the 9$^{th}$ Ohio Battery, on the preamble and resolutions submitted this evening, was entirely unanimous in the affirmative.

H. A. TALLMADGE      1$^{st}$ Lt. Comdg. Battery

March 2, 1863

SMITH D. ATKINS      Chairman
I.C. LAWYER      Secretary

On March 5, 1863, the Ninety-second Illinois Infantry moved their camp to Franklin, Tennessee in pursuit of Confederate General Earl Van Dorn.

## Chapter Seven
## Franklin, Tennessee

Congress passed the new Enrollment or Conscription Act on March 3, 1863 that said all able-bodied male citizens between the ages of twenty and forty-five who were able and called by the Federal Service had to enlist. The generals - Sherman, Rosecrans and Grant - were very pleased at the prospect of receiving new troops. They expected three million new soldiers, but in actuality, only one hundred seventy thousand men enlisted. [89]

Eugene knew the time was very close for his child to be born and he hoped for news soon.

*Franklin     18 miles south of Nashville, Tenn.*
*March 8$^{th}$ 1863*
*Dear Wife*
*I will try and write you once more. I have not writen to you since the 2$^{nd}$ nor have not heard from you in some time.*
*Last Thursday the 5$^{th}$ we received marching orders. Whilst on battalion drill our Col. doubled quicked us in to our Camp and gave us 5 minutes to get 2 days rations and 70 rounds of cartridges and form in line of battle. We done it. We then marched down to the rail road and jumped on board the cars and landed at this place. Slept on our arms all night in line of battle. Next morning up and stood attention till about noon. We drew some rations then and were ordered to get our dinner and not speak a loud word. We done so and about 5 o'clock our tents came. You see we had nothing with us but our guns and ruber blanket. We then pitched our*

---

[89] World Almanac Publications, *The Civil War Almanac*, Intro. by Henry Steele Commager, A Bison Book, New York, NY 1983, pp. 133-134

*tents and fixed for the night. It was raining all the time pretty near but we stood it very well.*

*You see, old Vandorn had advanced on this place in order to tare up the R. R. and Col. Cobern was ordered out to see and find out their strength but not to fight with them. But instead of obeying orders he went right into them and they cleaned him out and drove him back to town and you see that is why we are here. They are with in 3 miles of us with about 30,000. We are expecting an attact every day. Our force here is about 40,000 besides the forte. We will give them fits when they do come I think.*

After Confederate Braxton Bragg withdrew his troops from Stone's River, he occupied a position North of Tullahoma, Tennessee. His troops extended from Shelbyville to Wartrace to Fairfield along the Duck River. General William Starkie Rosecrans of the Union Army moved into Murfreesboro with his troops, north of the Confederate troops, occupying Auburn, Bradyville, Carthage, Eagleville, Franklin, Lebanon, Liberty, McMinnville and Woodbury. Until June, there were only minor skirmishes and engagements when pickets and expeditions went out.[90]

March 8, 1863 continued.

*My dirrhoea is very bad but I feel first rate every other way. I wrote to Mose the day we left Nashvill. I expect one from you to day but dont know as we will get any mail or not. I have writen you before this but had not time. Once a week is as often as I can possible write untill we get into quarters again. That may be soon and it may never be but I dont look on the darke side any more. I think there is as good a chance for me as for any one.*

---

[90] Frank J. Welcher, *The Union Army, 1861-1865, Organization and Operations, Volume II, Western Theater*, Indiana University Press, Bloomington & Indianapolis, 1993, pp. 818, 832-839

*Our Orderly seargeant E. English has got the erysippelas and I am afraid it will go hard with him. Wait Downs has been pretty sick but is some better to day. He has the sore throat.*

*I guess by the time you get this you will have some news for to write.*

*I dreamed it in such a way that I all most know it is over with. May be that I am to fast.*

Eugene was dreaming about the baby that was due very soon. March 8 continued.

*Good news. Gen. Rosecrans has promised to grant furloughs after while to all soldiers that are good in preforming their duties. Give my love to all. I will write as soon as I can. I am going on guard to night and must close. Remember me to Mother and Jennie.*

*I remain your loving Husband.*
*E. M. Swaggart*

The important event finally took place on March 4, 1863. Little George Swaggart II made his appearance into the war torn world.

*Camp near Franklin Tenn March 12$^{th}$ 1863*
*Dear Sister Dicky*
*I withe great pleasure read you kind and welcome letters bearing dates of Mar. 4th & 6th. I was glad to hear from you and more than all the rest to hear that our folks had a young soldier and that he was well.*

*We have been on a hard march since I have writen home. We left here to follow a band of rebles last Monday and just got back to camp this being Thursday. We followed them a bout 20 miles to a place called Columbia where there is a large force fortified so we had to skedadle back to our Camp.*

*We had to carry our own grub and take it in the rain soldier fashion. The boys stood it first rate but we would have liked it if we could have killed a fiew of them to pay us for our trouble.*

*Willis Ray was along. He belongs to the U. S. 4$^{th}$ Regulars Cav. He got a ball shot through his stirrup grazing the top of his boot, but did not hurt his foot. He likes the cavelry better than Infantry. I think some of joining them as soon as I can get a chance.*

*I hope they will do something in this term of Court. You say that they are having Court now.*

*Oh! Dear, I am so tired I can hardly scratch. I had a letter from Henry Lego today. He is well and hearty. We are 20 miles apart but expect to see each other when we move again.*

*Old Pap English is nearly gone by the board. He is crazy as a bed bug.*

*Tell Vira that my health is a great deal better since our jar a bush whacker.*

*Oh, but I would like to see my boy but I guess he will be quite a boy before that time. You must take good care of him. I know you will. What's is the use of writing such stuff. Dicky you will excuse my awfull crooked letter for you know my mind is like a whirl wind to hear of any good fortune.*

*You will find on the back of this sheet the 92ds resolutions in regard to our Northern traitors. We got them up ourselves. I think they will suite them first rate dont you.*

*Tell little Jennie Uncle Mack send his love to her with a kiss. Give my love to Vira & Jennie and all of the folks.*

*I remain your sincere Brother*
*Mack*

Eugene wrote to Elvira to let her know that he was happy about the news of the baby boy.

*Franklin Tenn.*            *March 13$^{th}$ 1863*
*Dear Wife*
*I will try and scrible you a fiew lines this morning to let you know how I am getting along. I am quite well at presant and hope this finds you the same but dont know as it will.*
*I had to letters from Dicky yesterday stating that you had a nice big boy. Very good. I was glad to hear that you was doing well. I can hardly controle my self. I want to see you so bad but I cant at presant. I suppose you have all the care that any one needs and that I guess will be sufficient to restore your health again.*
*We have been on a very hard and tedious march all week. We got in Camp last night so you can imagine about how I feel but that signafies nothing. It is just what we are here for and to put this damnable rebellion down we will have to endure hardships and privations.*
*I recd. a letter from you last night. It has been to Cairo twice. It had 4 stamps in it. You wished to know whether you sent me enough or not. I do not want for any. I have 12 you sent me now. I could not write at all if it were not for your kindness.*
*We expect to get our pay before long. I know you need it very much. Gen. Baird says we will need not muster for pay but once more. He thinks we will be set free by June next but he dont know. At any rate, I am not puting an dependance in it so if we are I will be happily disappointed.*
*I had a letter from H. H. Holt. He is well. They are 27 miles from Memphis guarding rail road. He say they have very easy times.*

*Wait and me are on good terms again. He has been very sick but is able for duty now.*
*Tobacco cant be had here at any price only the stuff the darkies raise here. The boys steal that and smoke it. It is not fit to chew. I never wanted any thing so bad in my life but I guess it wont kill me, will it. I think not.*
*But my boy, I cant hardly wait for the time to come for me to see him. It will come after while I guess if I am permited to live long enough. As for me sending him a name, I would rather not as I think you have the best right to that. If you wait for me to come home to name him, you will have to wait untill I come home for I could not send a name so far.*
*Well I guess I have writen enough for this time.*
*Good by my dear trusting you will be doing well when you get this. Give my love to family.*
*Your*
*Mack*

Little George, named after his grandfather, George Swaggart, had an uneasy first month, besieged with illness. His mother was doing well, however and Eugene was thankful. He was coping with fevers and no sleep when he received news of the baby's birth, but he was a proud father. He referred to his son as his "little solger", a term he often used in camp when he spoke to other soldiers about his son. The troops were on the move almost constantly from March 5 to March 12, 1863, in pursuit of the troops of General Earl Van Dorn. Camp set up in Franklin, Tennessee for Company I of the Ninety-second Illinois Infantry while others in the regiment occupied Brentwood, Tennessee.[91]

---

[91] *Illinois Troops (Union) Infantry, Record of Events, Volume 13, Records for the Ninety-second Illinois Infantry, September 1862 – June 1865*, pp. 497 & 547

*Franklin, Tenn.*            *March 18$^{th}$ 1863*
*Dear Wife*
*I will once more try and write you a fiew words. I am not very well, however, I hope this will find you in a flourishing condition. I just recd. two letters from Sister Dicky, one stating that our little solger was not very well but that you was quite smart. That is cheering news for me.*
*Dear Vira, you all appear to think that it is a very easy matter but it is not the case. A fellow must have a leg shot off or lay sick 4 or 5 months, then there is a show for him, a slim one if they were all like poor Dode Olney. I reported sick about a week ago. The Dr. says my liver is affected. Our 1$^{st}$ Liut. Colehour[92] died yesterday - no officer now, but old Cap. Colehours brothers are here. I guess they will carry the corpse home for interment.*
*Tell Dicky I will ans. her letter as soon as I feel a little better. No more for now.*
*Your loving Husband,*
*E. M. Swaggart*
*I will have someone write if I get worse but I guess I will be able to write a little myself.*

Other than guard duty on the Harpeth River and Nashville and Decatur Railroad, located in and near Franklin, Tennessee, the Ninety-second Illinois Infantry did not have a lot to do. Pickets went out frequently looking for General Van Dorn and guard details were on the perimeters on a regular basis. However, there were no skirmishes reported and things were quiet.

    Eugene was very sick. He contacted erysipelas, a streptococcus bacterial infection that causes a very painful

---

[92] 1$^{st}$ Lt. David B. Colehour, Mt. Carroll, 92$^{nd}$ Illinois Infantry, Co. I, died 3-17-63 Arthur Robbe and Richard Hinton, Booklet of *Rededication Ceremony of the Carroll County Soldiers & Sailors*.

cellulitis with lesions, general malaise, and high fevers,[93] usually in the afternoons and at night. It was very difficult to cure in some people, especially before antibiotics were available. He was feeling a little better when he wrote to Elvira from Hospital No. 2 in Franklin, Tennessee.

> *Hospital No. 2    Franklin Tenn    March 20$^{th}$ 1863*
> *Dear Wife*
> *I will once more try and let you know how I am getting. I have the eresipelas in my face and am writing with one eye. I am getting better. I have not heard from you since I have been here. I expect there is letter in camp for me but they cant get them to us. We have good care here, good food and beds. There is in the ward with me. They are getting well, but one. He is dieing now. I hope you will be able to write to me by the time you get this. I will write again in a day or so. Goodby.*
> *I remain your loving Husband.*
> *Mack*

On March 26, 1863, Eugene answered Elvira's letter. He was still in the hospital.

> *Hospital No. 2, Franklin Tenn.*
> *March 26$^{th}$, 1863*
> *Dear Beloved Wife*
> *I received a good long letter of you Dear, hand write, day before yesterday but did not feel my self quite able to ans. it untill the presant. You can not imajine the joy it gave me to hear that you were getting along so well. I am gaining some. The swelling has prety well all left my face but I am very*

---

[93] *The Merck Manual of Diagnosis and Therapy, Thirteenth Edition,* Merck Sharp & Dohme Research Laboratories, Division of Merck & Company, Inc., Rahway, New Jersey, 1977, p. 1576

weak yet. I have a pretty bad Dirrhoea and expect to have it as long as I remain in service.

I have not seen any of the Company since I have been here. They cant get passes to come so I dont expect to hear from you again untill I join the Co.

I am very lonesome here among strangers but I have very good care or I could not stand it at all but I will try and live through it.

I intend to be out of this in less than 6 months if I am spared that long, that is if the good lord sees fit to aid us in this rebelion a little while longer.

There was a skermish between us and Nashvill. They took 2 or 3 of our regiments prisoners and burned the rail road bridge so we will not get any more mail untill the bridge is repaired. That will not take more than 2 or 3 days. We did not get the particulars of the fight yet but we got whiped. That is certain.

It has cleared off and I think we are going to have nice weather.

Oh! Dear how I would like to see my boy. How can I wait so long. It seems to me now longer than ever but I guess it is not. Time rolls just the same now that it did three years ago, does it not. It has been but a short time since you and I first met if we only look back and consider one moment. It does not look very far back to me.

I am very sorry to hear of Mothers ill health. I am afraid that I will never get to see her more on this earth but will in a far better land than this. Tell her I have not forgoten my poor aged mother yet nor I never will while I am permited to stay on this earth.

Dear Vira, you said that C. E. Cross and wife had or was going to Racine to live and you wished it was you an my self. Dear I only hope to be out of this war and we will be with them. I dont think that I *can ever settle down on a farm if I ever should get a chance. No I would feel to much like a bird let out of a cage for that and you know I allways said I was going to be an Engineer and if the Lord spares me I will.*

*I am glad the lawsuit is over but the next will be the cost to pay and nothing to pay with. That is the worst of all.*

*I want you to stay on the place you are untill they drive you off. Freeze right to it. You was there first and there fore have the best right to it for your self and boy if should never get home.*

*Give my love to Jennie. Dicky, Mother, Annie and Mary Ann, John & Mose and kiss the baby for its Papa. I remain your loving Husband,*
*Eugene Swaggart*
*God Bless that little hand. Tell Moses and John to write to me as I have written to them last.*

Word from home stated that Elvira and the baby were doing fine. She had trouble breast feeding as many young mothers do, but that was not a great worry.

On March 27, the Ninety-second Illinois Infantry, Company I marched to Brentwood Station, on the railroad, where they camped until morning. The following day, they moved one and one half miles to a railroad bridge where they stayed until April 8,[94] fortifying the railroad.

*Brentwood Station Tennessee*
*March 30th, 1865*
*Dear Wife*
*I was once more made happy by the receipt of another letter from you. It brought news of your Dear health being poorly and also that our little*

---

[94] *Illinois Troops (Union) Infantry, Records of Events, Volume 13, Records of Events for the Ninety-second Illinois Infantry, September 1862 - June 1865*, p. 547

> baby was not so well but I hope that this will find you better.
>
> I am in camp now. I came up yesterday from Franklin. Our regt. came here together with the 96 to guard a R. R. bridge at this place last Thursday. The rebles run in here and gobbled up the 22d Wisconsin and 19 Michigan with out fireing a single gun but I dont think they will get the $92^{nd}$ quite so easy all though we are untried as yet.
>
> I am glad to get out of the Hospital. I was in 2 weeks but the eresipelas is still in my blood but I think they will bring me all right. You must not be alarmed a bit . Me, I think I have not suffered any to what you have.
>
> I wrote to you twice while I was in the Hospital but dont know as you will get them.
>
> The news is that Rosecrans is after Bragg. If so we will hear of some fighting before long. He is a man that will not fool a way much of his time.

After the capture of several of his regiments on March 4, 1863, by General Van Dorn[95], General Rosecrans readied his troops on March 9 to go after the "guerrillas" who "attempted to stop" the Union supply boats on the Tennessee and Cumberland Rivers. However, due to a crew shortage, his attempts were not effective.[96]

March 30, 1863 continued.

> I guess we will stay here a good while for we are fortifying here. The boys are on duty every day but they appear to stand it nobly for it is all for the union.

---

[95] World Almanac Publications, *The Civil War Almanac*, Intro. by Henry Steele Commager, A Bison Book, New York, NY 1983, p. 134

[96] Robert E. Denney, *The Civil War Years, A Day-by-Day Chronicle of the Life of a Nation*, Foreword by Gregory J. W. Urwin, Sterling Publishing Co., NY, p. 265

*There is no union people in this section of the country at all. Our cavelry is picking up secesh every day. They are hard looking beasts.*
*Caleb Ransome has got his discharge. He is a brother of Elsy Ransome.*
*I dont hear any news about our getting our pay soon and dont much look for it now untill the 1$^{st}$ of May. Then I guess we will get four months. I know you must need money bad. I would borrow some if I could but that is out of the question for the boys are all straped.*
*You have not mentioned Sylvester in a long time. You must tell me how he is getting along with old Stuart. I suppose he is enough for him as he allways was. Give him my respects and tell him to trot my boy on his knee for me and oblige.*
*I wrote Henry Lego to day. Him and me keep up a regular correspondence. He is well. They are at Murfreesboro yet. Give my love to Jennie and Mother good by Dear Wife, I remain your loving Husband.*
*E. M. Swaggart*

While at Brentwood Station, George Wait Downs and Eugene, who had made up sometime back and were great friends again, were out foraging for food one day when they had an adventure. Eugene wrote to Elvira to tell her all about it.

*Brentwood Station, Tenn     April 4$^{th}$, 1863*
*Dear Wife*
*It is with great pleasure that I am once more permited to write to you. I recd. a letter from Dicky today. It found Mc pretty well and was very glad to hear from you. I was afraid that you would have a time with your breasts, but hope that you will get better soon.*

The weather is very nice hear at presant and everything on a stir. We have fortified this place hear so that it will take a large force to take it from us, although, there is but two small regiments of us here and one battery. It is a very nice place, situated on a rise of ground, surounded by timber, which is begining to look nice and green. Peaches are all gone up.

I am afraid, we will not have any here to conficcate this fall. The earliest fruit was all froze.

We had a nice mess of greens for dinner. It was sour dock. Wait and I went over to an old secesh plantation, went in to his garden and was helping ourselves to pic plant, when the old devil came out and set his dogs on us. You better beleave we skedadled for dear life, but we got our plants, enough for a good old mess. That is the way it goes. We are on duty everyday, but after the fortify cations are done, it will not be so hard on us.

I recd a letter from Hen Holt today. He is well. They are at Memphis.

Dicky says the people begin to think the war is about to close. The prospects does look better now then they ever have since the war first broke out. It is a general supposition among us that the rebs are going to evacuate Richmond and come in here. They say they must have Tenn. & Ky. but we would like to see them get it. They are shiping all their big guns to the front of us. Old Rosecrans is wide awake enough for them. I think they will try one more kick and if they dont succeed, rebellion will be done gone - plaid out. We have several butternuts at work out on the forte that we picked up around here. They all say they are tired of it long ago and want to go home. Men will not fight very hard when they get homesick and tired as they are, unless there

is five or six to one. All that is wanting is for the niger heads at home to keep still, mind their own business, and our work will be short. Tell them so if you happen to see any, but I guess they are getting fiew.
Give my love to all. Kiss baby for Pap and I will stop for this time. From your husband.
Write as often as you can. Good by Mack

On April 8, 1863, the Ninety-second Illinois Infantry returned to the camp near Franklin. A couple of days later, Eugene wrote to Elvira to tell her he was back in camp.

*Franklin, Tenn,*          *April 10$^{th}$, 1863*
*Dear Wife*
*I will try and improve a fiew moments time in writing to inform you how I am geting along. I am quite well at presant and hope this may find you the same. I have not had a letter from you in a long time.*
*Well, Vira, we have not had any fight yet but expect one every day. The rebs are in force about 4 miles from us and we are waiting for them to make the attact. Whether they will or not is more than I can say.*
*We left Brentwood the 8$^{th}$ after we got it so we could hold it and came back to our old camp.*
*The weather is very warm and dry. Fruit trees are all in blow. I saw one man planting corn. Wheat is 6 inches high but there is not much of it. Wheat fields, corn fields and orchards is nothing but one vast field of camping grounds. That would look rather hard for some of your Northern farmers. Lots of times when we go in to camp near a mans farm, there is not a rail or board left on it but it is no more than right is it.*

*We have not been paid yet but expect it every day. They are paying off some of our brigade. We need it bad enough. You can bet on that.*

*How is baby boy? I want to see him. It dont seem hardly real to me to have a boy like that and not see him in less than a year if the Lord spares us both that long.*

*I suppose times are busy now among the farmers. I only wish I was one of them but as it is I dont know as I ever will be a farmer any more if I ever get back there.*

*They are fighting out the other side of town. I can hear the canon roar as I write.. I will stop a while.*

*Well I will try and finish. The rebs are skermishing with our out posts. I guess we will get fun before long.*

*I would have writen to you but this is the first chance I have had to write since I was sick as we are on duty all the time. Good by Dear. I will write again soon. Give my love to all. I remain your Husband, Mack*

That night, the Ninety-second Illinois Infantry went on a "scout after Van Dorn's forces on the Lewisville Pike - five miles."[97] The Ninety- second suffered no casualties as they were only backing up other troops. However, the Union troops led by General Gordon Granger attacked General Earl Van Dorn in a battle that left one hundred Union soldiers dead or injured and three hundred Confederate soldiers dead or wounded.[98]

Eugene was afraid the battle report in the newspapers would worry Elvira. Actually, it was only an engagement and she probably knew nothing about it until his letter of April 16 arrived. He also had some comments about the lawsuit that had

---

[97] *Illinois Troops (Union) Infantry, Records of Events, Volume 13, Records of Events for the Ninety-second Illinois Infantry, September 1862 - June 1865*, p. 547
[98] World Almanac Publications, *The Civil War Almanac*, Intro. by Henry Steele Commager, A Bison Book, New York, NY 1983, p. 139

been going on for sometime. He wanted his mother to have her one third and not end up with less because of his half-brother, John Miller. He also wanted to be sure his property was safe. As a gesture of love, he drew two hearts joined together with one arrow on the top of the letter.

> Franklin, Tenn, April 16th 1863
>
> Dear Wife
>
> I once more take my pen in hand to ans your letter of Apr. 8th which came to hand to day it found me well and hope this may find you the same. Well My Dear I will try and tell you about our big fight we had the other day for fear you have heard that we are all prisoners last friday the 40th Ohio went out on the front of our lines on picket and at 1 oclock P.M. the rebs made an attack on them with a large force and drove them in to the edge of town where they held them for about 2 hours by that time we were all drawn up in line of battle but would

*Franklin Tenn*      *April 16th 1863*
*Dear Wife*
I once more take my pen in hand to ans. your letter of Apr. 8th, which came to hand today. It found me well and hope this may find you the same. Well, my Dear, I will try and tell you about our big fight we had the other day, for fear you have heard that we are all prisoners. Last friday, the 40th Ohio went out on the front of our lines on picket and at 1 o'clock P.M., the rebs made an attact on them with a large force and drove them into the edge of town, where they held them for about 2 hours. By that time, we were all drawn up in line of battle, but would not let us go and help our poor boys untill it was too late, for when our old siege guns opened up on them, they fled for dear life leaving behind their dead & wounded. We took after them, then, and chaste them till dark, but could not make them fight, only, as they run, the bullets whistled around over our heads right smart. We lost 15 men, killed and wounded. Their loss was quite heavy. We picked up 57 dead and took betwen 40 & 50 prisoners.

We marched over the dead when we were after them, and in the night when we returned to our camp, we went over them as they lay there reaping their reward of merit. Old VanDorn was told by some of his sympathizers that our force was small, so he thought he would take us, but he was barking up the rong tree, but he still hangs around. One of our boys got shot, last night on picket, out of the 96th Ill. He was buried today. A fellow has got to keep his eyes open now when on picket.

Well, Vira, you say that the farm is to be divided. It is good news for me and, no doubt, as good for you, and, of course, you will all kick against mother having a childs portion, for a childs portion will do her no more good than for her to have the third her life time, nor half so much. I think it is all Johns doings, but, Vira, remember our place and not let anyone have it, if you can help it.

And, as for what is coming home from Harris, if you can draw it, I want you to use it to help you and Jennie. We were to get our pay today, but as it was so rainy and bad, we wont get it untill tomorrow.

Vira, I received the letter with the lock of babys hair. It is the only thing that is dear to me here in the army, it and Mothers and Sisters likeness. I want yours as soon as baby can be taken to town, do you understand. I cannot stand it a great while longer without seeing yours. Give my respects to the Mr. Smalls and give my love to Mother, Jennie, Vet, Annie and all. Kiss my boy. No more.

    With much love
    E. M. Swaggart

Tell Annie I will write to her in a day or so.

The next few days, camp was quiet and Eugene wrote to Elvira again.

*April 23$^{rd}$, 1863  Camp at Franklin, Tenn.*
*Dear Wife*

I will try and write a fiew lines. I am well at presant and hope these will find you the same. Dear Vira, I would like very much to hear from you but it seems as though I never would again. The last I heard from you was April 8$^{th}$. I guess the letters were way laid but never mind. They will come after while.

We are not troubled much now by the rebs. They are very quiet and I guess they are apt to remain so. Vira, I express $20.00 home in Moses name. I suppose it is there by this time. I also sent my over coat and Testament and Mothers likeness. It was *hard to part with it but we had to turn over our knapsacks and tents so I had to either send it home or throw it away.*

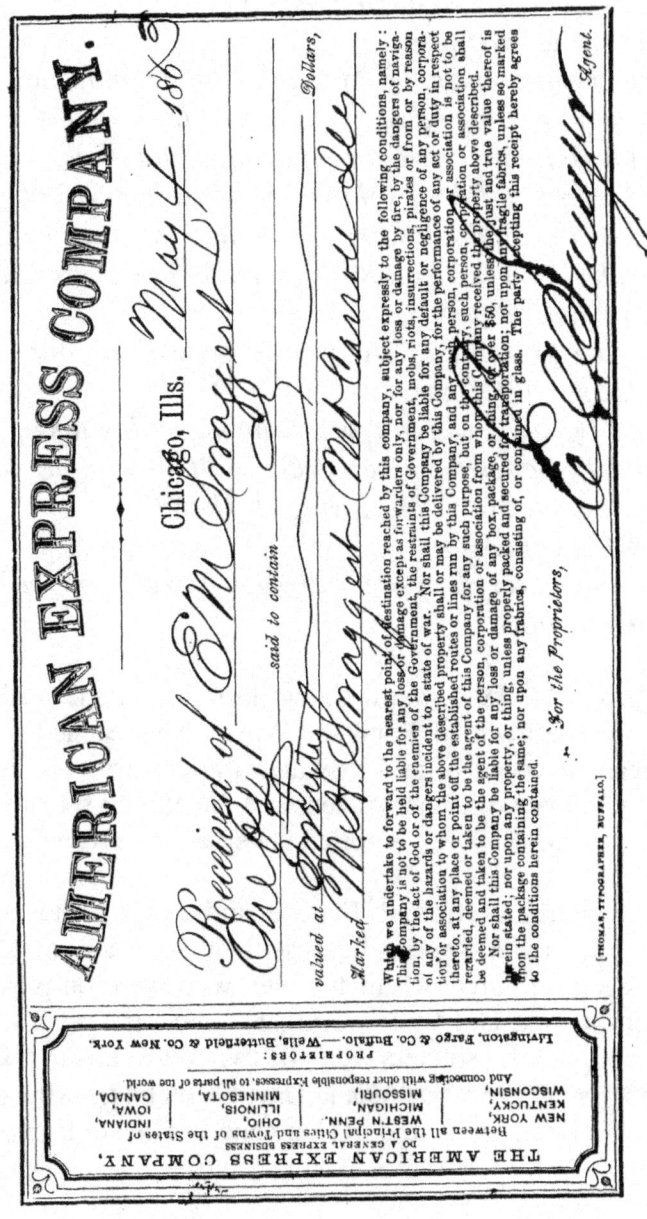

*We have shelter tents now and two in a tent and when on a march we carry them. I think Uncle Sam is to make mules of us but let him pitch in. We will go as long as we can and then quit.*

Referring to body lice.

*Oh, the graybacks is awfull thick. I found one on my shirt so big and old that he had U. S. on his back but it is nothing here to what you would think.*

*You can tell John I sold my revolver for $15.00. It got so it would not work so I bought another from a cavelry man for $14.00 - a regular old Colts Navy. I can depend on it.*

*I wrote to Annie a day or so a go with a couple of dollars in it for her.*

*Well I guess I will not write any more this time for I expect a letter from you every mail so with my love to all good-bye. Your loving Husband,*
*E. M. Swaggart*
*On duty every day we will soon have every hill in Tenn fortified.*

On April 27, 1863, the regiment left camp under orders and went into the town of Franklin. When they reached Franklin, they heard news of a fight in which the cavalry was involved. There were many prisoners taken, and the Ninety-second Illinois Infantry, Company I, escorted twelve to prison camp in Franklin. [99]

Union soldiers arrested Eugene and others who were on picket on the twenty-eighth because their Sergeant and Corporal were asleep on duty. All of the men who were on picket duty were questioned and kept overnight. Soon it was determined that the only guilty soldiers were the two in leadership positions.

The loss of First Lieutenant David Colehour, who died on March 17, 1863, left a void in Company I. The company wanted

---

[99] *Illinois Troops (Union) Infantry, Records of Events, Vol. 13, Records of Events for the Ninety-second Illinois Infantry, September 1862 - June 1865,* p. 547

to elect one of the men who had been with them from the beginning, Sergeant William H. Hollinger. However, General Baird had other thoughts in mind. A new recruit came in from Carroll County as a Lieutenant and General Baird moved him right into the vacant position although he had not served in the regiment before. Eugene and many others were very unhappy. Only two men in the regiment knew him well and wanted him as Lieutenant. The soldiers elected some officers and others served as officers because of people they knew or money in their families. The volunteers naturally resented an outsider. On April 28, Eugene wrote to Elvira to relate the happenings of the week.

*Franklin Tenn April 28<sup>th</sup> 1863*
*Dear Wife*
*I withe much pleasure write you a few lines. I am well and hope this will find you the same. I recd. Yours of Apr 22<sup>nd</sup>, it making the 2<sup>nd</sup> in this month.*
*I was on picket last sunday and in night, when the officer of the day came round. He found our Corporal & Seargeant asleep, so he arested the whole squad of us (12) and brought us before Col. Atkins. He sent us to the guardhouse to await our trial and, this morning, Col. Sheets came and released us all but the Corporal & Sergeant. They will be shot, I guess, so you see, your man has been in the guardhouse, once, to answer the fault of others.*

No evidence appeared in the records of Company I concerning the execution of a Corporal or Sergeant. Perhaps the Corporal or Sergeant was from another company or regiment.

*Vira, you are on your own farm now. I am glad of that, but I would like to know how it was divided and how the timber was run out. Give me the full particulars in your next, wont you. Our Cavelry had a skermish yesterday about 4 miles out. They took 728 prisoners and a lot of horses & mules.*

*They run into their camp while they were having their breakfast. Our men took all their camp equipage and put it all in one pile and burned them. They then chasted them about 10 miles, then returned to camp with their booty. We are still hard at work on duty everyday.*

*The weather is warm and dry. It suits for better tents first rate.*

*Oh! Vira, we have got a new Lieutenant. It is Viola Seymours beau, J. S. McRea. We was going to put Bill Hollinger in, but Brig. Gen. Baird put one in for us. He thought Co. I was not capable of electing their own Luit. The boys are all down on him, but 2. They are George Gotshale and J. A. Bigger. They are the only friends he has in the Co.*

*I wrote to Charlie Cross the other day, but have not heard from him. I dont get any news from up there, only what you write. I should think Moses would ans. my letters. Tell him if he dont write, I will stop also.*

*Vira, you will excuse a half sheet as I can write all I know on this much and this paper costs 60 cents per square, but that is nothing if I could get plenty of it. No more. Give my love to all.*

*I remain your Husband.         E Mc Swaggart*

Still operating out of Franklin, Tennessee, pickets and scouts continued without luck. It was very quiet and the talk resumed about the war ending soon.

*Franklin Tenn                April 30$^{th}$ 1863*
*Dear Wife*
*As this is a day set apart for feasting and prayr by Gen. Rosecrans and, as I will not do either, I will write you a fiew lines, of course, just to pass off time. I am well, never felt better in my life. We*

*have been on duty everyday for the last two months, so, I guess that is the reason we are so healthy. There has not been much sighns of the rebs since I wrote you last. The report is now that there is a force of 50,000 ready to pitch into us at most anytime. We are ready for them and waiting.*

*Some of the boys thinks that we will be at home in time to help you harvest, but thing does not look very favorable to me. I am waiting untill there is brake made on our lines be for I judge much about it. I think one general fight will either end this or prolong it.*

*Vira, I dont get my letters from anybody anymore. Is it because they have forgoten me or because they dont care for me. I am a poor soldier, I guess, is the reason. Vira, if you get that money I expressed, let me know.*

*I am afraid you will never get it. Wait Downs is well and Charlie Reynolds. They both send their love to you & the boy of yours & mine. Well, I guess I have writen quite enough so goodby. Love to Mother. I remain your loving Husband.*
*E. M. Swaggart*

Eugene saw beautiful trees falling right and left, the wood wanted for the forts going up near Franklin. General Gordon Granger said it would take three years to build the fortifications needed and Eugene had no plans to be around in three years, so he saw no purpose in destroying a beautiful forest.

In spite of his words to Elvira that he would not write to Moses anymore, Eugene still wanted desperately to know the details of the lawsuit and the division of the land.

*Franklin Tenn*           *May 7$^{th}$ 1863*
*Dear Brother*
*As it is a rainy day, I will write you fiew lines. I am well and hope this will find you enjoying the same great blessing. We have had very bad weather for the last 2 or 3 days, cold as the month of March. All quiet at presant, no accounts from the rebs in sometime. We are not on the front now. There is a brigade moved in front of us yesterday. It will make picketing much lighter, but makes fatigue harder.*
*Moses, I wish you could be here a week or so. You have no idea how things work. It caps anything ever I seen. When we came here about 2 mo. ago, there was nothing but a vast forest of miles. No forts ..and now, that timber looks as though some huge monster has pulled it up and threw it in every kind of shape. There has been three forts built and are about done with the 4$^{th}$. Gen. Granger says that it will take about 3 years to fortify this place, as he has it laid out, but I think we will not need them by that time.*
*The last news we had, Old Fightin Joe was givin them thunder, but had no papers today. I am afraid almost to hear the news, but, if he cant whip them, there is no General that can withe in Eastern troops.*

In Tennessee, General Joseph "Fightin Joe" Hooker supported by General John Sedgwick and others, were fighting General Robert E. Lee's army. The battle started in earnest on May 1, 1863 and lasted for three days leaving heavy losses on both sides. General Hooker confronted General Lee in Chancellorsville, but suffered a concussion. Possibly due to his injury, he was not as aggressive as he should have been. General Lee out maneuvered him with half as many forces.[100]

---

[100] World Almanac Publications, *The Civil War Almanac*, Intro. by Henry Steele Commager, A Bison Book, New York, NY 1983, p. 345

May 7, 1863 continued.
*Let them take some of the suckers up there and see how they will work. I expect old Rosecrans will have to take command there yet.*
*Cap. Becker is not very well but he is still around. Liut. York is still acting rank. He is 1$^{st}$ Liut. now and our 2$^{nd}$ Liut. Josh S. McRea is acting in capacity of the Brigade, think he knew better than to stay in the Co. He was put in by Gen. Baird, not by the boys. In fact, he is disliked by every man in the regt. I sent my overcoat home in a box with some other things. If the name is not on it, you can tell it by the brass ring on the collar and I sent some money by express. I wish you would see to it, if it comes, and let me know.*
*Moses, write me a long letter stating the whole affare of the dissolution of the place. Cap sends his love to you and Dicky, and, me also. Give my love to Mother. Kiss little Jennie and baby for me. Write soon from Your affectionate Brother.*

Elvira still asked questions about the nine-month men. She and the other wives conversed often at their meetings and none totally understood why some men served nine months and others three years. Eugene decided it was time to explain the program to her.

Eugene's friend, Henry Holt, was home on leave. While there, he married a girl from home. Henry finally gave up on Anna because she showed no interest in his courtship, but Eugene was surprised he was married.

Eugene related to Elvira some of his more pleasant experiences in his letter of May 21.

*Franklin Tenn    May 21$^{st}$ 1863*
*Dearest Wife*
*Withe great pleasure, I seat my old self to write you once more. I received your letter of May 12$^{th}$. It*

*found me well and in good spirits. I have resolved to content myself, come what will. I think that is the best plan as long as I am a soldier for freedom, dont you think it is best.*

*Poor prospects for a fight here at presant. The rebs has fell back on their main force at Columbia, about 20 miles from us. However, they may run in on us when we least expect them, for they are shy bugars, but if they dont soon come, it will be our turn to go there and just pay them a small tribute of our love.*

*Hooker has done as well as Burnside, got nicely floged, but General Grant, I guess, is doing good work down at, or near, Vicksburgh.*

General Ulysses S. Grant, in Vicksburg, was conducting successful raids due mostly to superior forces. He later took Vicksburg in July.

May 21, 1863 continued.

*Well, Vira, Holt has been gone and done it, as the nigers say down here. Well, I am glad of it. Maybe he will let me alone in regard to Annies not writing to him.*

*Well now, Dear, I will tell you all I know about the 9 months men. You know, we enlisted under the last call and the last call was for three hundred thousand drafted men, but instead of drafting us, Gen. Gates* [101] *got permision to raise the call with volunteers and was sworn in for the period of 3 years unless sooner discharged. Therefore, a good many think that they cant hold us any longer than 9 months, but we were sworn in for 3 years and will*

---

[101] Possibly General Elijah Gates of Missouri, but it is more probable he confused General Gates with Governor Richard Yates who is referred to in the Records of Events, 92nd Illinois Infantry, p. 494 by Colonel Smith D. Atkins who stated, "We are under orders from Governor (Richard) Yates to report to General (Julius) White at Cincinnati as soon as paid our bounty."

*serve the full time if old Abe wants us and I guess he will need us awhile yet.*

*I am so glad that our little fellow is so healthy and fat. I will hardly know him when I get home, will I. But, my Dear, I hope you dont think that I think you negligent, far from it. If it were not for you, I would not care to live and endure a soldiers hardships. Only for thy Dear sake, but I may not be spared. If not, my only hope is to meet you in realms above. As you say, we must live in hope. Oh, how I would like to have been with you down in Fare Haven. I have written to Hatheway twice and he has never ans. yet. Well, I have wrote the last time till he writes.*

*Vira, write how your renten are geting along. Down here they are plowing corn. I have seen corn in gardens a foot high. Wheat is all in heads and Oh! you cant guess what I had out on picket the other day. It was strawberry and cream. About a mile from where we picket is a union family of Irish. They milk 8 cows and have 2 acres of Berries, so you know the soges go right in. Potatoes are in blossom, green peas are large enough to eat or for use. Speaking proper, this is the nicest country in the world. I do believe the most common door yeard would be a great sight in the North. Cap Becker is well and beloved by all of the boys.*

*Vira, you will see a discription of our dog tents in your paper writen by our major. He dont exagerate a partacle.*

*I suppose Vet is gone by this time. Vira, he is you brother but, from what I have heard, I am done with him. Give my love to All. I remain your*
*Mack.*

*You cant say this sheet is not full of something. Give my love to kindred and sisters.*

It was slow in camp and boredom set in. Eugene wrote to Moses in answer to his letter.

> *Franklin Tenn*            *May 22$^{nd}$ 63*
> *Dear Brother*
> *With great pleasure I seat my self to ans. your kind letter which came in yesterday. I am well at presant with the exception of my eyes. They are very sore. I dont know what is the matter with them.*
> *We had orders for to dig out last night at 12 o'clock but the orders were countermanded. Our calvery is all out to day so if they find so if they find any rebs we will have to go out and get them out of the mess. The Cav. you know picks a fight out of them and the infantry generaly has to settle it but Cavelry is a good thing.*
> *They are raising hell in their ducks in Mississippi. It is thought here at presant that old Grant will have Vicksburgh in a fiew days. I hope he may have good success.*
> *But hold on in regard to the 9 months question. I am afraid G. W. Downs has been writing most to fast although it has created a big excitement here in our brigade as it consists of all the troops. I really beleave the 96 Ill. Reg. will stack arms if they are not musterd out of service the 4$^{th}$ of June. Our 9 months is out then but I wrote to Vira and tryed to explain it as well as I could so I will say no more about it. I have heard so much about it that it makes me sick to hear. I mentioned as there is no sense in it or the man ...........................a good pair of Colts for me till I get home. I will pay you for them as soon as I can.*
> *I would like you to see some of the mule teams we have here in the army. You never see any I bet that would come half way being as good as some we*

have here. We have a team in our brigade. They are all large as the common ones and white as old Buck ever was. The man what drives can make them go any where by word. Why they can go through the drill all most with a little training. That is the kind of teams with us. Us solgers have to haul our grub with us.

Well, I dont know as have any thing more to write about. I dont write very often of late. It is getting prety warm here.

Whiskey is worth $8 per canteen fill. I buy lager 10 cts for a taste - very few I taste. Potatoes 12 ½ cts per lb but thats nothing.

Such times I hope will not last all ways with me by thunder if I ever get out of this. I bet no damd Brigadier will order this child around again but at the same time, I like the service first rate because I cant help my self and I am fool enough to stay a while until I am discharged by proper authority.

Yes Luit. A. M. York has come back to the Co. and 2d Lt. McRea is Brigade Q.M. I am glad of it as is all of Co. I. 92. He is a poor coot. Any way he puts on more stile than Gen. Baird ever did. He wont last till he gets out eventually by degrees.

Well give my love to all. Tell little Jennie I will come home before long and see her. Write often.

I remain your sincere soger Brother.

E. M. Swaggart

Co. I, 92 Ill. Vol.

9 months men. Time out $4^{th}$ of June 1863

Moses mentioned in his letter to Eugene that he would give him a mule team and Eugene was excited about the prospect. He always loved working with horses and mules and really admired the mules used by the army.

John Miller wrote wanting his money for the revolver when he heard Eugene had sold it. Eugene was a little perturbed with John for more reasons than one. John had agreed to take payment later but wanted it now.

Eugene was also upset with John because he was trying to have an affair with Jennie in spite of the fact that Jennie was not interested and John was married to Mary Ann.

*Franklin Tenn                   May 25$^{th}$ 1963*
*Dear Wife*
*With the permission of kind providence, I write to you once more. I am not very well at presant but will soon be able for duty again. It has been near a week since I have heard from you but expect a letter today.*
*Vira, I sent my over coat home or not home but you will find it at Mrs. J. M. Noises Millner shop, formerly Miss Welthy Grant at Lanark. You will know the coat by the bright buttons. It is as good as new. Send an order for it as soon as you can.*
*I have never heard whether you got any money yet the other boys that sent money have heard of it going home safe. I hope it will not be lost.*
*Vira, John Miller wrote to me that he was prety hard up for want of a little money. If you get your money from Hams, use it up some way. Put it on interest if nothing else for I never should have taken his pistole if he had not agreed to take the rail road money for it but we are to be paid soon and I will send it to him. However you can do as you like in regard to paying him. If he needs it right bad, for Mothers sake, pay him.*
*Dont let any one see this. He is still after Jennie. For shure I have not much respect for him. Can you blame me for it?*

*There are some fiew agitating the 9 month question hard but am afraid it is a bore.*

*The weather is very warm. Flies are so thick that a fellow when eating has to fight hard to get his portion. We live prety well now. Good bakers bread but minus butter. Oh! if I was in Mothers old spring house just about this time of day, I bet I would go my length in good things.*

*We had charming news to day from Vicksburgh but it was not confirmed. Old Grant I guess will do the thing up right as he generaly does as well as any of our Generals and a little better. I think we will all have our winter quarters in Illinois some where this next winter. I may be disappointed but if we cant whip them by fall we cant in three years. That is an evident case.*

*Vira, Moses says he intends giving me a team when I come home. Do you think he will. He wrote me a very nice letter a short time ago which I have answered.*

*I understand that you have the land all planted. Bully for you. You can get along better with me away than if I were at home, cant you so I guess I shall stay a while longer yet and when I get home I will go to Engineering and let you farm. What foolish talk is it not to talk of home.*

*Vira tell me in your next who is waiting on Annie. I hear she is about to step of some good.*

*By. Give my love to Jennie & Dicky. Kiss the young Hooker for its old Dad.*

*Mack*


Anna had a new beau. It worried Eugene a little. He did not want Anna to be too intimate with her beau as he knew from experience what it led to and he felt Anna was too young for marriage. In addition, he did not want John Miller, their half-brother, taking advantage of Anna and getting her land. He did not feel Anna had the experience to handle John Miller if he started leasing it and things did not go well.

> Franklin Tenn        May 30$^{th}$ 1863
> Dear Wife
> It is withe pleasure I seat myself this best sabbeth morn for to write a fiew lines. I received 2 letters from you the other day which found me in good health and hope this will find you enjoying the same. I have nothing of consequence to write today, only we are to have general drill. We have no signs of moving from hear at presant. The news is, here, that the rebs has left and gone back to their fortify cations. The news from Vicksburgh is very favorable. I think a fiew days more will end that strife in our favor. It will be a hard blow to the rebellion if they loose that part and great will be the fall. The father of all waters will be in our hands. The Mississippi boys are in tolerable good health.

Many times the Union troops attempted to take Vicksburg but as of May 31, 1863, the Confederate armies still held on.[102]

The nine-month - three-year discussion took place around the campfires nightly. Eugene realized that many of the soldiers still believed their enlistment would end in nine months. He saw abundant disappointment as they realized what they signed.

> All are hoping the 9 months will come, but the question is somewhat subsiding, but let me tell you, it will be the ruination of some of our boys. It will be a hard shock for them when they find out that there is not such thing. They have so firmly beleaved it as to bet 4 or 5 months pay that we would get out in 9 months, but instead of going out, they will have to stay in and lose their money.

---

[102] World Almanac Publications, *The Civil War Almanac*, Intro. by Henry Steele Commager, A Bison Book, New York, NY 1983, pp. 144-154

*Besides, Vira, I have a bet of $15.00 staked that we will not be 9 months men, so if I lose, I shant care for it would let us hurry and get home. So, if I did gamble, it is one the safe side.*

*I had a letter from Ed. It was a hard old epistle, but it is all right. I paid him back in the answer.*

*It has been rainy for the last fiew days and we have had it easy, nothing to do when it rains. Here we do as the people do up north, just let it rain.*

*Vira, I am glad you got what money you did. If the other is lost, it cant be helped, but I know you need every cent of it and we expect some more pay in a few days. We have sighned and we never do that until the paymaster gives orders.*

*May 31$^{st}$ Well, inspection is over and I am glad, are you not. To day, I am not on duty. Therefore, I can spend part of my time with you, or as near as I can, and that will be in writing. I have not a thing worth reading, as I have said before, but if you are anything like me, anything is good which you write. I have the toothache here lately most all the time. I broke a piece off one of them and I guess I will have to get it jerked out and I afread worse than a battle. I will stop for a short time.*

*June 1$^{st}$. This is a beautifull day & not very warm. We had a hard shower last night. It blew our tents over and, oh, how wet we got, but that was nothing but fun for us. A soldier can stand more than I ever thought. Give them enough to eat and we are all right with a little sleep.*

*Oh! I am geting impatient for some thing to be done. I want to see things move so we will get home. I begin to think a good bit about home & I am going there before many months more passes by. That is my honest opinion of things at presant. If I get home by fall, it will be soon enough. If I was there now, it would be to late to do any thing so I would go leave soldier a while longer as not. It is not as hard as it used to be. Well, I must get out to target practice with my gun. Drill is over and my head aches so I can hardly write.*

Furloughs were primarily on everyone's minds. Eugene was hoping for one, too, but knew there were others who needed one more than he did.

*There is some talk of our regt. geting one hundred furloughs. If so, I can get one. I would like to see my son and its ma very much, but there is some in this Co. I would give way to, some that are sick and ought to go home for a short time, but if I can get one, I will come. In regard to my coming home, James Becker dont know as much as he thinks he does. I got a box of said stuff and am rid of the same but dont know how long I will be given. My love to all. I remain your loving Husband.*
*Eugene Swaggart*

Added to the letter dated June 1 was the following:

*I have the boy what you like best and it will be sent home.*
*I am very glad Annie has the beau you spoke of. I think more of him than any young man in that part of the country. All I hope is that their intimacy may prove for the best. You know what that is. She is arived at an age wich is sufficient for her to judge for herself and I hope she may do well, but it is not me to say what she must do. I have experience in that respect, have I not. John said he expected the young scotchman would take her of, but did not tell who the man was. He said he was about to ask Annies land for 3 or 4 years if she did not marry soon. You tell her not to let her land for any certain length of time and then, you know, if she should*

*happen to want it in a year or two, she could have it.*
*Mr. McCracken was here this week. His son is sick in Nashville. He is going to try and get Tom discharged from service. I hope he will be able to.*
*I wish you could come or some of our folks if I dont come home. I will write again. You need not write untill you here from me again. We are all well. I had the toothache last night like everything. I will have it pulled out in the morning by golly. I have quit swareing. That is good news, aint it? Dear, Oh how I would like to kiss you once more and I will be fore another sonday passes over our heads. I can tell you lots of news about warfare, so I can..........*
*Please excuse this dirty paper.*

John Russell sent his bill due in corn to Elvira and she sent it on to Eugene. It read as follows:

*Mt. Carroll May 27$^{th}$ 1863*
*G. W. Harris administrator of the Estate of George Swaggart deceased. Please pay the bearer the amount of my services rendered in division of Farm Employed by Corn and this will be your receipt.*
*John Russell*

Eugene was granted a furlough and he just knew he was on his way home to see Elvira and the baby. However, on June 2, 1863, orders canceled all furloughs and the Ninety-second Illinois was on the move again - this time to Triune, Tennessee, and twenty miles away.

## Chapter Eight
## The Hospitals, Triune and Nashville

Although the ultimate campaign to oust General Braxton Bragg from Tennessee did not begin in earnest until June 23, 1863, Union troops began to move slowly southward in preparation early in the month. Furloughs were cancelled. The Ninety-second Illinois Infantry marched twenty miles to Triune on the second and set up camp.[103]

> *Headquarters, Co. I, 92$^{nd}$ Ill.*
> *Triune Tenn June 6$^{th}$ 1863*
> *Dear Wife*
> *I will try and write you a fiew lines. I am well at presant and hope this will find you the same.*
> *We left Franklin, Tenn. the 3d and came here. We are now 14 miles east of Franklin & 12 miles from Murfreesboro. The next day after we left Franklin, the rebs run in there & tried to take the place, but I guess they got licked. We have not heard, yet, who was best. Our camp now is where the Murfreesboro fight comenced. I guess, from the appearance of things, that there will be a grand movement of Rosecrans army on towards the rebs front.*

General Rosecran's Union troops had a small skirmish with General Bragg's Confederate troops "south and east of Murfreesboro, at Franklin, and at Snow's Hill.[104]

June 6, 1863 continued.

> *News has just come in from Franklin that our boys give fits. A force of about 8 or 10 thousand went in there against to small regiments, but our old siege*

---
[103] *Illinois Troops (Union) Infantry, Records of Events, Volume 13, Records of Events for the Ninety-second Illinois Infantry, September 1862 – June 1865*, p. 547
[104] Robert E. Denney, *The Civil War Years, A Day-by-Day Chronicle of the Life of a Nation*, Foreword by Gregory J. W. Urwin, Sterling Publishing Co., NY, p. 291

*guns were to much for them. We have got off from any railroad now, so we cant get any mail, only when a supply train goes through to Nashvill. This is the third letter I have writen since I have had one from you, but I expect 2 or 3 when our mail comes through.*
*Grub is pretty scarce since our march. The boys swore they will raise ned if they dont give us grub, but I guess it will be all right- by and by.*
*Vicksburgh is ours, so the papers say.*

On July 4, 1863, General John C. Pemberton surrendered to General Ulysses Grant and the Federal troops took over Vicksburg.[105] The newspaper was about one month early with their announcement.

June 6th cont.

*I hope it is true and if it is true, I should not be surprised if we had to engage old Braggs army next. The fur will fly then, if the 92$^{nd}$ has anything to do with it, but I hope*
*We will be considered out, dont you.*
*This is the prettiest country I ever saw. The man that owns this where we are camped has a house that cost only $65.000 and owns 1600 acres of land, all in one body, no end to his nigers. He is a good union man since we come here or we would had the fun of burning his house and other buildings. Hostetters big house is a common smokehouse to the side of this one. Crops look fine, any amount of fruit. We will give it fits when it gets ripe if we are here that long.*
*The furlough business has played out, the order countermanded.*

---

[105] Robert E. Denney, *The Civil War Years, A Day-by-Day Chronicle of the Life of a Nation,* Foreword by Gregory J. W. Urwin, Sterling Publishing Co., NY, p. 301

*Give my love to all. Write as of as is convenient for you. Goodby. Kiss the boy for me.*
*I remain your loving Husband.       Eugene Mc*
*P. S. I have got to wash this afternoon and dont like to.*

Inserted in the letter of June 6 was a small booklet with a poem. The publisher was the Protestant Episcopal Book Society, 1224 Chestnut Street, Philadelphia.

*A Rainy Day in Camp*

*It's a cheerless, lonesome evening,*
*When the soaking, sodden ground*
*Will not echo to the foot-fall*
*Of the sentinel's dull round.*

*God's blue star-spangled banner*
*To night is not unfurled;*
*Surely He has not deserted*
*This weary, warring world.*

*I peer into the darkness,*
*And the crowding fancies come;*
*The night-wind blowing Northward*
*Carries all my heart toward home.*

*For I 'listed in this army,*
*Not exactly to my mind;*
*But my country called for helpers,*
*And I couldn't stay behind.*

*So I've had a sight of drilling,*
*And have roughed it many ways,*
*And Death has nearly had me;*
*Yet I think the service pays.*

# A RAINY DAY IN CAMP.

PHILADELPHIA:
PROTESTANT EPISCOPAL BOOK SOCIETY,
1224 Chestnut Street.

*It's a blessed sort of feeling,*
*That though you live or die,*
*You have helped your bleeding country,*
*And fought right loyally.*

*But I can't help thinking sometimes,*
*When a wet day's leisure comes,*
*That I hear the old home voices*
*Talking louder than the drums;*

*And the far, familiar faces*
*Peep in at the tent door,*
*And the little children's footsteps*
*Go pit-pat on the floor.*

*I can't help thinking, somehow,*
*Of what the Parson reads,*
*All about that other warfare*
*Which every true man leads.*

*And wife, soft-hearted creature,*
*Seems a-saying in my ear,*
*"I'd rather have you in those ranks*
*Than to see you Brigadier.*

*I call myself a brave one,*
*But in my heart I lie!*
*For my Country and her Honor*
*I am fiercely free to die;*

*But when the Lord who bought me*
*Asks for my service here*
*To "fight the good fight" faithfully*
*I'm skulking in the rear.*

*And yet I know this Captain
All love and care to be;
He would never get impatient
With a raw recruit like me.*

*And I know He'd not forget me
When the Day of Peace appears;
I should share with Him the victory
Of all His volunteers.*

*And it's kind of cheerful, thinking,
Beside the dull tent fire,
About that big promotion
When He says, "Come up higher!"*

*And though it's dismal, rainy,
Even now, with thoughts of Him,
Camp life looks extra cheery,
And death a deal less grim.*

*For I seem to see Him waiting
Where a gathered Heaven greets
A great, victorious army,
Surging up the golden streets;*

*And I hear Him read the roll-call,
And my heart is all aflame,
When the dear Recording Angel
Writes down my happy name!*

*But my fire is dead white ashes,
And the tent is chilling cold,
And I'm playing win the battle,
When I've never been enrolled.*

> *In Thine army vast receive me,*
> *Thou Saviour of the world!*
> *And I'll follow wheresoever*
> *Thy banner is unfurled.*
>
> *Oh, give me zeal and courage,*
> *My heart and life renew,*
> *That I firmly to my signet*
> *May set that Thou art true!*
>
> *To reach the Eternal City,*
> *I'll brave Death's sullen flood,*
> *My Saviour crossed before me:*
> *I'll triumph through His blood!*
>
> *Presented by*
> *U. S. Christian Commission*
> *Geo. H. Stuart*
> *Chairman*
> *Office, 13 Bank Street, Philadelphia*

On June 11, Confederate forces led by General Joseph Wheeler, attacked the Ninety-second Illinois Infantry and a skirmish developed. Immediately after the skirmish, Eugene complained of a bad headache. He had several headaches earlier, but this time, a high fever accompanied it. He reported to sickbay where the doctors diagnosed typhoid fever. Typhoid is a salmonella infection. The bacillus is a parasite of man that can contaminate food and water unless sanitary conditions exist. Because of lack of good fresh food, troops were eating whatever they could find and water was always a problem. One or both finally took Eugene down, as it did many other young men in the war on both sides. Disease was a reality of war, perhaps more so than fighting.

The ever-faithful George Wait Downs visited Eugene daily in the hospital and wrote to Elvira for him.

Triune Tenn.     Monday eve.     Jun 15$^{th}$ 1863
Affectionate Friend
I seat myself to inform you of your husbands illness. Mc is sick with a fever. He was taken ill on the eleventh of this month.
He has had quite a few fever days ever since. He restes very well nights. He is in the camp hospital. He is not very sick. He is well cared for. He has received two letters from home since he has been ill. We were attacked on the 11$^{th}$ by the enemy, but our battery soon sent them the way they came. Mc was out with the company, but as soon as it, that is the squirmish, was over, he complained of having the headache. He went to the hospital that night. He has not gained much but he is no worse. He does not want you to give your self any uneasyness about him. I think he will be allright in a few days. He sends his love to his wife and son. Also gives his love to all of his folks. Please write to him soon. he wants Annie to write to him. Receive my best wishes also.
    G. W. Downs
If he is in no better in a day or two, I will write again.

On Saturday, Eugene was still too sick to write, but again his friend George Wait Downs wrote for him.

Triune Tenn     Sat. eve.     June 20$^{th}$, 1863
Dear Mrs.
I seat myself once more to tell you that Mc is gaining health. It is very slow that he recovers, but he is geting along very well. He looks a great site, sight better, but it is so warm that a sick person cannot gain very speedily. He says to tell you that he will be able to write to you himself in a few days.

*He received a letter from you today. He was much pleased to hear from you. He bears his illness very well and is in good spirits. He also has very good care. They keep very good eatibles for the sick. He has a good bed to repose upon. He sleeps a good part of the time. He seems to rest very well. I think he will be well in a few days. I do not know how long we will stay in this place. I believe I have no news to write to you. If Mc is taken worst I will let you know it.*
*He sends his love to you and all of his friends. Hopeing soon to hear from you. Again recieve my respects. Also no more at present.*
*G. W. Downs*

On June 23, the Ninety-second Illinois Infantry began their march to Shelbyville, Tennessee and George Wait Downs left with his unit. The first day, they marched to Salem, a distance of twelve miles. On June 24, they marched to Walnut Grove, an additional twelve miles where they camped for three days.

June 27 found the Ninety-second Illinois Infantry on a side trip of eight miles to Guy's Gap along with other members of General Granger's Reserve Troops commanded by General Absalom Baird and led by David S. Stanley's cavalry. The infantry followed closely to drive General Wheeler's cavalry from there.[106] They returned to Walnut Grove on the twenty-eighth.[107]

June 29 and 30 took them thirteen miles into Shelbyville the first day and moved camp two miles on the other side of Shelbyville on the second day. There they stayed through the end of June, occasionally changing positions in the field.[108] Pickets and reconnaissance movements were frequent.

---

[106] Frank J. Welcher, *The Union Army, 1861-1865, Organization & Operations, Volume II, Western Theater,* Indiana UniversityPress, Bloomington & Indianapolis, 1993, *p. 833*

[107] *Illinois Troops (Union) – Infantry, Record of Events, Volume 13, Records of Events for the Ninety-second Illinois Infantry, September 1862 - June 1865,* p. 547

[108] Ibid.

Skirmishes developed between June 23 and July 7, 1863, associated with the Tullahoma Campaign.[109] Other companies in the Ninety-second Illinois occupied Shelbyville. Company I was one of the companies that moved about.

For Eugene McBride Swaggart, the Army and their whereabouts were unimportant. Orders came to transfer him to Nashville Hospital No. 13 for better care. In the absence of Wait Downs, others in the hospital, a little further along in their recuperation process, helped Eugene by writing his letters for him. On June 30, Mr. J. S. Ross, crippled from the war and a patient in the hospital, volunteered to write to Elvira while Eugene told him what to say.

*Hospital # 13, Nashville, Ten  June 30$^{th}$ 1863*
*Dear Wife*
*I have been very sick but I am getting better everyday, but I am too weak and nervous to write yet. I have been sick some four weeks with Typhoid Fever & I was transfered from Triune to Nashville on the 23$^{rd}$ of this month. Our whole Force has moved forward & left all who were unable to march behind.*
*I have received no letters from you for sometime & I want to hear from you - soon. You can write, for I am anxious to know how you are getting along. I expects you needs some money by this time. I will send 20 Dollars in this letter. Take good care of it & when you wants any, let me know, soon as you can. I dont want you to be nervous or alarmed about me for my case is not dangerous. I raved some at first, for a time, from the effects of the fever but, I remember all thats passed during that time. Give my love to Jenny & Mother & all inquiring friends. Respectfully  Your E. M. Swaggart*

---

[109] Frank J. Welcher, *The Union Army, 1861-1865, Organization & Operations, Volume II, Western Theater*, Indiana University Press, Bloomington & Indianapolis, 1993, pp. 832-842

The big news in Tennessee concerned General William Starkie Rosecrans and his Union Army who drove General Braxton Bragg from West Tennessee, thus forcing the Confederate Army to gather near Chattanooga.[110]

The Ninety-second Illinois Infantry was still in the field and on July 6, they detached from the brigade under orders and moved to Duck River Bridge. They built a permanent wagon bridge over the river. They did so with no tools but axes and shovels - in forty-eight hours. Wagon trains of the army used the bridge many times during the war.[111]

On July 8, they were permanently detached from the First Brigade, First Division Reserve Corps and assigned to the First Brigade, Fourth Division, Fourteenth Army Corps known as Colonel John Thomas Wilder's brigade of mounted infantry.[112] Colonel Wilder of Indiana was leading one of the cavalry units that fought bravely in the Tullahoma Campaign. The detachment to the unit pleased the soldiers of the Ninety-second Illinois Infantry. Their time to fight was here at last. On July 10, they returned to Wartrace and then moved on to Normandy on the twelfth.[113]

Elvira worried when she received the letters from George Wait Downs. She knew Eugene must really be sick if he could not write himself. She was ready to go to Nashville, find her husband, and take him home. After all, he had said others were going into Nashville to see their loved ones and had even invited her one time to make the trip.

The last thing Eugene wanted was for Elvira to travel into Tennessee. It was different before when he had told her to come. Now there was intense fighting going on and the trip was very dangerous. When he received her letter, he asked J. S. Ross to write another letter for him.

---

[110] World Almanac Publications, *The Civil War Almanac*, Intro. by Henry Steele Commager, A Bison Book, New York, NY 1983, pp. 156 & 158

[111] Thomas M. Eddy, *The Patriotism of Illinois, A Record of the Civil and Military History of the State*, Chapter XXII, Regimental Sketches, Ninety-second Illinois Infantry, 1865, p 371

[112] *Illinois Troops (Union) Infantry, Records of Events, Volume 13, Records of Events for the Ninety-second Illinois Infantry, September 1862 - June 1865*, p. 497

[113] *Records of Events*, p. 497

Hosptial # 13, Nashville, Tenn.     July 11$^{th}$, 1863
Dear Wife

I received your letter of the 4$^{th}$ today & it made me glad, sorry too, glad because you are well & getting along first rate, sorry to hear that you talk of coming after me, for I am all most well now. That, I can go about considerably. You say you would like to be here to give your little attentions in a thousand ways that others would never think of, admit it all, yet you must know that the Army is no place for a woman to be, but I thank you for your kindness in this man.

Vira, you know your heart. I know how you are uneasy concerning me, but if the mail route had been free from danger, you would have been satisfied long ago about me for I have sent several letters to you since I took ill. I told you frankly in each just how I was & now I am out of danger. I want you to rest easy about me. If I gets sick again, I will do all that a man can do to get home. I should like to come now, but I am getting well too fast to get off now, for if I never get well enough for field duty.

I sent you $20 Dollars some two weeks since & I will send you some more before long, anyhow, as soon as I think it will be safe to do so. Oh, Vira, I would like to see my little son & you guess who else. Well, maybe the first letters of her name are Vira. Give my love to all inquiring friends & tell Anna I will remember her next time, for I must think of you first, you know.

Done by J. S. Ross

Cripple who nursed me while sick -

I have not seen anything of the likenesses you spoke of in your letters.

Eugene's health improved. When his friend, J. S. Ross, left by discharge, he felt strong enough to write Elvira himself. He worried that J. S. Ross had told Elvira he received a promotion because he remembered raving about it when he was sick. It was not true and he wanted Elvira to know. After all, Eugene was not a model soldier. He left once without leave, had a fight, and was in the guardhouse because his Sergeant and Corporal fell asleep. The latter was not his fault, but the Army sometimes held things like that against a soldier. He was also sick and spoke with a German accent. He did not want Elvira to expect extra pay. On July 13, Eugene wrote to Elvira himself, from the hospital, for the first time since his illness.

> *Gen. Hosptial No. 13, Nashville      July 13$^{th}$ 63*
> *Dearest Vira*
> *I will try to write you a fiew lines myself. I am gaining everyday, as fast as I can. I recd a letter from you with the babies picture in it. He is quite a boy. I all so got one from Moses & one from Annie, but I dont feel able to answer them at presant.*
> *Dear Vira, you must not feel worried about me for I have good care & if I dont take a back set, I will be able to join my regiment in a month & if I should get worse, I will let you know as soon as the news can reach you. My Dear, I never knew what it was to be sick away from home before, but from all accounts, I guess we will all be home this winter.*
> *Old Bragg is chasted clear out of Tenn. and Gen. Meade has cut Gen. Lee's army all up & Vicksburgh has fallen.*

The Confederates formally surrendered Vicksburg, Mississippi to the Union Army on July 4, 1863. However, General Robert E. Lee, after withdrawing from Gettysburg, was moving southward along the Shenandoah Valley, in good condition although short of supplies and shoes.

> *The war has never progressed beter, since it first commenced, than it has in the last fiew weeks. Well,*

*I am getting so nervous I will have to bid you goodby, for the presant. My love to all.*
*I remain your loving Husband*
*E M Swaggart*
*J. S. Ross is discharged. He wrote I was promoted, but it is false. God bless you, Dear.*

Anna wrote to Eugene while he was sick and he answered her letter from the hospital. He knew Anna needed money for piano lessons and he wanted to help if he could.

*Hospital No. 13*                      *July 14$^{th}$ 1863*
*Dear Sister*
*I rec. yours of July, no date, with much pleasure to hear from you. I am geting quite smart. I have not been outdoors but twice. I am in the 4$^{th}$ story & can not get up & down stairs yet. I am so weak, but I guess I will soon overcome that. We have very good grub & Mc has an awfull appetite.*
*I wrote to Vira yesterday. I am so nervous & weak that I cannot write much at one time, but I will write to someone of the family everyday or so, so you will know how I get along. Dear Sister, of course you shall have what you requested of me as soon as we are payed up & that will be in the cours of a day or 2. The Paymaster is here now. I sent $20 to Vira not long ago. Well, I must close. Give my love to Mother, Jennie, Vira, John's folks & all. Everybody. Billy boy too. I remain your loving Brother. Mc S.*
*to sister Annie*
*Oh, my boy come yesterday. He is ugly as gehu.*
Eugene was referring to the picture that Elvira sent to him.
*Excuse half sheet*

Eugene also told Elvira the baby was not too pretty, but he used a little more discretion in his mention of the baby's looks.

*Hosptial No. 13, Nashville, Ten., July 14$^{th}$ 63*
*Dearest Wife,*
*The likeness of my boy com yesterday. I cant say he is pretty. He is too much like his dad, & me I guess, it would not be good for me to say so to you or I would get my ears pulled soundly.*
*I am lame in one leg. I dont know but it will gather & break, but however I am going to my regt. if it gets worse. There, why maybe I will get home with it. Vira, that fellow wrote for me to you told you I was orderly. He wrote a big lie. I said I was when I was sick but I was out of my head all the time.*
*Well, we was paid $20.00 today & I will get a check on the Carroll Bank and send it home. Vira, write to me if you can spare Annie some & if so, I will send her some to pay on her music lessons. Well, I suppose I must close. I got the boys like snuff in a case.*
*Your loving                    Mack*

The Ninety-second Illinois Infantry left Wartrace on orders from Colonel Wilder on July 19. On July 21, Colonel Smith D. Atkins of the Ninety-second Illinois Infantry and two hundred of his men and officers accompanied an expedition under Colonel John J. Funkhouser of the Ninety-eighth Illinois Volunteers. They moved west along the line of the Duck River to Columbia and other points. After two days, they returned with the detachment after killing several of the enemy and capturing close to thirteen hundred horses and mules and three hundred African contrabands, all pressed into service to fight for the flag. On July 22, because of their luck in finding so many horses, the Ninety-second Illinois Infantry returned mounted and thus became the Ninety-second Mounted Infantry, Illinois Volunteers.[114]

Eugene, who was still in Hospital 13, Ward 9, in Nashville, was feeling better. The time was approaching when he could rejoin his regiment. He had been to town once and was stronger everyday.

The women in Nashville, who were Confederate supporters, were not usually civil to the Union soldiers. There were many of them in the city although the Commander ordered them to leave. Eugene had seen some in town and found them very unfriendly.

On July 27, Eugene wrote his last two letters from the hospital before his discharge arrived. He mailed one to Amanda Ludisky and one to Elvira in the same envelope. He knew Vira would see that Dickey received hers.

*General Hosptial No 13, Ward 9, Nashville, Tenn.*
*July 27$^{th}$ 1863*
*Dear Sister Dicky*
*I recd your sometime ago & have neglected writing untill the presant. I am getting quite stout & hearty & will soon join the regiment. I have a very bad cough yet & a wheezing in my throat. I am afraid I am going to have Moses's complaint if I go back and go to sleeping on the ground.*
*I dont get any news from home now whatever. I have had one letter from Vira since here (5) months today & one from you & Moses. I guess my mail is in Louis Ville yet. I dont know why it dont come through, but I guess they will come afterwhile. I have writen home very often since here in the Hosp., but I dont know as you have recd them.*

---

[114] *Illinois Troops (Union) Infantry, Records of Events, Volume 13, Records of Events for the Ninety-second Illinois Infantry, September 1862 - June 1865*, p. 497 & Thomas M. Eddy, *The Patriotism of Illinois, A Record of the Civil and Military History of the State, Chapter XXII, Regimental Sketches of the Ninety-second Illinois Infantry*, 1865, p. 371

Dicky, I think I ought to be permited to go home to spend a fiew weeks, but it is surely imposible for me to come for the presant, but if I go to my regt. & my being will not stand it, I will try & come home. My lame leg is all most well. It is nothing more than a strain & weakness together.

Nashville is a nice city. I was out in town yesterday. I found it a very nice place. All the fault one can find with the place, it has most to many of the female sex. The Military Commander has sent off about five hundred and they are so thick yet, one can hardly get along on the pavements. I wish they were all in the bottom of the Cumberland.

There is not much business going on here except Uncle Sams. The government wagons are going night & day hauling stores from the wharfs and depots.

The war news is good. We got a dispach here that Charleston was taken. I dont know how true it is, but it is sure to fall if it has not all ready.

Well, I guess I will have to close. The Dr. is coming. Give my love to all.

    Your sincere Brother
    E M Swaggart

Write often if it is not more than 4 lines
Good by Vira

And in the same envelope was a letter for Elvira.

Hosptial No. 13, Nashville Tenn
July 21$^{st}$ 1863
Dear Wife

I, today, was overjoyed by the receipt of two good letters from you, but they were both directed to the Regt. Therefore, they were a good while coming, but better late than never. I am geting along Bully with the exceptions of a prety bad cough, but am in hopes it will not last long. I hope this will find you all well to enjoying good health.

I expect to leave here soon. I never wanted to get away from a place so bad in my life. Although it is very pleasant here fore those that are contented, it is more like a hotel than a hospital, everything right & nice when I was so low. I never wanted for anything. There was a kind old fellow stood by my bedside all the time. O' yea, there was something I wanted and that was my discharge. I called for it all the time, so they told me, but I don't want it so bad now, for I think this man will soon wind up everything. Looks more favorable for it now than it did by half.

Poor Lee Fish[115], he has retired from the battlefield in company with thousands of others that got to their long home, where the sabers & bayonets cease to glisten, but these names is & will ever be with us for the remembrance of honor & glory won by themselves.

I wrote to Dicky today before the reception of your letters & gave her a kind of off-handed discription of the town. I have nothing more to write about at presant. Only tell Annie I will remember her the next time & Willy also. Give My love to all. My duty Ona. I remain as ever
        your loving
        Mc Swaggart

On July 28, 1863, Eugene returned to his regiment.

---

[115] Major Leander B. Fish – Mt. Carroll, Staff Officer, 45th Illinois Infantry, killed in battle 6-25-63. Arthur Robbe and Richard Hinton, Booklet of *Rededication Ceremony of the Carroll County Soldiers & Sailors Monument*.

## Chapter Nine
## The Crossing

On July 23, 1863, "a detachment of Company E of the Ninety-second Mounted Infantry, Illinois Volunteers, started on a scout, passing by Shelbyville, Chapel Hill, Unionville, Columbia, Knob Creek, and Spring Hill. They returned July 28 through Unionville, Shelbyville and Tullahoma, to camp at Decherd". "They traveled one hundred sixty miles."[116]

The remainder of the Ninety-second Illinois Mounted Infantry "left camp under orders from General Joseph Jones Reynolds to report to Cowan, Tennessee," but when they arrived at Decherd Station, they moved into camp, under orders, just a mile or two north of Cowan.[117]

On July 28, Eugene left the hospital in Nashville and caught a train to rejoin his troops in camp near Decherd's Station. When he arrived in camp, he learned that the Ninety-second Illinois Infantry was now the Ninety-second Mounted Infantry, Illinois Volunteers. Assigned to First Brigade, Fourth Division, Fourteenth Army Corps, Department of the Cumberland and led by Colonel John T. Wilder of Indiana, the cavalry brigade was called Wilder's brigade by his soldiers.

His first week, he drew a horse that was one of the many confiscated from the Confederates in their raid while he was in the hospital. He also drew one of the soon to become famous, Spencer rifles. It was the first successful lever action repeater that held nine cartridges and used a rim fire round of .52 caliber. Referred to as "that tarnation Yankee gun they loads on Sunday and shoots the rest of the week" by one Confederate soldier, it was one of sixty thousand used during the war.

From camp, Eugene wrote to Elvira to let her know where he was and what was happening to him.

---

[116] *Illinois Troops (Union) Infantry, Records of Events, Volume 13, Records of Events for the Ninety-second Illinois Infantry, Company E, September 1862 - June 1865* p. 529
[117] Ibid., p 497

*In Camp near Dechards Station, Ten July 30th 1863*
*Dear Wife*
*I will try & write once more to let you know how I am geting along. I am well & hope this will find you the same. I left Nashville the 28th & got to the regt. the same day. We are now about 100 miles south of Nashville, 20 miles south of Tullihoma.*
*I saw Henry Lego at Tullohoma. You better believe there was a jolly-fication when we met. He is well. The car did not stop long for us to talk.*
*The 92nd is enough old set as sure as you are born. They have been out on one scout & brought in 600 niggers and over 150 horses & about as many mules. I have drew my horse, saddle & bridle. I guess we will advance soon.*
*Vira, I have not had my letters in a long time. I guess the mail has been stoped again.*
*Boys are well & hearty as pigs. We cant get much to eat here on account of them being such a large army to haul for. Our grub consists of ham, tack, sow belly & sugar & coffee, but when out, we live of the citizens.*
*I have no news of much importance to write at the presant, but will write you again soon. Give my best respects to all inquiring friends.*
*I remain your Husband.     Mack*
*Direct your letters    Co. I, 92nd Ill Mtd   Via Nashville Tenn*
*Co. I 92nd Regt Ill vol Via Nashville Tenn. Col. Wilders brig.*

When Eugene returned to the Ninety-second Illinois Mounted Infantry, he found some additional changes. For one, the men finally accepted Lieutenant Joshua McRea and liked him. He earned their respect.

The second big change was in the discipline and time schedules - everyday filled with training and jobs to accomplish. There was no time for rest, except at night. The troops had to care for their horses and condition themselves and the horses for the long hours they expected to pass without rest. However, at the time, Eugene knew none of the reasons for the training. He just knew he did not mind getting up at 4:30 A.M. and starting the day, not finishing up until twilight each night. In fact, he rather liked it. It reminded him of his days as a farmer and it made Sundays special. On August 8, he wrote to Elvira from his camp near Decherd Station to let her know he was content.

*Camp near Dechards Station Tenn August 8$^{th}$ 1863*
*Dear Wife*
*Once more, I am permited to write you a fiew lines to inform you how I am geting along. I am well & hearty, never felt better in my life. I am getting fat as fast as hard tack & coffee will make me. There is so many troops here that we cannot get any vegitables, not as much as a roasting ear. I am in hopes we will move soon.*
*Vira, I have not heard from home since I left the hospital. I am getting quite anxious to hear from you. I have not writen as often as I have been accostomed to, but I think I can give you a good excuse for not writing.*
*First, in the morning, is a bugle for roll call at 4 ½ o clock,*
*2$^{nd}$ is stable call from 4 ½ to 5 ½,*
*Breakfast at 6 to 7,*
*3d, water call,*
*4$^{th}$ is graze call till 9 ½,*
*then, we come in and drill till 11 ½ and eat our grub.*
*Afternoon, the same, so you see we have no time to do anything, only on Sundays & after night - although - I like the service much better than the*

way was. We have no guard duty, only to guard our horses, no fatigue. We have nigers to do our washing & cooking. If one does not do right, turn him off & get another.

5 days more and one year is gone. The boys are all in good cheer. Our officers all tell us that they are going to send us home this fall. About 4 months more will tell the good tale.

The Rebs are about played out in this state. Our boys were on a scout not long ago & captured a young bushwhacker, brought him into camp and is now a member of Company I. He makes a good soldier.

I suppose you have read in the papers the numerous battles our regiment have been through & never lost a man. I see in a Chicago paper that the ninty twosters were spoken of in the highest terms, but I never see anything about them so grand. Our young Liut. McRea, has come in to the Co. He is liked as an officer, first rate, much better than York. Our Cap is the man after all. I dont know what would become of us if it was not for E.Q. Becker.

Give my best respects To All  - Love to Mother. I remain your
*Affectionate Husband    Eugene M. Swaggart*
To Clara        Direct to 92 North
Via Nashville Tenn

August 16 dawn found the troops up and on the trail. It was raining, very hard, and the wagon train that accompanied the troops had a very hard climb up the mountain. The march was "from Decherd, Tennessee to the University of the South on the Cumberland Mountains". The first day, they were only able to make twelve miles, arriving the following morning.

After a short rest, the wagon train with the troops moved out again. They traveled thirteen miles, arriving at Firey Gizzard

Creek after dark. The decision made was that the crossing at night was too difficult so they waited until morning, posting guards.

August 18, the train crossed the creek and proceeded through Tracy City "through the hills and barrens on the road to Therman's in Sequatchie Valley," a distance of twenty miles. Altamont was to the left of them. The roads were good, except for "few rough places," but they were "dusty and water was scarce". However, the wagon trains were able to keep up with the troops.

When approaching Therman's on August 19, a slight skirmish developed that resulted with the capture of eleven Confederate prisoners. After the skirmish, the troops began the descent of the mountain. It was twelve miles long and very "tortuous and steep". Four miles up the valley took the troops and train into Dunlap, where they camped for the night on the "still Sequatchie". They traveled twelve miles.

The Ninety-second Illinois Mounted Infantry left Companies A & B, under Major John H. Bohn of the Ninety-second Illinois Infantry Staff, where Major Bohn was "in charge of the brigade, camps, trains, and forwarding of subsistence stores." The remainder of the troops began the march for "Chattanooga and Harrison's Landing via Poe's Tavern". "By sunset, they had crossed the Sequatchie River, ascended, crossed, and descended Walden's Ridge and encamped for the night in the Tennessee Valley below Poe's Tavern." They had traveled seventeen miles on August 20.[118]

By the twenty-first, it was evident that Bragg was following. Pickets were bringing in news that his troops were close. The brigade knew they had to do something to detract him so the trains could get through safely. One detachment, consisting of the 98th Illinois and the Ninety-second Illinois, with a portion of Eli Lilly's 18th Battery from Indiana, went to Harrison's Landing. The remainder of the brigade proceeded on to Chattanooga with Colonel John Wilder in command.

---

118 *Illinois Troops (Union) Infantry, Records of Events, Vol. 13, Records of Events for the Ninety-second Illinois Infantry, September 1862 - June 1865*, p. 498 – all information from August 16 to August 20.

At first, the detached party thought it would be a good idea to demonstrate at both places, but General John McAuley Palmer advised them not to demonstrate at Harrison's Landing. They met the enemy at Harrison's Landing, "strongly entrenched on the opposite side of the Tennessee River" and sharpshooters from the Confederate forces fired upon them. William Patterson, of the Ninety-second Illinois Mounted Infantry, Company D caught a cartridge in the arm, but it was only a flesh wound. The detachment moved out and traveled four miles before they bivouacked. They traveled a total of fifteen miles that day.

August 22, the detachment returned to Harrison's Landing where they tried to harass the enemy with shells, but the enemy was no longer present and there was no answer to their fire. The Union detachment "returned to Poe's Tavern" once again, a total of fifteen miles.

From Poe's Tavern, on August 23, the detachment started up the mouth of a creek and traveled for thirty-two miles in three days but saw no enemy. However, they "captured seventy-five bushels of wheat" and turned it over to the brigade.

Company A of the 98th Illinois went out on a scout the morning of August 26 to Harrison's Landing and they found part of the enemy on the north side of the Tennessee River. They charged and captured two members of the cavalry unit, killing one. The Confederate soldiers, captured by Company A, included one Lieutenant and one Private. The remainder of the company escaped. "Colonel Smith D. Atkins, with six companies" of his Ninety-second Illinois Mounted Infantry, "moved to the Captain's aid".

The following morning, the Union Army shelled the enemies' works, destroying some of their barricades, but no reply came forth. The sharpshooters, called forth, proceeded to shoot, but still no reply. They left with the assumption that the Confederates were gone. On the way back to Poe's Tavern, which was twenty-seven miles, on August 27, they met up with a picket at Dallas and shelled them heavily. That night and the rest of the month, they remained in camp at Poe's Tavern, "sending out scouting parties and pickets each day to Harrison's

Landing, Dallas, and Friar's Island."[119] The detachment and their "movements opposite and above Chattanooga, deceived the Army of General Braxton Bragg" and the troops were able to cross the Tennessee River without incident.[120] On the night of August 28, from a camp near Chattanooga, Eugene wrote to Elvira. He was very tired and beginning to realize what war really meant - possibly for the first time.

> *Camp near Chatnooga, Tenn    August 28$^{th}$ 1863*
> *Dear Wife*
> *With the greatest of pleasure do I now seat myself on the ground to ans yours of Aug 13$^{th}$ which I recd last night. I am well, never in better health in my life.*
> *Dear Vira, we have had hard times since I wrote you last. We have been on the march for 15 days over the worst roads in the world. We crost the Cumberland mountains after old Bragg & are now at the front where we can have the fun of shelling him everyday. I have been in two little fights with them, but we were on one side of the Tenn. river and them on the opposite side. I am in the 18$^{th}$ Indiana Battery now. I like the service first rate. I guess I will stay in the battery as long as I stay in the service. I guess that will not be very long.*
> *I will be at home in the spring, I think, if I live. Vira, I never was half so glad to get a letter as I was last night.*
> *We were out shelling them yesterday & made them raise the white flag, came into camp & found a letter for the first time in over a month. I guess we*

---

[119] *Illinois Troops (Union) Infantry, Records of Events, Vol. 13, Records of Events for the Ninety-second Illinois Infantry, September 1862 - June 1865*, pp. 498-499 – crossing of the Cumberland Mountains and activities of the detachment.
[120] Thomas M. Eddy, *The Patriotism of Illinois, A Record of the Civil and Military History of the State*, Chapter XXII, Regimental Sketches, Ninety-second Illinois Infantry, 1865, p. 372

will stay here quite a while and I can write to you oftener than I have.

> Camp Near Chattanooga Tenn
> August 25th 1863
> Dear Wife
>   With the greatest of pleasure do I now seat my self on the ground to ans yours of aug. 13th which I rec'd last night I am well never in better health in my life Dear Jim we have had hard times since I wrote you last we have been on the march for 15 days over the worst roads in the world we crost the Cumberland mountains after old Bragg I am now at the front where we can have the fun of shelling him every day I have been in two little fights with them but we were on one side of the Tenn. river

We have went over road that our teams could not, so we had to get our own grub where we could. You

can imagine the way yellow legs suffered. We got plenty of potatoes, corn, peaches & apples which we can live on very well. It is comencing to rain, so I will have to stop as we have no tents.
Give my respects to Ed and Flora. My love to Mother & Anna, Mose & Dicky, John & Maryann. Write often. I remain your
Mack
Direct to 18$^{th}$ Indiana batery.  Wilders Brigade Mounted Infantry 14 A.C.
Via Louisvill Ky

Eugene was spending a lot of time on the back of his horse and found it a completely different life from the one he had led before. The brigade he was in had been in a couple of skirmishes and his duty was to carry ammunition to the gun.

Gen. Wilders Brigade Camp
Near Chatnooga Tenn     August 31$^{st}$ 1863
Dear Wife
I will write you a fiew lines to let you know how I am. I am well & hope this will find you the same. I wrote 2 days ago & as we expect to move in the morning, I thought I would write.
Vira, in this Brigade, it is all together differant from being on foot. We are kept on the go all the while & the foot men are laying still. We get mail about once a week and ware a shirt till it is rotten, throw it away & get a new one. Oh, we are rough, ragged & dirty. You would scarcely know your Mc now if you could see him, but anything to dry up this show & they say Wilder's men have done more towards ending this war than any other in the service.
I have no duty to do now exepting our camp dutys and we are not in camp much at the presant. My duty in a fight is to carry ammunition to the gun.

*We have had two little fights. It made me work right smart. Well, we have to move camp, so I will close.*

On September 1, 1863, the detached regiment had some visitors. The Ninety-second Illinois Mounted Infantry moved from one campsite to another, probably to find a little better water. The visitors found them in camp. Eugene had never seen women that looked like the visitors from the mountainous region. He did not know exactly what to think about them, even if they were Union supporters.

Continued from August 31, 1863.

*Sept. 1$^{st}$. We have moved camp & are in a nice place, but cannot say how long we will stay here. The report is that the rebs are deserting. That is enough and I hope they are for I dont want to fight them here.*

*The Natives come in to see us. They are all union here. They come in ox teams with stars & stripes waving over them. The citizens here dont look as though they were a bit more than half civilized. The girls are all 6 footers and men in proportion. If you could see the women you would never get gealous, not saying that you ever was, but some men, you know, cant let anything alone, but if they were the last on gods earth, I could never have any pretentions, no, none for me.*

*Well, as for a likeness from me, will be hard to get in this country, but if I can get it, I surely will, but you can send me your photograph anyway. No other kind for I can not cary them.*

*There is 4 months due us now, but we may not get any pay for 4 months to come & I hope by that time we will get our pay and brake for home.*

*Give my love to all. I remain your loving Husband E. M. Swaggart*
*To Clara*

## Chapter Ten
## On to Chickamauga

General George Henry Thomas who was in the Army of General William Starkie Rosecrans as his Lieutenant General, was a "strong and pronounced Southerner" who served in "the battery of artillery in Corpus Christi, Texas in 1845" with General Braxton Bragg.[121] Now he was in pursuit of General Bragg along with others in the Union Army of the Cumberland.

On September 4, 1863, orders received by the Ninety-second Illinois Infantry stated they were to report to General Thomas at Bridgeport. Companies H & I, on picket at the mouth of the Chickamauga River and Harrison's Landing, received word they were to follow as soon as possible. When the regiment arrived at Therman's in Sequatchie Valley, Major John H. Bohn with Companies A & B joined them. They were escorting the regimental train. The regiment traveled by way of Jasper and arrived at Bridgeport at 10:00 A.M. on the seventh, only to find that General Thomas' headquarters moved to Trenton, Georgia. They spent the night at Cave Springs, Alabama.[122]

In the meantime, Colonel John Wilder and the remainder of his brigade along with Colonel Robert H. G. Minty, with a mixed cavalry, sent out patrols over a fifty mile radius, guarding every ford and landing along the waterfront.[123]

On the morning of the eighth, Companies E & F reconnoitered Lookout Mountain. Company E was within six miles of Summertown when night fell, compelling them to return to camp. However, they picked up enough information to believe an evacuation was in progress in Chattanooga. The information passed to General Rosecrans who ordered the entire regiment to proceed early the next morning to Raccoon Valley,

---

[121] *Battles and Leaders of the Civil War, Volume III - The Tide Shifts*, Edited by Robert Underwood Johnson & Clarence Clough Buel, of the Editorial Staff of "The Century Magazine", Castle, a Division of Book Sales, Inc., Edison, NJ, p. 639

[122] *Illinois Troops (Union) Infantry, Records of Events, Volume 13, Records of Events for the Ninety-second Illinois Infantry, September 1862 - June 1865*, p. 499

[123] Glenn Tucker, *Chickamauga, Bloody Battle of the West*, Konecky & Konecky, New York, NY, 1961, p. 16

pushing into it if possible.[124] At 3:00 A.M., the regiment moved out,[125] and at 10:00 A.M., the regiment entered Chattanooga. On the way in, they met with a "heavy cavalry picket" from the Confederate army that retreated safely after a skirmish across Lookout Mountain. Several companies from the Ninety-second Illinois Mounted Infantry were in pursuit for almost four miles, on several roads going south.[126]

The remainder of the regiment proceeded to Crutchfield House where they raised the regimental colors[127] along with the first Union banner since Tennessee became part of the Confederacy.[128]

The regiment rested for a short while, then pushed on by way of Harrison's Landing road, stopping for the night at the ford of the south Chickamauga River.

On Sept. 11, as the regiment approached within three miles of Ringgold, Georgia, it encountered the Louisiana cavalry led by John S. Scott and drove them into the town where they made a stand. A dispatch went to Colonel John T. Wilder and he quickly responded to the call. General Horatio Phillips Van Cleve from Minnesota, who was in the process of moving in with his division[129] on the north bank, set up additional batteries[130] and hearing the gunfire, started shelling on the enemies' flank. The Confederates broke to the right and ran leaving thirteen dead and many more wounded. The Ninety-second Illinois had three men wounded severely.[131]

An amusing story was told about one German soldier from the Ninety-second Illinois Infantry, Company F. who was in the

---

[124] *Illinois Troops (Union) Infantry, Records of Events, Volume 13, Records of Events for the Ninety-second Illinois Infantry*, September 1862 - June 1865, p. 499-500

[125] Glenn Tucker, *Chickamauga, Bloody Battle of the West*, Konecky & Konecky, New York, NY 1961, p. 18

[126] *Records of Events*, p. 500

[127] Ibid.

[128] Thomas M. Eddy, *The Patriotism of Illinois, A Record of the Civil and Military History of the State, Chapter XXII, Regimental Sketches, Ninety-second Illinois Infantry*, 1865, p. 372

[129] *Records of Events*, p. 500

[130] Tucker, *Chickamauga*, p. 20

[131] *Records of Events*, p. 500

line pressing the rebels back. He came out from the rebel ranks, horseless and hatless. As he approached Colonel B. F. Sheets of the Ninety-second Illinois, he said, "'O Col, they shoots mine horse, they shoots mine coat here and there; they shoots mine pants; they spoils mine gun, and I ish almost dead.' Sure enough, he had charged into the enemy, who had killed his horse and as he escaped on foot, three bullets went through his clothing with no harm to him and half the breech of his gun was missing."[132]

Upon leaving Ringgold for Lafayette, they took the road to Rossville since the direct road to Lafayette was not safe. Somewhere between Ringgold and Rossville, about midway, they encountered the rebel forces again. The rebel cavalry was charging a train, but after a small skirmish, they retreated quickly.

When the regiment reached Lee and Gordon's Mills on September 12, General Rosecrans ordered them to return to Summertown on Lookout Mountain "to open communication" with General Thomas' headquarters at Steven's Gap. A courier line needed establishing between the two points and companies C & K, of the Ninety-second Illinois, were picked to establish the lines. They succeeded by the end of the day on the thirteenth. The regiment had traveled forty miles in two days.

On September 14, the regiment of the Ninety-second Illinois Mounted Infantry moved down off the mountain by way of Cooper's Gap. Orders came from Major General Joseph J. Reynolds on the fifteenth to reconnoiter Crawfish Springs by way of Squire Mitchell's, thus opening communication with Major General Thomas L. Crittenden. They returned by way of Missionary Ridge Road to Pond Springs, thus scouting the country over an eighteen-mile range, including the Chickamauga Creek on the south bank where they discovered a line of rebel pickets. A skirmish followed. "Company E was detached with General John Basil Turchin to Catlett's Gap" on the sixteenth.

---

[132] Thomas M. Eddy, *The Patriotism of Illinois, A Record of the Civil and Military History of the States*, Chapter XXII, Regimental Sketches, Ninety-second Illinois Infantry, 1865, p. 372

A rebel force charged them and killed one of their soldiers, wounding another[133].

Company I stayed in camp on September 16 and Eugene used the time to write to Elvira and Amanda Ludisky. He seemed to grow from a boy into a man in his letters. There was no more talk of the war being over, only the hope that there would not be too many more battles. Elvira had problems at home with the farm. Eugene showed interest but not to the extent that he had before. Somehow the problems in Illinois seemed small and he was sure Elvira could handle them.

> *Camp in Chatnooga Vally, Ga.     Sept 16$^{th}$ 1863*
> *Dear Wife*
> *With the blessings of god, I am permited to write you once more. I am well as could be expected after marching the way we have in the last month & hope this will find Dear Vira & baby well.*
> *I recd a letter from you & Dicky today & 1 from Annie. Was glad to hear that you were well.*
> *Well, the Rebles are Cleaned out of Tennessee & we are still after them. We are about 20 miles in Georgia. Today is the first day without a fight in several days. We can get up a fight now at any Crossroads, but I dont think that it will be so long. Braggs army is completely surrounded. They must either fight & get whiped or surrender.*
> *I am sorry James Becker could not come clear through. I would like to see someone from home.*
> *Vira, in regard to the place, you can let it to any person you see fit & move the house if you can get it done. We have not drawn any pay since I was at Nashville and cant tell when we will get any, but hope we will get it soon.*

---

[133] *Illinois Troops (Union) Infantry, Records of Events, Volume 13, Records of Events for the Ninety-second Illinois Infantry, September 1862 - June 1865,* pp. 500-501 – covered all information from September 11-15.

*Oh! but I am dirty & ragged, but as soon as we stop I can get new cloaths.*
*Vira, I will write as often as I can & I think if we have the luck to clean them out here we will be home yet this fall. Goodby*
*My love to all    Your husband,*
*Swaggart*

One of their neighbors in Carroll County, Lottie Stouffer, who had a son in Company C, was angry with her son's wife. Perhaps they had been quarreling or perhaps she was one of the unfaithful wives. Eugene felt sorry for her and for her son, Daniel Stouffer, but he did not have much respect for Stouffer's wife and could not really understand why Daniel had married her in the first place. He reflected those thoughts when he answered Amanda Ludisky, his sister-in-law, in a letter on the same page as his letter to Elvira.

*Dear Sister*
*I will write you a fiew line as I am writing to Vira. I was very glad to receive your letter & to hear that you were well.*
*I suppose you think I am getting negligent that I do not write anymore often than I do, but beleave me, I write as often as I can get a chance & shall all ways do so.*
*I was sorry to hear of Lottie Stouffers bad luck on Dans account for he is one of the best little fellows in our Co. It is hard, but he ought to be in better luck than to have such a hag for a wife.*
*Yes, Dicky, I wish I was there to help thrash, but I have got a prety big job here to help out with & then I think I shall return. I thank you for praising my boy. He must be something for everyone says so. Well goodby. My love to all.*
*I remain your brother,            Mc*

*Direct to 18th Indiana Battery, Wilders Brig 14 A.C. Via Louisvill*

There have been many books written about Chickamauga, referred to as "the bloody battle of the West."[134] Suffice it to say that General William Starkie Rosecrans, up to the twelfth of September, in his passage of the Cumberland Mountains, spread his troops thin in an effort to move quickly and drive General Braxton Bragg and his Confederate forces out of Tennessee. General Bragg appeared to be falling back, but he was really regrouping his forces. General Rosecrans set up his headquarters in Chattanooga after General Bragg retreated. When General Rosecrans realized what was happening, he began to pull his troops together. The purpose of the Chicamauga battle, for the South, was to keep the northern troops divided and move in between the Union Army of the Cumberland and General Rosecrans in Chattanooga.

The battle involved many brigades of cavalry and infantry troops. On the Union side were such names as Major General George H. Thomas, commanding the Fourteenth Corps. His Corps consisted of Brigadier General Absolom Baird of the First Division, Major General James S. Negley of the Second Division, Brigadier General John M. Brannen of the Third Division, and Major General Joseph J. Reynolds of the Fourth Division which included Wilder's brigade and the Ninety-second Illinois Mounted Infantry. Major General Thomas L. Crittenden, commanding the Twentieth Corps, included Brigadier General Jefferson C. Davis of the First Division, Brigadier General Richard W. Johnson of the Second Division, and Major General Phillip H. Sheridan of the Third Division. Major General Crittenden also commanded the Twenty-first Corps with Brigadier General Thomas J. Wood of the First Division, Major General John M. Palmer of the Second Division, who appeared late in the morning, and Brigadier General Horatio P. Van Cleve of the Third Division. The Cavalry Corps' commander was Brigadier General Robert B.

---

[134] Glenn Tucker, *Chickamauga, Bloody Battle of the West*, Konecky & Konecky, New York, NY, 1961, title

Mitchell and the Reserve Corps commander was Major General Gordon Granger.[135]

The morning of September 18 found the Ninety-second Illinois Infantry, as well as the rest of Colonel John Wilder's brigade, near Alexander's Bridge on the Chickamauga River. From the North of the river, Dyer's Bridge and Dyer's Ford were unguarded. Colonel Robert Minty, who was serving under the Cavalry Corps, and his brigade were guarding Reed's Bridge where Confederate Colonel Bushrod Johnson was moving in to cross. Alexander's Bridge was in the middle where Wilder's brigade lay in wait for the columns of Confederate Major General William H. T. Walker moving in to cross the river.[136]

At 7:30 A.M., the men serving under Colonel Robert Minty found themselves involved in skirmish with troops led by General Nathan B. Forrest where they were "posted along Pea Vine Creek". With the arrival of General Bushrod R. Johnson and his Confederate infantry column, Colonel Minty was forced back in the direction of Reed's Bridge. Spotted earlier, moving toward Dyer's Bridge, was a Confederate column located one and one/fourth miles north of Colonel Minty. A detachment from Colonel Wilder's brigade moved in at noon to support him. Colonel Minty and his men had to fall back to Dyer's Bridge and then to Lee and Gordon's Mills with General Johnson in pursuit.[137]

At Alexander's Bridge, the remainder of Wilder's brigade were posted and they repulsed Major General William H. T. Walker as he approached the bridge with Brigadier General S. R. Gist and Colonel P. F. Liddell and their divisions. Colonel P. F. Liddell moved downstream to cross and threatened Wilder's left flank, but the brigade held the bridge until 5:00 P.M.,[138] with only a portion of the brigade and their Spencer rifles, thus

---

[135] Frank J. Welcher, *The Union Army, 1861-1865, Organization & Operations, Volume I, The Eastern Theater, Volume II, The Western Theater,* Indiana University Press, Bloomington and Indianapolis, 1993, and Glenn Tucker, *Chickamauga, Bloody Battle of the West,* Konecky & Konecky, New York, NY, 1961 - information came from both.
[136] Welcher, *The Union Army, The Western Theater,* pp. 536-537
[137] Ibid. pp. 536-537
[138] Ibid., p. 537

delaying the crossing. They withdrew under pressure, to the west toward Viniard farm field where Minty's dismounted cavalry joined them.[139] The Confederate armies crossed the river successfully throughout the night and lined up by morning with the Chickamauga River at their backs.

It was cold that September in north Georgia and the men used rails for fires and slept on frozen ground.[140] The woods were thick where the troops lined up and it was very difficult to see through the dense woods and fog.

September 19 found the troops of the North lined up with General Gordon's Reserve Corps four miles from the battlefield guarding the road from Rossville to Ringgold and Mitchell's cavalry guarding the fords along the upper portion of the Chickamauga.[141]

Facing the Union Forces were Confederate forces led by Brigadier General Nathan B. Forest, Major General William H. T. Walker, Major General Benjamin F. Cheatham, Major General Alexander P. Stewart, Brigadier General Bushrod Johnson, Major General John B. Hood, and General William Preston.

General Reynolds ordered Wilder's brigade, including the Ninety-second Illinois Mounted Infantry, to be held in reserve. When the battle broke out, the Union armies soon found that they had underestimated the strength of the Confederate troops. Colonel Edward A. King's brigade lined up next to General Van Cleve on the right. Wilder's brigade was some distance back. Colonel King's brigade broke under the onslaught of Confederate soldiers and the Ninety-second Illinois Infantry was thrown into the gap, but the disaster was too great for the regiment to control. They were "forced to fall back with heavy losses".[142] However, before they gave ground, the dismounted

---

[139] Frank J. Welcher, *The Union Army, 1861-1865, Organization & Operations, Volume II, Western Theater*, Indiana University Press, Bloomington & Indianapolis, 1993, pp. 536-537

[140] Glenn Tucker, *Chicamauga, Bloody Battle of the West*, Konecky & Konecky, New York, NY, 1961, p. 118

[141] Welcher, *The Union Army, Western Theater*, p. 538

[142] *Illinois Troops (Union) Infantry, Records of Events, Volume 13, Records of Events for the Ninety-second Illinois Infantry, September 1862 - June 1865*, p. 501

Ninety-second drove back part of the enemy force, advancing with their Spencer rifles, until Confederate forces came around their right flank. Colonel Atkins sent out patrols to locate the Confederates that broke through and when discovered, he immediately dispatched the information to Colonel Wilder.[143]

Throughout the day, General Bragg sent his strongest forces to the left, trying to cut off the Union armies from Chattanooga while General Rosecrans, sending "division after division" into battle, "extended his battle line north."[144] Late in the afternoon, Wilder's brigade helped to protect the enemy attacks on the left of General Jefferson C. Davis.[145]

At the end of the day, many lay dead and wounded and the hospitals were overflowing, but there was no clear victory on either side.

On September 20, Wilder's brigade reported to Major General Alexander McCook, who directed him to move his brigade about one-fourth mile south of Widow Glenn's on the crest of an eastern spur of Missionary Ridge.[146] General Rosecrans reportedly made a severe mistake in determining where his forces were in the thick brush. When he ordered Brigadier General Thomas J. Wood to support Major General Joseph J. Reynolds, he did not realize that there was a Confederate division between them. He meant only to tighten his line of defense. When General Wood moved out, he left a large gap through which Lieutenant General James Longstreet of the Southern armies charged, devastating a portion of the Union Army.[147] The Ninety-second Illinois, placed as an advance skirmish line for Wilder's brigade, held the line, until the charge made by General Longstreet's forces severed its right wing and almost cut it off, but a successful withdrawal took place.

---

[143] Glenn Tucker, *Chicamauga, Bloody Battle in the West*, Konecky & Konecky, New York, NY, 1961, p. 162

[144] World Almanac Publications, *The Civil War Almanac*, Intro. by Henry Steele Commager, A Bison Book, New York, NY 1983, p. 169

[145] Frank J. Welcher, *The Union Army, 1861-1865, Organization and Operations, Volume II, Western Theater*, Indiana University Press, Bloomington & Indianapolis, 1993, p. 541

[146] Ibid., p. 543

[147] *The Civil War Almanac*, p. 169

However, Colonel Wilder was able to keep his mounted infantry intact, and showed no signs of backing down. Charles A. Dana, Assistant Secretary of War, who was with General Rosecrans during the attack, advised Colonel Wilder to get his men out of there. He said they made up the only brigade left intact. Wilder did not believe him because he heard firing coming from the direction of General Thomas' division and he did not obey. Colonel Atkins of the Ninety-second Mounted Infantry came up with his intention to charge General Longstreet, but Mr. Dana ordered them not to make the charge, declaring the battle lost. He again ordered Wilder's brigade to Chattanooga to act as an escort for him. Wilder, in direct disobedience of orders, sent a guard. He and his brigade stayed behind, bringing in the hospitals from Crawfish Springs and saving part of the artillery that General McCook's Corps had abandoned on the field. That brigade, which included the regiment of the Ninety-second Illinois Mounted Infantry, was the only one on the Federal right that the Confederates did not drive away.[148]

General Rosecrans also fled to Chattanooga, thinking his Army had been destroyed. However, he was wrong again, as General Thomas had maintained total control of Snodgrass Hill, supported later by the troops of General Granger, giving him the title of the "Rock of Chickamauga".[149]

On the night of September 21, the entire Union Army withdrew to Chattanooga and the Ninety-second Illinois Mounted Infantry went to Harrison's Landing to guard the fords.

Through the end of September, pickets and scouts went out from both sides, but neither the North nor the South attacked. General Bragg started to attack Missionary Ridge, but he found the Federal troops dug in tight and backed off. Later he thought General Rosecrans would evacuate Chattanooga if he waited him out, but General Rosecrans held onto the city. At the end of the month, General Bragg learned that reinforcements for the Union army were on their way, so he contented himself with

---

[148] *Glenn Tucker, Chicamauga, Bloody Battle in the West*, Konecky & Konecky, New York, NY, 1961, pp. 317-318
[149] World Almanac Publications, *The Civil War Almanac*, Intro. by Henry Steele Commager, A Bison Book, New York, NY 1983, p. 169

attacks on the Union communication lines by General Wheeler.[150]

On September 23, Eugene finally sat down to write to Elvira, tired and grateful to be alive, but saddened by the loss of the men from his company. He disliked hearing that Henry Holt's wife had been unfaithful to Henry. A soldier had enough to worry about without that.

*Camp in Tenn.*          *September 23$^{rd}$, 1863*
A note at the top stated:

*Wilder is sick & we miss him very much. He has gone home.*
*Dear Wife*
*I am thankfull to my God that I am alive and well after being in three days of hard fighting, as ever war fought on this continent. The hard fighting comenced on Friday the 18$^{th}$ & is not ended yet & cannot tell when it will, as we have all most the whole reble force to contend with.*
*Old Lee's force is here, or a large share of it. Our battery was in Friday, Saturday & Sunday and then we were ordered on the Tenn. river to guard a ford which we are now fortifying. I never want to go in another such a fight, but perhaps I may, but doubt it, that is if we gain the day here in this & if we do not, this war will continue 12 months longer at least & if we come out victorious, it will not last 3 months longer, for then they are whiped.*
*Oh! that we may never witness another battlefield. I slept two nights where I could hear the wounded crying for help but none could we help. I suppose you will get the details in the papers before you get this, but when you get this, you will know I am all right. The 92d was in the fight in a very hot place,*

---

[150] World Almanac Publications, The Civil War Almanac, Intro. by Henry Steele Commager, A Bison Book, New York, NY, 1983, p. 170

*therefore, had to Skedaddle out of ...*
*about 60 men in killed & wounded. Co I had 3 wounded, Wm Price, 3d Sergt., Corpl. James Bigger, & Corpl. James A. Colehour. That is all that were hurt. Tell Tommy Lego that the 34 was in, but do not know whether Henry was hurt or not. The news is this morning that Rosy has heavy reinforcements. If so, we will come out all right yet, God grant that we may. I guess I will not write anymore about the battle untill I learn more about it.*
*Vira, you say I never mention my boy in my letters. If I do not, God knows I love him. Everybody that writes me says he is one of the finest boys in the Co. When Moses writes, he allways has something to say in regard to him. He is most to small to write yet, so I will write to his Ma. I would write to Jennie if I knew where to direct.*
*You say I can colect our railroad money by sending an order. You have Moses write an order and send it to me and I will sign my name to it, so you can draw it.*
*I should like very much to be there to attend the fair with you & Georgie, but hope the next, I will be on hand!*
*Well, goodby, with love to Mother & all the folks*
*From you loving Husband          Mack*
*Direct as before and your letters will come through all right.*
*Old Mrs. Holt is a regular old slut.*

Chapter Eleven
Guarding the River and the Railroad

Through October, 1863, the Ninety-second Illinois Mounted Infantry remained in camp at Harrison Landing, Tennessee, performing picket duties on the Tennessee River between Nelson's Ferry and Thatcher's Ford. They were on the move nearly all of the time, leaving at daybreak and returning after dark.

Wilder's brigade, however, had left the detached Ninety-second and gone after General Wheeler who was tearing up communication lines, destroying bridges and railroads in and about Chattanooga to halt supplies coming in. Eugene and William Reynolds were the only ones in the Ninety-second Illinois Mounted Infantry, Company I, detached to go with them. They served in the Eighteenth Indiana Battery with Wilder's brigade. Detailed also were twelve others from the regiment. The detachment picked up supplies where they could to feed the hungry armies. They skirmished often in places such as Hill's Gap, Thompson's Grove on the third, Murfreesboro Road on the fourth, McMinnville on the fifth, Sim's Farm, near Shelbyville and Farmington on the seventh.

In the next couple of weeks, Wilder's brigade continued to follow the railroad lines, foraging food while on pickets and patrols. The Army in Chattanooga was near starvation and food was necessary. One of the first duties of General Ulysses S. Grant, when he relieved General William S. Rosecrans in late October was to set up a line from Chattanooga to Bridgeport, Alabama, for transportation of food supplies, clothing, and badly needed equipment. The soldiers referred to it as "the cracker line". Wilder's brigade went into Alabama to help set up the line. Their duties included guarding the railroads while the Union army secured the Tennessee River for a supply line.

Confederates seriously challenged the "cracker line" only once when General Longstreet attacked on the night of October

28. However, due to extreme dark and confusion, the Southern forces were pushed back with losses.[151]

Because of his skills with horses, mules and a rifle, Eugene drove the mule team. He was encouraged to forage, as many of the soldiers were. They went out on pickets, sent by the officers, to warn the army of approaching troops and to bring in horses, mules, food or whatever they could find that was useful to the Army. The unwritten rule seemed to be that if they found something for themselves, that was fine, too, as long as the officers did not want it also. They were responsible for capturing many of the prisoners claimed by the Army.

The true foragers for the Army were often mounted and were usually good shots and horsemen who could outrun the other armies while driving in horses, mules or wagons filled with supplies. They had a daredevil personality with little fear. They usually moved in advance or on the flanks of the Army and "one Missouri colonel said, speaking of them concerning a later march to Savannah and the Carolinas, 'they were more valuable than cavalry protecting the front and flanks'" of the army.[152]

While out foraging, Eugene took a violin from a Confederate major who he captured. It was a Salzard Ataris violin and he scratched his name into it. He planned to send it home to his son so he, too, could become a good fiddler when he was old enough to play the fiddle.[153]

*Brownsboro Alabama                    Oct 22<sup>nd</sup> 1863*
*Dear Wife*
*With great pleasure, I seat myself to write you a fiew lines for the first in over a month. I am still well. Hope this will find you & baby well.*

---

[151] World Almanac Publication, *The Civil War Almanac*, Intro. by Henry Steele Commager, A Bison Book, New York, NY 1983, p. 173
[152] Joseph T. Glatthaar, *The March to the Sea and Beyond, Sherman's Troops in the Savannah and Carolinas Campaigns*, Louisiana State University Press, Baton Rouge & London, pp 122-123
[153] Violin is still in the family

Dear Vira, we have had hard times since I wrote you. Before, Old Wheeler, with about twenty thousand rebs, crossed the river above Chattanooga & made a raid through Tenn & we have been after them ever since but have stoped, at last, way down here in Alabam, where we cant get any mail nor send any away. We have drawn 5 days rations since we left Chattanooga, but Wilders Brigade will never starve as long as there is anything in the country.

We are now on Flint River on the Memphis & Charleston R.R. Gen. Grant is in command of our army & Gen. Rosecrans has gone to the Potomic to take command. We all hate to give him up, but I guess Grant is just as good. The $92^{nd}$ is not with us. I guess they will be with us soon. I want to see them bad, but not half so bad as I want to see you.

Well, my time is nearly half out, then, wont I see you, if I live. Oh! if I could only get a letter, but I dont look for any untill the 92 comes to us. The Battery is the place for me to soldier. I am driving mule team now. I go out 8 miles from camp everyday for forage. I captured me a fiddle the other day, worth about $50.00. I will send it home to my boy if I can get a chance. It belonged to a rebel Major, but it belongs to me now.

We had a prety hard fight with Wheeler at Farmington, Tenn bout 2 weeks ago. We whiped them and captured 3 pieces of Artilery & 8 or 9 hundred prisoners. We lost Col. Monroe of the 123 Ill & about 60 men killed. Bushwhackers are thick here at presant, but dont think they will last long.

I wish you could see our camp now. We have all built pool cabins and chinked up the cracks with cotton, so you see we are surrounded with king cotton.

Vira, you must excuse pencil & dirty paper for it is the best I can do here in this vast wilderness. I hope to do better next time. It may be so I can write again in a week and maby not in one month, but I will write as often as I can. Direct as before. Goodby to all. I remain your loving Husband
E. M. Swaggart

While Eugene was detached to Wilder's brigade, the Ninety-second Illinois Mounted Infantry moved out on October 27 and the first stop was Dunlap, Sequatchie Valley on the way to Bridgeport, where it procured, under orders, additional equipment, horses and arms from Nashville. October 28 found them still in the Sequatchie Valley, within four miles of Jasper. On the twenty-ninth, they arrived in Bridgeport where they reported to Major General David Sloan Stanley. "Companies C & K remained on courier duty at Chattanooga" and the regimental train remained behind with a strong guard and orders to follow as they could.[154]

Eugene and William Reynolds were in Maysville, Alabama, on the outskirts of Huntsville, still guarding the Memphis and Charleston railroad that ran from Memphis to Chattanooga Tennessee through Alabama. They were only twenty-five miles from the Ninety-second Illinois, but it could have been several hundred miles because Eugene & William never knew of the move the regiment made. Except for patrols and guard duties, Eugene had more time on his hands. It was wet and rainy, but the brigade built small cabins and stayed dry when they were in camp. He began to get involved in the news from home a little more. He decided to answer one of Elvira's letters that finally found its way to him when the Ninety-second Illinois moved closer.

> *Maysville, Alabama*            *Nov $5^{th}$ 1863*
> *Dear Wife*
> *Once more do I embrace the blessed opportunity of writing you a fiew lines. I am well, at presant, & hope this will find you enjoying the same great blessing. I received yours of Oct. $11^{th}$ last night. Was glad to hear you was well. I recd, also, one from Sister Annie.*
> *We are having a very wet time of it. It commenced raining about 2 weeks ago, has not stoped yet & dont as it will soon, but we dont care as long as we can stay in our nail pens covered with straw. We get lots of grub, but not much from Uncle Samuel.*

---

[154] *Illinois Troops (Union) Infantry, Records of Events, Vol. 13, Record of Events for Ninety-second Illinois Infantry, September 1862- June 1865*, pp. 501-502

In reference to the replacement of General Rosecrans by General Grant.

*As for the war, I have not heard much about it of late. Gen. Grant is in command of our army. I guess old Rosy is played out. Affairs are getting mixed up so that I dont bother my head much about them and I find it the best plan. I think this little war will dry up very soon. We have them where they cant get out, so they will either have to fight or surrender.*

*Oh! golly, but it beats any think I ever heard of that Jennie Graham is mama, dont it. She is the last one I thought of. I suppose there will be another of the Grahams moved not more than 15 miles from our house. ha ha. Dont tell Sis, will you.*

*I wrote to Jennie Van Alstien last week & Directed it to Chicago. I was sorry to hear of Sylvesters loss, for he trys hard to accumilate & it is hard for him to work & then loose it, but it cant be helped sometimes.*

*We musterd for pay, but the pay has not come as yet. It has been a long time since I sent you any money & I know you must be in need. That is the only thing that makes me unhappy here in the service. Only 21 months more & I am free, if I am permitted to live so long & that will soon pass off.*

*The 92d has not come to yet so I dont know how they are getting along. Vira, our brigade has left the 14 A.C. Col Wilder is a Brigadier Gen. now and has an independant command, so Direct to Wilders Brig. Mounted Inft. Via Nashville Tenn. No more. Give my love to Ma, Johns folks & Moses, also & Annie.*

*I remain your loving Husband,*

*E. M. Swaggart*

*P. S. my weight in 190 lbs. Small, aint it.*

Elvira had problems with the farm back home. She found it too much for her to manage alone. Jenny left for Chicago and Elvira moved in with Amanda Ludisky and Moses so she would not be alone. She thought of leasing it out to Sidney Morford, who leased farms from others. He had a bad reputation for not taking care of the land and Eugene did not want her to lease the land to him if she could help it. He preferred to see Moses, his brother, work the land, and so instructed Elvira to let Moses have it to plant.

*Maysville Alabama*                *Nov 11$^{th}$ 1863*
*Dear Wife*
*Once more I will write you, to let you know that I am well & hope my lettle wife & baby is the same. I recd. a letter from you writen Oct. 22d & also one from Dicky and as you are both together, I will make one in ans. for both. We are having pretty cold weather at presant, for no tents nor overcoats, but we expect to have an entire outfit as soon as it can be had from Nashville, Tenn.*

Referring to Captain Eli Lilly of Indiana who was in charge of the 18$^{th}$ Indiana Battery.

*Our Captain has gone home & on his return he will get everything we need.*
*I heard that the 92d were on the way to join the Brig. I hope so, for I am getting tired of Hosurdoom altogether.*
*We are to sighn the payrolls today. I suppose we get our pay tomorrow, but dont know how much as we have to settle for our last years clothes. My bill is $59.47 and if we only get two months, you see, I will hardly come out even.*
*You say your corn is very poor. I dont know what you are to do. Oh, if I was out of this d\_\_\_\_ war, I would see them perish before I would leave my own family to suffer, but it will not last all ways, thank God, & if I ever live to get out of this war & get*

*home, when I leave it again, it will be to go to any long home, thats whats the matter.*

*I suppose you had better let Moses have your place to work, but it is as I have told you before, you know better what to do with it than I can tell you, but never let any man like Morford have it, will you.*

*There is some talk of furlough being granted to this brigade. If there is, I want to be lucky once, but doubt whether I will be or not.*

*Rebs are very thick. They take some of our boys everyday, but I think we will soon clean them out of this. I am on detail and must close for the presant. Give my love to all. Kiss baby for pa.*

*Your loving husband,*
*Mack*

General Longstreet tried to cut off General Ambrose E. Burnside's retreat into Knoxville, but failed on November 16. He lacked troops for a siege. On November 29, General Longstreet attempted a second time to oust General Burnside from Knoxville, but due to extremely cold weather and lack of planning, that attempt failed also.[155]

In the battle of Chattanooga in late November, the Union won a decisive victory over General Braxton Bragg through the efforts of General Ulysses Grant with General William T. Sherman and General Joseph Hooker. They came very close to capturing General Bragg. Soon afterward, General Bragg resigned as Commander of the Army of Tennessee.[156]

The Ninety-second Illinois Mounted Infantry, Companies E & K, accompanied General Charles Cruft of the First Division, Fourth Corps to Missionary Ridge where a battle took place. They returned to the regiment on December 4 at Caperton's Ferry. The remainder of the regiment had scouting duty in Huntsville, Alabama until December 2 when they went to

---

[155] World Almanac Publisher, *The Civil War Almanac*, Intro. by Henry Steele Commager, A Bison Book, New York, NY 1983, pp. 175 & 178
[156] Ibid., pp. 176-178

Widow's Creek. On the return route, they rode over rough roads and had a difficult ford over Widow's Creek, arriving at Capterton's Ferry at 9:00 A.M. the next morning. Necessary guards were posted at ferries and fords. On Dec. 4, they returned to Ringgold, Georgia where they posted guard and stayed until December 18.[157]

Eugene was still near Huntsville, guarding the railroads. The brigade he was in did not fight in the battles stirring around them. He contacted malaria and was ill with high fever when he wrote to Elvira.

*Huntsville Ala Dec 10$^{th}$ 1863*
*Dear Wife*
*Once more do I attempt to write you a fiew lines . I am well & hope these fiew lines will find you enjoying the same great blessings. I said I was well, but am not very well, although, I am feeling much better than I did a day or two ago. I had a hard chill, but I guess it is all over with for the presant, at least, I hope so. I think I have had my share of sickness since I have been out, dont you. But it is in vain for a soldier to complain in most of things.*
*Vira, this makes about 20 letters I have writen and no ans. I sent money in 2 of them and, also some, in one. I wrote to Moses, but will send no more untill I get a letter from you.*
*I am detached to Wilders Pioneer Co. untill the regt. comes to us and how long that will be no one appears to know. Wm Reynolds and myself are the only ones from Co. I, so you can guess, we stick pretty close together.*
*Gen. Grant has been giving Old Bragg a nice little whiping and drove him a little closer home. I am*

---

[157] *Illinois Troops (Union) Infantry, Records of Events, Volume 13, Record of Events for Ninety-second Illinois Infantry, September 1862-June 1865,* pp. 502 & 530

*not sorry that I was not in it, by any means. I dont know how old Longstreet & Burnside are making it by this time, but hope all right. The general talk now among us Blue jackets is that we are going to be at home by next June now. You just bear this in mind and see if I am not as good as my word. There is nothing surer than this rebellion closing and that very soon. Well, I can think of nothing more at presant. Give my love to all. Kiss the boy. I remain as ever, Your loving Mack.*

On December 18, the Ninety-second Illinois Mounted Infantry received Department Headquarters orders to report to General Stanley of the Cavalry Corps, Army of the Cumberland. Their orders were to report for duty at Bridgeport, Alabama. The regiment encamped the first night on the north side of the Tennessee River between Stevenson and Bridgeport. The roads were impassable for the regimental train and Widow's Creek was inaccessible when they arrived. The train could not cross until morning of the nineteenth. They arrived at the river at noon but could not cross because General Sherman and his troops were crossing the bridge. On the twentieth, the Ninety-second Illinois crossed the river and proceeded into Hog Jaw Valley. There, on December 21, they received orders to proceed to Huntsville, Alabama.[158]

Eugene was still in camp at Huntsville, and had no idea his regiment would soon be arriving in camp. His malaria was still affecting him and, with Christmas coming up, he was not too happy. He could not help feeling a little envious when he thought of everyone gathering at his mother's house, around her new piano, while he was in camp, cold, sick, and miserable. However, on a more cheerful note, he had seen some Southerners making salt and decided to relate his observations to Elvira.

---

[158] *Illinois Troops (Union) Infantry, Records of Events, Volume 13, Record of Events for Ninety-second Illinois Infantry, September 1862 - June 1865*, p. 502

Huntsville Ala                    Dec 18$^{th}$ 1863
Dear Wife

Once more I will try and write you a fiew lines without any news from you. I cant say I am well this time for I am not. I have had the third day ague now for nearly three weeks and it still stops with me and is likely, for what I know.

I wrote to you on the 11$^{th}$ and sent you $5.00 in it. I dont know as you will get it or not, as there has been so many lost.

My Dear, I would like to be at home this Christmas with you, but hardly think I can be, nor the next one to come, without a great chance, but hope so. It will be a dull Christmas here for me this year. I thank God my time is as near half out as it is. 2 months and then time will go the other way.

Vira, I will tell you how the citizens get salt. In the first, they set up three or four leeches, and then, they fill them up with dirt dug out of old smoke houses. They, then, dreaned water through them and boil it down to salt. It looks just the color of the Butternuts. In this way, they make 4 & 5 lbs. per day. Prety hard to get it, but no harder than they deserve, do you think it is.

I suppose they have nice times down at Mothers now with their fine piano. I bet it makes Mary Ann feel big, but that is none of my business, is it.

Vira, rent your place as good as possible for the coming season. I think by the next, I will be around myself, if I am lucky. There is a great many crooks & turns for me to go through yet, but if I have luck, it will not take long anymore.

I have not heard from the regt. yet. I expect they are gone up the spout.

*Vira, I was down to get my picture the other day, but could not get it, but the man said he could take one for me next week.*
*I will send you the Storms of Chickamauga. I think it will please Vet to hear it read. Maby he can get a tune for it. It is true, every word of it.*
*Three cheers for old Grant & Thomas. My love to all. I remain your loving Husband.*
*E. M. Swaggart*
*Headquarters Wilders Brigade*
*14 A. C. in care of Cap Killbom    Via Nashville Tenn*

President Abraham Lincoln gave his Proclamation of Amnesty and Reconstruction on December 8, 1863, saying that a pardon would be granted to all Confederates who swore an oath of allegiance to the United States. The only exceptions were government officials, high-ranking officers, or those who mistreated prisoners of war, white or black. He also stated that their property would be restored. He promised that the Federal Statehood, of the states that supported the South, would be restored and recognized when one-tenth of the citizens swore allegiance and forswore slavery. The North approved greatly of his message,[159] as did Eugene.

He was still sick and dreading Christmas without his family when he wrote to Elvira from Huntsville.

*Huntsville Ala                    Dec 21$^{st}$ 1863*
*Dear Wife*
*Sadly & lonely, I seat myself to write you a fiew lines this morning. I have the ague every other day, with the exception of that, I am well. I hope this will find you and baby well.*

---

[159] World Almanac Publications, *The Civil War Almanac*, Intro. by Henry Steele Commager, A Bison Book, New York, NY 1983, p. 179

I suppose I have male at the regt. but have not had any in a long time, still I look for some everyday. Dear, I have no news of importance to write. All I can do is to let you know that I am well, or nearly so. If I could get that much from you, I would be content.

We got the Presidents Message last night & liked it very much. Old Abe is all right yet, by Jung.

Wm Reynolds is well. He is a friend of mine, I can assure you. Well, I guess I will close for today and finish when I can think of three cents worth.

Eugene closed his letter but did not mail it the same day. The next day he finished it.

Dec. 22d. Good morning, my Dear. I dont know as I have three cents worth yet. However, it is time my letter was mailed.

I was down to the city last night to get my picture, but could not get one. There is some talk of us moving in a day or so, but I dont know where we will go, unless we go farther south. That is our course and is likely to be for quite awhile to come. Then we will turn our faces to the North, then look out for the rush.

Christmas is very near and how I wish I were at the same place I was two years ago. Would I not have a gay old time, that so. I know how to appreciate good times now and think I can enjoy them if I am ever blessed with them again. I know I could live happy on the little farm with my Dear little Wife.

Give my love to Mother & Annie, Moses, Dicky & John & Mary and all the increase. Goodby. I remain your ever true & Affectionate Husband

P S   Direct as before

Excuse this short sheet

      from   Mack

Most of the detachments in the brigade moved out immediately to rejoin their regiments. However, the men from the Ninety-second Illinois stayed behind to spend Christmas alone. They spent the day packing but Eugene took time to wish Elvira a Merry Christmas.

> Christmas
> Huntsville Ala 25th 1863
> Dear Vira,
> I will try and write you a few lines but very few as I have not the time to write much I am well and hope these few lines will find you the same Dear Vira I wish you a mery Christmas it mine will not be so mery The Pioners is broken up and the whole Division has left Huntsville but 14 of us & we will leave to morrow morning for our regt. Direct to the regt. after this Give my love to all I remain your loving Husband
> E M Sergeant
> Excuse Haste

*Christmas*

Huntsville Ala                                  Dec 25$^{th}$ 1863
Dear Wife
*I will try and write you fiew lines, but very fiew, as I have not the time to write much. I am well and hope these few lines will find you the same.*
*Dear Vira, I wish you a mery Christmas, if mine will not be so mery. The Pioneers is broken up and the whole Division has left Huntsville, but 14 of us, & we will leave tomorrow morning for our regt. Direct to the regt. after this. Give my love to all. I remain your loving Husband*
*E. M. Swaggart*
*Excuse haste.*

Wilder's brigade met the Ninety-second Illinois Mounted Infantry on the trail into Huntsville. Their orders were to proceed to Huntsville to await the arrival of the train. It arrived on December 30. On the same day, scouting parties went out. They captured a number of horses and mules and Eugene was back in the war with Company I when they went to Fletcher's Ferry to capture a boat. They succeeded in their mission, destroying the boat and capturing three prisoners.[160]

December 31 found the Ninety-second Illinois Mounted Infantry on the move again, on pickets and scouting as they rode. New Year's Eve, they camped at Judge Hammond's where they found themselves in route to Pulaski, Tennessee. Companies C & K joined them at Caperton's Ferry when they returned from courier duty.[161]

---

[160] *Illinois Troops (Union) Infantry, Records of Events, Volume 13, Record of Events for Ninety-second Illinois Infantry, September 186 2- June 1865,* pp. 502-503
[161] Ibid. p. 503

## Chapter Twelve
## Operations in North Alabama

The New Year of 1864 rolled in, bitterly cold. Many of the men suffered from frostbite on their feet and hands. However, they started New Year's Day with a march of fifteen miles to Elkton Springs and on the second, another nine miles. Early on the morning of the third they crossed on pontoons one mile outside Prospect on the Elk River and near the Tennessee - Alabama line. After a seven-mile march, they forded Richland Creek, before they camped for the night. On the fourth, they finally reached their destination of Pulaski where they rejoined Wilder's brigade. There they stayed until January 12, posting pickets and scouting.[162] Eugene wrote to Elvira on the seventh. He was beside the campfire with snow swirling around his head, his feet and hands freezing.

*Camp in Tenn. Jan 7th 1864*
*Dear Wife*
*Once more, I seat me to write you. I am still well and hope this will find you and baby the same. I am in the Company once more. We have been on a march ever since New Years and have not had time to write.*
*We have had very cold weather for the last ten days and I am writing now by our campfire in the smoke and it is snowing like fun. I have not had a letter from you in 6 weeks. I have all most given up of ever hearing from you again.*
*I expect we will go to Columbia, Tenn and go in winter quarters and then I will write a longer and better letter, but it is to cold at presant. My love to all.*
*I remain Your loving  Husband            Mack*

---

[162] *Illinois Troops (Union) Infantry, Records of Events, Volume 3, Record of Events for Ninety-second Illinois Infantry, September 1862 - June 1865*, p. 493

On January 12, the brigade returned to Huntsville, Alabama. They forded the Elk River again at Elkton and the brigade arrived at Huntsville on January 14. On the fifteenth, they moved to Bridgeport, Alabama, returning to Huntsville again on the sixteenth.[163] Where they camped was not important. Every day and night, they were on their horses on pickets and scouts. There was not much time to write, but Eugene took time to pen a letter to Elvira.

*Camp in Tenn. Jan 19$^{th}$ 1864*
*Dear Wife*
*With pleasure do I attempt to ans. your more than welcome letter which came to hand last night. It found me enjoying good health, as usual, & I sincerely hope this will find you the same. You cannot imagine how thankfull I was to hear from you once more.*
*Vira, I have not wrote very often here of late, but wrote every opportunity I had and all ways will, as long as I remain in the U. S. service. We do not stay in one camp more than 3 or 4 days. It is not now like it was, before we were mounted, in regard to writing, but however, I will write often enough to let you know that I am well & I guess that will do, will it not....*
*Our time is nearly half out. Bully for that, I say. You say you are glad, now, that I came when I did. You are right and I knew it. The copperheads will have to come to it yet.*
*The boys are all well. Bill Reynolds got his hand hurt, very bad, but think he may recover. Kiss Georgie for me. Give my love to Mother and all the folks & excuse this short letter as I was on picket all last night and dont feel too purt. Besides, we have*

---

[163] *Illinois Troops (Union) - Infantry, Record of Events, Volume 3, Record of Events for Ninety-second Illinois Infantry, September 1862 - June 1865.* p. 493

marching orders tomorrow morning at 7 o'clock and my cloths are all dirty. Goodby. I remain your Affectionate Husband
E. M. Swaggart

Elvira worried that Eugene was not receiving her letters. It was so difficult to write and know the letters did not arrive. With that thought in mind, she wrote him.

Mt Carroll                    Jan $22^{nd}$ 1864
Dear Husband
With rather a sad heart I seat myself to write you a few lines, not thinking it will do any good, for you do not get them, the reason why, I cannot tell. I have directed it as you have told me, so you see that it is not my fault, dont you, my Dear. I know it must be hard to be off there and not hear from home once a month. It is well it is you instead of me, for I know it would kill me, but think for sure you have got back into the campaign. I hope we will be better able to keep track of you then we have for some time.
First - I am at Dickys now. I came over Sunday, shall go back in the morning. Sylvester and I are living alone. I shall stay there untill I get to spring house again.
Jennie is at Mrs. Sigmans, seeing her health. He is not very good.
The going folks are dancing themselves to death. It seems as though they thought of nothing else. They had a big party down to Eds last night. Annies teaching. She likes her school very mutch.
Old Mr. Hamilton is dead. He died with snakes in his boots.
Mack, I had got the bells of George, because you wished to me. I told him that you told me I could

*get the bells and keep them for the rest of the time we had and he gave them up. Mose has got them now.*

*I must close as it is bedtime. I will write again soon and you will have your match to read this, but will excuse it, as I have no ink here. Goodbye my Dear Your                          Vira*

January 23 found Wilder's brigade moving down Florence road to Athens, Alabama. They passed through Athens on the twenty-fourth, and after fording the Elks River, they camped on the south side. Over the next few days, they were in the saddle constantly, skirmishing as they went.[164]

Eugene hardened everyday, so much so, that he did not feel like himself anymore. He felt he did not resemble the young man that went into the Army but knew he was the same person because the others still called him Swaggart. Sometimes that was all of himself that he recognized – his name.

*Huntsville Ala.                        Jan 24$^{th}$ 1864*
*Dear Wife*
*With great pleasure I embrace the presant opportunity of ans̲ your welcome letter, which I recd̲ today bearing date of Dec 30$^{th}$ 63. It was long in coming, but not withstanding all of that, I was glad to get it. There must be about a bushel of mail for me somewhere on the road. I think it will come by time.*

*I am glad to hear you & my little Treasure is well, but am so sorry you did not get the money I sent you. I sent you $25.00 in 4 letters and in another, $2.00 for some stamps. I will not send anymore by mail. The reason I sent by mail was that I was in the battery and could not send by allotment.*

---

[164] *Illinois Troops (Union) Infantry, Records of Events, Volume 13, Record of Events for the Ninety-second Illinois Infantry, September 1862 - June 1865*, p. 493

*Dear Vira, you say you think me noble for keeping up so good spirits. My Dear, I find by experience (& that is a deer school), that it is far better for one to forget, in a measure, all the good times he ever had and look forward and hope for good times at the close of this <u>crewel</u> war. But you must not, my Dear, think that I can forget you and my boy. No, never, but you know what I mean. I guess you know me, or used to. I am not much now like I was 18 months ago, but the boys all call me Swaggart, anyway.*

*Bill Reynolds starts, or not start, but has applied for a furlough and I guess he will get it in about 2 weeks. He ought to have one and so ought I, but no go for me.*

*Vira, I have got the ague broke up and getting all right once more. You are about right when you say the rebs are about played out. They are plaid, but the army is not dispensed yet. I guess it will be so ever long, as soon as they learn that our old troops are coming in again. I think they will give one or two awfull kicks and then die an everlasting death.*

*Vira, I hear you about Jennie. Where is she, at your place, or in Chicago. I have writen several letters to her, but never rec<u>d</u> an ans as yet. I should like very much to hear from her in regard to my likeness. I sent it a long time ago. I supposed you had it before this and expected yours in return in the first letter I could get, but I did not see yours. I look at little Georgies everyday and kiss his dear little face. You cannot imagine the comfort of it is to me, though I guess it does not look much like him now.*

Early the next morning, Eugene heard the news that the brigade was moving again. The news spread through the camp like wildfire, but no one knew for sure where the brigade was going, except the officers – the rumor said Texas. He quickly wrote another page that he enclosed in his letter of January 24.

*Jan. 25$^{th}$ 64*

*Vira, as I have time, I will write a little more, as we expect to move from here soon and I may not have the opportunity of writing again soon. Where we are going, I cannot say, but expect to know when we stop. Some say our Brigade is to go to TEXAS. I hope not. It is still more of a wilderness than Tenn & Ala and they are bad enough for me.*

*<u>Deserters</u> are coming in from the rebel army everyday – not only privates, but officer of high rank. I saw two commissioned officers yesterday on their way home. They were permited to pass through our lines unharmed.*

*You say the boys are enlisting there. I would like to see some of them down this way, first rate. Who all are coming. Tell me in your next. Tell Ed Hatheway I have not received but one letter from him since I have been in the service and have writen more than a dozen, but cannot write anymore untill I get some from him. This writing & not receiving any in ans is played out with soldiers.*

*Lt. York got a furlough today. He starts for home next Saterday. I hope he will stay for all the good he does the Co. I. Give my love to all. My Duty and kiss the young Volinteer.*

*I remain Vira's Soldier man.*

*E M Swaggart*

*Co. I 92$^{nd}$ Ill M<u>td</u> Inft.*

*Wilders Brig 2$^{nd}$ Cav Div*

*Via Nashville Tenn*

*Care of Cap E Q Becker*

*They will come through if the foregoing is on them*

                    *E M S*

In Sweetwater, on January 25, there was a skirmish involving Company I, the advance guard. The Union soldiers of the Ninety-second Illinois Mounted Infantry captured six men, killed five and wounded several. They also killed twenty-five horses. They withdrew and proceeded down the Florence road and encountered enemy forces in a cluster of log buildings approachable only over open fields. Four Companies advanced and retreated under heavy fire. After reinforcements, they charged a second time and "completely routed them". The South lost fifteen men, including Lieutenant Colonel F. M. Windes, Captain W. B. Ingram and a commissioned Sergeant of the Fourth Alabama Cavalry. The regiment took several prisoners.[165] Six of the Union soldiers were wounded—two in camp with Eugene. One was Corporal James A. Colehour who had just recovered from his wound at Chickamauga, and the other was a Private, Daniel O'Brien from Wisconsin. Eugene wrote to Elvira from the campsite in Huntsville, relating to her the happenings during the skirmish.

*Huntsville Ala.*                      *Jan. 28$^{th}$, 1864*
*Dear Wife*
*Once more I have been spared to write you. I am well & hope this will find you enjoying the same great blessing. I recd a letter from you yesterday & today, was very glad to hear that you was well.*
*We have been out on a scout and I am very tired, but am not so tired but what I can write.*
*Well, I must tell you a little about our fun we had with the rebs.*
*Well, we (or the Brig.), started out and got about 25 or 30 miles from camp. Co. I was in front, was riding along, Old Cap at the head of the company when all at once, we noticed 8 or 10 horsemen in the road about a quarter of a mile in front of us and you ought to seen us go for them.*

---

[165] Illinois Troops (Union) Infantry, Records of Events, Volume 13, Record of Events for 92$^{nd}$ Illinois Infantry, September 1862 - June 1865, p. 493

*They run like so many D\_\_ \_\_ls untill they got into some timber where there was a whole brigade of them there. They made a bold stand and when our Co. came up they let us have it right and left till they found they could not drive us that way. Then they tried to charge on us, but Co I was not to be found runing from them, so they had to fall back on their old position, when at that time our whole Brig came up to our aid and we gave one shout for the Wilders boys and went at them. They run and I dont know as they have stoped yet. We killed about 20 of them. The wounded, they carried away with them. Our loss was 6 wounded, 2 in our camp, James Colehour, & Daniel O'Brien. James Colehour was wounded in the Battle of Chicamauga and had just got to the Co. 20 days before he was wounded this time. He will go home in a fiew days.*
*Give my love to all    I remain as ever*
*Your Mack*
*You have the adress now complete.  Mc*

On January 30, the brigade moved to Triana, Alabama. There they stayed through the months of February and March, with picket duties on the Tennessee River. On February 1, 1864, Eugene wrote to his brother, Moses, in answer to a letter.

*Triana Ala                    Feb $1^{st}$ 1864*
*Dear Brother*
*With pleasure, I assume the position of laying flat down on my belly to ans. your more than welcome letter I recd today, bearing date of Jan. $14^{th}$. Was glad to hear that the folks were all well. I, for my part, well & hearty, standing weight 190, small, I know, but a cuss for big.*
*We, (the 92), left Huntsvile last friday & came to this place, distance of 15 miles. It is situated on the*

Tenn. R. The river is very narrow here & lots of rebs on the opposite side. We have fine sport talking with them. They shoot at us & we shoot at them.

You say you have a span of the nicest mules that travail the roads. You ought to see some of our mules down here. I dont think you would say it then. Why we have mule teams that will draw anything that is loose at the two ends. I never in my life saw the like.

I would like if you could be here with me awhile, but not to soldier by any means. I was in hopes we could get some new recruits from Mt. Carroll, but am afraid not, as you say, they are going to join Cav. Moses, I will send you a photograph in this. I think it is a better one than Eds.

We had a little fight the other day. Our company had 2 men wounded. One was James Colehour. The other you do not know. He is an Irishman from Wisconsin[166]. Colehour will get a furlough home. I all most wish it was me. I wold like the fur pretty well, but would not take any lough in mine if I could help it.

Egbert is well and awfull close with the boys, but we get the start of him once in a while. He behaved nobly in the fight the other day, better than a good many expected. Mose, it is the prettiest fun anyone ever had to charge on them. Their old musket balls sing so nice, but they cannot stand the Spencer rifle. I have me a splendid horse, sadle & bridle and as good a gun as ever was fired.

Col. Wilder has got his star. He is now Brig. Gen. We expect him back soon. Give my love to all. I remain as ever    Your Affectionate Brother    Mc

---

[166] Daniel O'Brien from Wisconsin

*Vira has my adress.*
*Please write soon & often and I will do the same.*
*Mack*

Other than pickets and guard duties, nothing much happened on the Tennessee River out of Triana, Alabama. Colonel John Wilder left the brigade to get his stars. He became Brigadier General John T. Wilder. The men of the Ninety-second Illinois Mounted Infantry were in winter quarters and it was a slow time for them so furloughs came through. His good friend, William Reynolds left for home and Eugene knew that he had a furlough coming, too. He wrote to Elvira to tell her the news.

*Triana Ala.*                *Feb 11$^{th}$ 1864*
*Dear Wife*
*With pleasure, I attempt to write you a fiew lines. I am well & hope these fiew words will find you enjoying the same great blessing. I recd a letter from you about a week ago & have neglected writing untill now for the reason (I will tell some other time).*
*I have no news at presant but what I have writen before. Bill Reynolds started for home sometime ago. Mr. English started for Carroll yesterday & the best news I have for you is, Mack looks for his furlough everyday, but dont know as it will be approved or not. You must not look for me untill you see me coming. Then, you will not be disappointed. As I judge from your letters, that you would be glad to see me at home once more. There has been a great many applied for furloughs. Some gets them & some dont and as you know, I am lucky. I may not win.*
*I expect Henry Holt is at home by this time. Give him my respects & also Henry Lego.*

*We had a little fight the other day, but no one hurt as I know of.*
*Dear, excuse this short letter and if my papers come, I will make it all up in talking and if not, in writing. My love to all.*
*I remain your loving Soldier*
*Mack Swaggart*
*Triana Ala on Tenn River*

Enclosed in the letter was a piece of material – the color was a pale yellow butternut – with a bow tied around it, perhaps from the uniform of a Confederate soldier.

On February 16, 1864, Eugene's longed for furlough came through for twenty-five days. General George Henry Thomas signed it.

When Eugene arrived home, he saw immediately that Elvira could not handle the farm alone. Sylvester was with her, but he was nearly blind. She had much more than she could handle with Sylvester and the baby. Moses could not take the place either. With his bad lungs, he could only farm his own land, so Eugene did the very thing he asked Elvira not to do. He signed a lease with Sidney Morford, doing everything he could to protect Elvira in the lease.

*Article of Agreement Between Sidney Morford &*
*E. M. Swaggart*
*Salem February 29$^{th}$ 1864*
*Article of Agreement*
*Made between Sidney Morford of Carroll Co. Party of the first part and E. M. Swaggart, party of the second part. The party of the second part does agree to Lease or rent his farm situated in Carroll Co., Salem Township, it being part of Sec. (8) eight containing (70) acres, to the party of the first part, for the period of one year and the party of the first part does agree to give one third of the grain raised there. On all small grain is to be delivered in the*

bin. Corn delivered in the crib on said farm - and further, the party of the first part does agree to run his own risk in raising the crops in relation to the fences and the party of the first part does agree to give the party of the second part the one third of stalks & straw and the privilege of turning his stalk in said field and enjoying the same.
Sighned
(His mark)
Sidney X Morford

Eugene and Elvira had a wonderful time during his furlough. They attended to business, visited with friends and family and spent a lot of their time together. Eugene met his little son, George, for the first time and enjoyed playing with him everyday. Elvira cried when he left and he felt as if his heart was breaking, but the war was still in progress, so he returned to camp.

When he arrived back in camp from his furlough, he talked with several friends who had been home and they had sad tales to tell. Many of their wives were unfaithful to them while they were away, including William Reynolds and Henry Holt. Eugene felt it was his duty to tell Elvira what was going on so she would not fall into the same trap. On March 15, he wrote to her from Triana, Alabama to let her know he had arrived back in camp safely.

*Triana Ala*  *March 15$^{th}$ 1864*
*Dear Wife*
*With pleasure I once more take the opportunity of writing you. I am well & hope these lines may find you & baby enjoying the same great blessing. I arrived at the regt. last night, being one week on the road to an hour, but was in time. I found the boys where I left them, all well.*
*Will Skilling is here and Dan Galusha, also. Dan has been sick, but is around again.*

*I have no news of importance. Everything is dead, here, to me since I was at home, but I guess it will all come around right after while.*

*Vira, since I came back I hear a great deal of talk about the war widows not behaving in a proper style, but thank god, I found mine in the same way I expected. I know I all ways will, but you know how people talk and for your sake, not mine, beware. I can never be induced to beleave that you ever done anything wrong in my absence. Dear, do not think hard of me for what I have written for I feel is the duty of all Husbands to inform their better halves of what is going on.*

*My love to all. Kiss the boys.*
*I remain as ever your Husband,*
*Mack*
*Write soon. Send me one of Georgies photographs*

When Eugene arrived in camp, he found his horse unfit to ride. Perhaps while he was on leave, someone else rode him and did not care for him properly. He did not seem to mind too much that he was exempt from duty. It was too cold to go on patrols and guard duty.

While the troops were in camp, there were many shindigs going on and he loved the shindigs. It was a good way to stay warm. His string band played and he was one of the fiddlers.

William Reynolds, upset about his wife, Elizabeth, and the status he found back home, told Eugene his problems. Eugene understood how he felt and told Elvira about it when he answered her letter on March 23, extracting a promise that she would not tell anyone about the situation.

*Triana Ala   Mar 23$^{rd}$ 1864*
*Dear Wife*
*With pleasure, I seat myself to ans your more than welcome letter, which came to hand last night. It*

found me well as usual & hope this will find you all the same.

I was glad to hear that George was better. You say the little fellow misses me so much. I can assure you he does not miss me more than I do him.

We had an awfull snow storm last monday night. It was 7 inches deep, but it was rather a flying visit as it could not stop long with us. It did not cause many wet eyes, but a good many wet feet.

I am having pretty good times now. My horse is not fit for duty, therefore exempts me. We have 2 shindigs a week in a large hall here in this place built for the express purpose. We have a splendid string band. You see we are not going to go dead if we are away from home. Officers, private and all, we all rank the same there.

Vira, you say you are in good hopes. I am glad of it. It is the first time I ever heard you say you thought this war would close soon. I think this will close by fall, but we must not be to sure of it, only hope for it.

I wrote to James Becker the other day, but was a good deal as I am at presant , not much to write about.

Vira, dont say anything for the world, but Bill Reynolds is feeling very sore about matters and things up north, but do not tell anybody I wrote this to you, for you know it would go like wild fire.

Write all the news you can. I want to try and keep better posted hereafter. Give my love to all. Kiss my boy. I remain as ever
Your loving, bluecoated, brass buttoned, Soldier.
    Husband  Mack
P. S. Write soon and oblige.
Give my love to Jennie & Annie

On March 30, Eugene was still in camp without a horse so he wrote to Elvira once more.

> Camp near Triana Ala     March 30$^{th}$ 1864
> Dear Wife
> With pleasure I am once more at the delight full task of writing you that I am well & hope this will find you and Son the same. I have but one letter from you since I was at home, but I do not complain, as I know it is not your fault. I recd 2 letters from H. Lego the other day. He was well withe the exceptions of a very sore foot which rendered him unfit for duty.
> Everything is quiet here with us. Once in awhile we see a bushwhacker, but they are pretty scarce. I think we will move from here before long. The rebs has left from the opposite side of the river so we have no more fun shooting across at them. I have not been on picket-guard since I got back and am not sorry, either, for it, although, I do other duty to pay up for it.
> I understand that the draft is surely going to take affect. I hope, if it does, Moses will be exempt. Still, I will not believe they will draft untill I see them at it.
> I suppose you & Jennie are running a machine[167] of your own. I would like to happen around and see how you get along, but cannot do it for a few months yet - I will say five months, no more, that is if I live to see so long a time, you will see this rebellion close.
> Tell James Becker I wrote him directly after my arrival at this place & nothing would please me more than a line from him (Viras excepted allways).

---

[167] Likely a threshing machine

*I am watching every mail for one from him and am disappointed everytime.*

*Oh! My Dear little boy, if I only could see the dear little fellow once in awhile, I could get along as well again. You can not imagine the difference it made in me by seeing him. I thought I loved him before, but I see now I did not, not half like I do now. I will close for today.*

As often happened, Eugene did not get the letter mailed on the thirtieth, so he continued on the thirty-first..

*Mar. 31$^{st}$ I am on Headquarters guard today & do not feel any to well, but I am not sick, only sick of soldiering as I always have been. I am tired of laying at one place so long. We do not get our mail regular, nor more than half rations and you know when we lay still, we cant kill hogs.*

*I guess we can live, dont you. Dear Vira, I am in good hopes now that we will get home this Fall. Everything looks very favorable but we cant tell.*

*I am looking for a letter from you in the mail and if I get one, I will finish this to day. If not, I will finish when I get one, you know.*

Once again no letter arrived and Eugene finished the letter on April 2.

*April 2$^{nd}$*

*No letter yet and we march in the morning so I guess I will have to wind this thing up. Some pretend to say we are going up in to Mosouri. I hope so but think it is doubtfull. I think we will go to Columbia to draw Cavalry arms. Columbia is in Tenn. about 38 or 40 miles from Nashvill.*

*If we go there we can get our mail every day.*

*We are having very bad rainy weather now and you know that is any thing but pleasant for a soldier. I guess I have written enough for this time.*

*You can see by my discourse that I have not much to write about.*

*Vira, write me about Bill Reynolds wife - how she conducts her self. Bill is worried near to death about her.*

*My love to Every Body. Kiss Georgie for me. I remain as ever*

*your Loving Husband.*

*E. M. Swaggart*

## Chapter Thirteen
## Georgia - Skirmishing and Picketing

The regiment moved out again on April 3, 1864. The long bitter cold was over and it was time to get on with the war. Their first stop was Huntsville, Alabama, where orders awaited them from Brigadier General Kenner Garrard to proceed to Ringgold, Georgia. They traveled to Ringgold to join the First Brigade, Third Cavalry Division led by Major General Robert H. G. Minty. On April 17, General Eli H. Murray took over the command.[168] The Kentucky cavalry unit needed reinforcements and the Ninety-second Illinois Mounted Infantry was ready for the duty. The soldiers of the Ninety-second Illinois were uncertain where they were going and thought it probable they would be infantry soldiers once more.

After the departure of John T. Wilder, Colonel Smith D. Atkins of the Ninety-second Illinois Mounted Infantry had a disagreement with Colonel A. O. Miller, who was left in command in the brigade that was formerly Wilder's brigade. Consequently, the soldiers of the Ninety-second Illinois Mounted Infantry assumed the disagreement was the reason they left the brigade. The horses they were using were mounts requisitioned to the brigade led by Colonel Miller, and he wanted them back. After they arrived in Ringgold, the talk was of dismounting.

Eugene was very angry. He liked being on horseback better than a foot soldier because he always felt comfortable and safe on a horse. Most of the soldiers felt the same way. He expressed his feelings to Elvira when he wrote to her from Ringgold.

*Camp at Ringgold Ga*          *Ap 14$^{th}$ 1864*
*Dear Wife    Once more I am permitted the opportunity of writing you. I am well at presant . I*

---

[168] *Illinois Troops (Union) Infantry, Records of Events, Volume 13, Record of Events for the 92$^{nd}$ Illinois Infantry, September 1862 - June 1865*, p. 503

hope this will find you enjoying the same great blessing.

We have had a long and tedious march since I wrote last. We left Trianna the $3^{rd}$ and got here yesterday, being 10 days on the road and in swamps at that, most of the way. We are doing heavy picket duty here. We stand in sight of the rebs all day and at night, bushwhack.

When I wrote to you before, I told you we were going to Columbia, but our Col. & Col. Miller commanding Wilder's Brigade had a falling out and it resulted in our leaving the famous Wilder's Brig. We are now in some Brig., but do not know the No. of it yet. We have a very heavy force here of Inf. & Artillery but not much Cavelry, so you see it makes duty rather hard for the $92^{nd}$, still tho, Cavelry is coming. It will be here in a week or so.

I eat supper with Henry Lego last Monday night. He was well. We had a good time together. The $34^{th}$ is about 10 miles from here, but expect to move to the front soon. Then we will be together, I hope.

We had a large mail today, but poor me got none, so you see how I do when we get a large mail & I get none. I sit down and write some for you, is that not right. I think so & so do you. I have wrote to James Becker so you can tell him I am looking for him to reply as soon as possible.

Our Col. has just recd orders to dismount our regt. and I guess it will be did pretty soon, unless we are reorganized as Cavelry and I guess that will be pretty hard to be done, but if we are dismounted, here is one that will never do Uncle Sam much good afterwards.

I suppose farmers are getting along slow this spring, as it is so backward. It is cold & wet here

*now and is the middle of April. Time wheat was all up, but I guess it is not the case up there.*
*You better beleave the boys are mad about this order[169] and I am so mad that I cannot write anymore. Give my love to Jennie & Annie, Dicky, well, all. Kiss all the little ones for me and bub twice. No more at presant. I remain as ever,*
  *your loving Husband.*
*E. M. Swaggart            Co. I 92 Ill Vol*
*Via Chattanooga Tenn*
*No Wilder about it            E. M. S.*
  *Give my love to Mother.            Mack*

By April 15, all the troops were in place and the Ninety-second Illinois discovered they had not lost their status as Mounted Infantry. Instead, they were on duty day and night, on pickets and guarding. When they were not on duty, they had a very tight regimen to follow. Eugene informed Elvira of his duties when he wrote on April 22.

*Ringgold Ga            Apr 22$^{nd}$ 1864*
*Dear Wife*
*Once more I have the extreme pleasure of writing you a few lines as I am off duty long enough. Dear Vira, I would like to receive a letter from you, but it appears as though I cannot. I have not had one since we came to this place and we get our mail regular, but my Dear, you must not think that I blame you. No! far from it. I know you write and very often.*
*Our Regt. is doing heavy picket duty at presant. I will tell you our duty that we are doing at presant. In the first place, in the morning, is pickets. They go nine miles to their posts & stay out 48 hours, so you see, that is no sport, but after all, the boys all*

---
[169] Order to dismount.

say they would rather picket out in front in sight of the rebs than any other way - number of men for picket from Regt is 120.

Next, is camp guard. It takes 50 men per day from Regt.

Next, is fatigue which some days takes 100 men and again, there is none.

Next is our time table which is as follows.

$1^{st}$, reville, ½ past 5 A.M. - that means get up, come out under arms to rool call.

$2^{nd}$, is feed & stable call, ¼ to 5 - we feed and groom our horses.

$3^{rd}$, we get breakfast at 6.

$4^{th}$, is water at 8 A.M.

$5^{th}$, is drill from ½ past 8 to 10.

$6^{th}$, is dinner & rool call from 10 to 1 P M.

$7^{th}$, from 1 P M to 3 - graze.

$8^{th}$, from 3 to 5 P M - feed, groom, get our supper & get ready for dress parade.

$9^{th}$, Dress parade at 6 P.M.

$10^{th}$, Retreat & rool call at 7 P.M.

$11^{th}$. Tattoo & rool call - ½ past 8.

$12^{th}$, go to bed, so you see we are kept pretty busy.

Oh! yes, I am well & hope this will find you the same. I am on picket tomorrow. I will write again as soon as I come in. Give my love to all.

Kiss the boy for pap. As ever, I remain your sincere Husband

E. M. Swaggart

Dismounting is plaid out, I guess.

On April 23, a detachment, consisting of sixty-four men, under the command of Lieutenant Horace C. Scoville of Company K, was on picket at Nickajack Gap. William Reynolds, Eugene's friend was with them. They were "attacked by an overwhelming force of the enemy." They were "surrounded and defeated with a loss of five killed"—one outright and four after they surrendered. Three were severely wounded and twenty captured.[170] William was one they killed - after he surrendered! Eugene was sad and angry when he wrote to Elvira.

> Ringgold Ga             Apr 25$^{th}$ 1864
> Dear Wife
> With rather a sad heart, I seat myself to pen you a few lines. I have some very pain full news to write you. That is, on the morning of 23d Inst., our pickets, 7 miles from Camp, were attacted & a horrable massacre of our boys took place. There were 64 men on from our regt. Out of that No, 31 came to camp, the remaining 33 men all killed & taken prisoners.
> Among them, from Co I, was Wm. Reynolds[171] & James Rhodes[172], killed, & from Co I, C. W. Reynolds & Wm. McWorthey[173], captured.
> I will try and tell you some of the particulars. The posts were cut off from camp by some rebel Inft., attacked in the rear by reb Cav., (this being early in the morning, not quite light) and drove our boys right into their trap & after the boys surrendered, they shot them down in Cold blood. Bill Reynolds surrendered. One reb rode up to him an told Bill he wanted his boots, but Bill did not hear him at first,

---

[170] *Illinois Troops (Union) Infantry, Records of Events, Vol. 13, Record of Events for the 92$^{nd}$ Illinois Infantry, September 1862 - June 1865*, p. 503

[171] William H. (Bill) Reynolds, Salem, 92$^{nd}$ Illinois Infantry, Company I, killed at Nickajack, GA. on 4-23-64. Arthur Robbe and Richard Hinton, Booklet from *Rededication Ceremony of the Carroll County Civil War Soldiers and Sailors Monument.*

[172] James W. Rhodes, York, 92$^{nd}$ Illinois Infantry, Company I, killed at Nickajack, GA. on 4-23-64. - Robbe and Hinton, Booklet from *Rededication Ceremony*

[173] William P. McWorthy, Mt. Carroll, 92$^{nd}$ Illinois Infantry, Company I, captured at Nickajack, GA. Died at Andersonville prison. Grave # 9710 Robbe and Hinton, Booklet from *Rededication Ceremony*

Charles W. Reynolds - captured and sent to Andersonville prison. He was a brother of William Reynolds, killed at Nickajack Gap and Josephine Reynolds Woodin/Swaggart, Eugene's second wife.

*and then was a reb Captain came up, drew his revolver and shot him, (Bill), through the bowels, and said," now, God damn you, you will give up your boots". He lived about 4 hrs. I did not see him before he died. The dead were buried today. There is 2 men living, yet, that was wounded. I dont know how many was killed in the regt. You will see all in a short time, no doubt, in the papers.*

*I am well. I came in from picket today being out 2 nights. I do not feel in a very good way for writing. No letters from you yet.*

*Give my love to Every boddy. Kiss my boy. I remain your loving Husband*

*P. S. I suppose Capt. has written to Lib and will send his things home.*

At 2:30 A.M. on April 29, the Ninety-second Illinois Mounted Infantry formed a part of a column that moved through Ringgold Gap and drove the rebel cavalry to Tunnel Hill. In the skirmish, there were four wounded out of the regiment, one mortally, one severely and two slightly. Twelve horses were lost, either killed or wounded.[174]

May 1 found the Ninety-second Illinois at Stone Church where skirmishing broke out with a column of General Bushrod R. Johnson's troops. Still on the move the following day, the regiment was on a reconnaissance to Tunnel Hill, Georgia, when they charged across an open field to gain possession of a wooded hill. One man, Sergeant John L. Strock of Company C was wounded.[175]

Many times, during stressful events such as a war, the only sanity one can hold on to, is assurance of the family and children. Perhaps that was why Eugene, back in camp after the reconnaissance, wrote a letter to his little niece, Jennie Swaggart

---

[174] *Illinois Troops (Union) Infantry, Records of Events, Volume 13, 92$^{nd}$ Illinois Infantry, 1862-1865*, p. 503
[175] Ibid., p. 504

to thank her for a little pail she had given him. He wanted her to know he still had it and cherished it.

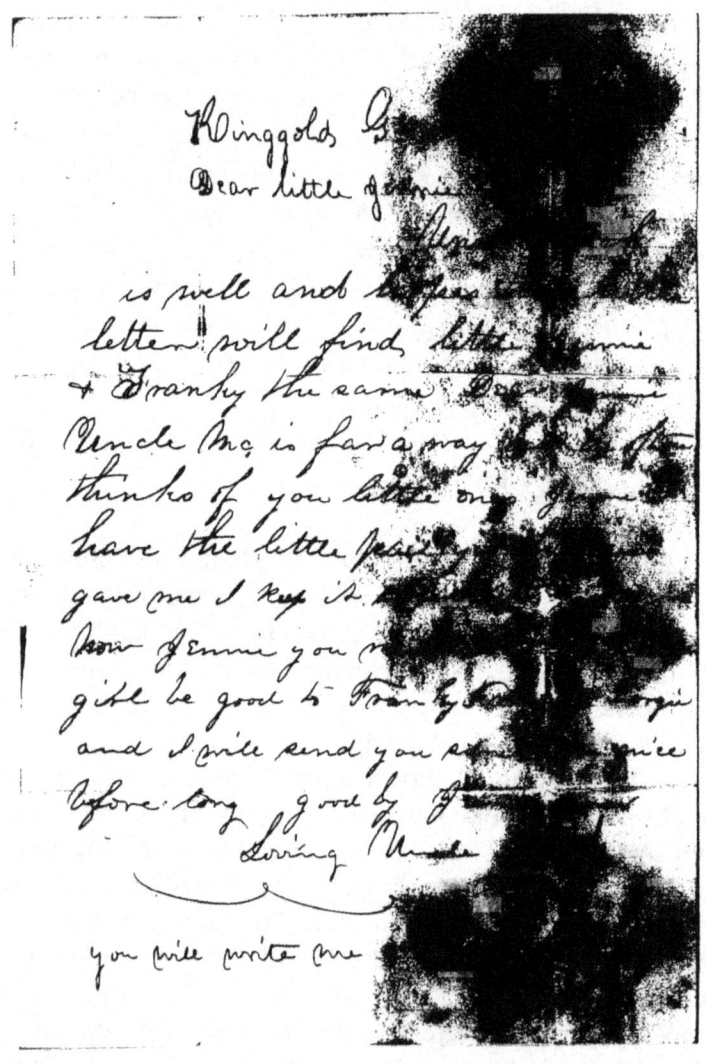

Ringgold Ga                        May 1$^{st}$ 1864
Dear little Jennie
Uncle Mack is well and hopes this little letter will find little Jennie & Franky the same. Dear Jennie, Uncle Mc is far away but he often thinks of you little ones.

*Jennie, I have the little pail yet that you gave me. I keep it to put my sugar in. Now Jennie, you must be a good little girl. Be good to Franky, Freddy & Georgie and I will send you something nice before long. Goodby, Jennie.*
*Your loving Uncle,    Mack*
*You will write me a letter, wont you.*

The next two days, the pickets had skirmishes at Leet's Cross Roads and again near Ringgold Gap. Unknown to the soldiers of the Ninety-second Illinois Mounted Infantry, Headquarters was reorganizing again. This time, the Military Division of the Mississippi was under General William Tecumseh Sherman. He commanded the Armies consisting of the Army of the Cumberland under General George H. Thomas, the Army of the Tennessee under General James B. McPherson, and the Army of the Ohio under General John M. Scofield. Brigadier General Judson Kilpatrick was in command of the Third Cavalry Division and Colonel Eli H. Murray of the Third Brigade in the Third Cavalry Division.[176] The Third Brigade became the new post of the Ninety-second Illinois Mounted Infantry as well as the Third and Fifth Kentucky Cavalry.

The Ninety-second Illinois and a portion of the Third Kentucky were the only ones who held an exposed and extended line to the West of Ringgold, Georgia.[177] They were in front of the forces and skirmishing daily.

Eugene ran into his old friend, Henry Lego of the Thirty-fourth Illinois, who told him some gossip from home that hit him hard. He knew there was nothing he could do about it, but the thought galled him that Elizabeth Reynolds, the wife of his friend William Reynolds, who had just lost his life, was unfaithful to her husband with his half-brother, John Miller.

---

[176] Frank J. Welcher, *The Union Army, 1861-1865, Organization & Operations, Volume II, Western Theater*, Indiana University Press, Bloomington & Indianapolis, 1993, pp. 351 & 414
[177] Colonel Eli Murray, *The Official Records of the War of the Rebellion, No. 422*, p. 888.

John Miller told Henry Holt that he planned to leave his pregnant wife, Mary Ann, for Elizabeth.

Elvira, in her letter, also gave Eugene some news that concerned him. She was pregnant again. His furlough was fruitful.

> Ringgold, Ga            May $5^{th}$ 1864
> Dear Wife
> With great pleasure, I am permited to write you a few lines in ans. to yours of Apr 26, which came to hand day before yesterday. I was happy to hear that you was well. I am well, as usual, & hope this will find you the same.
> You said you heard we were dismounted. It is a mistake. They will never dismount our regt as long as we can get horses. Genl. Killpatrick says we are the best Cavalry regt. he ever see go into a fight and he says we shall not be dismounted.
> We are having very nice weather at presant, only rather warm & lazy.
> My Dear, you need not ever fear any alarm about me telling anything you write me, never. The $34^{th}$ is here now camped about one mile from us. I see Henry Lego everyday. He was telling me that John Miller was going to leave Mary Ann (say nothing about it). He says John is going to have the game as well as the name with Miss Lib, you know. I am sorry but I cant help it, so let them go.
> Sister Jennie is going to Chicago. Tell her she must write me when she gets there & I will ans. Give her my love.
> In regards to the pregnancy. I am very sorry I ever applied for a furlough now, as it is, but you know it was all a mistake, dont you, but I only hope and pray I may be at home by the time. I have but little

hopes. I shall feel quite content if you have Jennie with you.

In regard to the photos, send them as quick as is convenient. I have no chance to get any here at the front, everything is on the moove now. We are expecting a big fight here, now, everyday and as soon as it comes off, what is left of the 92d will go to the rear to recruit up our horses. Then, I guess I can get a photo for you.

Some say our mail will be stopped for 1 month. If so, you need not look for any more letters till the said 4 weeks are passed. There will be a great change in military affairs in that length of time. The rebellion will be crushed, or prolonged, clear out of sight the other way. Both rebel & Federal are, from appearances, doing everything in their power to resist other in the coming campaign. Mark what I have said and see if it is not true.

I hope Annie has not sold her farm. It does not seem bad to me. Oh, I only wish I could have said a few words to her before she sold it. I think she would have kept it, but I would rather see Sylvester have it than anyone else but her. If we move soon, I may not have a chance of writing again very soon. Kiss my Dear little boy. My Duty, Ma. Give my love to all the family. I remain as ever your Affectionate Husband

E. M. Swaggart

Not much sighns of any pay soon.

The Atlanta Campaign began, led by General William Tecumseh Sherman. His Union army, which included the Army of the Cumberland, the Army of the Tennessee and the Army of the Ohio prepared to meet General Joseph E. Johnston's Confederate Army of Tennessee, and lesser armies including General John Bell Hood's Army of Texas. General Sherman's orders were "to move against Johnston's army, break it up and get into enemy's country, inflicting as much damage as possible against their war resources".[178]

On May 7, General Sherman began to advance and the Ninety-second Illinois Mounted Infantry entered the new campaign at 4:00 in the morning, leading the advance of General Sherman's Army. Colonel Eli Murray, Commander of the Third Brigade reported, "The brigade, at the moment of the commencement of the campaign was unorganized. After two reconnaissances in the direction and to Tunnel Hill, resulting in heavy skirmishing, the brigade moved with the division as the vanguard of the Twentieth Army Corps, crossing Taylor's Ridge at Nickajack Trace, through Trickum, and thence to a point two miles from Buzzard's Roost, skirmishing with the enemy's cavalry." One of General Hooker's brigades relieved them and they moved in between the Twentieth Army Corps and the Army of Tennessee. They went into camp at Gordon's Gap.[179]

Before daylight the next morning, the Ninety-second Illinois moved out again. They moved "six hours in advance of the Army of Tennessee". They moved in the direction of Resaca. Nightfall found them in possession of Villanow and the mouth of Snake Creek Gap where they encamped with the army of General James Birdseye McPherson. Scouting parties, sent out in the direction of Resaca and Tilton, both had rebel encounters. Pickets moved out to guard the Villanow Cross Roads.[180]

From Villanow, on May 9, the brigade moved in the direction of Tilton where they encountered many rebels and drove in the rebel picket line of General Pat R. Cleburne, returning to Gordon's Gap to camp.[181]

The troops stopped for a rest and stayed in camp until 12:00 noon when they resumed the march and after twelve miles,

---

[178] World Almanac Publications, *The Civil War Almanac*, Intro. by Henry Steele Commager, A Bison Book, New York, NY 1983, p. 198
[179] Colonel Eli Murray, *The Official Records of the War of the Rebellion, Reports, Army of the Cumberland*, No. 422, p. 888
[180] Ibid., p. 889
[181] Ibid., p. 889

camped in Sugar Valley at the mouth of Snake Creek Gap.[182] It was one of "the most natural places to fortify" they had seen.[183]

The rain and wind came hard the next morning and the troops stayed in camp, but on the twelfth, they moved out. Company I, along with others in the regiment, went to Tilton Road where they skirmished hard with a rebel force, driving the enemy two miles and then lay in the line of battle until dark. They took one prisoner and killed or wounded several others.

As the Union armies moved toward Resaca, where they hoped to unseat General Joseph E. Johnston's army, General Leonidus Polk's Army of the Mississippi moved in to Resaca to join General Johnston.

The battle at Resaca broke loose on May 13 when, at daylight, the division, in advance of the armies, moved upon the rebel line of communication. Colonel Baldwin's Fifth Kentucky Cavalry joined the brigade advancing on the main Resaca road, covering the formation of infantry lines. "General Kilpatrick was wounded while driving the pickets in." Colonel Murray assumed command of the division and Colonel Atkins assumed command of the Third Brigade. At the command of Colonel Murray, the Ninety-second Illinois was dismounted and placed in a position to hold Smith's Cross-Roads, between the Snake Creek Gap and Resaca, covering the flank of the regiment along with the Fifth Kentucky Cavalry. They held the position with slight skirmishing until General John A. Logan's Corps moved forward in line. One man in the Ninety-second Illinois was badly wounded.

At 1:00 P.M., the Ninety-second Illinois moved to Lay's Ferry. There they found the enemy posted behind the earth works, guarding the ferry, but were under orders not to attack. When they returned, the Fifth Kentucky Cavalry left to picket the ferry for the night while keeping an eye on the enemy.

Over the next two days, skirmishing went on in the city. The Ninety-second Illinois Mounted Infantry split up and Companies

---

[182] Colonel Smith D. Atkins, *Official Records of the War of the Rebellion, Reports, Army of the Cumberland*, p. 895
[183] Charles E. Cort, *Dear Friends, The Civil War Letters and Diary of Charles Cort*, Helyn W. Tomlinson, ed., n.p., 1962, p. 143

went out to Newton Ferry, Gideon's Ferry, Calhoun Ferry and Lay's Ferry. There, pickets and guards set out along with sharp shooters across the Oostenaula River. Their pickets covered the Snake Creek and Smith's Cross Roads. At night, they went into line behind rail barricades on the road to Calhoun Ferry and Lay's Ferry. Near Resaca Road, they engaged the enemy and held the crossroad. One man, Joseph Taylor of Company A, was wounded in the head.[184]

The battle did not gain advantage for the North or the South. However, a pattern formed whereby General Sherman moved from one flank of the Confederate army to the other trying to move in behind them or pass them on the way to Atlanta. Each time, General Johnston retreated so the Union army was unsuccessful in their attempts to pass or move in behind the Confederate army. On May 15, the Union Army was able to cross the Oostenaula River and was moving to the rear of General Johnston's Army. When General Johnston heard the news, he ordered a retreat.[185]

That night, near the campfire, Eugene wrote to Elvira to let her know he was all right.

*May 15, 1864           South Dalton*
*On the Battlefield         20 miles*
*Dear Wife*
*In haste I will try and let you know how I am. I am well at presant & hope this will find you and baby the same.*
*Well, we are right into it. We have been fighting near a week & have gained a complete victory at every point so far and the rebs are in full retreat in our losses. I am not posted. Hooker is still after them full chizel.*

---

[184] Colonel Eli H. Murray, *The Official Records of the War of the Rebellion, Reports, Army of the Cumberland, Report No. 422* p.889; Colonel Smith D. Atkins, *Official Records, No. 423*, pp. 892-893; *Illinois Troops (Union) Infantry, Records of Events, Volume 13, 92$^{nd}$ Illinois Infantry, 1862-1865*, p. 505

[185] World Almanac Publications, *The Civil War Almanac*, Intro. by Henry Steele Commager, A Bison Book, New York, NY 1983, pp. 201-202

> May 15th 1864
> On the Battle field 20 Miles South Dalton
> Dear Wife
>             in haste I will try and
> let you know how I am. I am
> well at presaint & hope this will
> find you and baby the same
> well we are right in to it
> we have been fighting near
> a week & have gained a
> complete victory at every
> point so far and the rebs
> are in full retreat in
> our losses I am not posted
> Hooker is still after them
> full shigel I had a letter
> from you since the fight
> commenced & was glad.

I had a letter from you since the fight commenced & was glad to hear from you, that you was well. I am writing by firelight, so you must not complain at this. Our Genl. (Killpatrick) was severly wounded in the first skermish. Our regt. brought on the fight and then we limbered to the rear and watched the *flanks. It is getting late and I must close. My love to all.*

*As ever your Husband     Mack Swaggart*

*I write again as soon as I can*

On May 16, the Ninety-second Illinois Mounted Infantry and the Fifth Kentucky, commanded by General John A. Logan, reported to Brigadier General John M. Corse who was commanding the Fourth Division of the Fifteenth Corps of the Detachment Army of the Tennessee under General Sherman. They accompanied General Corse to Rome to set up communications with General Kenner Garrard who was commanding the Second Division of the Cavalry Corps near Rome, Georgia. The crossing at Lay's Ferry was by pontoon. After opening communications with General Gerrard, whom they found at Floyd's Springs, the Ninety-second Illinois returned across the Oostenaula River to the South side where they camped for the night. They traveled forty miles in one day.[186]

It rained most of following day. The Fifth Kentucky stayed with General Logan, but the Ninety-second Illinois returned to the brigade and moved to Adairsville, Georgia. On the eighteenth, they proceeded on to Kingston, which was known as a "hospital town, where most every house had been a reb hospital"[187]. After marching twenty-five more miles, they arrived at Cassville and camped for the night.

Colonel Atkins resumed command of the Ninety-second Illinois on May 20, just in time for a detail to return to Resaca to pick up stragglers that were sent back to their regiments in the front. The Third Kentucky and the Fifth Kentucky Regiments were detailed to guard an ammunition train[188]. The Ninety-second Illinois detached Eugene to go with them. On the trip

---

[186] *Illinois Troops (Union) Infantry, Records of Events, Volume 13, 92nd Illinois Infantry, 1862-1865*, p. 505

[187] Charles E. Cort, *Dear Friends, The Civil War Letters and Diaries of Charles Edwin Cort*, Helyn W. Tomlinson, ed., n.p., 1962, p. 145

[188] *Records of Events*, p. 504; Colonel Smith D. Atkins, *The Official Records of the War of the Rebellion, Reports, Army of the Cumberland*, No. 423, pp. 892-893. Described events from May 16-20.

back to Resaca, he decided to get a letter off to Elvira. She received the letter about William Reynolds' death and wanted more details.

*Rasaca Ga*                        *May 21$^{st}$ 1864*
*Dear Wife*
*With great pleasure, I once more attempt to write you. I am still well & hope this will find you & baby the same. I had a letter from you a fiew days ago & was glad to here that you were well. I wrote you once before, since we commenced this campaign. That was the 4$^{th}$ of this month and we have been on the go everyday, since, & expect to be for one month yet & probably longer, but I hope (& so does everyone else) that the thing will be brought (ink) to a close.*
*Our Army here is still after the rebs full chase. Our regt. left the main army at Kingston, Ga. about 25 miles from this place. We came back to this place to guard an Amunition train through to the front. The rebs left the R Road in good order, so you see the cars follow us right up. Our boys were so close to the rebs that they could not do any harm to the roads, in any respects. This place here is well fortified. Our loss here in killed, wounded & captured was Ten Thousand but, after all, we out flanked them and made them skedaddle. We get no news from Genl. Grant. We cant tell how he is getting along, but hope all right.*
*Well, my Dear, you wished to learn something in regard to Wm. Reynolds. I went on picket the morning he was killed, therefore did not see him before he died, but Hi Hay Ward was with him when he died.*
*He said Bill was to far gone when he found him to say much. He wished Hi to write to Lib was about*

*all he said. Bill was buried decent as could be expected, according to Military orders. Eg sent Bills things home, or started them. Charlie Reynolds was captured and has not been heard from since, but expect to help liberate him soon, providing all works right & we must look to God for our success.*

Regarding the pregnancy.

*Well, you little dove, you are in a pretty fix now, are you not & all just for wanting me to come home on a furlough. Are you not sorry. I will ans. for you ((I am), but am still in hopes that I will be there in time to take command in person, myself, do you not, I bet.*

*Oh! yes those photos. I will look for them one of these fine days. We are to start for the front at 6 in the morning. We are in the prettiest country I ever saw except Illinois. I will write again as soon as I can. Untill then, goodby. I remain as ever your*
*Affectionate Husband*<br>*E. M. Swaggart*

    The Ninety-second Illinois returned to Adairsville, again to pick up stragglers along the way. They found twelve but only three were really stragglers. The other nine wounded and sick were trying to return to their regiments.[189] The next few days, pickets and scouting resumed for the Ninety-second Illinois. Company D went to Cassville, Georgia. When they returned, pickets from the regiment proceeded to McDon's house on Cassville Road. They returned to camp on May 25.[190]

    In the last few days of May, a lot of activity took place in the direction of the Dallas area. However, General Kilpatrick's cavalry, including the Ninety-second Illinois Mounted Infantry,

---

[189] Col. Smith D. Atkins, *The Official Records of the War of the Rebellion, Reports, Army of the Cumberland*, p. 895

[190] *Illinois Troops (Union) Infantry, Records of Events, Volume 13, 92$^{nd}$ Illinois Infantry, 1862-1865*, p. 505

stayed behind to guard the line of the Etowah River from the North bank, and the railroads. Several skirmishes broke out on the line from Pumpkin Vine Creek to Allatoona Hills, with battles in Dallas near the New Hope Church. The Union Army suffered heavy losses, but captured Allatoona Pass and its railroad. The key to General Sherman's success was in controlling the railroads. General Johnston knew the key to the success for the Confederacy was to destroy the vital lines needed by the Union Army to bring in supplies.[191]

Eugene received a letter from Elvira and one from Amanda Ludisky, his sister-in-law, protesting the actions of her brother-in-law, John Miller and his illicit romance with Elizabeth Reynolds. He had only one reply to Elvira—stay away from Elizabeth Reynolds. To Amanda, there was reassurance that he trusted her sister, Elvira.

*Camp Near Adairsville Ga  May 26$^{th}$ 1864*
*Dear sister*
*With great pleasure, I write you a few lines in ans. to yours of the 11$^{th}$. I was glad to here that you were all well. I have nothing of importance to write. We have not been to the front for several days, therefore, know but little of what is going on, only the army is still advancing.*
*Our regt. has been picking up stragglers for 3 or 4 days. You see, when an army mooves, there are a great many get tired and fall back & some play off & it has been our business to gather up these fellows and take them to their respective commands, but that job is done. We are now waiting for Rebel Wheeler to make his appearance on some of our wagon trains or R. R. Bridges, then we will let him*

---

[191] Frank J. Welcher, *The Union Army, 1861-1865, Organization & Operations, Volume II, The Western Theater*, Indiana University Press, Bloomington & Indianapolis, 1993, pp. 431-441 and World Almanac Publications, *The Civil War Almanac*, Intro. by Henry Steele Commager, A Bison Book, New York, NY 1983, pp. 204-205

*know the 92$^{nd}$ is around. Till then we may not have much to do.*

*I suppose you get all the news from Grants Army and also from ours. We get no news atall except papers by mail.*

*Dicky, in regard to the war widows procedings, it does not worry me in the least, only I pity their Husbands. In regard to myself, I have no fears, whatever, nor never had, nor do I think I ever will have, any occasion, do you, but it is as you say, a disgrace to the entire neighborhood, the way one or two have been acting. They will play out some of these days, I think. The soldiers that live to see September next, will see the end of this war, then they can help some of them devils at home that have laid back doing nothing for the last 2 or 3 yrs but try and miss use the reputacion of poor soldiers and their wives.*

*Give my respects to All & Dicky, when you have time that you cannot use no other way more profitable, please write me & it will be welcomly received and ansd.   Your Brother*
*A kiss to all the babies.   Mack*

He wrote to Elvira and mailed it in the same envelope to save postage.

*Camp near Adairsville, Ga.   May 26$^{th}$ 1864*
*Dear Wife*
*I rec<u>d</u> yours of the 12$^{th}$ some time ago, but had no opportunity of writing till to day.  I am well at presant & hope this will find you & my boy the same. I have written three to you since we have been on this Campaign.*
*To day is the first day we have not saddled up since we left Ringold & we may have to saddle yet before*

May 26th/1864
Camp Near Adairsville Ga.
Dear Wife

I rec'd yours of the 12th some time ago but had no opportunity of writing till to day. I am well at presant & hope this will find you & my boy the same. I have written three to you since we have been on this Campaign. To day is the first day we have not saddled up since we left Kingsld & we may have to saddle yet before night. we are now in the rear of our Army watching for a reble raid — Old Wheeler has made his appearance captured a few wagons & left as soon as he came. but there is no telling when he wile be back again. Our Army is still on the advance & hope it will not stop this side of Atlanta we get but little news now from the Potomac but hope they are all right back again. Our Army is still on the advance & hope it will not stop this side of Atlanta.

We get but little news, now, from the Potomac, but hope they are all right. I suppose you hear all the late news and that is all I care for. I get your letters regular now, so that point is settled. I recd a letter from Dicky and ans. it & sent it with this one.

You said George was sick and was better. I wish I could see him. You will send me the said photos, as soon as you can.

I did not know that Tom Magee was at home or I should of told him to go and see you as he is one of my old regimental friends. I guess there will be no more furloughs granted to men this summer, but you can send them by mail. I dont think there is any danger. The Boys all think that this will be the last campaign. They are all in good spirits. Every one is doing his part. The thing looks quite favorable at presant.

Jennie has left you again, but you seem to think she will come back in the fall and you think my presence should be acceptable. May be you will see me there by that time, if I should be spared to live so long.

I am sorry Ma's health is so very poor. Dicky says she is very bad. Does she Doctor any or not. I wish I was home. I would have her live with us, but here I am, & what can I do (nothing). You can not imagine my feeling at times. I would not give a straw whether I died or lived, but when I would think of my Dear little family, it would revive me, and would revive any man that had, & knew he had, as good a wife as I have.

Oh! I am Thankfull I am not in Elsy Hebringtons situation. If I was I know what the results would be, but he is not the only one in that fix. Every day most

*I hear of some such occurance among the war widows.*
*You say you & Lib Reynolds are not quite as good friends as you were. I would not like to hear of you associating with any such person, for you are worth of better company - if not better, none.*
*I am glad Morford is getting along so well. I think, if he meets with no bad luck, he will do pretty well. Down here the rebs have put in large crops, but the Yanks have drove them off of it. Well, I guess I have writen enough for this time.*
*Give my love to Mother & Sylvester. All of them*
*As ever your                                     Mc*
*P. S. Papa sends a kiss to Mama & George*

Eugene, still in camp a few days later, decided to write to Elvira again. He had heard they were moving and wanted to be sure she received a letter in case they did. He wanted to assure her he had no interest in glory. He just wanted to stay alive until he could go home.

*May 28$^{th}$ 1864            In Camp Near Adairsville Ga*
*Dear Wife*
*Once more I will try and write you a few lines, as I expect we will moove from here today or tomorrow. I am well as usual & hope this will find you & boy enjoying the same great blessing.*
*I wrote to you & Dicky the other day & also to James Becker*
*They are fighting now at the front. I can hear the canonading very plain, cannot tell how they are making it. It has been quiet at the front for 3 or 4 days, untill this morning. We suppose our men are advancing on them rather faster than is pleasant for the rebs. We have not heard much from old Wheeler yet, but are looking for him, almost hourly.*

I have not heard from Henry Lego since we left Ringold, but his Division has not done much fighting yet, so I think he is safe.

Adairsville is a small place. It is situated on the railroad and is between 60 & 70 miles south of Chattanooga. Getting good ways south, but hope we will not have to stay long. Well, I must go and graze my plug.

May 29$^{th}$

I will try & finish my poor sheet. We did not moove yesterday, nor do not expect to moove today.

Oh! but we are having nice weather. It seems as though we were favored by the supreme high power for this campaign to put an end to this cruel war and everything works admirably towards it. Col. S. D. Atkins made us a short speech last night and he said in sixty days from this date all fighting would be over and he said if we did not go to the front during this time, we would share none of the great glory of putting down this rebellion. You see, he wanted to dismount us and take us in on foot, but we could not see it in the same light. As for my part of the glory, I care but little for it, if what I have done amounts to nothing. Our Col. is nearly plaid.

Well, today is sunday & how I wish I was on the the old native primis of Carroll. I think I could enjoy myself some, dont you. Still, I do not complain for the simple reason that this war can be seen clear throug without doubt, but after all, we do not know what great change might take place. News came yesterday to our Div. Commander and he sent to all his regiments, that Gen. Grant had completely routed Lees army and that all he wanted was food & plenty of ammunition. He said he had all the men he wanted (that is good).

General Ulysses Grant and General Robert E. Lee were battling in Virginia where General Grant did eventually beat General Lee, but he had not reached that accomplishment when Eugene wrote to Elvira. On May 12, 1864, the Union Army charged General Robert E. Lee's Confederate army at the Spottsylvania courthouse and a bloody battle took place which was later dubbed as "the Bloody Angle", where casualties in killed and wounded were six thousand eight hundred Union soldiers and five thousand Confederate soldiers. An additional four thousand Confederate soldiers were captured. "General Grant was accused of butchery" in the newspapers of the North because of the large numbers of soldiers lost, but the South took the biggest blow because of the difficulty in replacing lost soldiers. Again on May 19, General Grant's armies lost many more soldiers than the South in a difficult battle in the same area, but again, the North could afford the loss and the South could not. Battling between the two continued for many weeks.[192]

*May 29th cont.*

*Our army here is within 25 miles of Atlanta and you know, or I know, they will soon be closer. Atlanta is in a level country where the enemy will have no advantage over us as they have to fore. They never would stand a fair fight on open ground and for that reason I think that point can be easly obtained and that is their 2nd Richmond, as it cuts off all of their R. R. communications. Well, I have gassed plenty about that, so I will quit.*

*Oh! yes, sowbelly is very scarce as it all goes to the front. I will close withe much love to all. My love to Mother.. Except this, Yours as ever.*

*Soldier boy*

---

[192] Robert E. Denney, *The Civil War Years, A Day-by-Day Chronicle of the Life of a Nation,* Foreword by Gregory J. W. Urwin, Sterling Publishing Co., NY, pp. 406 & 410

## Chapter Fourteen
## On to Atlanta

The weather was rainy and warm[193] in Adairsville. The fields were deep with clover and the horses needed a rest and time to graze. Pickets went out daily, but the Ninety-second Illinois Mounted Infantry was not on the move.

Atlanta was evacuating, with the presence of Union soldiers so near. Eugene told Elvira about some of the women who were coming into their lines.

*Adairsville Ga*                              *June $4^{th}$ 64*
*Dear Wife*
*With great pleasure I am once more permited to write you in ans. to your of May $17^{th}$, which came to hand day before yesterday.*
*I was glad you and boy was well. I am well & hope these few lines will find you enjoying the same great blessing. By this letter, I see that you are fretting yourself entirely to much. You see, it does no good and will do you great harm. You must be pacient as ever. Trust in God & I trust all will come out right.*
*Tell Sylvester he is about, in regard to the termination of the war. I am of a little differant opinion. I think it will be over in just one half the time. I may be rong. You must hear some dreadfull news, news for the $92^{nd}$, in regard to reenlisting. That will never do, as long as we know ourselves & we think we do. Here is the promise you requested, (I will not reenlist). Here it is, in black & white.*
*I was on picket yesterday & last night, consequently feel rather spongy. Our regt. is getting the horses up in good order. We have nice large clover fields*

---

[193] Charles E. Cort, *Dear Friends, The Civil War Letters and Diary of Charles Edwin Cort*, Helyn W. Tomlinson, ed. n.p., 1962, p. 146

to graze our horses. Rebs are pretty scarce now in these parts. I have not heard from any of them in sometime.

The Rebs sent all of their nude wimen away from Atlanta when they fell back and a goodly number of them found their way inside of our lines. Those of them that I see, were barefooted & naked almost to the skin. There is not many of our boys that notice them atall and I am glad for it. It shows they have some respects for those they left behind.

I am so glad Morford is doing so well on your account. If the farm does well, I will think you can get along another year if I should not get home, but if it does not, well, I cant tell what will become of you. I hope & pray for the best, is all.

You say Mr. Downs folks do not hear from Wait. He is with the Company & has been all the while, except 8 or 10 days. He was sick, but he is all right now. He says he cannot hear from home, therefore, will not write unless they write him. I cannot blame him much.

Tell the folks I hope they had a gay old time on the excursion to Chicago & wish I had been with them. Never mind. We will have a nice ride sometime yet, wont we. Give my love to everybody, whether they wish it or not, my Duty to Mother, kiss all the babies for me & be sure and not let Georgie get into the ashes again.

With much love. I remain as ever
your devoted Husband.
E. M. Swaggart
I am looking for some photographs everyday. I will send Annie's soon.

On June 7, orders arrived to march into Kingston. The brigade moved one and a half-mile south of Kingston and camped. The next morning, the Ninety-second Illinois moved to Rome, where they met the enemy on Van Wert Road and a small skirmish developed, but the following day, they returned to Kingston and camped for four days.

The Army advanced again, this time to Marietta. The Ninety-second Illinois, operating as rear guard on June 10 when the movement began, stayed in camp a few days longer, while pickets went out.[194] While there, Eugene wrote to Elvira asking her the news concerning John Miller and Elizabeth Reynolds. He had quit writing to John when he heard about his affair with Elizabeth because of his disgust with his half-brother, John, and because of his friendship with William Reynolds, who died at Nickajack. Elvira did not mention the affair anymore because she was afraid it would upset him. However, he wanted to know what was going on, and, it was something to discuss around the campfire at night.

> Kingston, Ga.                                June 10$^{th}$ 1864
> Dear Wife
> With pleasure, I seat myself to ans. your more than welcome letter, which came to hand yesterday. Was very glad to hear that you was well. I am well as usual & hope this will find you the same.
> Our Div mooved here the 7$^{th}$ from Adairsvill, being 10 miles farther south on the Atlanta R. R. We are 15 miles from Rome. Our Co. went to Rome, on account they say it is a very nice place & was well fortified by the rebs, but they had to leave it without much fighting. What the army is doing out front now, I am unable to say. I suppose you get all the news from both armies so I will not say much about them.
> My Dear, you ask if the wounded in our Co. will be sent home or be left to die. All that were wounded

---

[194] *Illinois Troops (Union) Infantry, Records of Events, Volume 13, 92$^{nd}$ Illinois Infantry*, 1862-1865, p. 548; Smith D. Atkins, *The Official Records of the War of the Rebellion, Army of the Cumberland,* p. 895-896

Kingston Ga. June 10th 1864

Dear Wife

With pleasure I seat my-self to ans your more than welcome letter which came to hand yesterday was very glad to hear that you was well. I am well as usual & hope this will find you the same. Our Div mooved here the 7th from Cldairsville being 10 miles farther south on the Atlanta R.R. we are 15 miles from Rome our Co. went to Rome on a scout they say it is a very nice place & was well fortified by the rebs. but they had to leave it with out much fighting What the army is doing out front now I am un able to say. I suppose you get all the news from both armies so I will not say much about them. My Dear you ask if the wounded in our Co. well be sent home or be left to die. all that were wounded in our Co. is dead long

in our Co is dead long ago. That was poor Will & James Rhodes, but the wounded, in a general thing of our army, I think is well cared for, as far as the skill of man is concerned, but the weather is very hard for them.

*The weather here now is warm, warmer than it ever gets up in Black Oak, at any rate, seems so to me, very showery. We have just been visited with a heavy Thunderstorm. The lighting killed one of our Horses.*

*Oh! you naughty girl for taking Georgies dinner from him. Oh I would like to see the little fellow and receive some of his prescious little kisses from him.*

*Yes, Annie says she will write all about her excursion, but that is about all. The write, I seldom see. Tell her I am not mad yet, but will be afterwhile if she does not do better in the future.*

Concerning a deserter who they both knew well – possibly Herr Browning.

*And yess, he starts out again. I guess the big bounty has caught him, too, and he has gone in the 100 days service, ha ha. I hope I shall be there to work with him this winter. I guess we will all be at home by that time.*

*You speak of that as if Grant is successfull in this campaign, which we have all reason to beleave he will be.*

*How does Lib get along. What is she doing & what is John Miller doing. Tell me all such news. It may not seem interesting to you, but it is to me & what you are doing. I guess I want to know that, dont I.*

*Vira, you must excuse this sheet, for it is the best I have at presant. I will try and get some better by next week, if I am spared that long. I guess I have scribled plenty for this time. Water call has just blowed and I must close. My love to Mother & all the family. Kiss the boy. I remain as ever your Affectionate Husband*
*E. M. Swaggart*

On the last page of this letter is a very pretty church drawn in pencil with a bell tower and what appears to be a weather vane on top.

Eugene, concerned about the expected baby, wanted Jennie's assurance that she would be there. Jennie had not heard from Elvira but dreamed about her and wanted to assure her she would come when Elvira needed her.

*Chicago, Ill Sabbath Morning      June the 12$^{th}$ 1864*
*My Dear Sister Vira*
*I have not had a letter from you in a long time. I received one from Mack last week. I was glad to hear from him, you may well believe. He was well and had just received one from you.*
*I dreamed last night that you sent for me to come home. We see if you wants me, before I come. Georgie will be quite a big boy. I cannot hardly wait to see him. I am afraid Mrs. Shrimkel will not have little Harry very long. He declines so fast but your vis may do him good.*
*How I long for one breth of air. To think this is the summer that I shall spend in Chicago. I never did like it and dislike it more than ever this summer. The perfumes from Bridgeport are almost unbearable. They are burning a great time about but say the cause cannot be removed this summer, is it not stresful.*
*Dicky said that Sylvester went to Rockford. I have not seen, but Freddie Merrell tells me, he was in Salem. Did Annie receive a letter from me with fifty cents in it. Tell her to write me. Give my best love to all the children and kiss them for me.*
*Mrs. Shekel has given me a very funny little white dress fur. You, she speaks of very often and sayes she is sory for you . I tell her it is all right and she*

*sayes, stop my muse, that I dont know anything about it. I think I did write some lines to your Mother and everyone else on the place.*
*I feel anxious about John and Mary Ann. Write me how they get along. What a pitty that everybody cannot be happy. Clara gave me a very pretty bedstead for Jennie. It is almost large enough for a baby. I cannot hardly wait to bring it but I must close, for the lunch bells are ringing and I am going to get ready. Love to Moses, Dicky, and a large share to yourself. Goodbye.*
*Write soon to your affectionate Sister*
*Jennie*
*I feel weak and my hand trembles like some Old Lady when I think I shall never get better.*
*Patience*

Part of the brigade moved out to return to Resaca on June 13. They were after the rebels, but instead found an outlaw gang, led by a man named Jordan, that was operating in the town. Union supporters helped them find and wipe out the band of outlaws.[195]

Company I of the Ninety-second Illinois was left scouting the area, while the rest went to Resaca. One company scouted in the field and one in Villanow, but neither found anyone, so they returned to camp before 3:00 P.M.[196] Rumors were flying around the camp and they were all good. Eugene wanted Elvira to know the good news he heard even if he did not know whether to believe it or not.

*Kingston Ga                  June 15$^{th}$ 1864*
*Dear Wife*
*Pardon me for my neglect in not writing you before this & I will try and make it all satisfactory. I recd*

---

[195] Colonel Eli Murray, *The Official Records of the War of the Rebellion, Reports, Army of the Cumberland*, No. 422, p. 889
[196] Smith D. Atkins, *Official Records*, pp. 895-896

Kingston Ga. June 15th/1864

Dear Wife

Pardon me for my neglect in not writing you before this & I will try and make it all satisfactory. I rec'd one of May 29th and ans. it but was ordered out on a scout and was out 3 dys, so when I came in I found another one of June 5th so I will ans. both with one. I was glad to hear that you are still well & hope you will remain so. Well we or our Brig has just got in camp from a 3 dys scout we found no rebs. for the simple reason that they skedaddled to fast for us to catch them. There is 4 or 5 hundred of them around here some where that is trying to do damage to our R.R. but they keep pretty close. We are having good news now and plenty of it we heard to day that Fort Darling is ours and that Genl Sherman has Atlanta

no rebs, for the simple reason that they skedaddled to fast for us to catch them. There is 4 or 5 hundred of them around here somewhere that is trying to do damage to our R.R., but they keep pretty close.

We are having good news, now, and plenty of it. We heard today that Fort Darling is ours and that Gen. Sherman has Atlanta and Col. Wilder has been dressing old Wheeler out again. Also, old John Morgan has been whiped good in Ky. If it is all true, it is good enough for anybody. I expect, and so does everyone here, that the next good news will be the fall of Richmond.

You do not say much about the crops, how they appear to be coming, but still I can all most know that they are very backward. The crops here, what has not been destroyed by the army passing over them, look nice. The wheat is turning yellow fast and there is a good quanity of it growing in this state. Corn is not so good here as it is in Ala, Tenn, for a general thing.

Our Co is pretty small at presant, as there is a great many dismounted and horses cannot be had for some unknown reason to me. Our Co. musters 74 men and in that number, there is about 30 for duty and you know, in a raw country like this, makes duty pretty hard, but I suppose we will get horses in a short time, but I am afraid we will not get them afterwhile.

Wait Downs is well, but you know, him and me are not very intimate. One of our boys was telling me yesterday that I was the means of breaking up corrispondence between him and Sis. He had made his brags to this person that he could, and intended, having Anna, so you see, in his way of thinking I have done a wicked act, for all of which, I plead not guilty.

*I heard the 34th had been in a heavy fight, but did not learn who was hurt. If you hear anything from Henry Lego, by Tommy, please let me know.*
*The 15th passed by here the other day, but I did not see any of them. I suppose they are at the front now.*
*You say Sylvester is going to travail this summer. Tell him, if he happens down this way, to call and see a body. I will regail him with coffee, sowbelly & hard tack, and have a good time in general. Anyway, give him my best wishes and all the rest. My duty, Mother. Kiss that boy of ours for me. As ever your Affectionate Husband*
Referring to the church he had drawn on the previous letter.

*P. S. I guess I will send both as I have got a very nice picture drawn on one. E M S*

    Although Sherman moved forward, fighting all the time, the Ninety-second Illinois Mounted Infantry, left in the rear, had pickets and scouts along the railroad. Because of a lack of horses, they had to take turns using the steeds, so soldiers did not go out everyday. They had returned to Kingston on June 15. It started raining on the eighteenth and rained all night.
    Eugene had been out scouting along the Etowah River and an amusing incident occurred.

*Kingston Ga. June 20th 1864*
*With pleasure I write you to inform you that I am well & hope this will find you & boy enjoying the same great blessing. I have not had a letter for the past few days, but will write anyway.*
*We are having very good times now, our duty not being very hard. All we do now is to picket & scout along the R R, which brings any man on duty once a week.*

*The news from the front is still good. Grant appears to be doing well where he is. Sherman, I guess, is enough here for them. I hope so. We cannot get much news, only the dispatches.*

*Well, I guess I will tell you about a little scout we had the other night. Our Co put out on the Etowah river, part of them to picket and part to patrol on the other side. Well, Sergeant Price from Mt. Carroll, myself & others were sent out just at dark on the opposite side of the river, we having strict orders not to fire if we should meet any Johnies, but to report to Headquarters. Well, we started & proceeded out about 2 miles where we came to a cross roads, so we took the right hand road, went on near a mile, then we turned about & came back to the cross roads and took the left hand road, went about 1 ½ miles, about faced & started for the cross roads. Well, we got back to the crossroads & started for Camp. We came about ¼ miles, when to our surprise we heard a number of men coming after us, fast as their horses could carry them. Then you ought to have seen us poor coots leg it. As good luck would have it, we all had good horses. We rode in thick, heavy timber & the road very muddy & stony & to top off with, pretty dark. Well, here we went fast as our horses could carry us and the supposed rebs close behind us, for over a mile, where we came out on an open field & here we made a bold stand, got loads in our guns and everything all ready. Sure enough, here they came, but slow. We halted them as soon as they came near enough and they turned out to be our own men - <u>pretty good joke</u>.*

*My love to All both great & small Goodby*
*Your E. M. Swaggart*
*P S Please send me a few stamps.*

On June 27, General Sherman ordered an attack on Kenesaw Mountain. It was a failed attempt, so his movements to the Chattahoochee River resumed.

Colonel Smith D. Atkins was sick and had been for some time. He badly needed a rest. On June 29, he announced to the soldiers that he planned to resign and go home. Major Albert Woodcock, described as a faithful and efficient Christian officer,[197] took over Colonel Atkins' command, under General Judson Kilpatrick who was still in command of the division that included the Ninety-second Illinois Mounted Infantry.

*Camp 92$^{nd}$ Near Kingston Ga  July 2$^{nd}$ 1864*
*Dear Wife*
*Once more I will try & pen you a few lines in ans. to yours, which brought the photos. I was very glad to hear that you were still well & was also happy to receive the photos. Georgies looks very natural, but yours, I think, is very poor. However, I am more than thankfull to get it. The boys all think Geor is a nice boy and well worth fighting for. I tell them they are right.*
*I wrote you the other day, had no news worth writing & it is about the same with me today.*
*The 92$^{nd}$ mooves tomorrow, but where I am not to say, although we will not go far. The news from the front is still good. Deserters from Johnsons Army say they are in the last ditch. Sherman is good for Johnson. If Gen. Grant succeeds on to Richmond, which he will no doubt, if they only give him time.*
*The boys in the Co. are all well and full of fun. Some say we are going to spend next 4$^{th}$ of July at home. I hope so, for from all appearances, we shall have a ptry 4$^{th}$ this time.*

---

[197] Thomas M. Eddy, *The Patriotism of Illinois, A Record of the Civil and Military History of the State*, Chapter XXII, Regimental Sketches, Ninety-second Illinois Infantry, 1865, p. 373

*Col. S. D. Atkins has resighned & will leave us in a few days. He goes on account of ill health. Who will be our next Col, I cannot say, yet.*

*Wilson Gotshall[198], wounded in a skermish near Dalton, Ga., has since died. He was a brother of Jacob Shinks wife and was a good soldier, well liked by all that know him well. 13 months more will tell (if I am spared that long) where I am. You can imagine where I, and a great many more, at the end of that time, that is whats the matter, if the war does not close.*

*Oh! Dear, I was on picket last night & it rained all night & I caught such an awfull cold. I can scarcely breathe and you bet, I dont feel pleasant by any means. Think I will live through it.*

*Huckle Berries are here by the Bushell. We have all we can use of them. Black Berries are beginning to ripen fast. Black Berries, in this country, are not like they are North. One of these is as large as three of them north and as sweet as candy. You better believe we go for them fast. Apples are very plenty & are getting quite good. New potatoes are pretty much all the go now. The Wheat & Oats here is all dead ripe and no one to cut and take care of it. It looks hard but cant be helped very well just now. Give my love to Mother & all & except this from your devoted Husband*

*P. S. I will endeavor to get some larger paper in a few days.*

---

[198] Wilson S. Gotshel, Mt. Carroll, 92nd Illinois Infantry, Co. C. – Died at Nashville on 6-18-64 - Arthur Robbe and Richard Hinton, Booklet of *Rededication Ceremony of the Carroll County Civil War Soldiers and Sailors Monument.*

Operations began on the Chattahoochie River for General Sherman's Army on July 1, 1864.[199] The Ninety-second Illinois Mounted Infantry, moved, under orders, to Resaca on July 3. There, they scouted and sent out heavy pickets between Resaca and Calhoun until July 25. On July 19, 1864, Colonel Smith D. Atkins was relieved of his command by order of Colonel Eli Murray.[200] Eugene wrote to Elvira describing their days.

*Resaca Ga                                  July $19^{th}$ 1864*
*Dear Wife*
*Pardon me for not writing you before this, as we are on the go now allmost night & day to keep the rebs from tearing up the R. R. I am well as usual and hope this will find you enjoying the same great blessing. I recd yours of the $1^{st}$, also one from Annie, which I will ans. soon.*
*My Dear, I am not in very good spirits at presant. There is bad news from the Eastern Army, but I cannot say what it will amount to yet, but I hope it will all come out right. And, we have bad news from the North in regards to the Corps & frankly, ours will be a slim one.*
*I think I shall be able to send you some money before long. In regards to you sending me some, you must have any fears about me. I will get along fine and wish you could be half so well cared for as I am. I could be happy, then, & content with my lot, but as it is, I cant be as long as I am in the service. I feel it my duty to be in the army, but feel it my duty, by tenfold ratio, to be with my family.*
*Our regt. is about to get orders to re-enlist and I would be one among them first to enroll my name if*

---

[199] Frank J. Welcher, *The Union Army, 1862-1865, Organization & Operations, Volume II, Western Theater*, Indiana University Press, Bloomington & Indianapolis, 1993, p. 451
[200] Albert Woodcock, *The Official Records of the War of the Rebellion, Reports, Army of the Cumberland, No. 427, Second Report*, p. 898

*I were single, but I never will. Well, I guess I will tell you how we start out at night. Generaly, 3 or 4 squads of 100 each take different roads, march all night, and next day we all come together & then, you see driven these squads of rebs, all in among us, they get themselves gobled.*
*The country now is full of what the boys like to eat & when out, we do about as we please, you know. We have some great times and some pretty hard times. Sometime we are out for a week at a time that we get no rest, only while we graze our horses, and our turn to get to camp. We stay long enough to get one nights rest and we are out again. I hope this campaign will soon be over so we can settle down in camp for awhile.*
*Give my love to all. I remain as ever,*
*your Affectionate Husband*
*E. M. Swaggart*
*P. S. If I am in camp 2 days, I will write again, but there is no certainty*

The regiment stayed in camp another day and Eugene kept his promise to Elvira.

*Resacca Georgia          July 18$^{th}$ 1864*
*Dear Wife*
*With pleasure I am once more permited to write you a few lines. I am well as usual & hope these lines will find you & boy enjoying the same great blessing. It has been sometime since I had a letter from you, but I guess it is no more than right if I should not get more than one for not writing oftener to you of late. I told you in my other letter how it is about writing at presant, so I deem it unnecessary to say more about it.*

*Times are very difficult with us. We are in Camp with 2 Ky Regts. & 1 hosoure, and we like them nearly as well as we do the rebles. Our Camp is on the old battleground so you can imagine how cheering it looks. The good thing is we get our mail & papers very regular & plenty of rations & as I. M. Doc Will says, we get plenty of onions, potatoes, cucumber, string beans, in fact, all vegetables that the southerners know how to raise & Black Berries to no end.*

*There is a camp rumor out today that we are to be dismounted. Where it came from, I dont know or whether there is any truth in it or not, and dont care much. Thank Providence, 2 long years of our time has fled and the one to come, if I am spared, I can put in most anyway and not complain, I suppose.*

*The 15$^{th}$ boys are having good times now. At least, I hope they are. I shall expect it if I should be one of the lucky ones. Moses Barlow has been and married, not whom I expected, far from it. I guess he is suited. I know I am.*

*You can tell Annie I keep pretty good watch of the marriages in the Mt. Carroll Mirror, but do not take notice of hers as yet.*

*Oh! I must let you know. One of our boys got a sixty day furlough. There was a squad of 9 men that went out in the Country to pick up cattle for beef. While they were out, they were attacked by a squad of rebs. The boys gave fight & whiped the rebs, killed 2 & wounded the Captain. The rebs captured one of our boys (who had his horse shot) & took him clear in the rear of the reble army, 12 miles south of Atlanta, and was under guard by to men, who thought he was not liable to get away. Went one morning about geting their breakfast, supposing all was right & in the mean time, our boy sneaked away*

*from them & made his way safe into our lines. On his way home, he saw all the rebs works & went & reported to Gen Thomas who had him draw a plot of the works, so near perfect that the Gen wrote Col Atkins an order & sent it with the man to make out said furlough and forward it to him to be sighned. Bully for him, I say, dont you think he deserved it. Dress parade now, so I will close for this time.*
*Your Affectionate Husband.*
*E. M. Swaggart*

In late July, the camp moved from Resaca to Calhoun where the brigade camped in the field until August 2 when they received orders to move forward.[201] Eugene seized the opportunity to write Elvira another letter. Prisoners were coming through the camp in vast numbers and Eugene believed General Sherman was in Atlanta.

*Calhoun                              July 26$^{th}$ 1864*
*Dear Wife*
*With pleasure I embrace the opportunity of writing you. This is the 3$^{rd}$ time since receiving one from you. I am well and hope these few lines will find you & baby enjoying the same.*
*We left Resaca yesterday and came to this place. Calhoun is a nice little place. It has been, in time of peace, a buying town.*
*Bushwhackers have been pretty whise for several days. We heard of regiments of them, yesterday, & I guess we will go for em shortly.*
*Sherman has Atlanta. He sent 900 prisoners by here today.*
*We have had no news from Grant lately. I suppose, though, he is doing well enough. I am willing to*

---

[201] Major Albert Woodcock, *The Official Records of the War of the Rebellion, Reports, Army of the Cumberland,* No. 427, Second Report, p. 898

beleave it all of him. I guess he can flax them, give him time enough.

We have pretty hot weather, but not as hot as we will have next month. Crops in this country, that the armys did not destroy, are looking very good. I wish crops looked half as good North. I fear here will be hard times, both in the Army and at home, but I am still in hopes that the Army will be disbanded this fall or winter. In regard to my time, I can bet little whether the war closes in 2 years or not. I am willing to serve my little year. You know & I know that I should be at home now and never ought to been away. Well, I guess there will be some drafting, then, before long. I tell you, wont some of them Copperheads hunt their holes fast. Oh, what a poor pen.

The news has just come that Sherman has captured 11,000 prisoners, some say more and some say less, but I guess he has a pile of them. We hold one part of Atlanta, & the rebels, part.

I mailed 2 of our military papers to Moses today. They do not contain much, but you can see what they are like.

I have just fell heir to an old mare that has been in our Co. ever since we were mounted. It is the one that I told Moses, looked so much like Poll.

My bunky was detailed to go to the front for a regular scout. Bill Skilling says to give Vira his love. He is well and makes a pretty good soldier for $402, as the boys say. Wait is well. He recd a letter from Ed yesterday. Tell James Becker I should like to hear from him. I have writen twice since he wrote me.

There is rumor in Camp that we will move camp tomorrow. Where we turn up next will be hard to

*tell, at presant. Give my love to all. Kiss the baby for papa. As ever, your Affectionate Husband*
*E. M. Swaggart*

On July 28, the Ninety-second Illinois Mounted Infantry was still in Calhoun. In answer to two letters, Eugene mailed another letter to Salem. Unlike before, he was not sure General Sherman had taken Atlanta, but he thought things were going well anyway.

At home, the farm was not producing as it had in the past and Elvira finally decided she had to go to work. Pay was not coming through from Eugene and she had a child and one on the way to support. Eugene was concerned when he wrote to her.

*Calhoun Ga.                                July $28^{th}$ 64*
*Dear Wife*
*I will try and answer your more than welcome letters, one of July $3^{rd}$ & one the $21^{st}$, both mailed the $22^{nd}$. They found me enjoying good health & hope this will find you the same.*
*I wrote to you a short time ago. I wrote Jennie today in care of J. W. Shinkle. Was that right? I had forgotten the number of his box. I cannot see why James M. Becker does not write anymore. He certainly has time enough. Probably he has other fish to fry. In regard to writing Moses, I have writen to you at every oppotunity and thought that would answer as long as we are on the go so much. I mailed 2 of our papers to Moses. Those letters that you spoke of were of no importance, only I should not like to have my composition exposed to strangers.*
*I am very sorry that you have to go out to work. I hope it will not be the case long. We have musterd for pay, but will not get it untill the $1^{st}$ of Sept. There will be $96.00 coming to us if we are paid*

clear up. My Furlough arrangement was heavy on me. Besides, I have something over twenty dollars that I could not collect the last pay day which I was going to send you.

I am sorry crops are so very poor. There is going to be hard times if this little mess is not dryed soon, thats whats the matter.

You say you think the news is not very encouraging to you. I think it is Bully good news from our Army. Old Billy Sherman has been flaxin old Hood nicely the last few days. We did not get any news from the front yesterday nor today. Cant tell whether we have Atlanta or whether the rebs holds it. One thing certain, if we have not got it, it was not because we could not get it.

Vira, I wish you to not get discouraged now. You have stood it like a major 2 years. Try and stand it 1 more & all will be well, if we are spared so long. I wrote to you in my other that I had recd your photo & liked them very much indeed.

The letter you mailed me at Fair Haven has not come in yet. I guess it is absent without leave. Oh! I wish I could see you and Georgie, once in awhile. I could soldier then, good. Well, only one year more. Bully for this year, I say, dont you. Tattoo has sounded so I must close until morning. Good night.

It is $29^{th}$. Again, I will wind up. We are having very nice weather at presant, cool as we could expect in Illinois. Give my love to Sylvester, Mother & all the family. I remain, as ever, Your Loving Husband.

E. M. Swaggart

P. S. I will send you a little money in my next.

I will write to Annie in a few days. Tell her she must not wait for me to write, just send always, the mail.

At 5:00 A.M., on the morning of August 2, the brigade moved out toward Atlanta. Company I of the Ninety-second Illinois skirmished with a rebel squad when they reached Glasses Bridge. The brigade camped in Cartersville for the night.

The march resumed the following morning to a creek four miles south of Allatoona, on the Sandtown Road, where they camped for the night. The following day found them on the Chattahoochee River, four miles above Sandtown, where pickets and scouts went out until August 9. The Ninety-second Illinois Mounted Infantry, along with their brigade, moved forward to the front and guarded the right flank of the Army. They heard fighting in front of them and rebel soldiers were all around. There were constant skirmishes for several days, but on Sunday, it stopped. Both armies observed the Sabbath. Later in the afternoon, the fighting resumed.[202]

*Aug 7th 1864*                      *In Camp in Ga.*
*Dear Wife*
*With pleasure I once more attempt to write you. I am well and hope these few lines will find you and Georgie the same.*
*We are now on the front at the extreme right of the Army, protecting its flank. We are about 12 miles southwest of Atlanta. There has been very hard fighting for the past two days. This morning it stoped. I guess because it is the sabbath.*
*Today is 3 months since this campaign opened and not yet ended. The rebs say will not end till they gain their Independance. I fear they are mistaken.*
*It is warm enough to roast meat in the sun. One thing we are blessed with is plenty of rain that you know, it keeps from being so bad.*

---

[202] *Illinois Troops (Union) Infantry, Records of Events, Volume 13, 92nd Illinois Infantry, 1862-1865,* p. 549 and Major Albert Woodcock, *The Official Records of the War of the Rebellion, Reports, Army of the Cumberland, No. 427, Second Report,* p. 898

*Our mail has come in but none for me. You have not written if Tommy Lego hears from Henry or not. I wish you would if you can hear from him. The 15$^{th}$ is not very far from us now but do not know exactly where.*

*Wait Downs is not very well at presant. He is still with the company. Health is very bad throughout the regiment. When sick call blows now, there will be 2 or 3 report when a year ago 15 or 20 would report every morning.*

*Some of our boys were in a cornfield this morning, for shucks for their horses, and were drove out by the rebs. We can see them every hour of the day from camp. It seems as though the whole country was alive with the Johnnies and the largest portion of the reble army has gone to bushwhacking.*

*Artillery is booming again. They have forgotten that it is Sunday. However, I suppose that there is but little respect paid to such things in a time like this. We have divine services in our regt. once a week, sometimes oftener. Our old chaplain is very punctual. If ever there was a good man, he is one, sure.*

*Well, I suppose you know, by this time, how the grain is going to yield. I hear from our Town in Wisconsin, which will not have 30 bushels of wheat in it.*

*We heard the officers say that Petersburg was in our hands. We have not heard anything to the contrary, yet. I only hope that it is true.*

After an explosion in a mineshaft designed to create a crater where a troop of African Union soldiers could enter, the Confederates, who lost close to three hundred men, trained artillery on the hole. White soldiers entered first but were repelled. African soldiers sent in were "cut to pieces". By the ninth, the siege was quiet and the damage repaired. The Confederates still held Petersburg.[203]

Aug. 7$^{th}$ cont.

> *If you hear it reported that Atlanta is ours, you need not beleave it, for it is neither ours nor the rebs. I guess there is not a living thing in the city, but, unless it be mice & rats. I guess they are kept pretty much confined to their holes.*
> *My love to Mother, Annie & all the married folks in general. Kiss my boy & accept much love from*
> *you loving Husband*
> *Mack*

The morning of August 9 found the Ninety-second Illinois, along with the brigade, moving in the direction of Sandtown. When the brigade reached the river, they demonstrated crossing the river to deceive the enemy forces. Shots were traded with the rebel forces across the river. The artillery shelled Sandtown. When night fell, the brigade moved back a mile and camped. The next morning, they returned to their previous campground, where they stayed until the morning of August 12.

Orders went out for all regiments to report for an inspection by General Judson Kilpatrick. After inspection, they returned the five miles to camp. The next day contained the usual duties. Lieutenant G. R. Skinner, the Brigade Inspector, called a second inspection on August 14.

Action began again on August 15 when the brigade moved with the division to throw out a pontoon bridge across the Chattahoochee River. The troops crossed at noon, moving in the direction of the Atlanta and West Point railroad where Lieutenant Colonel Robert Klein of the First Brigade commanded a strike force. The division arrived at Fairburn, opposite Sandtown, and camped at the Bethel Church. Along the way, they drove the enemy, killing, wounding and capturing several.

---

[203] World Almanac Publication, *The Civil War Almanac*, Intro. by Henry Steele Commager, A Bison Book, New York, NY 1983, pp. 217 & 219

At dawn of morning, the brigade marched to the Atlanta and Macon Railroad, between Atlanta and East Point. They were hoping to find Brigadier General William Jackson's rebel division, but had no luck and returned to Sandtown after crossing the river. On August 17, the brigade stayed in camp near the Chattahoochee River.[204]

*In Camp on The Chattahoocha River*
*August 17$^{th}$ 1864*
*Dear Wife*
*With much pleasure do I seat myself to ans. yours of July 31$^{st}$, which I recd. sometime ago, for which, I ask your forgiveness for not writing sooner. I had just mailed you a letter when I recd yours and thought I would put off writing for a day or two & it has been weeks instead. I am well as usual & hope this will find you & baby well.*
*Vira, our good time is over, laying around in the rear. We are now at the front, rebs on every side of us. We are on the Extreem right of the army, where the dirty rebs are a considerable trouble to us. We came in of a scout raid yesterday & will go on another tomorrow. We seldom have more than 2 days & one nights rest at a time.*
*Our mail was all gobled yesterday on the way from Marietta to us, so I will not look for any mail from home in sometime to come. Our rations consist, now, of hard tack & coffee. We are so far away from the R R that we cannot get any sow belly & it makes pretty dry living. Corn has plaid out. It has got too hard for us to eat.*
*The poorest country I ever saw in my life is here. It is 30 miles from one house to the next.*

---

[204] Major Albert Woodcock, *The Official Records of the War of the Rebellion, Reports, Army of the Cumberland, No. 427, Second Report*, p. 898, covered all action from August 9$^{th}$ to August 17$^{th}$.

*The mail goes away immediately so I will close. I hope to write more next time. My love to all*
*Your loving Husband*
*E. Mc Swaggart*
*P. S. I have ten dollars to send you, but where we are, it is not safe to send you it. I do not think we will be so far away from the railroad long. Then I will send it.*
*E. Swaggart*
*Excuse blank paper as my thoughts are absent and the mail goes out soon.*

## Chapter Fifteen
## Atlanta is Ours

General Judson Kilpatrick began his cavalry raid around Atlanta on 18 August. The Third Brigade, including the Ninety-second Illinois Mounted Infantry, played a part in his raid. Lieutenant Colonel Robert H. King reported that the brigade "moved from camp on the North bank of the Chattahoochee River on the evening of the eighteenth, moving in the direction of the railroad leading from Atlanta to West Point."[205]

Major Albert Woodcock, commanding the regiment of the Ninety-second Illinois Mounted Infantry wrote "regiment had the advance of the column as it moved out from Sandtown in the evening. Companies D, E, K, in charge of Captain M. Van Buskirk, acted as advance guard. These companies skirmished with and charged the enemy's scouts and pickets during the entire night, driving them steadily before them. One rebel died, several wounded, and five captured. Company D had one man wounded slightly in the foot and Company K had a horse shot."[206]

At 3:00 A.M., the remainder of the division started in the direction of McDonough and Fosterville. When they reached Jonesboro, a station on the Macon Railroad, at 8:00 P.M., they crossed the railroad and proceeded, under orders, to tear up the railroad for several miles. While they were working, heavy enemy fire started in front of the Second Brigade and the Third Brigade hastened to their aid. The firing stopped and the Third Brigade formed, slightly to the left and partially in the rear of the brigades commanded by Colonel Minty and Colonel Long. The center of the Third Brigade, which included the Ninety-second Illinois, was behind barricades with one side protected by heavy timber and the other resting on the railroad itself. Their orders

---

[205] Lt. Col. Robert H. King, *The Official Records of the War of the Rebellion, Reports, Army of the Cumberland,* No. 424, p. 893
[206] Major Albert Woodcock, *Official Records,* No. 427, pp. 896-897

were to form for a charge. During the night, the enemy tried unsuccessfully to dislodge the Union command.[207]

Morning of the twentieth found the regiment of the Ninety-second Illinois "thrown out on the left flank," guarding the division traveling in the direction of the Flint River. As they neared the river, "the column halted and fed". Companies A, G, H, and I, along with a detachment of the Third Kentucky, had orders to proceed to the river and cross the bridge of the Flint River three miles south of Jonesboro. They were under the command of Captain John M. Schermerhorn. The bridge was down and the ford blockaded. On their way back to report the problem to the division, they skirmished briefly with the rebels.

The Ninety-second Illinois moved in advance, under orders of the brigade, to tear up and burn the railroad track. At Lovejoy Station, an attack on the division came from the south end of town. The Ninety-second Illinois moved forward to keep the rebel forces from advancing in that direction. They held the enemy in check until the rest of the command mounted and formed to march. At 3:00 A.M. of the twenty-first, they moved out, leaving one dead on the field.

All day, the regiment was frequently in the line of battle but not fired upon until they charged the rebel forces. In the charge, the rebel lines broke, but several of them rallied and charged the Union ambulances. The left column, of the Ninety-second Illinois, near the ambulance train at that time, wheeled around, charged and drove the enemy away from the train.

That night, the companies of B, C, and I were advance guard to the regiment that was leading the division. Captain Egbert Q. E. Becker was in command. Frequently, they charged the enemy, capturing one prisoner.

Upon reaching McDonough, Captain Van Buskirk of the Ninety-second Illinois and Captain Cummings of the Third Kentucky, each with one hundred men, received orders to proceed to and hold South Bridge. Captain Matthew Van Buskirk took the lead, with fifty of his men. In approximately one mile, they ran into a body of rebels and chased them for

---

[207] Lt. Col. Robert H. King, *The Official Records of the War of the Rebellion, Reports, Army of the Cumberland, No. 424*, pp. 893-894

three miles, driving them from the area. They took the bridge at 9:00 P.M. and held it until 2:00 A.M. when an infantry brigade relieved them. Losses suffered were one private killed, one lieutenant wounded, and four privates wounded with one sergeant and two privates missing.[208]

A tired division returned to camp without incident where they stayed for several days, resting up. On the twenty-fourth, word came that the postmaster had been captured.[209] Knowing Elvira worried, Eugene wrote to her.

*In Camp on Chattahoocha      Aug 24th 1864*
*Dear Wife*
*Once more, I am, Thank God, permited to write you. I am well, as to health, but never was so tired in my life. We have just came in of a raid & have not had time to recruit up much yet. I have had no mail from you in nearly 4 weeks. Our mail has been captured 2 or 3 times & it appears as though mine was among the lost. I dont care a darn, if you are only well. If the rebs wants my mail worse than I do, let them have it. We capture theirs everytime we can & they ours, turn about fair play.*
*Well, I suppose I ought to say something about our great raid, although you will see accounts of it in all the papers, as it is the first of the kind ever made. We, the 3d Div., with 2 Brigads of the 2nd Div., Brigadier Genl. Killpatrick in command, started from the right wing of our army & went clear around their army, tore up all their Rail Roads, burned a great many stores & took a few prisoners & fought them all the time on all sides of us & came*

---

[208] Major Albert Woodcock, *The Official Records of the War of the Rebellion, Reports, Army of the Cumberland, No. 427*, p. 897, All information concerning August 20 & 21.
[209] Charles E. Cort, *Dear Friends, The Civil War Letters and Diary of Charles Edwin Cort*, Helyn W. Tomlinson, ed., n.p., 1962, p. 153

back all right, for which we should all feel very thankfull.
Our loss in the regt. was 9 killed & captured. In the whole expedition was 270. All our wagons & 2 ambulances were lost by fording a river. Our company is all well.
There is a camp rumor that our Brigade is to go to the rear again, to drive old Wheeler away from our hard tack line. I hope it is true. I have got enough of the front to last me some time.
War news, we get none atall, I might say, only what we see for ourselves, and that you know is very little. I have not seen a paper in 2 weeks, except the Mirror which came in our last mail & it had nothing in it, as usual. We are looking for the paymaster soon. I hope he will come before we moove again.
Vira, I am writing this on reble paper, genuine reb, as I had bad luck with my stationary, paper, pens & ink, so you will excuse this. I will close this miserable sheet. Give my love to all. Accept as much as you like for yourself.
I remain as ever
Your loving Husband
E. M. Swaggart

August 26 came with orders to prepare to move out again. Eugene, back from scouting, wanted to get a letter off.

*In Camp on Chattahoocha River August 26$^{th}$ 1864*
*Dear Wife*
*As I have a few leasure minutes, I will pass them in writing to you. I am well & hope these few lines may find you enjoying the same great blessing. I received a letter from you today, but was pretty old, still better than none. I was glad to hear Georgie was getting better. I trust he will get over them. I*

*wish I was with the dear little fellow and his dear Ma. I would be happy once more.*

*Well, one more long year & our time is up. I mailed a letter for you yesterday. I just got it mailed when the whole Division had to go on a scout. We went out about 6 miles, layed in the brush all night, & then returned to Camp. We expect lively times now for awhile as the whole army is on a moove of some kind. I guess Sherman is going to try another of his favorite flank moovements. Well, I will have to close for today.*

Eugene did not mail the letter. He just stuck it in his pack, hoping to complete it soon. He hated to leave space on precious paper.

At midnight, the regiment moved out toward the Atlanta and West Point Railroad again. They crossed Camp Creek and stopped for what remained of the night at Bethel Church, holding a barricaded position.

At daylight, the division moved once more to the railroad between Red Oak and Fairburn where they struck the railroad and the enemy cavalry attacked them. All the regiments in the division engaged with the enemy, and the Ninety-second Illinois, under orders, took the hill near the railroad and held it. While taking the hill, Lieutenant Cooling of Company B was wounded slightly. At 11:00 A.M., a regiment of infantry relieved the Ninety-second Illinois and they took a position on the right where they threw up breastworks to protect the guns before going into camp. The Ninety-second Illinois spent the rest of the day and the following on pickets and guarding the railroad.

On the thirtieth, all hell broke loose for the $92^{nd}$ Illinois Mounted Infantry. Told to take the lead to Jonesboro, they skirmished all the way, steadily driving the Confederates before them until they neared Bethsaida Church where the enemy barricaded behind heavy rails. The Ninety-second Illinois charged with one Battalion, reported Major Albert Woodcock, through "dense, almost impenetrable wood" into an open field.

"Not a man hesitated, but all went in with a yell, and poured into the enemy a deadly volley the moment he reached the barricade." The enemy fled, but left twelve of their soldiers behind them, dead. The Ninety-second Illinois had one private killed and First Lieutenant James Dawson of Company H severely wounded.

The regiment then proceeded in "advance of the infantry skirmishers, driving the rebels steadily until they neared Flint River," where the rebels held the bridge and east bank. The Ninety-second Illinois Mounted Infantry dismounted and charged. The rebels fled leaving the river and bridge in the possession of the Ninety-second Illinois. After mounting, they crossed the river and moved south until southwest of Jonesboro where the Confederates lined up on a hill. The Ninety-second Illinois dismounted again and charged the hill, driving them back to their breastworks. Darkness fell and it was difficult to determine how many of the rebels were in front of them, but the soldiers felt outnumbered. They persevered under heavy crossfire until they ran out of ammunition and withdrew. Their loss was two, dead, and twenty wounded including Lieutenant Oscar F. Sammis.[210]

Major General Oliver O. Howard, who saw the charge take place "complimented the men by telling them he had never witnessed a more brilliant charge."[211] Colonel Eli Murray stated in his report, "Here was a most bloody conflict, and here so well and so manfully did our men do their work, charging a hill held possession of by the enemy, and under a heavy cross-fire, after ammunition was expended, holding it until ordered to withdraw; engaged thirty minutes with two hundred men........The part taken and the noble bearing of these men is a source of just pride, for which too much praise cannot be given them."[212]

---

[210] Colonel Eli Murray, *The Official Records of the War of the Rebellion, Reports, Army of the Cumberland, No. 422*, p. 890 and Major Albert Woodcock, *Official Records, No. 427*, p. 897, covers from midnight 27th through the 30th.
[211] Thomas M. Eddy, *The Patriotism of Illinois, A Record of the Civil and Military History of the State, Chapter XXII, Regimental Sketches, Ninety-second Illinois Infantry*, 1865, p. 373
[212] Murray, *Official Records, No. 422*, p. 890-891

At dawn on August 31, the division held in reserve crossed the river to provide relief. They returned across the river with the men that fought the day before and had breakfast. After breakfast, they moved to Anthony's Bridge where the Fifth Kentucky and Company I of the Ninety-second Illinois remained in reserve. While there, General Pat R. Cleburne's rebel infantry attacked them. The engagement was severe and again, ammunition exhausted. The Union forces had to fall back until relieved by the brigade.[213] Other companies of the Ninety-second Illinois "engaged at Harris Bridge". The "Color Corporal" was hit and two privates died.[214]

The first of September was quiet and on the second, at 10:00 A.M., Colonel Smith D. Atkins returned from his leave to retake his command of the Ninety-second Illinois Mounted Infantry. After a long rest, he recuperated and decided not to retire from service but to rejoin his troops.

The Ninety-second Illinois Mounted Infantry was on their way to Glasses Bridge near Lovejoy Station, moving in advance of the division. At the bridge, a rebel picket waited, but was quickly driven away but not before they destroyed the bridge so it could not be crossed. The ford was full of "fallen trees" but one company quickly forded by foot and guarded while the others cleared the ford. The regiment crossed and moved to Bear Creek Station and Lovejoy's Road. The Ninety-second Illinois returned across the river and held it in spite of considerable skirmishing.[215]

They remained at Glass Bridge on the third until late in the afternoon when the division returned, crossing the river. They covered the crossing and moved in behind to guard the right flank of the Army. Right after they moved into position, the enemy engaged with artillery shells. Several horses died in the barrage of shells, but Colonel Atkins and the Ninety-second Illinois stayed firm. At night, the "brigade moved in on rear and right flank of the rebel army, joining the division of the

---

[213] Colonel Eli Murray, *The Official Records of the War of the Rebellion, Army of the Cumberland, Official Reports, No. 422*, p. 891
[214] Major Albert Woodcock, *Official Records*, p. 899
[215] Colonel Smith D. Atkins, *Official Records, No. 425*, p. 894

Seventeenth Army Corps near Lovejoy Station," a position held until the fifth, on pickets and scouting heavily.[216]

Unknown to the soldiers of the Ninety-second Illinois, on September 4, 1864, General John Hunt Morgan of the Confederate Army, who had plagued them so over the years, was shot and killed in Greenville, Tennessee as he tried to escape from a trap.[217]

At 3:00 A.M. of the fifth, the Ninety-second Illinois moved as rear guard of the brigade to Anthony's Bridge, near Jonesboro, and at 3:00 A.M. of the sixth, proceeded into the camp on the north side. At 7:00 A.M., they covered the crossing of the Seventeenth Army Corps from a position behind barricades. As soon as the Seventeenth Army Corps crossed, the Ninety-second destroyed the bridge and the ford as ordered by General Kilpatrick. At 4:00 P.M., they returned to camp after leaving the left wing of the regiment to picket the bridge. Early the next morning, on 8 September, the picket took fire from a Confederate picket and a small skirmish developed. However, by 8:00 A.M. they were ready to proceed to the West Point railroad with the brigade. They stayed there until September 28.[218]

On September 11, General Sherman and General Hood entered a truce for ten days. The purpose of the truce was to allow private citizens to leave Atlanta.[219]

Eugene found his letter he started on August 27 and finished writing to Elvira.

*Sept. 12<sup>th</sup>*
*In camp 9 miles South West of Atlanta*
*Dear Wife*
*I will now try & finish my letter, which you will see commenced a long time ago & have not had the*

---

[216] Colonel Eli Murray, *The Official Records of the War of the Rebellion, Reports, Army of the Cumberland, No. 422*, p. 891
[217] World Almanac Publication, *The Civil War Almanac*, Intro. by Henry Steele Commager, A Bison Book, New York, NY 1983, p. 222
[218] Colonel Smith D. Atkins. *Official Records, No. 425*, pp. 894-895
[219] *The Civil War Almanac*, p. 223

*time since to write. I am well, as fat as ever, if any thing a little fatter, as sweet potatoes are plenty.*
*The day after we left the Chattahoocha River, I recd a letter from you, was glad to hear that the boy was all right again.*

a letter from you. was glad to hear that the boy was all right again. Well we have had a hard time for the last 3 weeks & a pretty serious one too however Atlanta is Ours the Confedrates Gate City as it opened to all their supplyes & munitions of war, besides the taking of the City the reble army got the worst whipping they have ever got yet Their loss was very heavy & ours right so the reverse. Our Division was on the extreme right & in the front as our army swung around to the right so you see that put us in a place where we had to go for every thing that came in front of us in our Div. there is 9 Regs.

*Well we have had a hard time for the last 3 weeks & a pretty serious one to, however **ATLANTA is OURS**. The Confederates Gate City, as it opened to all their supplys & munitions of war. Besides the taking of the city, the reble army got the worst whipping they have ever got yet. Their loss was very heavy & ours, right so, the reverse. Our Division was on the extreme right, so you see, that put us in a place where we had to go for everything that came in front of us. In our Div., there is 9 Regts., so they say, but I cant see them when there is any danger. Our regiment was in the advance every day & night for nearly a week and when our army fell back to Atlanta, the 92sters were in the rear, so you see we make good guards for the Cavalry. Our loss in regt. is some 40 killed & wounded.*
*The 3d Ky lost 3 or 4 men is all the loss our Div. had.*
*The $92^{nd}$ mustered for pay today. I guess it will come soon. I will write again in a day or so, when I get my bunk & shebang all fixed up.*
*Give my love to Ma & Annie, Dicky & Moses, John & Mollie. Kiss Georgie for me.*
*I remain your loving Husband*
*E. M. Swaggart*

    The Ninety-second Illinois Mounted Infantry was still busy with pickets and scouts. They were on duty nearly every day. However, it was easier duty and the soldiers welcomed it.

    Back home, the draft called John Miller. He left his wife and children for Elizabeth Reynolds but she did not care as much for him as he did for her. He left Mt. Carroll in a huff without telling anyone good-bye, including his family. The One Hundred Forty-sixth Illinois Infantry formed on August 29, 1864, and he, as well as James Becker left with the unit. Both were in Company A. The One Hundred Forty-sixth Illinois Infantry was a unit not destined to fight. Their assignment was to "guard the draftees and substitutes at Camp Butler, Illinois."[220] Eugene thought the service would be a good place for John Miller where he might learn to appreciate his home and family.

*Sept 26th 1864          Camp in Ga. near east point*
*Dear Wife*
*Once more, I will try and write you a fiew lines in ans to two of yours, one of Aug 27th, one of Sep 10th. I would have written before, but was on duty everyday, so I could not.*
*We have got our Camp and Quarters fixed up, jointly well, & pickets start at three days at one time, so you see we will have more time than we have had here before.*
*I am not sick now, but will be, if uncle does not give me some sow belly. He says he will give it to us again, the first of next month. We are looking for the man, what is to pay us. Our pay rolls are all made out. I guess we will be paid soon.*
*Cap Eg has applied for some leave of absence. If he gets it, I will send money by him.*
*I am glad you have the chance of staying with Dicky. Save your oats & corn, or sell it. Do just what think is best. If you can get along and keep it till spring, it will bring more, but you will need all you can scrape up to winter yourself & babies on.*
*You say John went away & said nothing to nobody. He must of went off mad. Wait till he soldiers awhile. He will soon think of home & no other place.*
*I do think you have had a hard time getting along and am sorry I could not send you money before this, but it is impossible for me to get a cent that is*

---

[220] Arthur Robbe and Richard Hinton, Booklet from *Rededication Ceremony of the Carroll County Civil War Soldiers and Sailors Monument*, p. 19

owing to me and by going home, you know, put me in debt enough to take four months pay, but that is all on the square now.

You say you are looking for Jennie in 5 or 6 weeks, but do not say when she is, so I cannot write anymore. I am glad she is going to live with you this winter. I shall feel just as well, on your account, as if I were there myself, & ten times more so.

I do not hear much about Sylvester anymore. Where has he been & what is he doing. He had better lay low or he will be drafted yet.

There is considerable talk of the Illinois & Indiana troops going home to vote. I cant hardly believe it. I dont believe I should go, if it was to be our luck. I never want to travel that old road, but once more & then, I want my own time to come back. In 11 months, I will want to go, but not to vote exactly. My president is elected already.

Co. I is all well & I believe all that is in the Company, we have only 19 privates for duty. I guess we will draw some horses before long. Then we will have more men for duty. Well, I guess I'd as well close for this time. Probably by the next, I will have something to write of more importance.

I heard that Henry Lego was wounded, but not dangerously. Give my love to Ma & Annie and Dicky & Jes. Kiss Georgie for me.

As ever your loving          Mc Swaggart

## Chapter Sixteen
## In Pursuit of Hood

General John B. Hood, of the Confederate Army, pulled south to Lovejoy's Station as he left Atlanta. However, on September 18, 1864, he moved northward along the Western and Atlantic railroad, hoping to destroy the communication line to the North used by General William T. Sherman. Another Confederate general, General Joseph Wheeler was also in northern Georgia trying to destroy the railroad. By October 1, General Sherman was convinced that General Hood was moving toward Marietta, Georgia to attempt to tear up the railroad south of the Etowah River. On October 3, General Sherman and his army moved toward Marietta.[221] The Ninety-second Illinois Mounted Infantry was with General Sherman's army, hoping to find General Hood.

On October 3, the Ninety-second Illinois, Company I, engaged the enemy at Noyes Creek.[222] Later, there was a severe engagement at Powder Springs where a large number of men were killed or wounded.[223]

As the army moved forward, on October 5, there was a battle at Allatoona with heavy losses on both sides, but the Ninety-second Illinois was not involved. After the battle, General Hood proceeded past Dallas and Van Wert.[224] On October 10, one of his pickets met the Ninety-second Illinois in Van Wert and after a short skirmish, they were repulsed.[225] General Hood moved on, striking the railroad north of Resaca. His destructive path proceeded on to Tunnel Hill through Dalton to Villanow moving

---

[221] Frank J. Welcher, *The Union Army, 1861-1865, Organization & Operations, Volume II, Western Theater*, Indiana University Press, Bloomington & Indianapolis, 1993, pp. 583-584

[222] *Illinois Troops (Union) Infantry, Records of Events, Volume 13, 92$^{nd}$ Illinois Infantry, Company I*, p. 549 – referred to Noyes Creek as Nose Creek.

[223] Thomas M. Eddy, *The Patriotism of Illinois, A Record of the Civil and Military History of the State, Chapter XXII, Regimental Sketches, Ninety-second Illinois Infantry*, 1865, p. 373

[224] Welcher, *The Union Army, Western Theater*, p. 584

[225] *Records of Events*, p. 549

toward LaFayette, Georgia.[226] General Sherman, with part of his Army, pursued General Hood's Army on to Gaylesville, Alabama, arriving there on October 20. He stayed in Gaylesville until the end of the month, but the Ninety-second Illinois stayed behind in Georgia with the brigade of General Judson Kilpatrick, to guard the river.

Eugene wrote to Elvira from a campsite near the Etowah River eleven miles from Cartersville, Georgia.

*Monday Oct 24<sup>th</sup> 1864*
*Dear Wife*
*Once more, thank Providence, I have the opportunity of writing you. I am well & hope these lines will find you & boy enjoying the same. I have not heard from you since the last of Sept & I know you have not, from me, for the R.R. has been tore up for nearly a month, but Mr. Hood, with his host, are driven away off in Alabam & our Road is all right again.*
*We have never seen soldiering before, untill the last month. We have went night & day most of this month. We are in camp now 11 miles S. West of Cartersvill . That place is where the road crosses the Ettawah river. How long we stay here is more than I can tell. We have not done much fighting. Still, we have done some. Our loss in the regt this month, killed, is 8 & 3 or 4 wounded & as many more gobbled. We lost one man out of Co. I. His name is Baltzer Apple[227] from Black Oak. He was captured at Van Wert.*

---

[226] Frank J. Welcher, *The Union Army, 1861-1865, Organization & Operations, Volume II, Western Theater,* Indiana University Press, Bloomington & Indianapolis, 1993, p. 584
[227] Balsar Apple, 92<sup>nd</sup> Illinois Infantry, Co. I, mustered out on 6-3-65. Arthur Robbe and Richard Hinton, Booklet from *Rededication Ceremony of the Carroll County Civil War Soldiers & Sailors Monument.*

*Oct 25$^{th}$*
*I recd a letter from you last night, never was so glad to hear from you before. You said in your letter that you had not recd any letters from me in 3 wks. I hope the time will not come again, while I am in the service, that we cannot correspond. The time is only 10 months, you know.*
*War news is good from all parts. Sherman, they say, is giving Mr. Hood fits. The Armies are both in Alabama. There is a rumor that our Division is to be releaved and back to the rear to reorganize. I should like a little rest & camp life once more, only we would miss our good living.*
*Oh, I must tell you what we live on, & have, all fall. In the first place, we draw from U. S., salt & coffee. 2$^{nd}$, we forage the rest of the country, which is full of nice fat hogs and an acre or two of sweet potatoes, on every farm. I have dug several that had young Chinamen hanging to the roots. Since we can get by the barrel, the people make more of it than we can use, so we leave a little, great country for honey. I wish you could just step around and take dinner with me today. Maby you think I could not get up a good one.*
*Well, I was saying, we would be releaved. If we are, we will be paid, but will not be untill we are. We have 8 months due now. I do not know what you will do without money. There is no money here I can get. The boys are all straped, or I could send you some. As for my self, I need none atall. If there is anything we want in this country, we simply go and get it & tell them to book it to Uncle Sam. If you can borrow, some do it. I think we will be paid in the course of a month and I will send it.*
*You told me not to forget and say something about some Shirts. I do not know what you mean by that.*

*Please explain. Sylvester has bought him a farm. Bully for him, if he has the filthy lucre to back it up, he is all right. Give my love to him & Jennie. Tell Jennie I have never recd that letter nor photo yet. My love to Mother & Annie & all Every body I remain your devoted     Mack*

The Ninety-second Illinois Mounted Infantry moved to Marietta, Georgia before the end of the month, along with General Judson Kilpatrick's Third Cavalry Division of the Cavalry Corps. They spent the next two weeks in preparation for a move. Their horses were tired, as were the soldiers. New mounts were issued to the other regiments but not to the Ninety-second Illinois so Eugene assumed the Ninety-second would rest for a while. He looked forward to that possibility.

*Marietta Ga                              Oct 31$^{st}$ 1864*
*Dear Wife*
*With pleasure, I seat myself to ans to yours of the 4$^{th}$, which came by Luit McRea. Was sorry to hear of your ill health, but hope your complaint will proove nothing fatal.*
*I am well as usual, with the exception of a bad cold. I will get over that in a day or two. You wished to know why I do not write oftener. The reason is that our communications are cut about half the time, or we are on the march. I pledge you my word that I write as often as I can. That is all I can do.*
*We sighned the payrolls the 28$^{th}$ and expect our pay in a day or so.*
*Henry Holt is here, but I have not seen him since I have been here. I guess I will see him today. H. S. Bradley is here & Charley Holt also. I saw Bradley yesterday. He looks fine. I suppose you have heard that the old 15$^{th}$ was all captured but a very few.*

*Old Braureguard & Hood are in middle Tenn. and are making their way for Ohio. Somebody will be hurt before he gets back. It is a death struggle with them. They will eather compel Sherman to fall back, or get their entire Army annihilated.*

*We are now south of the whole reble Army & still, we get our regular Tack, but the good fare I was telling you about has pretty much paid out. We can get forage of the Country by going 15 & 20 miles.*

*I should like very much to hear my boy sing papa. You say is it possible that we only have 11 months to serve, yes, only 10.*

*Do not feel any way alarmed, but we will rest & have good quarters, if the Johnnies will not pester us. Our Division has all the old broken down horses in this Department and the other two Divisions have drawn new ones. Therefore, we will be releaved, in a measure, from active field duty, probably untill spring. There is no geting at these things close, you know.*

*Do not send me any shirts. I can get shirts from Govt. for one half what they would cost there and are good enough for any Lincoln man to weare, thats whats the matter.*

*In regards to the command, you was mistaken in the time in which I was to take it, by about 12 months, thats all, My Dear.*

*Mrs. Steams sees the good of eloping by this time.*

*Vira, if there should be another time this winter that you do not get your letters from me, regular, do not think that I am neglecting you. That would kill me to have you entertaining such thoughts. I know you do not. There has been times that I did not receive one single word from you in a month, but I knew that it was not Dear Viras fault.*

*Richmond is not ours, yet, as I know of, but am looking for the great fall everyday. I trust you will understand the mail. I think I have said enough for this time. My Love to Jennie & Vet. Kiss the boy good by.*
          *As ever, your devoted Husband*
*Mc*
*P. S. Send me nothing, if you please.*
*Mack*

    In October, General Sherman presented a plan for a "march to the sea", hitting Savannah. General Grant approved it on November 2, 1964. He immediately began refurbishing his army for the move.[228] His theory of war was to destroy the "South's will to fight" by using military demonstrations against Confederate civilians as well as the Confederate Army.[229]

    All of the men picked for the march to Savannah and on to the Carolinas were examined by doctors who slated them physically fit and able. They had to move against great odds while living off the land. General Sherman wanted General Judson Kilpatrick in spite of his reputation as a "cocky little powderkeg"; insisting Kilpatrick and his cavalry were just what he needed for his march.[230] He did not want a large cavalry but one known as fighters who would be a help to the Army as they were to be used to forage, picket, and flank or lead the armies – their first line of defense. The cavalry usually started the fight and the infantry came in and finished it.

    General Sherman led one of "the toughest armies in history".[231] The cavalry commanded by General Kilpatrick, fit in well with his plans, but they were also an undisciplined lot

---

[228] Frank J. Welcher, *The Union Army, 1861-1865, Organization & Operations, Volume I, Eastern Theater*, Indiana University Press, Bloomington & Indianapolis, 1993, p. 1000

[229] John G. Barrett, *Sherman's March Through the Carolinas*, The University of North Carolina Press, Chapel Hill, 1956, pp. 15-16

[230] Mark Coburn, *Terrible Innocence, General Sherman at War*, Hippocrene Books, Inc., New York, NY, p. 158

[231] Ibid.

with a reputation.[232] General Kilpatrick had the reputation of throwing his cavalry into precarious and dangerous situations. For his disregard of his men, he had the nickname of "Kilcavalry"[233]. The Ninety-second Illinois Mounted Infantry fought with General Kilpatrick in the Atlanta Campaign. They fought well and he picked them as one of the regiments in his two brigades to move with his cavalry. The next couple of weeks were busy in preparation for the move. Eugene did not know where they were going, but he knew they were moving.

Henry Holt's wife left him and he told Eugene he was not returning to Illinois after the war. His marriage was short-lived.

Elvira was ill and expecting a baby – not a good thing for expectant mothers anytime, but especially difficult that year for her. Food was so scarce and she was working to make ends meet.

*Marietta Georgia          Nov. 5$^{th}$ 1864*
*Dear Wife*
*With great pleasure, I seat myself to write you a few lines in ans to two of yours, bearing date of Sept 26$^{th}$ & Oct. 25$^{th}$, which brought me the sad news of your ill health, but hope this will find you better. I wrote you a few days ago, therefore have nothing much to write, only there is a large expedition being fited out to go off somewhere, of both Infantry & Cavalry & we are among the rest to go. So, you will have to do without mail for awhile. I cannot tell where we are going nor how long it will be before we can write.*
*We are getting our pay today, but I dont know as it will be safe to send you money now, as the rebles*

---

[232] Cox, General Jacob D., *Sherman's March to the Sea, Hood's Tennessee Campaign and the Carolina Campaigns of 1865,* with New Introduction by Brooks D. Simpson, Da Capo Press, New York, 1994, p. 40

[233] Stonesifer, Jr., Roy P., *Biographical Dictionary of the Union/ Northern Leaders of the Civil War, Judson Kilpatrick,* Edited by John T. Hubbell, Greenwood Press, Westport, Connecticut, 1995

are on the R. R. between Chattanooga & Nashville. However, I will send it if there is any show.

Henry Holt was telling me that he wife had left him without a cause and I told him, if she was that kind of woman, it was a blessing for him to get rid of her as soon as he did. He does not appear to mind it at all. He is different from what I would be, in the same case. He says he will never go back to Ill.

Oh, I am so glad that Jennie has got out there with you. I can feel perfectly contented now, as to yourself.

Tell Sylvester I will write him a huge old letter, as soon as this moove is over, that is, if I am spared so long.

You say Annie & Mother has mooved to their new home. I wish they may have a plesant time in their city home.

Yes, one thing you have done you had no business to do, that was to pay Mr. Cambell. He promised to wait on me untill I would come home. You see, you would have had the use of the money and you are in great need of it, I should think, at this presant time. Let Mr. Morford have the place for one year more. That was the understanding between him and me, if he done what was right, and you know all about that.

We have had no war news lately. Cant say much about war.

Hurrah for Old Abe everytime, that is the voice of the Army & should be of every loyal heart. Much love to all.

I remain as ever your devoted Husband.
            E. M. Swaggart

P. S. Do not look for another letter for sometime and then you will not be disappointed.
            Eugene

Election Day came on November 8, 1864 in the North and re-elected was Abraham Lincoln. Eugene voted for himself on November 7 when the men voted absentee, but only as a joke. He felt President Lincoln did not need his vote to be re-elected. He wanted Moses to know what he had done in case it came out in the newspapers.

He knew the Army was moving to Savannah and he sent $50.00 to Elvira via Moses. He wanted Moses to look for it and see that she received it.

*Marietta Georgia       Nov. 7$^{th}$ 1864*
*Dear Brother*
*Rather Solmnly , I seat myself to write you a few lines and they must be very brief, as everything is in confusion preparing for a long & tedious march. We expect to start tomorrow or next day.  Our destination is not known, yet, by privates soldiers but we are going to Savannah, Ga.*
*I wrote to Vira a few days ago & told her I did not think we could be paid, but we were, & I sent $50.00 by H. Thomas Sutler of the 92 to be delivered to Willis in Mt. Carroll, in your name, for Vira. He may not get through in a month & he may make it sooner. It depends on what kind of luck he has.*
*I suppose after we leave this place, our chances will be very poor for writing. You must not look for any more letters untill we have time to march & fight 200 miles. Then, they will have to cross the old Atlantic Via N.Y. City, although we do not anticipate much fighting untill we get to Savannah or Charleston, S. Carolina. We are all drawing plenty of clothing, rations & the boys all feel bully. We do not belong to the "army of the cumberland" anymore. Ours is the "army of the Mississippi", Comd. by old Billy Sherman.*

*Mose, if you see an account of our regt. voting, you will see one vote for little Mc in our comp. & it was this Mc that put it in. I did it just to be contrary. I knew it would not count anyway. The boys give me fits for being disloyal, but I am just as patriotic as any of them. My love to all.*
*Your Affectionate Brother*
*E. M. Swaggart*
*P. S. Vote for old Abe everytime. Mc is a good man, but the company he keeps are d\_\_\_\_d rebles.*
*E. M. S.*

By November 14, 1864, the army had concentrated, ready to move.[234]

---

[234] Frank J. Welcher, *The Union Army, 1861-1865, Organization & Operations, Volume I, Eastern Theater*, Indiana University Press, Bloomington & Indianapolis, 1993, p. 1001

## Chapter Seventeen
## March to the Sea - Savannah

In the "march to the sea," General Judson Kilpatrick, of the Military Division of the Mississippi, commanded the Third Division. The First Brigade of the Third Division was commanded by Colonel Eli H. Murray, and the Second Brigade by Colonel Smith D. Atkins, former commander of the Ninety-second Illinois Mounted Infantry.[235] The Ninety-second Illinois was a regiment in the Second Brigade, commanded by Lieutenant Colonel Matthew Van Buskirk.[236]

Troops began to move out on November 15, 1864 headed toward Savannah. The entire tour was one of destruction. "Railroads, factories, mills, farms, cotton gins, and storehouses" were demolished or burned and "cattle, food, forage and supplies" were taken or destroyed by the troops.[237] In spite of the destructive attitude of the Union army, rape and murder were almost unknown. General Wheeler's Confederate army was as destructive and, many times, more feared by the citizens than the Union army.[238]

General Kilpatrick, who led the cavalry division under General Sherman, drew considerable criticism as he tore through Georgia to Savannah and on to the Carolinas. His two brigades held their own against General Wheeler's six on many occasions. No one could criticize the fighting ability of the soldiers under his command. For that reason alone, the leaders, especially General Sherman, tolerated his actions and complaints against him and his men met deaf ears. General Sherman felt that in order to win the war, it was necessary to

---

[235] Frank J. Welcher, *The Union Army, 1861-1865, Organization & Operations, Volume I, Eastern Theater*, Indiana University Press, Bloomington & Indianapolis, 1993, p. 1008

[236] Thomas M. Eddy, *The Patriotism of Illinois, A Record of the Civil and Military History of the State, Chapter XXII, Regimental Sketches, Ninety-second Illinois Infantry, 1865, p.* 373

[237] Welcher, *The Union Army, Eastern Theater*, p. 1001

[238] General Jacob D. Cox, *Sherman's March to the Sea, Hood's Tennessee Campaign and the Carolinas Campaign of 1865*, with New Introduction by Brooks D. Simpson, Da Capo Press, New York, 1994, p. 41

defeat the spirit of the citizens as well as the soldiers. However, General Kilpatrick went overboard in his weakness for women and moral attitudes.

Foraging was necessary for the army to exist. It took place on both the Union and Confederate sides. General Sherman instructed the army to live off the countryside and touch the supplies only when necessary. But, foraging had regulations and disciplines as guidelines. One such guideline was an order not to enter homes.

One twentieth of the men and an officer from each regiment were detailed to forage each day. The men, chosen from the best horsemen and best shots, possessed daring self-confidence. Their lack of fear and hesitation often kept them alive. They acted as pickets and advance scouts for the troops as they foraged the countryside. Seldom injured or killed in spite of their constant contact with the enemy, they had the advantage of the long reach of their Spencer rifles and dare devil tactics.

General Kilpatrick did not encourage foragers to follow the rules. He condoned and encouraged foraging to such a degree that many soldiers in his army were referred to as "bummers". They took what they wanted whenever they wanted it, usually before they burned the property. General Kilpatrick, himself, had a reputation for taking his share along the way for his own use, leaning toward carriages and horses.[239] Eugene was no exception to the rule. While out on pickets and scouts, he foraged nearby homes. His weakness was musical instruments.

General Wheeler's Confederate bummers were as feared as General Kilpatrick's Union bummers. [240] The part foraging played in the Civil War was probably as large as illness when stacked against honor and glory in an ordinary soldier's life.

As the troops neared Macon, Georgia on November 19, Sherman's right wing was sent along the Macon railroad to deceive the enemy and drive off General Wheeler's cavalry and the Georgia militia that had assembled at Lovejoy Station.

---

[239] General Jacob D. Cox, *Sherman's March to the Sea, Hood's Tennessee Campaign and the Carolina Campaigns of 1865*, with New Introduction by Brooks D. Simpson, Da Capo Press, New York, 1994, pp. 40-42
[240] John G. Barrett, *Sherman's March Through the Carolinas*, The University of North Carolina Press, Chapel Hill, 1956, p.58

General Judson Kilpatrick and his cavalry were on the flank of the Seventeenth Corps. They drove the enemy's skirmishers before them to Lovejoy Station. When they reached Lovejoy Station, they found "two brigades of cavalry with two pieces of artillery." Dismounting the men, he had them "charge the works on foot."[241] The Ninety-second Illinois Infantry engaged, "fighting three or four times its number, driving the rebels from their works, capturing, killing, and wounding quite a number."[242] The attack was successful and he followed it with another attack, capturing the guns and chasing the Confederates toward Macon. They continued on nearing Forsyth, deceiving the enemy into believing an advance was moving in that direction. They then turned and crossed the Ocmulgee.

November 20, 1864 found General Kilpatrick's cavalry striking the railroad a little east of Macon. They destroyed "a train of cars and tore up track for a mile."[243] General Kilpatrick's division moved to the extreme right of the armies led by General Sherman and by passed Griswoldville and Milledgeville. However, on November 26, General Kilpatrick was directed "to the front and left" of the moving armies where the action was.

As General Kilpatrick left Milledgeville, his orders were to reach Briar Creek, near Waynesboro, and destroy the railway-bridge and trestles, then proceed to Millen to release the prisoners held there. Two regiments of General Eli Murray's First Brigade fell behind and General Wheeler's Confederate forces attacked them in the middle of the night. They fought their way back to the brigade and General Kilpatrick had to abandon efforts to destroy the bridge and trestles. He learned that the prisoners had been moved to another location so he proceeded to rejoin the forces. The two brigades of General Atkins and General Murray took turns guarding the rear of the column and skirmishing with General Wheeler's forces. At

---

[241] General Jacob D. Cox, *Sherman's March To the Sea, Hood's Tennessee Campaign and the Carolina Campaigns of 1865,* with New Introduction by Brooks D. Simpson, Da Capo Press, New York, 1994, pp. 26-27

[242] Thomas M. Eddy, *The Patriotism of Illinois, A Record of the Civil and Military History of the State, Chapter XXII, Regimental Sketches, Ninety-second Illinois Infantry,* 1865, p. 373

[243] Cox, *Sherman's March,* pp. 26-27

Reynold's plantation, General Kilpatrick took a stand because of a destroyed bridge. General Kilpatrick and his cavalry repulsed General Wheeler and his rebel forces and General Kilpatrick rejoined his forces. However, General Wheeler claimed victory.

Two days later, General Kilpatrick was still angry and asked permission to pursue General Wheeler. His cavalry, backed by the Fourteenth Corps, who never seemed to engage, attacked General Wheeler in Waynesboro and drove him by three lines of barricades, out of town and over Briar Creek.[244] The Ninety-second Illinois led the charge, "under heavy fire," and "captured more than its own number".[245] Eugene's friend, George Wait Downs was killed in the charge.

The next day, December 5, General Kilpatrick moved with his division to Jacksonboro. From Jacksonboro, they followed the coast to near Savannah,[246] arriving on December 10,[247] with the armies of General Sherman.

General Kilpatrick and the cavalry had orders to capture Fort McAllister, but after a reconnaissance, decided it was too strong for the cavalry alone. General William B. Hazen and the Second Division of the Fifteenth Corps took the fort using nine regiments with eight in reserve.[248]

Savannah was important to General Sherman because he needed to control the sea port city to supply his troops from ships arriving from New York. With a new stock of supplies coming in, General Sherman requested that General William J. Hardee of the Confederate troop, holding the city of Savannah, surrender. The request was denied. However, on December 20, the Confederate General and his troops evacuated Savannah and

---

[244] General Jacob D. Cox, *Sherman's March to the Sea, Hood's Tennessee Campaign and the Carolina Campaigns of 1865*, with New Introduction by Brooks D. Simpson, Da Capo Press, New York, 1994, pp. 31-34

[245] Thomas M. Eddy, *The Patriotism of Illinois, A Record of the Civil and Military History of the State*, Chapter XXII, Regimental Sketches, Ninety-second Illinois Infantry, 1865, pp. 373-374

[246] Cox, *Sherman's March*, p. 53

[247] *Illinois Troops (Union) Infantry, Records of Events*, Volume 13, $92^{nd}$ Illinois Infantry,1862-1865, Company I, p. 549

[248] Frank J. Welcher, *The Union Army, 1861 - 1865, Organization & Operations, Volume I, Eastern Theater*, Indiana University Press, Bloomington & Indianapolis, 1993, p. 1006

General Sherman moved in. On December 13, the Ninety-second Illinois Mounted Infantry "crossed the Ogeechee River, marched to the Altamaha River and returned."[249]

The trip was a long one and Eugene did not have much opportunity to write to Elvira. Along the way, he confiscated some spoons, a guitar, and another violin which he planned to send home when he could.

Eugene was not the same person who left to fight for his country. War had hardened him to the point that he accepted the death of his friend George Wait Downs, almost as an occurrence he expected to happen. He was sorry for Wait's parents, but perhaps relieved Wait died instead of him. He mentioned Wait's death as another soldier – not one of his friends.

*Dec 19th 1864           Camp in Ga. Near the Coast*
*Dear Wife*
*With great pleasure, I am once more permited to write you a few lines. I am tolerable well, at presant, but have been rather poorly all the way through our march.*
*We left Marietta Ga. on the 14th of Nov. & was on the road 34 days. We had a very good time. We subsisted on the country and had plenty untill we got to Savannah. Then, we seen pretty hard times for a few days, as our Communications had to be opened before our fleet could land, but they are all right now.*
*We recd a large mail on the 17th. Poor me only received 1 letter from you & 1 from Annie. Yet, I will not compain for I know you have not had many from me in the last month, but I guess I can write now, as usual.*
*Our Div. of Cav. done about all the hard fighting that was done on the march. Our loss in the 92nd*

---

[249] *Illinois Troops (Union) Infantry, Records of Events, Volume 13, 92nd Illinois Infantry, 1862-1865,* p. 549

was 5 killed & 9 wounded. Loss in Co I, was Wait Downs[250] killed and Abner Cumy wounded. Wait was killed on the 4$^{th}$, in a charge. He never spoke after he was struck. It will be sad news for his folks, but you know in battle, there is no distinction.

The Co. is all in good health, but will not stay so long if we stay here very long. Oh, it is the darndest place in America. There is nothing here but swamps & canebrakes, but the prettiest weather you ever saw. We can go all day in our shirt sleeves & hunt for a shade, to boot. I think we will be out of this before hot weather. I hope so, at any rate. If we are not, we can never stand the heat. We must trust to kind providence and I guess all will be well. Well, I guess you have the money by this time, which I sent to Wills for you. The amount was $50.00. I have 4 large tablespoons & 13 small ones for to send you as soon as I can express them. Also, a fine guitarrh, and one of the best violens in the world. Direct your letters as before. Only Savannah Ga. Via N. Y. City. My love to All. Kiss the baby. No more at presant.

As ever your         Sincere Husband

E. M. Swaggart

    The wagon trains with all the camp supplies and equipment were still coming in near the end of December. The Ninety-second Illinois Mounted Infantry was detailed to meet them and bring them in safely on Christmas Day. It was not a pleasant day for Eugene and he was envious of the Christmas he was sure his family enjoyed at home.

    He had the opportunity to go into Savannah and enjoyed the visit. The citizens were actually nice to him and especially one

---

[250] George W. "Wait" Downs, Salem, 92$^{nd}$ Illinois Infantry Company I, killed at Waynesboro, GA. 12-4-64 - Arthur Robbe and Richard Hinton, Booklet for *Rededication Ceremony of the Carroll County Civil War Soldiers & Sailors*.

young woman. Speaking with her was a pleasant experience and he wanted Elvira to know.

The only letter from home was dated November 10.

*Dec. 30$^{th}$ 1864*
*In Camp 8 miles from Savannah Ga.*
*Dear Wife*
*Once more I am seated for the purpose of writing you. I am well at presant & hope this will find yourself & babies enjoying good health. I have not heard from home since Nov. 10$^{th}$, but look for some mail soon as a large fleet is just in from N. Y. City.*
*Our grub line has been pretty short for a short time, but is some better, & prospects of being good.*
*I was in the city of Savannah the other day. It is a far nicer place than I expected to find. It is far ahead of any place we have captured before. Everything looks nice & clean, lots of citizens & ladies. They are what attracts the attention of a Soldier, down in this forsaken country, more than anything else. I had the pleasure of quite a long chat with a lady from the state of Vermont, who was on a visit here when the war broke out, and has been here ever since. You bet she was glad when the Yanks marched into town. She is not the only one in the same fix, but they can go now.*
*The rebs left us 200 large seige guns, 900 of their men & 30,000 Bales of Cotton, when they left the place. Dont you think them generous. I do. One more, as successfull a moove as this last one of Shermans and all is well, and that is not far distant eather. I think 6 months will be a long time to end this little thing. It may be longer, but I cant see it.*
*Oh, I have got the itch and cant get anything for it. What shall I do, Scratch, I guess that is what you*

would say. I am using sulphur and think I could cure it with sulphur, if could get half enough of it, but that I cannot do, at this presant time.

Well, I reckon I must tell you how I spent Christmas. In the first place, it rained hard all day. $2^{nd}$, we was on the march, $3^{rd}$, through a big swamp of about 5 miles wide. 4, our regt was detailed to help the train, wagon train, through it, which took us all day Christmas. Went to no dance at night, Did not eat much turkey. I hope youens all had a better time than I did and wish you a happy New Year. My Love to All. Write soon. Direct as before only Via. N. Y. City.

As ever your        Affectionate
                 E. M. Swaggart

P. S. Send me a good Violin E String in your next. Have Moses get it for you.      E. M.

Eugene still had no news from Elvira. He was lonely, thinking about all of his friends who were gone, due to death, illness or discharge. They were gone, but he was moving on, in the campaign.

He knew a baby was due in November and he worried. He had every reason to be worried because Elvira was weak and ill. The baby girl, born on November 25, 1864, was a full term baby, but very small. It weighed a little over five pounds possibly due to the lack of food Elvira had encountered during the pregnancy because of a money shortage, or because Elvira had been sick for weeks before the baby arrived.

The baby was small, cold, and did not seem to be breathing when she made her appearance into the world. Jennie wrapped her in a blanket and laid her on a log pile beside the fireplace. She meant to clean her up and dress her for the burial after attending to Elvira. While she was busy helping Elvira, she heard a soft mewling sound coming from the fireplace and ran over to the baby. She found it alive, but cold. She began to rub the arms and legs vigorously until they turned pink and the baby cried for the first time.

It took Elvira another two months to regain her strength so she could care for the baby alone. The baby girl held her own, but everyone worried about her health and wondered if she was "bright". She seemed to be healthy, but she was just too small.[251] No one wanted to write to Eugene right away and tell him the news. What could they tell him? He was busy fighting a war. They feared the news of his wife's bad health, and the baby, too, would be too much for him to bear. They agreed they should wait and see what happened before alarming Eugene who had enough to cope with in war.

Eugene, however, was very worried about Elvira and, in spite of his efforts to shut out the death of friends, the thoughts of them kept returning. He knew home would never be the same again.

*Camp Near Savannah*      *Jan 15<sup>th</sup> 1865*

*Dear Wife*

*With pleasure, I am once more permited to write you. I am well at presant. I hope this will find you enjoying the same blessing.*

*Dear Vira, you cannot imagine how anxcious I am to hear from you. I stand and listen for my name when the mail is read, but cannot hear my name anymore. I cannot tell why the mail does not come. I would not care a button for it, if I only knew that you were well, but I cant here a word from home now, by no one.*

*All the boys that was in our Co. from our neighborhood are gone. Wm & Charlies Reynolds, Wait Downs, Loy Frasier, George Finlayson. The latter will be back. Myself & Egbert are left, yet, I mean. Our old acquaintance, Dutch Jake, started home yesterday. I went to see him, but was to late.*

---

[251] Story told by my grandmother about her birth.

*He had left. I wanted to send some things by him. Ive received orders yesterday to get ready for another campaign of 6 weeks. We are to start on the 20$^{th}$ so you must not look for anymore mail untill in March sometime. It will seem a long time, but not much longer than on our last campaign. I will write every opportunity I have. I dont know where we are going, unless it be to Willmington, North Carolina.*
*I have not had a letter for so long, that I dont know what to write.*
*Oh yes, our old Col. Smith D. Atkins has been promoted to Brigadier General. He got his commission last night. He says the 92$^{nd}$ is what got it for him.*
*Well, I guess I will close after sending much love to all. Kiss babies. I remain your loving   Husband*
*E. M. Swaggart*

Eugene's worry increased, but he did not know what to do. Several mails had come and no word from home. Christmas passed and New Years Day. Still, no letter arrived from Elvira wishing him a Merry Christmas. He knew with certainty that something was wrong when he wrote to her to inform her of the new campaign.

*In Camp Near Savannah Ga     January 20$^{th}$  1865*
*Dear Wife*
*With rather a sad heart, I seat myself to write you a few, not in ans. to any of yours, for I have had none from you or anyone else, for 2 months and now I do not expect any for 2 months more, as we start tomorrow morning on a long Campaign. It will not end untill March, so you must not look for anymore from me.*

In Camp near Savannah Ga
January 20th 1865

Dear Wife
    With father a sad heart I seat my self to write you a few not in ans to any of yours for I have had none from you or any one else for 2 months. and now I do not expect any for 2 months more as we start tomorrow morning on a long Campaign it will not end untill March so you must not look for any more from me I cant tell where our destination will be some where in South Carolinas Traitorous Soil I suppose. I mailed Moses some Savannah papers a day or so ago. I also mailed you some. We have had the nicest times imaginable

I cant tell where our destination will be, some where in South Carolinas Traitorous Soil, I suppose. I mailed Moses some Savannah papers a day or so ago. I also mailed you some.

*We have had the nicest times imaginable for Solders to have since we have been here, but they all end today. Tomorrow we expect to meet ol Wheeler and his band of rebs, and if we do, he will eather get whiped, whip us, or run, one of the above three things. He has all ways got the first and last. He generaly prefers running.*

*I would just give anything I possessed in this world for three words from you and they that, <u>I am well!</u> I could then start out with a cheerfullness, other ways I cannot do. You must think hard of me for not writing oftener than I do, for it is the best I can do. If we should stop a day or so, anyplace, and we have a chance to mail letters, you can rest assured I will write. This coming Campaign, and one more, will finish up soldiering for the 92 & those that are lucky enough to see them through, I hope well be done this war, or any other. You can bet it will be my last if I live through it.*

*Well, I suppose I have said enough for this time. Give my love to Jennie & Sylvester, Moses & Dicky, Mother & Annie, Mary & everybody*
*I remain your      Affectionate Husband*
*E. M. Swaggart*

The long awaited letter finally came. Elvira was strong enough to write and she mailed him a letter on January 8, 1865, giving him the news of his daughter who was born six weeks earlier. Eugene pulled out of Savannah with peace in his heart concerning his wife and baby. When he wrote Elvira a quick letter, he asked that she let him name the baby.

He told her how he had obtained his confiscated property. It was evident he was not following the orders concerning entering private homes.

He and his companion, Kato, had been stuck in the mud that was so prevalent on the march. He almost drowned in it, but finally freed himself.

*In Camp Near Savannah Ga*     Jan 23 1865[252]
Dear Wife

With pleasure I write you this in ans to yours of Jan 8$^{th}$. You cannot imagine the joy I anticipated with the news which it brought. It stated that <u>our</u> folks had a grand daughter six weeks old the first of January and it is well and is hapy to hear you are very good at the biz done twice and I saw none of it. Quite lucky for me. Maybe you dont mind so I must. I shall be more attentive in the future. Oh! yes, I wish you to name it, no, let me name it. I think I can find a good one for the darling.

Vira, I write quite differant from what I did when I sent the last. I did not expect at that time that I would get a letter until our campaign end but we have such bad evil weather that our move was postponed for a short time.

So you thought...........of are hearing of.......... of giving a ............I hope we are staying here awhile and ending it. It cant continue he doesnt think in this darned secish ......soil.

I was out the other day and my old man (....Kato) he was withe me in a deep kinda hole and nearly drowned himselfe and me also. His foot was caught in the stirrup and Kato would not stay still long enough to get loose nor I could not get by. You can picture it now how we looked after bumbling around in the mud four feet deep for half an hour or so. I got loose at last as you see by this but there never was another such a looking dashing cavalry man mounted such as I was at that time.

Vira, you have never writen whether............................

---

[252] This letter was in very bad shape and difficult to read. However, after computer enhancement, many of the words could be read. The missing portions are words that could not be read at all.

and said.............about it...................on your place. Answer in another....................cut your wood for your lumber...............
I do not wish you to punish yourselfe for any thing you want as long as you have money. If I ever get home I can work..............
You wish to know something about those spoons. There is two sets of teaspoons and four large tablespoons. They are pretiest of silver there. I got them I captured them in an old rebles house in his Chest but all such Articles are Contraband of War and soldiers from the U. S. Armies confiscate and keep part so I have a safe place to keep them and I will do it. The violin I sold but did not get paid for it yet.
Tell Sylvester ...... cut home visiting folks. I wish I might do the same.
You asked if I seen Wait after he was killed. I did not but he was buried by our own Company near Wayneboro in this state on the 4$^{th}$ of Dec. 1864.

The rest of the letter was too faded to read.

## Chapter Eighteen
## The Carolina Mud March

General William T. Sherman and his armies started advancing from Savannah to the Carolinas on January 3, 1865.[253] The entire march through the Carolinas consisted of almost insurmountable logistics by expert woodsmen. The area embodied swamps and rivers that were treacherous in the consistent rain that fell.[254]

General Judson Kilpatrick and his division of cavalry, which included the Ninety-second Illinois Mounted Infantry, did not leave Savannah until January 20. His orders were to cross "the Savannah River above Savannah at Sister's Ferry and advance to Augusta to threaten the city."[255] "General Kilpatrick gave a party to the officers of his command and in his speech, said, 'In after years, when travelers passing through South Carolina shall see chimney-stacks without houses, and the country desolate, and shall ask, Who did this, some Yankee will answer, Kilpatrick's cavalry.'"[256]

From the first, General Kilpatrick's old enemy, General Joseph Wheeler and his Confederate cavalry were nearby and determined to "contest Kilpatrick's advance." The Union cavalry accompanied General Jefferson C. Davis' Fourteenth Corps. On January 29, they arrived at Sister's Ferry on the south side of the river.[257] The river was three miles wide at the crossing due to a lot of rain and flooding. Long trestle bridges laid by General H. W. Slocum of the Union Army connected the ends of the pontoon bridge with the shore.[258] The river crossing by the cavalry took place on February 3. They marched to

---

[253] Frank J. Welcher, *The Union Army, 1861-1865, Organization & Operations, Volume I, Eastern Theater,* Indiana University Press, Bloomington & Indianapolis, 1993, pp. 639-641

[254] General Jacob D. Cox, *Sherman's March to the Sea, Hood's Tennessee Campaign and the Carolina Campaigns of 1865,* with New Introduction by Brooks D. Simpson, Da Capo Press, New York, 1994, p. 171

[255] Welcher, *The Union Army, Eastern Theater,* pp. 639-641

[256] Cox, *Sherman's March to the Sea,* pp. 175-176, taken from General Smith D. Atkins, *The Ninety Second Illinois.,* p. 211

[257] Welcher, *The Union Army, Eastern Theater,* pp. 639-641

[258] Cox, *Sherman's March to the Sea,* p. 168

Robertsville with the Twentieth Corps and Fourth Division of the Fifteenth Corps.

At Robertsville, General Kilpatrick and his cavalry, along with another division, started their advance into Augusta moving "ahead of the infantry along the line of the South Carolina railroad", skirmishing with General Wheeler and his Confederate forces all the way. [259]

The first real problem occurred as they neared the Salkehatchie River, near Barnwell. General William Hardee waited with ten thousand troops; many entrenched along the river. "After three days of skirmishing and laying corduroy roads for the wagons", the troops reached Whippy Swamp. The divisions of General Joseph Mower and General Giles E. Smith,[260] as well as the Ninety-second Illinois Infantry, charged from earthworks on the other side. The Ninety-second Illinois Mounted Infantry, led by Lt. Col. Matthew Van Buskirk, "dashed through the swamp, the men wading in water up to their armpits, crossed the stream on trees felled by the pioneers, and under cover of rapid fire of artillery, gallantly carried the works, driving the enemy in confusion toward the town of Barnwell."[261] The crossing took three hours.[262]

On February 10, they arrived at Johnson's Station near Augusta.[263] General Kilpatrick's cavalry raided the area near Augusta as they passed on August 11. Twenty miles from Augusta, in a little town called Aiken; General Wheeler posted two thousand of his men on the side streets to prepare for an ambush on General Kilpatrick's cavalry. The Ninety-second Illinois Mounted Infantry, followed by the rest of the brigade,

---

[259] Frank J. Welcher, *The Union Army, 1861-1865, Organization & Operations, Volume I, Eastern Theater,* Indiana University Press, Bloomington & Indianapolis, 1993, pp. 640-641

[260] Burke Davis, *Sherman's March, The First Full-Length Narrative of General William T. Sherman's Devastating March through Georgia and the Carolinas,* First Vintage Books Edition, May 1988, pp. 146-147

[261] Thomas M. Eddy, *The Patriotism of Illinois, A Record of the Civil and Military History of the State, Chapter XXII, Regimental Sketches, Ninety-second Illinois Infantry, 1865,* p. 374 reported by Colonel Bowman, a staff officer of General Sherman.

[262] Davis, *Sherman's March,* pp. 146-147

[263] Welcher, *The Union Army,* pp. 639-641

approached the town first with General Smith D. Atkins in the lead. As they charged into town, a sharp fight broke out and[264] the Ninety-second Illinois found itself trapped, but in a "hand to hand encounter, cut their way out."[265] Several soldiers were shot and others surrendered. General Kilpatrick, almost captured, lost only a hat. The Union cavalry made a stand about five miles out of Aiken on a bank of a stream behind barricades. They withdrew the following day, carrying their wounded in wagons.[266]

After the demonstrations against Augusta and the skirmish in Aiken, they headed for Colombia, marching on the left of the Fourteenth Corps whose soldiers were going to Lexington. At Lexington, on February 16, the cavalry encamped for the night. The following morning, General Kilpatrick turned north and proceeded toward Monticello. His forces reached there on 20 February after crossing the Saluda River at Mount Zion Church and passing through Alston.

During this period, The Fifteenth Corps destroyed Columbia while the Seventeenth Corps tore up the railroad tracks. On Feb. 22, the Seventeenth Corps met the cavalry and together they proceeded toward "Rocky Mount Ferry on the Catawba or Wateree River, above Peay's Ferry." General Kilpatrick and his cavalry led the march. February 23 and 24, the cavalry and the Twentieth Corps crossed the river and waited for the Fifteenth Corps, who could not cross because of bridge destruction due to rising water.[267] On 27 February, all were able to cross and the cavalry moved with General Slocum westward to Abbeville, tearing up railroad as they traveled. After Abbeville, the cavalry and other troops moved to Winnsboro tearing up the railroad. Part of General Sherman's overall plan was to destroy as much

---

[264] Burke Davis, *Sherman's March, The First Full-Length Narrative of General William T. Sherman's Devastating March through Georgia and the Carolinas*, First Vintage Books Edition, May 1988, pp. 150-151

[265] Thomas M. Eddy, *The Patriotism of Illinois, A Record of the Civil and Military History of the States, Volume XXII, Regimental Sketches, Ninety-second Illinois Infantry*, 1865, p. 374

[266] Davis, *Sherman's March*, p. 151

[267] Frank J. Welcher, *The Union Army, 1861-1865, Organization & Operations, Volume I, Eastern Theater*, Indiana University Press, Bloomington & Indianapolis, 1993, p. 642

railroad as possible, thus damaging communication lines between General Pierre Gustave Beauregard's and General William Hardee's armies.

He also wanted to leave the impression that the Union armies were moving to Charlotte, not to Raleigh.

The next crossing for the cavalry, moving on the extreme left flank, was eastward on the Catawba River. After the crossing, they moved through mud caused by the incessant rains to the Great Pedee at Cheraw.[268] The crossing on the Great Pedee took place on a bridge completed by March 6 at Pegue's Ferry. The cavalry was the first unit to cross, followed by the Fourteenth Corps.[269]

General Kilpatrick's cavalry split following the crossing. They were assigned to three different crossroads in a triangle. On March 9, General Smith D. Atkins brigade, including the Ninety-second Illinois Mounted Infantry, detected an attack by the Confederate Army but were skirmishing and unable to reach General Kilpatrick in time to warn him.[270]

At Monroe's Crossroad, just after leaving Solemn Grove,[271] General Kilpatrick and General George E. Spencer were asleep in a house when surrounded, but woke up and General Kilpatrick managed to escape, leaving most of his clothes and his arms behind. The other brigades, "used to rough and tumble fighting," rallied under the cypress trees when joined by General Kilpatrick, charged the enemy and took the cannon back, which they used on their adversaries.

When General Atkins arrived with his brigade, the fight was over. General Kilpatrick reported losing two hundred men and

---

[268] General Jacob D. Cox, *Sherman's March to the Sea, Hood's Tennessee Campaign and the Carolina Campaign of 1865*, with New Introduction by Brooks D. Simpson, Da Capo Press, New York, 1994, p. 178
[269] Frank J. Welcher, *The Union Army, 1861-1865, Organization & Operations, Volume I, Eastern Theater*, Indiana University Press, Bloomington & Indianapolis, 1993, p. 642
[270] Cox, *Sherman's March to the Sea*, p. 179-180
[271] Welcher, *The Union Army, Eastern Theater* pp. 642-643

the Confederates lost over one hundred men in death with many wounded, including several officers.[272]

On March 11, General Kilpatrick and his cavalry moved toward Fayetteville, following the rest of the army that moved out the previous day. "He camped a few miles from town."[273] Other than small skirmishes, the army moved in, virtually unopposed.

In Fayetteville, General Sherman ordered the destruction of the arsenal.[274] From there, he ordered General Kilpatrick's cavalry to move "up the Plank Road along the east bank of the Cape Fear River to the vicinity of Averasboro." General Henry Warner Slocum and four divisions followed them. As they moved out on March 15, General Atkins and his brigade, including the Ninety-second, were in the lead. "Seventeen miles north of Fayetteville and six miles from Averasboro," they found a stronghold of enemy and immediately barricaded, moving the two brigades following them on either side. They were facing General Hardee and his Confederate forces. General Kilpatrick determined the enemy was too strong for the cavalry alone and sent for backup.

When General William Hawley's Second Brigade moved in, they moved into the center relieving General Atkins' brigade who moved to the rear. In the morning, General Atkins' brigade joined General Thomas Jordon's brigade on the right. With General Atkins in command of the cavalry, the Union forces attacked and drove the enemy back. As other Union brigades arrived and moved in to join the attack, General Atkins' brigade kept moving to the right to guard the right flank until they ended up facing General Lafayette McLaw's rebel brigade.[275] At 10:00 A.M., they almost lost the right flank when they ran short of

---

[272] General Jacob D. Cox, *Sherman's March to the Sea, Hood's Tennessee Campaign and the Carolina Campaigns of 1865*, with New Introduction by Brooks D. Simpson, Da Capo Press, New York, NY, 1994, pp. 180-181

[273] Frank J. Welcher, *The Union Army, 1861-1865, Organization & Operations, Volume I, Eastern Theater*, Indiana University Press, Bloomington & Indianapolis, 1993, p. 643

[274] Cox, *Sherman's March to the Sea*, p. 181

[275] Welcher, *The Union Army, Eastern Theater*, pp. 644-645

ammunition but the Twentieth Corps moved in and saved them.[276]

General Hardee and his Confederate force retreated that night. General Wheeler's rebel cavalry guarded the rear flank and General Kilpatrick's cavalry followed the retreat to the North.[277] When they doubled back, they joined up on the left flank to the rear of the Twentieth Corps, "making their way back to the principal column."

When the cavalry joined the main unit, they rode with General Slocum and his Army of Georgia, also known as the left wing, consisting of the Fourteenth Corps and Twentieth Corps. The cavalry "crossed the Black River and took the Smithfield road to the right and in front of the infantry." Advancing was slow and arduous because of muddy roads. As the left wing advanced, the right wing was moving in on Bentonville.

On the morning of March 18, the Fourteenth Corps of General Slocum's wing was attacked. They skirmished until sunset and both sides withdrew. Held up a day, on the nineteenth, General Slocum's forces again moved forward. At 10:00 A.M., a battle that began with foragers from the Union Army skirmishing with General Wade Hampton's cavalry took place and expanded, ending on the twenty-first. When the battle was over and the Confederates retreated, it left one thousand five hundred casualties on the Union side and two thousand six hundred on the Confederate side.[278] General Kilpatrick's cavalry, including the Ninety-second Illinois Mounted Infantry, took part in the battle on the far left; leaving several injured, including Captain Robert M. A. Hawk of Company C, who lost his leg.[279]

---

[276] John G. Barrett, *Sherman's March through the Carolinas*, The University of North Carolina Press, Chapel Hill, 1956, p. 153

[277] Frank J. Welcher, *The Union Army, 1861-1865, Organization and Operations, Volume I, Eastern Theater*, Indiana University Press, Bloomington & Indianapolis, 1993, pp. 643-646

[278] Ibid., pp. 646-649

[279] Thomas M. Eddy, *The Patriotism of Illinois, A Record of the Civil and Military History of the State, Chapter XXII, Regimental Sketches, Ninety-second Illinois Infantry, 1865,* p. 374

On March 23, General Sherman's armies arrived in Goldsboro, North Carolina and camped on the north side of town. General Kilpatrick's cavalry moved to Mount Olive, north of Faison's Station, on the railroad. While General Sherman and a large count of his armies remained at Goldsboro for seventeen days, he heard about General Lee's surrender that took place on April 11 at the Appomattox Courthouse in Virginia.

General Kilpatrick's cavalry left Mount Olive and moved "westward, south of the Neuse River" toward the "North Carolina and Atlantic railroad between Smithfield and Raleigh." They were trying to move in on the rear of General Joseph Eggleston Johnston's Confederate army but missed them and General Johnston's army arrived in Raleigh on April 12. The night of April 12, General Johnston's army moved out of Raleigh with General Wheeler following the next morning. On April 13, the citizens of Raleigh surrendered to General Judson Kilpatrick. However, General Kilpatrick left the city the same day in pursuit of General Wheeler, after General Sherman moved in to take control of the city. His cavalry pushed on to Durham and, at that point, he sent General Smith D. Atkins and his brigade, including the Ninety-second Illinois Mounted Infantry to Chapel Hill while he held Durham.[280]

General Wheeler, who held Chapel Hill until April 16, decided to withdraw without a fight. On the April 17, General Atkins and his brigade rode into town. Their first action was to raise the American flag to fly from university buildings. They stabled their horses in the library of the university and placed guards at the homes, but did not damage the buildings.

While in Chapel Hill, General Smith D. Atkins fell in love with the daughter of Governor David Lowry Swain, Eleanor "Ellie" Swain. Their courtship was infamous and looked upon with disdain by the supporters of the Southern cause. When General Atkins brigade left Chapel Hill on May 3, however, he and Eleanor had announced their engagement to be married.

---

[280] Frank J. Welcher, *The Union Army, 1861-1865, Organization & Operations, Volume I, Eastern Theater*, Indiana University Press, Bloomington & Indianapolis, 1993, pp. 654-655

General Atkins married his Southern belle after the war ended on August 23, 1865.[281]

While Eugene was in Chapel Hill, Elvira heard the march was nearing an end and that General Johnston had surrendered. She was ecstatic about the news until the announcement concerning the assassination of President Abraham Lincoln.

Elvira, concerned that Eugene did not mention the baby girl nearly as much as he did Georgie, thought she would assure him that the baby was fine. She was small, but intelligent. She wanted Eugene to understand that the news she suspected he was hearing from home concerning the baby's mental and physical development was untrue.[282]

*Mt. Carroll                         April 18<sup>th</sup> 1865*
*Dear Husband,*
*With a gladened heart, I seat myself to pen you a few lines. I received another long looked for letter last night. I had almost given up ever hearing from you again but I will not complain.*
*Good news come at last - the best of all was that you was well after having such a long and tedious march and is hopefull this will be the last.*
*Providence has seen fit to smile upon us again. Peace is at hand. News come last night that Jonson had given up, but Oh, while we were rejoicing over the fall of Richmond the aoughfull and sad news of the death of our dear president. Sutch a time before it was known and then, everybody looked as though they had lost their best friend, but as the old saying is allways like darkest just before day. The day is not far distant, you will all be at home. Oh! the wait of your comming home, My Dear, I can hardly stand*

---

[281] John G. Barrett, *Sherman's March through the Carolinas*, The University of North Carolina Press, Chapel Hill, 1956, pp. 256-266

[282] Until Nellie Eugenia Swaggart was one year old and walking, many in her family thought she was mentally handicapped because of her size. She was only 4'9" when she reached adulthood.

it. To think, you will come for good and with good health, the best of all.

Oh, Annies piano come last night. She is very mutch delited with it. It is a splendid instrument, so mutch that the others get along with music very fast.

Oh Mack, I am so sorry about the spoons. They would of been so nice for the Children to of kept in remembrance of the great rebellion, but we will not mourn for a few spoons will we, in this time of rejoicing, as well as mourning.

Mack, I am, in your words, once again enjoying bully good health. Your letter sent the children love and a kiss to Georgie, but thought the other to little. I wish you could see her. She is the smartest little darling. You will see. She only weighs 13 pounds and is five months old the last of this month, but Georgie is a noble boy. He has to read your letters and look at them as much as I do. He is writing Papa a letter now. You must write him a little letter. He will think so mutch of it.

Mack, there is nothing like living in the silly life. I think you put more stress on the silly than I do.

Morford, about the place this fall, he has rented out all of the nice ground and puts in nothing but twenty acres of oats this side of the rail and I am glad he is not going to put in the corn. I do not think the corn turned out as well as it mite. Fanily got twenty six dollars for all my share. Something wrong down where he is, dreadfull slack, hope he will leave for away in September, good for that.

John Russell is working part of Moses land. They are all well. Moses poor health is going on with him.

Our Presidents funeral will be preached tomorrow. Mack, what do you think of men we are standing I am told about in Chicago, and made the comments

that they are glad that Lincoln was dead. They no more than sed it before they both lay dead on the side walk. They were shot instantly. Good for them, dont you agree.
Sylvester is all right. Oh dear, I hope I can look for you before long. The baby is crying, so I will half to stop.
Your loving wife
Vira
Write as often as you can. I know you will. I will send you all the stamps I have.

   Anna was not good about writing to Eugene, but it seemed he was finally coming home and she was happy. He wrote to her often while serving and she thought that perhaps she had better make it up to him since it seemed he was on his way home soon.
   Eugene did not give Elvira a name for the baby girl. She was five months old and everyone called her "little sis." Elvira and Anna thought it was about time the child had a name. Every child deserved a name.

Mount Carroll    April 21$^{st}$ 1865    Friday morning
Dear Brother
I received your kind and ever-welcome letter last evening. I will hasten to answer you and, in answering, atone for my past neglect. We are all well and enjoying ourselves as well as could be expected without my big Brother. However, we expect to see you soon. We think this war is most over and that is enough to lighten our troubles, if nothing more. Vira and Jennie think you will be home the last of June and I hope so. At least, by the appearance of things at presant, you are done fighting and, of course, will be home as soon as you can be mustered out. Well, Brother mine, we are ready for you.

*My new Piano has arrived and is a perfect gem. Georgie points his finger at it and says, "no no, Annie, me won't". Dear little fellow, he never touches it, but he loves it. He stands by me half an hour at a time listening with all attention. I sold my old one to a gentleman in Lanark for one hundred and fifty dollars and my new one was four hundred and fifty, but Mrs. Thimen ............of thirty per cent, so I got it for $330.*
*Dont you think that was reasonable.*

Charles Reynolds, captured at Nickajack on April 24, 1864, was released and home. His friend, William P. McWorthy, captured at the same time, died in Andersonville prison.

*Charly Reynolds has been home two months and is quite well now. I have not seen him yet. I suppose he starts to his Reg. in a few days to be mustered out. I hope you will all be here the fourth. Oh! wont it be splendid though.*
*John Smith and Barbara McKay are to be Marriade next May the 1st, public announcement & suppose they will have a grand wedding. Bell has gone to Hazel Green, teaching music. She told me to remember her to you when I wrote. She is a splendid girl. Anna has gone home. I will send your letter to her next mail. I believe she proposes teaching at Mt. Pspt. next summer. Sue Dulibar teaches our school this summer.*
*Mose & Dicky talk of traveling this summer. Jennie will take care of the children. They propose viewing Iowa to find a home that will suit them better than this one. Mose talks very strongly of selling. I hope he will. I will go with them, I guess.*
*It is snowing very hard. I guess we will have sleighing this month. There is to be a party at Olive Maclures tonight given by two young ladies.*

*I promised to attend, but I fear the weather will not permit me to do so. These parties dont amount to much, my general opinion.*
*Are you going to name the baby. We are waiting very patiently.*
*We have not heard from John very lately.*
*The Presidents funeral is to be preached next sunday. The relatives were not prepared to have it the appropriate day.*
*The rebs have done their fatal wave but its my opinion they will suffer for it and they had ought too.*
*Vira says she will write to you next sunday. She is looking for a letter from you tonight. Georgie sends a kiss to Papa. Mother is well and send her love. Hoping to hear from you soon. Will inscribe myself your loving sister.*
*Anna Swaggart*

Eugene wrote a letter to Elvira before he left Chapel Hill. He received a letter from her that was a month old and wanted to answer it right away. He was happy about the surrender of General Johnston and ready for the war to end.

"From Chapel Hill and members of the Ninety-second Illinois came the most common reaction to peace. These Illinois cavalrymen certainly were not afraid of civilian life as was the Illinois infantryman who wondered what he would do with himself at home; nor did they look upon peace merely as no more bullets and no more screaming shells. To them peace meant mustering out and discharge from the army. These two facts occupied their minds. Just why were they not being discharged as were some infantry regiments, they asked."[283]

---

[283] John G. Barrett, *Sherman's March Through the Carolinas*, The University of North Carolina Press, 1956, p. 272 taken from *Regimental Committee, Ninety-second Illinois Volunteers*, Freeport: Journal Steam Publishing House and Book Bindery, 1875, p. 247

Chapel Hill   Orange Co.   N.C.   April 22nd 1865
Dear Wife
With pleasure I write you in ans. to yours of March 28th, which came to hand last night. It found me in good spirits & was very glad to learn that you and babies were well.

*Dear Vira, we are having good news now. Lees Army has all surrendered & Johnsons is all surrendered. In fact, the whole Confederacy has give up, on conditions. We are waiting for the returns from Washington. If Johnsons propositions are excepted, we will be on our way home in 2 weeks, so our Generals tells us. I will be home in time for harvest, if I live. Now Vira, you must not be excitable over this news.*

*We are in one of the most pleasant places we have ever been in, in the south. Our Brigade is here by itself. No others of our troops in less than 12 miles, but the Johnnies do not molest us whatever. We have orders not to fire another gun & they have the same orders, under the penalty of death, so you see the thing is about done. We are issuing rations to the reble army now, in our front. Camp is lively, everybody happy over the Termination of our diffculties. We will get the news for certain in about 3 days more & of course, you will get it just as quick.*
*Your Husband*
*E. M. Swaggart*

While the Ninety-second Illinois Mounted Infantry, along with the Second Brigade of the cavalry was in Chapel Hill, General Kilpatrick, in Durham Station, received a message from General Johnston involving a negotiation with General Sherman to "end hostilities." The message was delivered to General Sherman. A meeting took place on April 17 whereby an agreement was reached. However, General Ulysses Grant arrived on April 24 with the news that the truce was not acceptable. On April 26, General Johnston surrendered under Union terms.[284]

---

[284]World Almanac Publications, *The Civil War Almanac*, Intro. by Henry Steele Commager, A Bison Book, New York, NY 1983, pp. 264-266

## Chapter Nineteen
## The War Is Over

Near May 1, 1865, the Ninety-second Illinois Mounted Infantry transferred to the Department of North Carolina. Their days of war were over. Their assignment was Concord, North Carolina where they awaited orders to muster out.

Back home Elvira was excited and all she could think about was Eugene's arrival. She felt he should come home right away. The war was long and he had fought in many battles. It was time for him to be at home with his family.

Eugene's niece by his half-sister, Mary Ann, died in 1861 but word concerning her death was slow in arriving. Her mother, died some years before and part of George's estate was to go to young Leticia. Elvira was hoping they could afford to buy her land that adjoined Eugene's land. She had not given up the idea of farming.

*Mt. Carroll     May 8$^{th}$ 1865*
*My Dear Husband,*
*Hastily I seat myself to write you a few lines while the baby is asleep. She has got a hard cold and is not very well. I am anxious to hear from you again. I have not heard one word since you first got to N. Carolina and that is a long time.*
*Oh Dear, I do think it is to bad that you are not comming home now, as well as the rest. The papers state that Shermans Calvary are going to be kept until their time is out, but the infantry are going to be discharged and come home. I think those that have done the hard fiting and marching ought to have their time done up, but I am thankfull the fighting is out, but I guess not more so than you poor soldiers are.*
*Marshal Harington was here yesterday. He is home on a 30 day furlough. His wife is sick. They think*

*she has the quick consumption and looks very bad. It makes it hard for Marshal, as he is a poor man. He is as fat and ruged as a bair.*

*Oh Dear, I am so lonesome. Jennie is out to Dickeys. She has been out there for two weeks. Dickey has been quite sick but is better now. I expect Jennie home next Saturday. I have been so sad & lonely that Mt. Carroll would not keep me long without you or Jennie. She stands with yourself in my afections and well I may think of her, for she has been all that a devoted sister could be to me and my children. I hope she will reap the rewards of it some day. Bring her a nice presant from you, Mack.*

*Mr. Wilson has had a letter from Mr. Price. He says that Letties dead, that she died in 1861 with the typhoid fever. He also said there are some demands against her estate to be settled up, her factor bill and a few others, little. The land is going to be sold. I wish you could buy it. It lais right along side of yours, clear through to Hasbler. It would improve yours so much. It is for about a thousand dollars. Annie sais that if you will buy it, she will let you have the house. Purchased on time, you would have, then, the demands against the estate to pay up, also, Moses and Nelson to pay. Price writes that she has no other friends living that he knows of, consequently, it come back to your children. Shores has taken out letters and Moses acts as administrator.*

Leticia's land ended up in a lawsuit initiated by Mrs. Leticia Lundy who was 85 years old and young Leticia's grandmother. Her son, Clifton, married Mary Ann and both were gone. Her grand daughter lived with Eugene as a child after the death of her parents. The 85-year-old Leticia Lundy filed in behalf of her children and grandchildren on March 28, 1868.

> *Mack, we are all very well with the exception of hard colds. We have been making garden and has got most done. Oh Mack, I long for the time for you to come. I am sick of silly-life as you call it there.*
> *The baby is scuawling at the top of her lunges. I must go and take her. Master Georgie has taken the advantage of the time and been padling in the water and has wet himself from head to foot. Oh, what a site. He ses Papa is comming and is going to fetch him a gun. You must fetch him something when you come. He is a noble boy. Little Sissy can almost sit alone. She is as pretty as a little pinky.*
> *Mother send her love to her boy. Good by for this time and except lots of love from your ever loving Wife.              Vira*
> *Write often, please & time is so long, long.*
> *Georgie sends a kiss, he sais, to his Dear Papa.*

The Ninety-second Illinois Mounted Infantry was assigned the task of restoring order in the area. Peace was the factor and both sides wanted to be sure that nothing happened to break the truce. Soldiers who had been encouraged to burn and loot were now supposed to be gentlemen. Some did not comply and paid for their disobedience with their lives.

Eugene had mixed emotions concerning the war. He burned and looted along with the rest, but it after the war was over, he had time to think about his actions. He never approved of killing private citizens and felt justice was served when he heard about a soldier who was put to death because he murdered a citizen for his money, but he was not sure how others felt. The soldiers had to learn to comply to polite society again.

In Camp Near Concord N. C.   May 14$^{th}$ 1865
Dear Wife
With pleasure I seat myself to write you. I am well as usual, hoping these lines will reach you & babies, enjoying good health.
I wrote to you about a week ago, but could not mail the letter, on account of having to moove. We are now in regular Camp & expect to remain so untill we start home. The 92$^{nd}$ is all there is here at presant.
We are looking for the rest of our Brigade here tomorrow. They halted yesterday to execute a soldier of the 9 Mich. Cavalry for murdering a citizen for his money. It looks hard for him, to be killed by his own men after living through all the dangers of Battle, but Civil laws must be established. That is all that is keeping us here now & I hope it will not take us long to do it.
I wish I could tell you when to look for me home, but I cant. We may start home in a month & we may stay our time, which is 3 month from the 4$^{th}$ of next month.
I had a letter from Annie a short time ago, but cannot ans. untill I get some ink. This is mud.
Vira, there is a large cotton factory close to our Camp & 100 mighty nice girls in it. Look out, or I am gone up. You know I will keep out of their way. My love to all Wife & babies.
As ever your            Loving Husband
                    E. M. Swaggart

Elvira, reading the papers, was keeping up with the news better than Eugene was. She read in the newspapers about the review that was occurring in Washington, D. C. on May 24. She knew there was usually a review before the release of troops.

The Ninety-second Illinois, however, did not move with General William Sherman's forces, or with General Judson Kilpatrick's cavalry. They stayed in North Carolina to help bring peace to the area.

A package arrived from Eugene. He sent home what he could to make his trip easier. There was a lot of theft that occurred involving the soldiers as they mustered out and headed home – possibly by Southern citizens who just wanted to retrieve their own goods that were stolen from them, and possibly by others who knew the soldiers had valuables with them. He wanted to be sure he traveled light.

*Mt. Carroll*                              *May 19$^{th}$ 1865*
*Dear Husband,*
*Once more I am permited to write a few hasty lines to you. Oh Dear, I am feeling so happy that I do not know what to do with myself, to think that you are comming home and Georgie is better. Georgie has been sick for 2 weeks. He has a very severe actacked of the fever. He has been very sick, but Dock Bill has brought him out all right but, Oh, he is so cross. Mother, also, has been quite sick, but is now better.*
*Oh Mack we are looking for you home by the first of June. The last nights paper states their will be a review of Medes and Shirmans Armys.*
*If that is so, you will all be home soon, wont you. Oh, I can hardly wait for the time to come when you will be your own master and, to think, that when you come, it is for good. Oh Mack, what a time that will be, wont it, My Dear.*
*I read a letter from Mrs. Staffer last night stating that I had package thare from the Army, to advance one dollar and she would send it. Annie is going up in the morning after it. Oh, I want to know so bad what is in it, something nice, I expect.*

> *Will Graham is at home on furlough. He was here to tea the other night.*

John Miller, away from home, finally came to his senses. His affair with Elizabeth Reynolds was over when he left for the Army and he wanted his wife and family back. He started writing Mary Ann, who was more than ready to take him back. The family felt if Mary Ann could forgive him, they could also.

> *Annie had a letter from John Miller last night. They think they will all be home before long. Their Company is out guarding our Presidents remains. I should not think it would be very plesant business. It would not be for me at any rate. I would rather guard the living then the dead, would you not.*
> *Well, what do you think of their getting old Jefferson. If wasnt that a good hall, but the idea of this miserable rebeliase going out in petticoats. We do not think mutch of rather a disgrace to them.*

Jefferson Davis, President of the Confederacy, was surprised in his tent by a Union picket when he was in the process of escaping at the end of the war. It was cold and rainy outside and when he heard the horses, he threw a shawl around his shoulders which he later claimed was his riding shawl. As he was going out into the rain, his wife threw her full-length raincoat over him to prevent him from getting wet.

The Northern newspapers, as well as showman P. T. Barnum, capitalized on the story saying he was dressed in women's clothing trying to escape.[285]

> *Marshal Harington is at home. His wife is sick.*
> *Olive Harington has acted so that her Mother has turned her out of the house. She is a poor miserable thing. Her Mother keeps the child. I do not know where she is. She better be dead than alive.*
> *Jennie is at home now. Dicky is better but not very well. Poor thing. I feel sorry for her. The Children*

---

[285] Joseph McElroy, *Jefferson Davis*, Konecky & Konecky, New York, NY, pp. 510-518.

*are both fretting, so I will close for this time. Good by for this time    from you loving Wife.*
*Vira*
*Mack, do write often. Please do till you come home. I do not get any mail, letters, hardly. I do not know the reason.*

Eugene tried to stay occupied to help pass time. He was tired of the officers and their orders. He took a detail driving a mule team so the officers left him alone.

The soldiers in the Ninety-second were still unpaid. They were due several months' pay, but Eugene knew he and Elvira needed that so desperately to start over. The war was hard on him and he and his family suffered financially. He saw others in the family buying land and pianos. However, he knew it would take every cent he had just to get back on his feet. Was patriotism worth it?

John Miller wrote to Eugene and Eugene answered him. The war was over and it was time for families to reunite and forget the past.

*Concord   North Carolina      May 24$^{th}$ 1865*
*Dear Wife*
*With unexpectible joy, I seat myself to ans. your May 9$^{th}$, it being the only letter recd in Co. I in I dont know when.*
*I am well & hope this will find you & babies the same.*
*I was very sorry to hear of Letties death at the same time. I was expecting to hear of bad news from her. In regard to buying the place, I guess it will be a hard matter, as they would want the money down and I could not raise enough. If we would be paid, I could raise $200.00 & you know that we will need.*
*Vira, two or three days ago, the news was very favorable for going home, but since, it is all a blow up. We find as we are Mounted Infantry, we are*

*not included with neather Cavalry nor Infantry. Consequently, there must be a special order from War Department to muster us out of service. Some seem to think there will be such an order before long and others think we will have to serve our time out. For my part, I would like to go home, but I could not do much now if I was at home, so late in the season. I will feel very Thankfull if I get home all right in the fall, wont you. Fighting, as you say, is over, but there is numerous dangers, you know, that you are all exposed to, but I must to him who has so long protected us and all will be well.*

*I do not know when we will get our pay, but one thing, the longer it runs the more we will have when we do get it. Our officers put on more stile now than they ever did, but Mc is not in their clutches. I got a detail to help drive team, so you see, I can do about as I please. I sleep in the morning as long as I want to & have no sholder scab to pull me out to rool call and you that is my best holt to sleep in the morning, I suppose.*

*Henry Lego is at home by this time. Well, our time will come next.*

*Give my love to all and except much love from your Devoted            Mc Swaggart*

*P. S. I wrote to John the other day and told him we was to be musterd out right away, but we have found out different - since.*

*William Skillings is well and sends respect to all.*

Eugene spent some of his time trading with the southern ladies. They needed coffee and sugar and that was Government Issue. He wanted eggs and butter. A few of the ladies, who still had chickens and cows and were tired of doing without, were willing to trade with a Yankee.

He went to a dance and played the fiddle one set. He wanted Elvira to believe he did not dance with anyone.

Everyone at home waited for the baby girl's name. Eugene would not give it to them, perhaps because he wanted to discuss it with Elvira first.

> *Concord North Carolina         June 1$^{st}$ 1865*
> *Dearest Wife*
> *With pleasure, I renew my old bask in receipt of yours by Jake Hudling, which came to hand by todays mail. I was glad to see the photo of my boy and I am in good hopes I will see the original by the 4$^{th}$ of July. The 92$^{nd}$ is now waiting for the Paymaster to pay us so we can start home. I guess we will be on our way home in less than 10 days. Still, you must not look for me till you see me, for you know there is many a slip between the cup and the lip.*
> *Oh! yes, I am well and enjoying myself as well as I can. I have no duty to perform, so you see, I can go and come when I like. I was out today 15 miles from camp, trading sugar & coffee for butter & eggs with the Weans, or southern ladies, just as you like. I gave 2 lbs of coffee & 3 lbs of sugar for 8 dozen eggs & 5 lbs. butter. Big speculating, that.*
> *I will not write again in the course of a week if we stay that long. If not, this is the last you can look for, for sometime. I have no news worth writing. Camp is very dull, everybody mad, because they dont start us home sooner. Oh yes, you are mighty right.*
> *I was to a big dance the other night. I went to see and learn. I did not dance any. I plaid for one set and lit out. I recd a letter from J. Miller. He said our folks were well, but I could not take his word for it as he is not at home more than I.*

*Well, good by. Love to all. Kiss the boy. As ever.*
*Your Affectionate Husband*
*E. M. Swaggart*
*P. S. I can not send that name. I will have to bring it.                           EMS*

The long awaited news finally came. Eugene was going home. He heard the tenth as a date and thought it was June 10. However, they left camp in North Carolina on June 21, 1865 and were discharged in Chicago, Illinois on July 10, 1865. Eugene wanted Elvira to have the news.  It was his last letter to her while he was in the Union Army.

*Camp in Concord  North Carolina*
*June 3$^{rd}$ 1865*
*Dear Wife*
*With joy, I now write you in ans. to yours of May 22d. It found me well & hope this will find you the same. I wrote you day before yesterday stating that we expected to start home soon, but it still remains uncertain when we will start. One thing certain, we will go as soon as we are paid & Genl. Atkins went for the Pay Master this morning and we expect him here tomorrow sometime and it is thought we will get off by the 10$^{th}$ of this month.*
*You wrote in your letter as you expected home. You must not be impatint. The time will come now very soon.*
*I am looking forward and anticipating some good times in the course of the next 6 months, are you not. Oh, I want to see you & the babies so bad. I cant hardly content myself.*
*Vira, you said the package I sent in Mrs. Stouffers Box had arrived. I sent 1 over with a silver cup in it and a bound book of magazines. I forget whos. I suppose she will know what to give you. I would*

have sent more books, but I had no idea they would ever go through.  I wish I had now what I threw away, but I will be very thankfull if I get myself home safe, thats whats the matter.

Vira, I dont know as I will write anymore.  I hope not, but if we do not start soon, of course I will, you bet.  I will close hoping our next will be closer than the pen.  Much love to all.

       As ever your loving         Mc

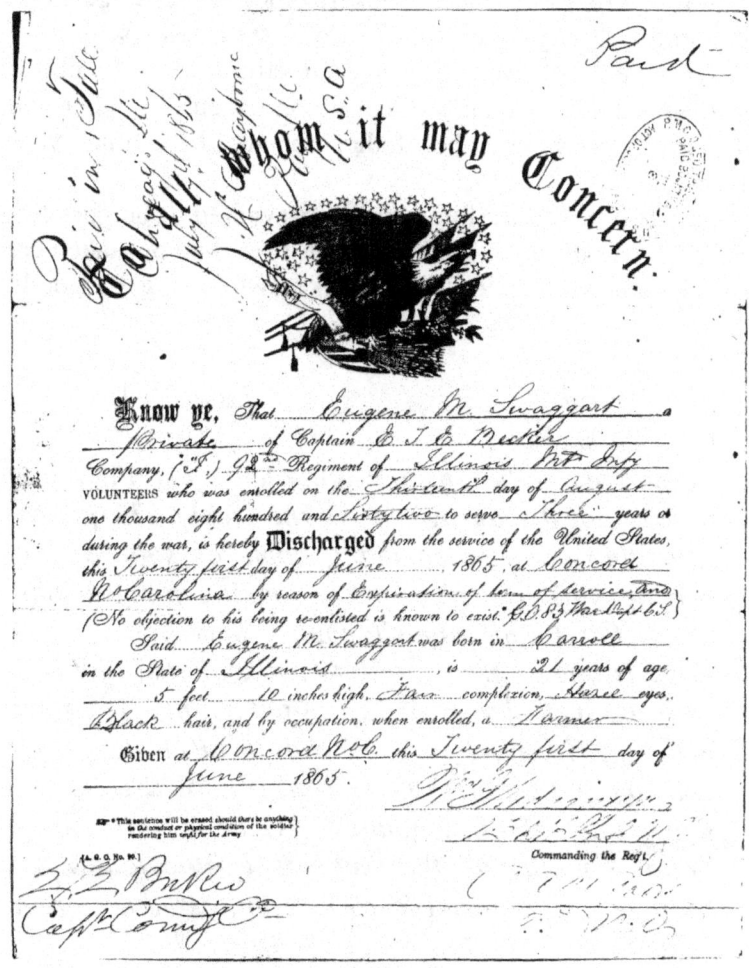

Discharge papers for Eugene McBride Swaggart

*Vira, since writing this, we find that we will be on our road home by the 10. Our papers are being made out at this present time so you need not write any more. You hear.        From Mc*

Before Elvira received Eugene's letter, she wrote to him. John Russell, who had gone to live with the family as a young man to help out, was helping Sylvester dig a well for Moses and Amanda Ludisky.
Anna heard from James Becker, who was a Sergeant in the One hundred Forty-sixth Illinois, Co. A with John Miller
Elvira wanted Eugene to bring something for the children. It had been a long time since Georgie had seen his father and the baby girl would meet her father for the first time when he arrived.
The farm looked terrible and Elvira wanted to prepare Eugene for the worst before he got home. Morford had not taken care of it and Elvira was afraid it would take awhile to get a good crop again.

*Mt. Carroll                June $6^{th}$ 1865*
*Dear Husband,*
*I recd your rather discouraging letter last night, but it does not discourage me in the least. The papers state that you are comming home as soon as you can be mustered out. I am looking for you next week. Oh, I hope you will come, Mack.*
*Their is one request I want to make of you, that is, if you are in Chicago or Springfield long enough to get your likeness taken, have it taken large for D....ism and bring it to me, wont you, please do.*
*Bring the babies something. Georgie talks about Papa comming all the time. The little fellow has been very sick since I last wrote, but is better again. Little Sissie is well and fat as a little ball.*

Mother has gone out to Mr. Garners on a visit, she went home with Jim Garner last friday. Annie has gone to Church. Jennie did not go this morning.

We are having beautifull weather now, still it is very dry as we have not had any rain in a long time. They predict that crops will be poor this year as the bugs are taking everything. Oh, if crops fail, it will go hard on us as it will be like our starting anew again this fall.

Oh Dear me, you never saw such a looking place in all your life. It was as like some old Dutch level it. It will take us awhile to get the filth and livestock out, I can tell you. They have the first of September. You better believe I am glad for once that they are going to leave the country. They is puttering, as usual, not doing much of anything.

John Russell and Sylvester are diging a well for Mose. I believe they have got it about done. They have brought splendid water. They have also dug a roothouse. I hope poor Dicky will have it a little easier than she has allways had it. Her health is real poor this spring.

Mary Anns baby is very sick, or has been, with the longue fever. They did not think it would live. It is four months old. It is a little boy.

Annie got a letter from James Becker last night. He says that news states that the 92$^{nd}$ would be mustered out this week either in Springfield or Chicago. He also said that the Guviner had orders to muster out all the state troops. If it is so, you will all be home early.

Your devoted Wife<br>Vira

P S  Sylvester and John Russell has come in. They walked in yet. Ses tell him to express his violin *home as soon as you can for fear it will be stolen. He thinks it not safe to bring it through the states. Mack, write often as you can. If it is every other day, it seems long. Vira*

When Eugene returned home, there were many parties in town to welcome all the soldiers home and many friends dropped by to say "hello". It was too late to plant for the season, but Eugene was not too upset about that. It was not something he looked forward to doing.

One of his first responsibilities was to name the baby girl who had been almost six months without a name. He named her using the feminine version of his own name, Eugene, for her second name. Her name was Nellie Eugenia Swaggart.

With all the soldiers returning home with little money, economy was low. Everyone had a hard time. Families had to dig deep to help those that returned to get started again.

Many of Eugene's friends were killed in the war and never returned. Home was not the same anymore. Eugene and Elvira decided to move to Minnesota where Eugene had the farm. They lived in Minnesota for awhile and returned to Mt. Carroll but after a few years, they moved to Caldwell, Kansas where Eugene became a successful building contractor. They had two children besides George and Nellie who they named Josephine and Charles Swaggart.

George Swaggart, son of Eugene and Elvira, was taken by Apache Indians when he was fourteen years old and was "held captive for six days, escaping by riding to a home forty miles without bridle or saddle." He later moved to New Mexico as a pioneer where he was foreman of a large ranch and was active in combating hostile Indians in that part of the Southwest. In 1901, he moved to Cochise County in Arizona where he and his children purchased a ranch. He died in 1922 at the age of sixty.[286]

Nellie Eugenia Swaggart married Joseph Henry Briggs and they moved to Palestine, Texas where he was a mailman and

---

[286] Information came from newspaper clippings that were sent to Nellie Eugenia when he died. It is unknown which newspapers printed the accounts.

journalist as well as assisting his mother, Adeline Perry Briggs/Ford in the furniture business. Nellie was a dressmaker. She died in 1951 and is buried in Palestine, Texas.

John and Mary Ann Miller followed Eugene and Elvira to Minnesota. When Eugene and Elvira returned to Mt. Carroll, they moved on to Caldwell, Kansas and were later followed by the family. At some point, they moved on to Moore, Oklahoma where both are buried.

Moses and Amanda Ludisky moved to Caldwell with Elvira and Eugene. Sarah, mother of Eugene, Moses, Anna and John Miller, was due to move with them, but she died just before the move in 1872. Moses and Amanda Ludisky had, as known children, six boys and two girls. Jennie, their daughter, was still living in Caldwell, Kansas in 1908.[287] Moses died in 1898. They have many descendants still in the Kansas and Oklahoma areas.

Anna Swaggart married Albert H. Nyman in November of 1866. They stayed in Carroll County, residing in Mount Carroll with Anna teaching music in Lanark part-time, where Henry Lego lived until his death. They had no children.

Sylvester, who eventually lost all of his sight, married a girl from Carroll County named Ellen A. Myers in 1873. They had three children. Sylvester became a traveling medicine salesman.[288]

It is not known what happened to Jenny Jane but she was mentioned in a letter in 1899.

Elvira died in Kingfisher, Oklahoma in 1908 and Eugene, in Chickasha, Oklahoma at the age of ninety in 1930. After the death of Elvira, Eugene married Josephine Reynolds Woodin in 1910. She was the sister of his friends, William and Charles Reynolds and his childhood sweetheart before he met Elvira.

---

[287] Information on back of photo submitted by Richard and Lynda Swaggart of Geary, OK.
[288] Van Alstine, Lester - *Van Alstyne - Van Alstine Family History, Volume 3*, Publisher J. Grant Stevenson, Provo, Utah, and marriage records of Illinois.

# BIBLIOGRAPHY

*A Rainy Day in Camp*, Protestant Episcopal Book Society, 1224 Chestnut Street, Philadelphia, PA, Presented by U. S. Christian Commission, George H. Stuart, Chairman

Barrett, John G., *Sherman's March through the Carolinas*, The University of North Carolina Press, Chapel Hill, 1956. © 1956 by North Carolina Press

*Battles and Leaders of the Civil War, Volume III - The Tide Shifts*, Edited by Robert Underwood Johnson and Clarence Clough Buel, of the Editorial Staff of "The Century Magazine", Castle, A Division of Book Sales, Inc., 114 Northfield Avenue, Edison, NJ 08837. © by Castle.

Coburn, Mark, *Terrible Innocence, General Sherman at War*, Hippocrene Books, Inc., New York, New York. © 1993 by Mark Coburn

Cort, Charles Edwin, *Dear Friends, The Civil War Letters and Diary of Charles Edwin Cort* - Helyn W. Tomlinson, ed. n.p.: 1962

Cox, General Jacob D., *Sherman's March to the Sea, Hood's Tennessee Campaign and the Carolina Campaigns of 1865*, with New Introduction by Brooks D. Simpson, Da Capo Press, New York, 1994. Introduction © 1994 by Brooks D. Simpson.

Davis, Burke, *Sherman's March, The First Full-Length Narrative of General William T. Sherman's Devastating March through Georgia and the Carolinas*, First Vintage Books Edition, May 1988. © 1980 by Burke Davis

Denney, Robert E., *The Civil War Years, A Day-by-Day Chronicle of the Life of a Nation*, Foreword by Gregory J. W. Urwin, Sterling Publishing Co., Inc.. New York, © 1992 by Robert E. Denney.

Dyer, Frederick H., *A Compendium of the War of the Rebellion, Illinois Regimental Histories, Ninety-second Regiment Infantry*, Des Moines, Frederick H. Dyer, 1908

Eddy, Thomas Mears, *The Patriotism of Illinois: A Record of the Civil and Military History of the State in the War of the*

Union, Chapter XXII, Regimental Sketches, Ninety-second Illinois Infantry, 1865, Chicago, Clarke and Company, 1866

Glatthaar, Joseph T., *The March to the Sea and Beyond, Sherman's Troops in the Savannah and Carolinas Campaigns*, Louisiana State University Press, Baton Rouge & London. © 1985 by New York University and Joseph T. Glatthaar

*History of Carroll County, Illinois*, Published by H. F. Kett & Co., Chicago, IL 1878 and Reproduction by Unigraphic, Inc. Evansville, IN, 1976

*Illinois Troops (Union) Infantry, Records of Events, Volume 13, Record of Events for Ninety-second Illinois Infantry, September 1862 - June 1865*

Lyman, Darryl, *Civil War Wordbook Including Sayings, Phrases and Slang*, Combined Books, Conshohocken, PA. © 1994 by Darryl Lyman

McElroy, Joseph, *Jefferson Davis*, Konecky & Konecky, 156 Fifth Avenue, New York, New York 10010, ©1937 by Robert McElroy

Robbe, Arthur and Hinton, Richard, *Rededication Ceremony of the Carroll County Civil War Soldiers and Sailors Monument*

Stonesifer, Jr., Roy P., *Biographical Dictionary of the Union, Northern Leaders of the Civil War*, Edited by John T. Hubbell, Greenwood Press, Westport, Connecticut, 1995

*The Civil War Almanac*, Introduction by Henry Steele Commager, World Almanac Publications, A Bison Book, New York, New York 1983. © Bison Books

*The Merck Manual of Diagnosis and Therapy, Thirteenth Edition*, Merck Sharp & Dohme Research Laboratories, Division of Merck & Company, Inc., Rahway, New Jersey, 1977. © 1977 by Merck & Co.

*The Official Records of the War of the Rebellion, Reports, Army of the Cumberland, No. 422, Report of Colonel Eli Murray; No. 423, Report of Colonel Smith D. Atkins; No. 424, Report of Lieutenant Colonel Robert H. King; No. 425, Reports of Colonel Smith D. Atkins; No. 426, Report of Captain Matthew Van Buskirk; No. 427, Reports of Major Albert Woodcock.*

Tucker, Glenn, *Chickamauga, Bloody Battle in the West*, Konecky & Konecky, 156 Fifth Avenue, New York, New York 10010, 1961. © 1961 by the Bobbs-Merrill Company, Inc.

Van Alstine, Lester, *Van Alstyne - Van Alstine Family History, Volume 3*, Publisher: J. Grant Stevenson, 230 West 1230 North, Provo, Utah 84601. © 1981 by Lester Van Alstine

*Webster's New Universal Unabridged Dictionary*, Barnes & Noble Books, New York. © 1994 by dilithium Press, Ltd.

Welcher, Frank J. *The Union Army, 1861-1865, Organization and Operations*, Volume I - *The Eastern Theater*; Volume II - *TheWestern Theater*, Indiana University Press, Bloomington and Indianapolis, 1993. © 1993 by Frank J. Welcher.

## SOURCE LIBRARIES

Illinois State Historical Library, Springfield, IL
Indiana State Historical Library, Indianapolis, IN
Wisconsin State Historical Library, Madisonville, WI

Carroll County Library, Savannah, IL
Valparaiso Public Library, Valparaiso, IN

Wabash College Library, Crawfordsville, IN

## OTHER SOURCES

Battlefields Revisited, New Cumberland, PA
Bigelow, Lucille, Clackamas, OR
Boulineau, William
Bruner, Cathy, Mount Carroll, IL
Griffin, Dr. Larry, Dyersberg, TN
Harris, Jerry, Scottsdale, AZ
John F. Walter Institute for Civil War Research, Middle Village, N.Y.
Robbe, Arthur O., Mt. Carroll, IL
Swaggart, Richard & Lynda, Geary, OK
Swaggart, Thomas, Belmont, CA
Welcher, Dr. Frank W., Indianapolis, IN
Whiteside, William R., Cottage Hill, IL

# GLOSSARY

Many letters written in the Civil War period were written by soldiers who had minimal education. Most who attended school at all had only a sixth grade equivalent education. Officers were usually more educated than the average enlisted man although that was not always the case. However, a few of the letters were written by people who were teaching in the schools, so the language differences could denote the time period or the Dutch and German influence.

Some words are spelled correctly but used incorrectly. There are also perfectly good words that are not generally used in conversation anymore so I included those. When I felt it helpful, an explanation or meaning was given. It is my hope that all who read this book will understand it and thus, enjoy it. I feel sure most Civil War enthusiasts, historians, or people who read a lot would have no problem just as it is, but I am hoping to also make it interesting for those who do not necessarily fit into the categories above.

Some definitions were taken from * Webster's New World Dictionary of the American Language listed in the Bibliography, some from the Civil War Period were taken from the **Civil War Wordbook by Darryl Lyman, but many were from Mack and his family and were words used by them. Those are my interpretations from reading the letters many times and others may have different interpretations for them.

<u>When Mack and His Family or Friends Said - They Probably Meant</u>

4 ½ - 4:30
11 ½ - 11:30
40 pounder – used when describing General Absolom Baird, probably comparing him to a cannon.
100 days service – prison time

-A-

abomanable – abominable
abut – about
accostomed – accustomed
accumilate – accumulate
accumudate – accommodate
acounts - accounts
actacked – attacked or attack
Adairsvill - Adairsville, Georgia

351

adress - address
afections - affections
affare – affair
afread – afraid
afterwhile – after a while
agitant - adjutant
ague – *malaria
aint – ain't
Alabam - Alabama
all the increase – all the children
all ways - always
allmost – almost
allright – all right
amunition – ammunition
ans – answer
ansd - answered
anxcious – anxious
aoughfull – awful
Ap - April
arested – arrested
arived – arrived
armey – army
armys – armies
artilery – artillery
asure – assure
atacted - attacked
atal – at all
atall – at all
attact – attack
attacted – attacked
aways – away or a short distance

awfull – awful

-B-
batchelor - bachelor
bair – bear
bare - barely
barrell – barrel
barricks - barracks
bask – *enjoy pleasant warmth
batery - battery
bbls. – barrels
beare – bear
beatting - beating
beautifull – beautiful
be caus – because
because – because
begining - beginning
beleave – believe
best holt – Mack's term for the best thing that is happening
beter – better
betwen – between
bigest - biggest
bilious fever – *bilious fever described as a bilious cholera or fever associated with yellow diarrhea and/or problems with the liver
bin – been
bitters – *a beer made of a bitter weed or a medicine made of a bitter herb

bivouacked – *camped in an open field
Black Berries – blackberries
blowed – blown
blue jackets – Union soldiers
brake – break
Braureguard - General Pierre Gustave Beauregard
breth - breath
brig. – Brigade
Brigads - Brigades
bub – *brother, boy, buddy
bugars – buggers – *a fellow or a lad
bugy – buggy
bummer – an independent forager who left the ranks and plundered for the North or the South. Also used for soldiers in Sherman's army who foraged and also acted as pickets or scouts for the army.
bunky – bunkie or bunk mate
bushell – bushel
bushwhacker – **a Confederate guerrilla who lurked in the woods engaging in plundering or irregular warfare
buternuts - butternuts
butternuts – * & **Confederate whose uniform was dyed with an extract from butternuts or walnuts. The uniforms were usually yellow or yellowish brown.
By - Bye
by jung – a swear word without meaning. It was always assumed by this person that it referred to Carl Gustav Jung, the Swiss psychiatrist. However, he was not born until 1875 and it was obviously used prior to that time.

-C-

C. S. A. – Confederate States of America
canebrakes – canebrake rattlesnakes
cannot hardly – can hardly
canon – cannon
canonading - cannonading
cant –can't
Cap – Captain
car – railroad car
carefull – careful
carfull – careful
carpit - carpet
Cartersvill - Cartersville, Georgia
cary – carry
carys – carries

353

catradges – cartridges
caus – because
Cav. - cavalry
cavelry – cavalry
Charley - Charlie or Charles Reynolds
Charly Wright - Charlie Wright
chaste – chased
chasted – chased
Chatanooga - Chattanooga, Tennessee
Chatnooga - Chattanooga, Tennessee
Chatnooga Valey - Chattanooga Valley
Chattahoocha - Chattahoochee River
cheerfullness – cheerfulness
Chicamauga - Chickamauga, Georgia
chizel - chisel
choping – chopping
Cin. O - Cincinnati, Ohio
cloaths - clothes
cloths – clothes
Co – Company
Col – Colonel
Col. Cobern - Colonel John Coburn from Kentucky
Col. Hardee - Colonel Chester Harding
colect - collect
com – come

comd. - commanded
come out – came out
comenced - commenced
comensed – commenced
commensed – commenced
comensing - commencing
comming – coming
comp. – company
compain - complain
conficate – confiscate
confiscats – confiscates
canonading – cannonading
consumtion – consumption or tuberculosis
consumtium – consumption or tuberculosis
contre bands – contrabands, slaves who escaped or were brought into Union lines
controle - control
Copperheads – **Northerners who sympathized with the South or opposed Lincoln's war policies
corispond – correspond
Corpl - Corporal
corps – corpse, body
corrispondence – correspondence
cosin - cousin
cours – course
crewel – cruel

croany – crony or close companion
cronic - chronic
crost – crossed
ct or cts. - cents
cume – come
cut home – went home

-D-
damd – damned
Danvill - Danville, Kentucky
darke – dark
darkies – Africans
darndest - damnedest
deer – dear
delight full - delightful
delited – delighted
dependance - dependence
deuce - *devil
Dicky - Dickie or Amanda Ludisky Van Alstine/Swaggart
dictory – dictum
differant - different
dieing – dying
diffculties - difficulties
diging – digging
dirrhoea – diarrhea
disapointed – disappointed
disapointment - disappointment
discription – description
dispach - dispatch
dispair – despair

distruction - destruction
Dock – Doctor
doctrin – doctoring
doesnt – doesn't
donatd – donated
dont – don't
door yeard – door yard, *yard in front of the door of the house
doubtfull – doubtful
dread full – dreadful
dreaned – drained
droped – dropped
dryed - dried
dutys – duties

-E-
earthe – earth
easly – easily
eat – ate
eather – either
eatibles – eatables
Edg. - Captain Egbert Q. E. Becker
encamp – make into a camp
enoug - enough
enquiring - inquiring
entrenched – placed in a position of strength
envelop – envelope
epistle – a letter
equipage – *carriage with horses and liveried servants

355

but used in his letters to mean army equipment.
ere – before
eresipelas – erysipelas, an acute disease of the skin
erysippelas – erysipelas
Ettawah River - Etowah River
eve – evening
every boddy – everybody
exagerate - exaggerate
except – accept
exceptable – acceptable
excepted - accepted
excitable – excited
exepting – with the exception of
expects - expect
extravigant – extravagant
extreem – extreme

-F-
familys – families
fanily – finally
Fare Haven - Fair Haven, Illinois
fer – for
fiew – few
fifes – flutes used in military or marching bands
fighte – fight
fightin - fighting
fireing - firing
firkin – *quarter of a barrel

fited - fitted
fiting – fighting
flank – *the extreme right or left side or moving to the left or right side of an army to pass them
flatering – flattering
flaxin – fighting with the winning edge
floged – flogged
fore – for
forgoten – forgotten
Fort Donolson - Fort Donaldson in Tennessee
forte – fort
fortify cations – fortifications
Fredricksburgh - Fredricksburg, Virginia
french furlough – unauthorized furlough or AWOL, Away Without Leave
fret – worry
frog coffee – coffee made with water out of frog ponds
fryed – fried
fulough - furlough

-G-
ganders – a condition whereby the mind wanders and one sits and stares into space
gass – *empty talk

356

gassed – talking in a boastful manner
gealous – jealous
gehu – Jehu – a slang word referencing a character from the Bible in Kings II
Gen - General
Gen Bird - General Absalom Baird
Gen Buel - Brigadier General Don Carlos Buell
generaly – generally
Genl - General
Genl Killpatrick - General Judson Kilpatrick
Geo. Fomlinson - George Finlayson
Geor. - George
Georgie - George Swaggart II
geting – getting
gets - get
git – get
gladened – gladdened
gobbled – eaten, but in the Civil War it meant to steal, defeat or capture
gobled – gobbled or eaten or to steal, defeat or capture
goodby - goodbye
gooms – gums
Gorge - George
gound – ground

GQ – General Quarters or Quartermaster
grayback – **a Confederate soldier or a body louse
grub – informal word for food
guard hous - guardhouse
guitarrh – guitar
guviner – governor

-H-
half – have
hapen - happen
hapened - happened
hapy – happy
hard tack – **hardtack or salt less hard biscuit or cracker made of plain flour and water
have drew – have drawn
haver sack – * & **haversack, made of canvas and similar to a knapsack, it strapped over the right shoulder with the weight on the left hip and was used for provisions
hear – here
heer - hear
hedgepen – *fence with hedges
herd – hard
himselfe - himself
holt – *wooded hill
hom – home
hopefull - hopeful

hopeing – hoping
horrable – horrible
hosoure – hoosier – a term used for people who reside in Indiana
hosp. - hospital
hospitial - hospital
hosurdoom – Indiana Brigade or environment where many Indiana people are together
house – jailhouse
Huckle Berries – huckleberries
hugg – hug
humbug – *sham or dishonest person
hussled – hustled

-I-
I be – I will be
I V – Illinois Volunteers
Ive – I've
imajine – imagine
impatint – impatient
imposible – impossible
independance – independence
independant – independent
indipendant – independent
Inft - infantry
ish – am
its – it's

-J-
Jake Hudling - Jake Hedling

Jaxson Judge - Jackson Judge from Wisconsin
jehue – Jehu, a slang word referencing a character from the Bible in Kings II
Johnies – Johnny or Johnny Reb,** a Confederate soldier
John Russel - John Russell
Johnson - General Joseph Eggleston Johnston
Jonson - General Joseph Eggleston Johnston
jolly fication – a very happy time
jorney – journey
jurs harp – Jew's harp

-K-
Kanosha - Kenosha, Wisconsin
Kenusha - Kenosha, Wisconsin
Kentuck - Kentucky
kinda – kind of

-L-
laid – layed
lais - lays
late fare – traveling or arriving late
layed – laid
laying – lying
leasure - leisure
Lebonon - Lebanon Station

leeches – *instrument used to draw blood
leetle - little
lef – left
leundt – lieutenant
likeness – picture or photo
little mixed – slightly confused
little plant – unborn baby
Liut. – Lieutenant
longue – lung
longue fever – lung fever or pneumonia
lonsome - lonesome
loose – lose
los – loss
Louis Ville - Louisville, Kentucky
Louisvill, Ky - Louisville, Kentucky
lucre – money
luit. - lieutenant
lung fever – pneumonia
lunges - lungs

-M-
maby – maybe
male – mail
marriade – married
marrid - married
Marshal Harington - Marshall Harrington
measels – measles
med - medicine

Medes - General George Gordon Meade
mersys – mercy used as a slang word
mery – merry
Millegeville - Milledgeville, Illinois
millner - milliner
minse - mince
miss use – misuse
mite - might
moove – move
mooved – moved
moovements – movements
mooving – moving
Mosouri - Missouri
mostach – mustache
Mount Stearling - Mount Sterling, Kentucky
Mrfreesboro - Murfreesboro, Tennessee
mtd. - mounted
Mt. Pspt. - Mount Prospect, Illinois
mudy – muddy
muse – meditate or reflect
musterd – mustered
mutch – much
my self – myself

-N-
nail pen – a shack that consisted of whatever wood

or scrap material they could
find and nails, possibly
wooden nails
nap packs – knapsacks
napsacks - knapsacks
Nashvill - Nashville, Tennessee
neather – neither
neusance – nuisance
new - knew
niger – African
niger head – niggerhead – **a
term used by the
copperheads or southern
sympathizers for the
northerners who thought
violent means should be
used to resolve the slavery
issue.
niggas - Africans
nigger – African
ninty twosters – 92$^{nd}$ Illinois
Infantry Volunteers
no – know
No. - number

-O-
occurance – occurrence
of – off
offise - office
oftener – more often
ol – old

old set – old timers or
something that someone is
tired of hearing or doing
oppinions – opinions
oppotunity - opportunity
ordelys - ordelies
owd – owed
oweing – owing

-P-
pacient - patient
padling – paddling
pain full – painful
parad – parade
parde - parade
partacle – particle
patroll – patrol
payed - paid
peck – *one-fourth of a bushel
or eight quarts
pefict – perfect
pen – to write or the instrument
used in writing
pepr – pepper
perfict - perfect
perfumes – odors
permision - permission
permited – permitted
Perryvill - Perryville, Kentucky
peticular – particular
pic - pick
pich – pitch

picket – soldier placed on a forward line to warn against enemy advance
picture man – photographer
pistole - pistol
pitty – pity
plaid – played, used as played out
plasure – pleasure
pleasent – pleasant
plesant – pleasant
plug – reference to his horse
posescion – possession
posted – informed of events
Potomic - Potomac
prayr – prayer
preformed – performed
preforming - performing
presant – present
prescious – precious
presum – presume
pretentions – pretensions
pretiest - prettiest
prety – pretty
primis – premise
privations – deprivations, lack of necessities of life
procedings - proceedings
proove - prove
Provest Marshel – Provost Marshall
ptry – paltry
purt – pert

puting – putting

-Q-
quanity - quantity
quareling - quarreling
quick consumption – pneumonia or a fast acting tuberculosis

-R-
R. R.– railroad
raise ned – raise hell
Rasaca - Resaca, Georgia
Resacca - Resaca, Georgia
rebs - rebels
rebbles – rebels
rebeliase – rebellious or rebel
rebelion – rebellion, a term used often by Union sympathizers to describe the Civil War
reble – rebel
rebles - rebels
rebs – rebels
recd – received
receaved – received
receipt – recipe, used when requesting the medicine recipe or mixture used
recieve - receive
recived - received
recolect – recollect or remember

reconnaissance – *search made for useful military information by examination of the ground
redy - ready
reg – Regiment
regt – Regiment
regts - Regiments
regail – regale or entertain
regt – regiment
releaved – relieved
remainet - remained
renten – rendering, extracting fat from lard to use in cooking or making soap or he could have been referring to the land she was renting
repose – rest upon
reputacion – reputation
res - rest
resighned – resigned
ress – rest
restes – rests
reville - reveille
Rily Stoddard - Riley Stoddard
Ringold - Ringgold, Georgia
rong – wrong
rool call – roll call
roothouse – cellar where potatoes or other root crops were kept
Rosy - General William Starkie Rosecrans

ruber – rubber
ruged – rugged
runing – running

-S-
sabath – Sabbath
sabbeth - Sabbath
sadle – saddle
sais – says
sale stable – horse stable
Saterday – Saturday
sayes – says
scampes – scamps
scatered - scattered
scout – sent out to obtain information
scrible – scribble
scribled – scribbled
scuawling – squalling
Seargeant – Sergeant
seargeons – surgeons
secesh – person who withdrew from the Union by secession
secish – secesh or person who withdrew from the Union by secession
sed – said
seige – siege
seperate – separate
Sergt – Sergeant
ses – says
settleing – settling
severly – severely

shant – shall not
shiped – shipped
shiping - shipping
Shirman - General William Tecumseh Sherman
sholder – shoulder
sholdered - shouldered
sholder scab - **shoulder strap or officer
shure – sure
sighn – sign
sighned - signed
signafies – signifies
silver band – arm band
simtoms – symptoms
Sis - sister
site – sight
skedadle - skedaddle
skedadled – skedaddled, **retreated quickly from the battlefield
skermish – skirmish, a small battle
skermishing - skirmishing
slipe – slip
snoozin - snoozing
snubed – snubbed, caught or taken
soger - soldier
soges – soldiers
solger – soldier
solmnly – solemnly
som – some

Sonday – Sunday
sood – stood
sory – sorry
Sothern – Southern
sour dock – *coarse, weedy plant with long tap roots
sow belly – side meat or salt pork
spase - space
spoon up close – **because of crowded conditions, soldiers slept close together in a spoon formation with their knees drawn up – when one rolled over they hollered "spoon" and all would turn at the same time
squirmish – skirmish
steel – steal
stile – style
stinkin - stinking
stol – stole
stoped – stopped
straped – strapped, needy or wanting
stresful – stressful
Suaint Louis - Saint Louis, Missouri
successfull – successful
sulphur – sulfur
suplies – supplies
supose – suppose
supplys - supplies

supprised – surprised
surounded – surrounded
suspence – suspense
sutch - such
sutter – sutler, *one who followed the Army to sell food, supplies or liquor to the soldiers
swareing – swearing

-T-
tare - tear
tarnation – *damnation or hell
teames – teams
tel – tell
Ten. - Tennessee
Tenesee - Tennessee
thankfull – thankful
thare – there
thats – that's
thear - there
their - there
ther – there
there – their
they was – they were
tho – though
thomb – thumb
thoug – though
thrash – thresh or *remove seeds from grain such as wheat or rye
thrasher – thresher, *machine used for threshing or removing seeds from grain such as wheat or rye
throug – through
throwed out – threw out
tifoid fever – typhoid fever
till - until
to – too
to day – today
toat – tote
togather – together
train – *procession of animals, vehicles & men accompanying an army to carry supplies, baggage and ammunition
transfered – transferred
trapes – traipse
travail – travel
Trianna - Triana, Alabama
tryed - tried
trys – tries
Tullihoma - Tullahoma, Tennessee

-U-
Uncle Samuel - Uncle Sam or U. S. government
uneasyness – uneasiness
unexpectible – unexpected
untill – until
useing – using

364

-V-
vacinity – vicinity
Vandorn - General Earl Van Dorn
vegitables – vegetables
Vicksburgh - Vicksburg, Mississippi
vis – advice
Vol - Volunteers
volinteer – volunteer

-W-
wach – watch
wants - want
war widows – **wives left behind while their soldier husbands went to war
ware – wear
watchfull - watchful
wate – wait
Wayneboro - Waynesboro, Georgia
we seen – we saw
weans – children or Southern ladies
weare - wear
welcomly – will be welcome
wellcome - welcome
Westley Rowley - Wesley Rowley
westrn – western
wether – whether
whar – where

wharfs – wharves
whats – what's
whezing – wheezing
whilst - while
whiped – whipped
whiping - whipping
whise – wise
whos – whose
wich – which
wil – will
Willmington - Wilmington, North Carolina
wimen - women
Wis. - Wisconsin
withe – with
withe in – within
withe out – without
won - one
wonderfull - wonderful
wont – won't
wouldent – wouldn't
wrest - rest
wright - write
wrighting - writing
writen – written

-Y-
yess – yes
youens – you
youre - your
your self – yourself
yourselfe - yourself
youself - yourself

yu - you

<u>Z</u>
Zimer - Peter Zimmer

\* *Webster's New World Dictionary of the American Language, Concise Edition,* The World Publishing Company, Cleveland and New York

\*\* *Civil War Wordbook including Sayings, Phrases, & Expletives* by Darryl Lyman, Combined Books, PA

# INDEX - PEOPLE

## A

Adams Christian, Mary - wife of Andrew Christian - 75, 109

Aldrich, Mrs. John - neighbor of John and Mary Ann Miller in Winnebago - 20

Aldrich, Warren - Mt. Carroll, $92^{nd}$ Illinois Infantry, Company I, died at Mt. Sterling Hospital on 2-18-63 - 43, 111

Apple, Balzar - Salem, $92^{nd}$ Illinois Infantry, Company I, mustered out 6-9-65 - 294

Atkins, Smith D. - Colonel who was later a Brigadier General, Staff Officer, $92^{nd}$ Illinois Infantry - 25, 30, 40-42, 44, 46, 53, 55, 58, 70, 81, 115, 117, 119, 139, 144, 169, 178, 191-192, 229-230, 241-242, 244, 246, 252, 257, 261, 266-268, 271, 287-288, 303, 305, 312, 317, 319-321, 323-324, 340

## B

Backman aka Boughman, Christian - Salem, $34^{th}$ Illinois Infantry, Company I, mustered out 7-12-65 - 79

Baird, Absolom - Union General - 39-40, 43, 45-46, 53, 63, 82, 87, 114-115, 123, 139-140, 143, 147, 163, 188

Baldwin, Colonel - $5^{th}$ Kentucky Cavalry - 241

Barlow, Moses S. - Carroll County, $15^{th}$ Illinois Infantry, Company K, mustered out on 5-24-64 - 270

Barnum, P. T. - showman - 336

Bashaw, Henry - Corporal from Mt. Carroll, $92^{nd}$ Illinois Infantry, Company I, mustered out as Sergeant on 6-21-65 - 30

Beauregard, Pierre Gustave T. - Confederate General - 297, 320

Becker, Egbert Q. E. - Captain from Salem, $92^{nd}$ Illinois Infantry, Company I, mustered out 6-21-65 - 32-33, 35-36, 41, 70, 101, 103, 143, 145, 176, 216, 282

Becker, James M. - Sergeant from Mount Carroll, $146^{th}$

Illinois Infantry, Company A, mustered out 7-8-65 - 152, 186, 224-225, 230, 251, 272-273, 290, 342-343

Bell – music teacher – 327

Bennett aka Bennitt, Edger - Fair Haven, 92nd Illinois Infantry, Company I, died in Lexington, Kentucky on 2-19-63 - 111

Bermers, Mrs. - friend of Mary Ann Miller – 20

Bigger, James A. - Corporal from Mount Carroll, 92nd Illinois Infantry, Company I, killed at Chickamauga on 9-19-63 - 140, 194

Bohn, John H. - Major, Staff Officer, 92nd Illinois Infantry - 42, 65, 177, 183

Brace, Charles - 34th Illinois Infantry, Company I, transferred to 4th U. S. Cavalry - 80

Bradley, Horace - Mount Carroll, 15th Illinois Infantry, Company K, discharged 3-2-65 - 296

Bragg, Braxton - Confederate General - 46-48, 62, 69-70, 72, 77, 80, 120, 129, 155-156, 165, 167, 177, 179, 183, 186, 188, 191-192, 202-203

Brannen, John M. - Union Brigadier General - 188

Briggs, Joe Henry - husband of Nellie Eugenia Swaggart many years after the war - 344

Browning, Henry - 92nd Illinois Infantry, Company I, died in Danville, KY prior to 2-14-63 - 103-104

Browning, Herr - 92nd Illinois Infantry, Company I, deserted - 111, 259

Brownloe, W. G. - wrote verse on stationary - 17

Bucks, Mr. - friend of Mary Ann Miller in Winnebago - 20

Buell, Don Carlos - Union Brigadier General - 46-47

Burlin, Jesse N. - 34th Illinois Infantry, Company I - 79

Burnside, Ambrose - Union General - 52, 70, 86, 144, 202, 204

Butler, Mrs. - fortune teller - 95, 107

C

Campbell, Mr. - neighbor - 300

Champion, Thos. E. - Colonel, Staff Officer, 96th Illinois Infantry - 117

Cheatham, Benjamin F. - Confederate Major General - 190

Christian, Andrew J. - Mount Carroll, 92nd Illinois Infantry, Company C, discharged with a wounded thumb on 2-2-63 - mentioned as Mary Adams' man once and Mary Christian's man on another page - 75, 109

Christian, David - mill owner in Mt. Carroll - 2

Clara - friend of Jennie Van Alstine - 261

Cleburne, Pat R. - Confederate General - 240, 287

Coburn, John - Union Colonel from Kentucky - 120

Cochran, Col. - Kentucky Colonel - 41

Colehour, Captain - father of David Colehour - 125

Colehour, David - First Lieutenant from Mount Carroll, 92nd Illinois Infantry, Company I, died on 3-17-63 - 110, 125, 138

Colehour, James A. - Corporal from Mount Carroll, 92nd Illinois Infantry, Company I, mustered out 6-21-65 - 194, 217-219

Cooling, Lt. - Lieutenant, 92nd Illinois Infantry, Company B - 285

Corse, John M. - Union Brigadier General - 244

Couple, Liz - friend of Emma Miller - 37

Crittenden, Thomas L. - Union Major General - 185, 188

Crosit, David - uncle of Elvira Van Alstine Swaggart - 15

Crosit, Mary - cousin of Elvira Van Alstine Swaggart - 16-17

Crosit, Nehsuh - wife of David Crosit and aunt of Elvira Van Alstine Swaggart - 16, 29

Cross, C. E. - friend and probably family of Charles E. Cross of the 7th Illinois Cavalry, Company B, who mustered out 11-4-65 - 127, 140

Cruft, Charles - Union General - 202

Cummings, Captain - Captain in the 3rd Kentucky - 282

Cumy, Abner - possibly in 92$^{nd}$ Illinois Infantry, served with Eugene McBride Swaggart in March to the Sea - 308

**D**

Dana, Charles E. - Assistant Secretary of War of the Union - 192

Davis, Aunt - aunt of Elvira Van Alstine Swaggart - 47, 49, 71

Davis, Jefferson - President of the Confederacy - 336

Davis, Jefferson C. - Union General - 188, 191, 317

Dawson, James - First Lieutenant, 92$^{nd}$ Illinois Infantry, Company H, severely wounded on 8-30-64 - 286

Delia - friend of Mary Ann Miller - 21

Dodge, John - grandfather of Elvira Van Alstine Swaggart - 4

Dodge, Sarah Serepto - grandmother of Elvira Van Alstine - 4

Dodge, S. Whitman - Uncle of Elvira and Amanda Ludisky - 4, 6

Dodge Van Alstine, Emeline - mother of Elvira Van Alstine Swaggart - 4-6

Downs, George Wait - 92$^{nd}$ Illinois Infantry, Company I, killed at Waynesboro, Georgia on 12-4-64 - 3, 32-34, 41-43, 45, 49, 51, 53, 55, 62, 86, 99, 101, 103-104, 121, 124, 131, 141, 146, 161-165, 189, 256, 263, 272, 276, 306-308, 311, 316

Downs, Simeon. - father of George Wait Downs - 86, 256

Duerke, Martie - teacher - 23

Dulibar, Sue - teacher - 327

**E**

Eaton, William - handyman - 2, 15, 50, 53

Emmert, Catherine - wife of George, neighbor in Salem - 87

Emmert, George - husband of Catherine, neighbor in Salem - 111

Emmest, Desiree - wife of Thomas Emmest - 23

Emmest, Thomas H. - Carroll County, 8$^{th}$ Illinois Cavalry, Company G, died at

Alexandria, Virginia on 1-15-62 - 19-20, 23

English, Edward W. - Sergeant from Salem, 92$^{nd}$ Illinois Infantry, Company I, Orderly, mustered out 6-21-65 - 76, 121-122, 220

Eshelmon, Benjamin F. - Mount Carroll, 92$^{nd}$ Illinois Infantry, Company I, died at Danville, Kentucky on 1-19-63 - 84

Eula - possibly a sister of Emma Miller - 37

F

Farrell, Peter - Mount Carroll, 34$^{th}$ Illinois Infantry, Company I, discharged for wounds on 4-21-63 - 79

Finlayson aka Fomlinson, George - Salem, 92$^{nd}$ Illinois Infantry, Company I, mustered out 6-21-65 - 105, 311

Fish, Leander B. - Major from Mount Carroll, 45$^{th}$ Illinois Infantry, Staff Officer, killed in battle on 6-25-63 - 172

Forest, Nathan B. - Confederate General - 97, 190

Foster, John - Wisconsin resident - 29

Frank - soldier friend of Emma Miller - 60

Frasier or Frazer, Loy - 92$^{nd}$ Illinois Infantry, killed or discharged due to wounds - 311

Funkhouser, John J. - Union Colonel - 169

G

Galusha, Daniel E. - Fair Haven, 92$^{nd}$ Illinois Infantry, Company I, mustered out on 7-13-65 - 222

Garner, Jim - friend of Sarah Whiteside Miller/Swaggart - 343

Garrard, Kenner - Union Brigadier General - 229, 244

Gates, General Elijah - Union General from Missouri - 144

Gaylord, Actias – Rock Creek, 34$^{th}$ Illinois Infantry, Company I, discharged for wounds on 2-3-63 - 75, 84, 105-106

Gelwich, John Phillip - Corporal from Mount Carroll, 34$^{th}$ Illinois Infantry, Company I,

discharged for wounds on 5-9-64 - 79
Gist, S. R. - Confederate General - 189
Gotshall aka Gotshell, George - Salem, 92$^{nd}$ Illinois Infantry, Company I, mustered out 6-21-65 - 34
Gotshel aka Gotshall, Wilson S. - Mount Carroll, 92$^{nd}$ Illinois Infantry, Company C, died in Nashville on 6-18-64 - 267
Graham, Jennie - neighbor - 200
Graham, William - First Lieutenant from Mt. Carroll, 146$^{th}$ Illinois Infantry, Company A, mustered out 7-8-65, in another regiment prior to this one, but information unknown - 26, 336
Granger, Gordon - Union General - 39, 90, 133, 141-142, 163, 189, 192
Grant Noises, Welthy - wife of J. M. Noises who owned a shop in town - 148
Grant, Ulysses S. - Union General - 119, 144, 146, 149, 153, 156, 194-195, 197-198, 200, 202-203, 206, 245, 248, 252-253, 259, 265-266, 271, 298, 330

## H

Hall, Samuel - Fair Haven, 4$^{th}$ U. S. Cavalry, Company E, mustered out 11-3-64 - 108
Hamilton, Mr. - neighbor - 213
Hampton, Wade - Confederate General - 322
Hardee, William - Confederate General - 306, 318, 320-322
Harding, Chester - Union Colonel - 97
Harper, George Washington - father-in-law of Nelson Swaggart - 4
Harper Swaggart, Mary Adeline - wife of Nelson Swaggart - 4
Harrington aka Harington, Marshall D. - Mount Carroll, 7$^{th}$ Illinois Cavalry, Company B, mustered out 11-4-65 - 331, 336
Harrington, Olive - 336
Harris, G. W. - Administrator of George Swaggart's Estate - 136, 153
Hatheway, Ed - neighbor - 145, 151, 181, 216
Hatheway, Flora - wife of Ed Hatheway - 106, 181

Hawk, Robert M. A. - Captain from Lanark, 92$^{nd}$ Illinois Infantry, Company C, lost his leg on 3-18-65 - 322

Hawley, William - Union General - 321

Hazen, William B. - Union General - 306

Hebrington, Elsy - neighbor - 250

Hedling, Fred - 34$^{th}$ Illinois Infantry - 104

Hedling, Jake aka Dutch - 34$^{th}$ Illinois Infantry - 104, 311, 339

Higgins Harper, Louisiana - mother-in-law of Nelson Swaggart - 4

Hitt, Samuel H. - mill owner in Mt. Carroll - 2

Hobart, Mark H. - Fair Haven, 92$^{nd}$ Illinois Infantry, Company I, discharged 6-25-63 due to illness - 43

Hollinger, William H. - Sergeant from Mount Carroll, 92$^{nd}$ Illinois Infantry, Company I, discharged for promotion in colored troop on 8-17-63 - 139-140

Holt, Charles Putnam aka Charlie - Mount Carroll, 45$^{th}$ Illinois Infantry, Company I, mustered out 6-3-65 - 296

Holt, Henry - Fair Haven, 15$^{th}$ Illinois Infantry, Company K, mustered out 9-16-65 - 3, 11-15, 123, 131, 143-144, 193-194, 220, 222, 238, 296, 299-300

Holt, Mother - Henry Holt's Mother - 14

Holt, Mrs. - wife of Henry Holt - 194

Hood, John B. - Confederate Major General - 190, 234, 275, 288, 293-295, 297, 299, 303-306, 317, 320-321

Hooker, Joseph aka Fightin Joe - Union General - 142, 144, 202, 240, 242

Howard, Oliver O. - Union Major General - 286

I

Ikerman, Frederick - York, 34$^{th}$ Illinois Infantry, Company I, mustered out as Corporal on 7-12-65 - 8$^{th}$ Illinois Cavalry - 79

Ingram, W. B. - Confederate Captain - 217

## J

Jackson, Stonewall - Confederate General - 52

Jackson, William - Confederate Brigadier General - 278

Jes - friend or relative of Swaggart family - 292

Johnson, Bushrod R. - Confederate General - 189-190, 235

Johnson, Laurentine aka Larntine - Wysox, 34th Illinois Infantry, Company I, transferred to 4th Cavalry on 12-18-62 - 80

Johnson, Richard W. - Union General - 188

Johnston, Joseph E. - Confederate General - 239-242, 247, 266, 323-324, 328, 330

Jordan, Outlaw - Outlaw in Resaca, Georgia - 261

Jordon, Thomas - Union General - 321

Judah, Henry Moses - Union General - 45

Judge, Jaxson - Wisconsin soldier - 29

Justin - friend of Emma Miller - 37

## K

Kilpatrick, Judson aka Kilcavalry - Union Cavalry General - 237, 241, 246, 266, 277, 281, 288, 294, 296, 298-299, 303-306, 317-323, 330, 335

King, Edward A. - Union Colonel - 190

King, Robert H. - Union Lieutenant Colonel - 281-282

Kinnman, William - 115th Illinois Infantry - 117

Klein, Robert - Union Lieutenant Colonel - 277

## L

Lauver, Adam - Elkhorn Grove, 34th Illinois Infantry, Company I, mustered out 7-8-65 - 79

Lawyer, I. C. - Adjutant, Staff Officer, 92nd Illinois Infantry - 115, 117

Lee, Robert E. - Confederate General - 142, 167, 193, 252-253, 323, 330

Lego, Henry - Salem, 34th Illinois Infantry, Company I, Musician, mustered out as Corporal on 7-12-65 - 3, 77-80, 87, 89, 93, 99, 104, 108, 122, 130, 174,

Liddell, P. F. - Confederate Colonel - 189

Lilly, Eli - Colonel who was a Captain when Eugene McBride Swaggart served under him, 8th Indiana Battery - 177, 201, 203

Lincoln, Abraham - President of the United States of America during the Civil War - 17, 86, 113, 206, 292, 297, 301, 324, 326

Logan, John A. - Union General - 241, 244

Longstreet, James - Confederate Lieutenant General - 191-192, 195

Lower, Levi - Salem, 34th Illinois Infantry, Company I, mustered out 9-12-64 - 79

Lower, Martin L. - Salem, 92nd Illinois Infantry, Company I, died in Nashville on 2-20-63 - 75, 102, 108

Lundy, Clifton - Son-in-law of George Swaggart and father of Leticia Lundy - 332

Lundy, Leticia aka Lettie - grandchild of George Swaggart, daughter of Clifton Lundy and Mary Ann Swaggart and half sister of Eugene McBride Swaggart - 60, 331

Lundy, Leticia - Grandmother of Leticia Lundy who was George Swaggart's grandchild and Clifton Lundy's mother - 332-333

## M

Mackay, John - built brick schoolhouse in Salem - 4

Maclure, Olive - friend - 327

Magee, Thomas aka Tom - York, 92nd Illinois Infantry, Company C, mustered out 6-21-65 - 250

Marsh, C. Carroll - Union Colonel - 34

Mary - friend of Mary Ann Miller in Winnebago - 20

Masters, James - Corporal from Mt. Carroll, 34th Illinois Infantry, Company I, killed at Stone's River on 12-31-62 - 87-88, 104

Maynard, Hiram H. - York, 34th Illinois Infantry, Company I, died from wounds at Stone's River - 79

McCook, Alexander - Union General - 191-192

McCracken, Mr. - father of Thomas McCracken - 153

McCracken aka McKracin, Thomas - Mt. Carroll, 92$^{nd}$ Illinois Infantry, Company I, mustered out 6-21-65 - 72, 153

McKay, Barbara - neighbor and friend of the family - 327

McLaw, Lafayette - Confederate General - 321

McPherson, James B. - Union General - 237, 240

McRea, Joshua A. - First Lieutenant from Mount Carroll, 92$^{nd}$ Illinois Infantry, Company I, mustered out 6-21-65 - 140, 143, 147, 174, 176, 296

McWorthy, William P. - Mount Carroll, 92$^{nd}$ Illinois Infantry, Company I, died at Andersonville Prison, Grave # 9710 - 233, 327

Meade, George Gordon - Union General - 167, 335

Merrell, Freddie - friend of Jennie Van Alstine - 260

Merston, Mr. - friend of Mary Ann Miller in Winnebago - 20

Miller, A. O. - Union Colonel - 229-230

Miller, Emma - friend of Anna Swaggart - 37-38, 60

Miller, Genie - daughter of John & Mary Ann Miller - 19

Miller, John - foster brother of Eugene McBride Swaggart - Mt. Carroll, 146$^{th}$ Illinois Infantry, Company A, mustered out 7-8-65 - 2, 7, 19, 21, 24, 31, 35, 54, 85, 95, 103, 134, 148-150, 237-238, 247, 257, 259, 261, 290-291, 336-337, 339, 342, 345

Miller, Mary Ann - wife of John Miller - 7, 19-21, 24, 31, 54, 128, 148, 205, 238, 261, 336, 343, 345

Minty, H. G. - Union Colonel - 183, 189-190, 229, 281

Mitchell, Robert - Union Major General - 188-190

Mitchell, Squire - 185

Monroe, Col. - Colonel, 123$^{rd}$ Illinois Infantry - 198

Morford, Sidney - leased farm - 201-202, 221-222, 251, 256, 300, 325, 342

Morgan, John Hunt - Confederate General - 51-52, 62-65, 69-70, 72, 84, 263, 288

Morton, Oliver - Governor of Indiana - 117
Mower, Joseph - Union General - 318
Murray, Eli H. - Union General - 229, 237, 240-242, 261, 268, 286-288, 303, 305

**N**
Ned - friend of Swaggart family - 32
Negley, James S. - Union General - 188
Nehsuh, Aunt - aunt of Elvira Van Alstine Swaggart - 16, 29
Nyman, Albert H. - husband of Anna Swaggart after the war - 345

**O**
O'Brien, Daniel - Wisconsin soldier - 217-219
O'Neal, James - Wysox, 92$^{nd}$ Illinois Infantry, Company I, died in Danville on 1-17-63 - 84
Olney, Dorace E. aka Dode - York, 92$^{nd}$ Illinois Infantry, Company I, discharged 2-2-63 due to illness - 125

Orb, Samuel - Lieutenant Colonel, 84$^{th}$ Indiana - 117

**P**
Palmer, John M. - Union Major General - 178, 188
Patch, B. L. - Lawyer & Judge who performed marriage ceremony of Eugene McBride Swaggart and Elvira Van Alstine - 9-10
Patterson, William - 92$^{nd}$ Illinois Infantry, Company D - 178
Pemberton, John C. - Confederate General - 156
Pitman, Robert - Wysox, 92$^{nd}$ Illinois Infantry, Company I, died in Danville on 1-6-63 - 74
Polk, Leonidus - Confederate General - 241
Preston, William - Confederate General - 190
Price, Mr. - friend of Leticia Lundy - 332
Price, William H. - Corporal from Mount Carroll, 92$^{nd}$ Illinois Infantry, Company I, mustered out as Sergeant on 6-21-65 - 194, 265

## Q

Queckbranner aka Quickbrener, Phillip - Fair Haven, 34$^{th}$ Illinois Infantry, Company I, discharged with wounded thumb - 87

## R

Raines - relatives of Emma Miller and the Swaggarts - 37

Ransom aka Ransome, Caleb S. - Second Lieutenant from Elkhorn Grove, 34$^{th}$ Illinois Infantry, Company I, discharged for bad eye, enlisted in 142$^{nd}$ Illinois Infantry, Company G on 6-18-64, mustered out 10-27-64 - 79, 99, 104, 130

Ransome, Elsy - sister of Caleb Ransome - 130

Ray, Willis - Sergeant from Mount Carroll, 34$^{th}$ Illinois Infantry, Company I, transferred to 4$^{th}$ U. S. Cavalry on 12-18-62 - 80, 122

Reynolds, Charles W. - Salem, 92$^{nd}$ Illinois Infantry, Company I, captured at Nickajack, mustered out 6-21-65 - 3-4, 104, 141, 233-234, 246, 311, 327, 345

Reynolds, Elizabeth aka Lib - wife of William Reynolds - 21, 26, 237, 247, 251, 257, 290, 336

Reynolds, Joseph Jones -Union Major General - 173, 185, 188, 190-191

Reynolds, William H. aka Bill - Salem, 92$^{nd}$ Illinois Infantry, Company I, killed at Nickajack, Georgia on 4-23-64 - 3, 195, 199, 203, 207, 212, 215, 220, 222-224, 227, 232-234, 237, 245, 257-258, 311, 345

Reynolds Woodin Swaggart, Josephine - sister of William & Charles Reynolds, 2$^{nd}$ wife of Eugene McBride Swaggart - 9, 234, 345

Rhodes, James W. - York, 92$^{nd}$ Illinois Infantry, Company I, killed at Nickajack, Georgia on 4-23-64 - 233, 258

Robbins, George - Salem, 34$^{th}$ Illinois Infantry, Company I, died in Nashville on 3-9-63 of wounds - 79, 108-109

Rosecrans, William Starkie - Union General - 62, 69-70, 77, 80, 90, 113, 119-121, 120, 131, 140, 143, 155, 165, 183,

185, 188, 191-192, 194-195, 198, 200
Ross, J. S. - Union soldier, cripple in hospital in Nashville who wrote letters for Eugene McBride Swaggart - 164-168
Rowley, Louis Westley - Mt. Carroll, 45th Illinois Infantry, Company A, died at St. Louis on 10-30-63 - 55
Russell, John - handyman & friend - 50, 53, 88, 110, 153, 290, 325, 342-343
Russell, Mollie - wife of John Russell - 290

**S**

Sammis, Oscar F. - Lieutenant, 92nd Illinois Infantry, Company D, killed at Flint River - 286
Sara - friend of Emma Miller - 38
Sawer, Joseph - Mt. Carroll, 34th Illinois Infantry, Company I, died of wounds at Stone's River - 79
Schermerhorn, John M. - Captain, 92nd Illinois Infantry, Company G - 282
Scofield, John M. - Union General - 237

Scott, John S. - Confederate Colonel - 184
Scoville, Horace C. - Lieutenant, 92nd Illinois Infantry, Company K - 232
Sedgwick, John - Union General - 142
Seymour, Viola - 22-23, 140
Sheets, Benjamin E. - Lieutenant Colonel, Staff Officer, 92nd Illinois Infantry - 42, 44, 84, 117, 139, 185
Sheridan, Phillip H. - Union Major General - 188
Sherman, William Tecumseh - Union General - 73, 76-77, 86, 119, 196, 202, 204, 237, 239-240, 242, 244, 247, 263-266, 268, 271-274, 285, 288, 293-295, 297-299, 301, 303-307, 309, 317-324, 328, 330-331, 335
Shink, Jacob - brother-in-law of Wilson Gotshall - 267
Shinkle, J. W. - friend of Jennie Van Alstine - 273
Shrimkel, Harry - son of Mrs. Shrimkel - 260
Shrimkel, Mrs. - friend of Jennie Van Alstine - 260
Shipton, J. E. aka Ed - Corporal, 96th Illinois

Infantry, discharged 2-13-65 due to illness - 47-48, 76, 81

Shore, Thompson M. - York, 92$^{nd}$ Illinois Infantry, Company I, died at Danville, Kentucky on 2-26-63 - 102

Shores, Mr. & Mrs. - landlords of Anna Swaggart - 18, 22, 332

Sigman, Mrs. - patient of Jennie Van Alstine - 213

Skilling, William W. - Mount Carroll, 92$^{nd}$ Illinois Infantry, Company I, mustered out 7-13-65 - 222, 272, 338

Skinner, George R. - Lieutenant, 92$^{nd}$ Illinois Infantry, Company D, Brigade Inspector - 277

Slocum, Henry Warner - Union General - 317, 319, 321-322

Small, William aka Bill - neighbor - 71, 85, 87, 136

Smith, Edmund Kirby - Confederate General - 61-62

Smith, Giles E. - Union General - 318

Smith, John F. - Mount Carroll, 92$^{nd}$ Illinois Infantry, Company I, died at Danville, Kentucky on 2-26-63 - 111

Smith, John - neighbor and friend of the family - 327

Spencer, George E. - Union General - 320

Stanley, David Sloan - Union Major General - 163, 199, 204

Starnes, Hamilton - brother-in-law to Sam Hall - 109

Steames, Mrs. - friend of the family - 297

Stephenson aka Stevenson, Nathan - Fair Haven, Staff Surgeon, 92$^{nd}$ Illinois Infantry - 106

Stewart, Alexander P. - Confederate Major General - 190

Stoddard, George Riley - Sergeant from York, 34$^{th}$ Illinois Infantry, Company I, discharged for wounds on 2-4-63 - 75

Stouffer, Daniel H. - Sergeant from Lanark, 92$^{nd}$ Illinois Infantry, Company I, mustered out 6-21-65 - 187

Stouffer, Lottie - mother of Daniel Stouffer - 187, 340

Stouffer, Mrs. - wife of William Stouffer - 88

Stouffer, William - Captain from Mount Carroll, 92nd Illinois Infantry, Company I, died 1-21-63 of illness - 88

Strock, John L. - Sergeant from Mount Carroll, 92nd Illinois Infantry, Company C, mustered out 6-21-65 - 235

Stuart, George H. - Chairman of U. S. Christian Commission - 161

Stuart, Mr. - employer of Sylvester Van Alstine - 130

Sutler, H. Thomas - possibly in 92nd Illinois Infantry - served with Eugene McBride Swaggart in March to the Sea and possibly was a name they used for the sutlers that followed the army - 301

Swaggart, Alice - daughter of Nelson Swaggart - 4

Swaggart, Ann - daughter of Nelson Swaggart - 4

Swaggart, Anna aka Annie - sister of Eugene McBride Swaggart, married name Nyman after the war - 2, 4, 7, 10, 15, 17-19, 21-24, 26, 31-32, 37, 47, 49, 53, 56-60, 67, 72, 88, 102, 113, 128, 126, 138, 143-144, 149-150, 152, 162, 166-169, 172, 181, 186, 199-200, 207, 213, 224, 231, 239, 256, 259-260, 263, 268, 270, 274, 277, 290, 292, 296, 300, 307, 314, 325-328, 332, 334-336, 342-343, 345

Swaggart, Charles - son of Eugene McBride Swaggart and Elvira Van Alstine Swaggart - born after the war - 344

Swaggart, Eugene McBride aka Mack - Salem, 92nd Illinois Infantry, Company I, mustered out 6-21-65 - 1-4, 7-11, 15, 19, 21, 29, 37, 39-67, 69-78, 81-91, 93-99, 101-113, 119-153, 155-157, 161-177, 179-182, 186-187, 193-194, 196-209, 211-227, 229-233, 235-239, 242-253, 255-279, 283-285, 288-292, 294-302, 307-316, 324-345

Swaggart, Frank aka Frankie - son of Moses Swaggart & Amanada aka Dickey Van Alstine Swaggart - 8, 19, 83, 236-237

Swaggart, Fred aka Freddie - son of Moses Swaggart & Amanda aka Dickey Van Alstine Swaggart - 237

Swaggart, George Samuel - father of Eugene McBride

Swaggart - 1-2, 4, 7, 60, 124, 153

Swaggart II, George aka Georgie - son of Eugene McBride Swaggart and Elvira aka Vira Van Alstine Swaggart -121, 124, 128-129, 132-133, 136, 143, 153, 169, 186, 194, 196, 201-202, 206, 211-213, 215, 221-224, 227, 242, 245, 250-251, 256, 259-260, 266, 271, 273-275, 278, 284, 290, 292, 308, 324-325, 327-328, 333, 335, 342, 344

Swaggart, George - son of Nelson Swaggart - 4

Swaggart, Jennie - daughter of Moses Swaggart and Amanada aka Dickey Van Alstine Swaggart - 8, 16,19, 87, 112-113, 122, 143, 147, 235-237, 261, 345

Swaggart, Josephine - daughter of Eugene McBride Swaggart and Elvira Van Alstine Swaggart, born after the war - 344

Swaggart Lundy, Mary Ann - half sister of Eugene McBride Swaggart and mother of Leticia Lundy - 332

Swaggart, Moses aka Mose - brother of Eugene McBride

Swaggart - 2, 4-5, 7-8, 15, 19, 21, 36, 46-48, 54, 56, 59-60, 64, 71, 87-89, 102-103, 105, 111-112, 120, 128, 136, 140-143, 146-147, 149, 167, 170, 181, 194, 200-203, 207, 214, 218-219, 221, 225, 261, 270, 272-273, 290, 301-302, 310, 313-314, 325, 327, 332, 342-343, 345

Swaggart, Nellie Eugenia - daughter of Eugene McBride Swaggart and Elvira Van Alstine Swaggart, married Joe Henry Briggs many years after the war - 310-311, 314, 324, 326, 328, 331, 333, 339, 342, 344-345

Swaggart, Nelson - half brother of Eugene McBride Swaggart - 2, 4, 60, 103, 332

Swain, David Lowry - North Carolina Governor - 323

Swain, Eleanor aka Ellie - Southern girl who married Smith D. Atkins - 323

Swingley, Nathaniel - mill owner in Mount Carroll - 2

T

Tallmadge, H. A. - First Lieutenant, 9$^{th}$ Ohio Battery - 117

Taylor, Joseph - 92$^{nd}$ Illinois Infantry, Company A - 242

Teeter, Joseph - Captain from Mount Carroll, 34$^{th}$ Illinois Infantry, Company I, shot through the body at Stone's River, mustered out 7-12-65 - 79

Thimen, Mrs. - sold piano for Annie - 327

Thomas, George Henry - Union General - 183, 185, 188, 192, 206, 221, 237, 271

Thomas, Henry - 92$^{nd}$ Illinois Infantry, Company I, died at Nashville on 12-10-62 - 52

Thompson, Ev - friend of Emma Miller - 37

Tod, David - Governor of Ohio - 117

Trake, Bill - student of Anna Swaggart - 23

Trims, Mary - friend of Van Alstine family - 17

Turchin, John Basil - Union General - 185

U

Unity - soldier friend of Anna Swaggart - 60

V

Van Alstine, Alonzo - father of Elvira Van Alstine Swaggart - 4

Van Alstine, Jane aka Jennie - sister of Elvira and Amanda Van Alstine Swaggart - 5, 8, 15-17, 20-21, 26-29, 31, 34-35, 37-38, 41, 43, 45, 52, 54, 56, 71-72, 77, 83, 87-90, 95, 97, 99, 103, 107, 109, 112-113, 121-122, 128, 130, 136, 148-149, 168, 194, 200, 213, 215, 224-225, 231, 238-239, 250, 260-261, 273, 292, 296, 298, 300, 310, 314, 326-327, 332, 336, 343

Van Alstine, Sylvester aka Vet - brother of Elvira Van Alstine Swaggart - 8, 10, 15-16, 21, 28-29, 31-32, 43, 45, 50, 56, 66, 71, 87-89, 95, 102, 106, 109-111, 130, 136, 145, 200, 206, 213, 221, 239, 251, 255, 260, 264, 274, 292, 296, 298, 300, 314, 316, 326, 342-343, 345

Van Alstine Swaggart, Amanda Ludisky aka Dickey - wife of Moses Swaggart and sister of Elvira Van Alstine Swaggart - 4-10, 19-21, 31, 33, 36, 38, 56, 71, 87-90, 102, 106, 112, 121-123, 125, 128, 130-131, 143, 149, 170-172, 181, 186-187, 201, 207, 213, 231, 247-248, 250-251, 260-

261, 290-292, 314, 327, 332, 336, 342-343, 345
Van Alstine Swaggart, Elvira aka Vira - wife of Eugene McBride Swaggart - 6, 8-10, 15-36, 39-45, 47-58, 60-67, 69-77, 81-91, 93-99, 101-113, 119-141, 143-145, 148-153, 155-157, 161-176, 179-182, 186-187, 193-194, 196-209, 211-218, 220-227, 229-233, 235, 238-239, 242-253, 255-279, 283-285, 288-292, 294-301, 307-316, 324-326, 328-345
Van Buskirk, Matthew - Captain, 92$^{nd}$ Illinois Infantry, Company E - 281-282, 303, 318
Van Cleve, Horatio Phillips - Union General - 184, 188, 190
Van Dorn, Earl - Confederate General - 118, 124-125, 129, 133
Vled, James - 1$^{st}$ Wisconsin Cavalry - 16

# W

Walker, James - Mount Carroll, 34$^{th}$ Illinois Infantry, Company I, discharged for wounds on 2-3-63 - 75

Walker, William H. - Confederate Major General - 189-190
Ward, Alfred aka Hi Hay - Mount Carroll, 34$^{th}$ Illinois Infantry, Company I, mustered out 7-12-65 - 79, 245
Wheeler, Joseph - Confederate Brigadier General - 97, 161, 163, 193, 195, 197-198, 247, 249, 251, 263, 284, 293, 303-306, 314, 317-318, 322-323
White, Julius - Union General - 31, 144
Whiteside Swaggart, Sarah - Mother of Eugene McBride Swaggart and fifth wife of George Swaggart - 1-2, 4, 7, 19, 23, 36, 56, 60, 62, 64, 67, 72, 75, 77, 83-84, 87, 90, 97, 102-103, 106, 109, 112-113, 121, 127-128, 130, 134-136, 141, 143, 148-149, 164, 168, 176, 181, 194, 204-205, 207, 212, 231, 251, 253, 256, 259, 261, 264, 267, 274, 277, 296, 300, 314, 328, 333, 335, 343, 345
Wilder, John Thomas - Union Brigadier General who was Colonel when Eugene McBride Swaggart served under him - 165, 169, 173-174, 177, 181, 183-184, 188-

193, 195, 197-198, 200, 203, 206, 209, 211, 214, 216, 218-220, 229-231, 263
Will, Doctor I. M. aka Doc - doctor in Mount Carroll or with the 92$^{nd}$ Illinois Infantry - 270
Willis, J. Platt - Salem, 92$^{nd}$ Illinois Infantry, Company I, mustered out as Corporal on 6-21-65 - 72, 75
Willis, Mr. - neighbor - 301
Wilson, Mr. - friend of Leticia Lundy - 332
Windes, F. M. - Confederate Lieutenant Colonel - 217
Wood, Thomas J. - Union General - 188, 191
Woodcock, Albert - Major in 92$^{nd}$ Illinois Infantry, Company K - 266, 268, 271, 275, 278, 281, 283, 285-287
Wright, Charlie aka Charly - 1$^{st}$ Wisconsin Cavalry - 16

## Y
Yates, Richard - Governor of Illinois - 31, 117, 144

York, Alexander M. - Second Lieutenant from Lanark, 92$^{nd}$ Illinois Infantry, Company I, promoted at end of war - 64, 143, 147, 176, 216

## Z
Zimmer, Peter - Fair Haven, 34$^{th}$ Illinois Infantry, Company I, mustered out 7-12-65 - 104

# INDEX - OTHER

## A

Abbeville, South Carolina - 319
Abolition Regiment - $92^{nd}$ Illinois Infantry - 41
Adairsville, Georgia – 244, 246-247, 251-252, 255, 257
Aiken, South Carolina – 318-319
Alabama - $4^{th}$ Cavalry - Confederate - 217
Alexander's Bridge on Chickamauga River – 189
Allatoona, Georgia – 275, 293
Allatoona Pass, Georgia – 247
Alston, South Carolina - 319
Altamaha River, Georgia - 307
Altamont, Tennessee – 177
Anthony's Bridge on the Flint River – Georgia – 287-288
Apalachicola, Florida – 8
Appomattox Court House in Virginia - 323
Army of Tennessee - Confederate - 70, 202
Army of Tennessee - Union - 239-240
Army of Texas - Confederate - 239
Army of the Cumberland - Union - 70, 102, 183, 188, 204, 237, 239, 301
Army of the Mississippi - Confederate - 241
Army of the Mississippi - Union - 301
Army of the Ohio - Union - 237, 239
Arnold's Grove, Illinois - 1
Athens, Alabama - 214
Atlanta, Georgia – 239-240, 242, 250, 253, 255, 263, 270-275, 277-278, 290, 293, 299
Auburn, Tennessee – 120
Augusta, Georgia – 317-319
Averasboro, North Carolina - 321

## B

Barnwell, South Carolina – skirmish – 318
Bear Creek Station, Georgia – 287
Bear Wallow, Kentucky – 62
Bentonville, North Carolina – 322
Bethsaida Church near Jonesboro, Tennessee - 285
Black River in North Carolina - 322
Bradyville, Tennessee - 120
Brentwood Station, Tennessee – 128, 130

Brentwood, Tennessee – 132
Briar Creek near Waynesboro, Georgia – 305-306
Bridgeport, Alabama – 183, 195, 198-199, 204, 212
Bridgeport, Illinois - 260
Bummers - 304

C
Caldwell, Kansas - 344-345
Calhoun Ferry, Georgia – 242
Calhoun, Georgia – 268, 271, 273
Camp Baird in Danville, Kentucky – 50, 54, 58, 61, 63, 65, 69, 73, 75, 81, 83, 85, 88, 90
Camp Butler – 291
Camp Creek, Georgia – 285
Camp Dick Robinson, Kentucky - 50
Camp Fuller in Rockford, Illinois – 25-26, 28, 30-31, 33, 35, 37, 42
Carolina mud march – 317
Cape Fear River in North Carolina - 321
Caperton's Ferry in Tennessee – 202, 209
Carroll County, Illinois – 1, 4, 7-8, 15, 25, 31, 35, 54, 139, 187, 345
Cartersville, Georgia – 275, 294

Carthage, Tennessee – 120
Cassville, Georgia – 244, 246
Catawba River in South Carolina – 320
Catlett's Gap – engagement – 185
Cave Springs, Alabama - 183
Chancellorsville, Virginia – 142
Chapel Hill, North Carolina – 323-324, 328-330
Chapel Hill, Tennessee – 173
Charleston, South Carolina – 171, 301
Charlotte, North Carolina - 320
Chattahoochee River, Georgia - 266, 275, 278, 281, 283-284, 289
Chattanooga, Tennessee – 165, 177, 179, 181, 183-184, 186, 188, 191-192, 195, 197, 199, 202, 231, 252
Cheraw, South Carolina - 320
Cherry Grove, Illinois - 1-2
Chicago, Illinois – 37, 40, 176, 200-201, 215, 238, 256, 260, 325, 340, 342-343
Chickamauga Creek - 185
Chickamauga, Georgia – 183, 188-192
Chickamauga River – 183-184, 189-190
Chickasha, Oklahoma - 345

Cincinnati, Ohio – 17, 31, 40, 144

Civil War Clothing - obtaining and care for - 22, 28, 30, 34, 45, 53, 55-56, 74, 81-82, 101, 110, 136, 143, 148, 185, 201, 213, 224, 233, 235, 295, 297, 320, 336

Civil War Countryside Descriptions - 1, 13-14, 49, 75, 101, 113, 132, 141-142, 145, 156, 177, 219, 246, 251, 253, 263, 267, 269, 272, 278, 287, 303, 317-318, 320

Civil War Enlistments - 8, 21, 23-26, 29, 75, 79, 88, 90, 111, 119, 144, 146-147, 150-151, 216, 225, 255, 268, 272

Civil War Food & Water - Obtaining, preparing, & descriptions - 5, 12, 14, 26, 30, 35-37, 39, 42, 44-47, 49, 51, 54-56, 60-63, 71, 75-76, 80-82, 84, 88, 93-94, 97, 102, 107, 109-110, 119, 122, 126, 130-132, 145, 147, 149, 156, 161, 168, 174-175, 177, 180-182, 195-197, 199, 201, 205, 222, 226, 230, 232, 252, 259, 263-264, 267, 269-270, 272, 276, 278, 284, 289, 291, 295, 299, 301, 303, 309, 310, 325, 330, 338-339, 343

Civil War Foraging - 75-76, 130, 169, 174, 195-196, 209, 270, 303-304, 307-308, 316, 340

Civil War Furloughs - 15, 31, 33-35, 71, 121, 152-153, 155-156, 202, 215-216, 219-222, 238, 246, 250, 270-271, 274, 291, 331, 336

Civil War Holidays - 9, 60-64, 66, 70-71, 105, 108, 204-209, 211, 266, 308, 310, 312, 339

Civil War Life at Home - 1-10, 14-24, 29, 43, 54, 59-60, 64, 71-73, 88-89, 95, 102-103, 106-107, 109-112, 123, 128-129, 133, 135, 139, 141, 143-145, 147-149, 153, 186-187, 193-194, 201-202, 206, 221-222, 225, 237-239, 251, 256, 259-261, 270, 273, 296, 299-300, 310-311, 314, 324-328, 331-333, 335-337, 340, 342-345,

Civil War Mail - 7, 15, 17, 29-30, 33, 36, 41, 43, 50-51, 53-54, 56, 58, 64, 71, 73, 77, 80-81, 84-85, 88-89, 91, 97-99, 101-103, 105, 107, 109-110, 113, 120-121, 123, 125, 127, 136, 138, 141, 143, 150, 156, 162, 164-166, 170-171, 174, 176, 181-182, 188, 194, 197-198, 200, 203, 207, 209, 213-215, 224-226, 230-231, 235, 239, 248, 250, 265, 270, 272-274, 276, 278-279, 283-285,

295, 297-299, 301, 307-314, 326-327, 334, 337, 339, 343
Civil War Medicine & Illnesses - 15, 29-30, 33-34, 36, 40, 42-43, 45-46, 48, 52-54, 56, 60-61, 64-66, 69, 72, 74-76, 82, 84-85, 87-88, 101-104, 106, 108-109, 110-112, 120-121, 124-127, 129, 133, 152-153, 161-167, 169, 193, 203-206, 215, 222, 246, 250, 256, 266-267, 276, 296, 310, 331-333, 335-336, 342-343, 345
Civil War Pay -14-15, 26, 28, 31, 42-43, 45, 47, 49, 54, 56, 58-59, 64, 70, 73, 87-89, 102-103, 113, 123, 128, 130, 133, 136, 148, 150-151, 164, 167-169, 182, 186, 194, 200-201, 203, 214, 239, 268, 273-274, 284, 290- 292, 295-297, 299-301, 308, 310, 337-340
Civil War Prisoners & Prisons - 12-13, 52, 72, 77, 79-80, 97-99, 127, 129, 135, 138-139, 169, 176-178, 196, 198, 206, 209, 217, 233-234, 241, 245-246, 253, 270-272, 277, 281-284, 294, 296, 305-306, 327
Civil War Punishment - 34, 53, 101, 103, 116, 139, 167, 259
Civil War Religion - 30, 36, 136, 260, 264, 275-276, 328, 343
Civil War Sutlers - 54, 61
Civil War Weapons - 13, 31, 34-36, 40, 45, 51, 82, 96-99,

119, 129, 131, 135, 146, 148, 152, 155-156, 173, 181, 184-185, 189, 191, 196, 219, 265, 285, 304-305, 309, 330, 333
Civil War Weather - 6-7, 9, 14, 19, 41, 45, 48-49, 51, 53, 58, 60, 63, 65, 75, 83-86, 93, 97, 101, 103-104, 110, 120, 122, 132, 136, 140, 142, 147, 149, 151, 157, 160, 162, 176, 181, 190, 199, 201-202, 204, 211, 223-224, 226, 229-230, 238, 241, 244, 255, 259, 264, 267, 275, 310, 317, 320, 327, 336, 343
Columbia, North Carolina - 319
Columbia, Tennessee – 121, 144, 169, 173, 211, 226, 230
Concord, North Carolina – 331, 334, 337, 339-340
Confederate States of American - C. S. A. - 101
Cooper's Gap – 185
Corpus Christi, Texas – 183
Covington, Kentucky – 40, 43, 83
Cowan, Tennessee – 173
Crawfish Springs, Georgia – 185, 192
Crutchfield House, Chattanooga, Tennessee - 184
Cumberland Mountain – crossing – 176, 179, 188

Cumberland River in Tennessee - 94, 129

**D**
Dallas, Georgia – 79, 178-179, 246-247, 293
Dalton, Georgia – 242, 2467, 293
Danville, Kentucky – 46, 48, 50-51, 54-55, 58, 60-61, 63-65, 69, 72, 74-75, 81, 83-85 88, 90, 93, 97, 101-104, 106, 111
Decherd Station, Tennessee – 173, 175-176
Duck River in Tennessee – 331
Dunlap, Tennessee in Sequatchie Valley – 177, 198
Durham Station, North Carolina – 330
Durham, North Carolina - 323
Dyer's Bridge on Chickamauga River – 189
Dyer's Ford on Chickamauga River - 189

**E**
Eagleville, Tennessee – 120
Elizabethtown, Kentucky – 62
Elk River, Elkton, Alabama - 211-212
Emancipation Proclamation - 65, 113

Enrollment or Conscription Act - 23, 119
Etowah River, Georgia – 247, 264-265, 293-294

**F**
Fairburn, Georgia – 277, 285
Fairfield, Tennessee – 120
Fair Haven, Illinois – 1, 111, 145, 274
Faison's Station near Mount Olive, North Carolina - 323
Farmington, Tennessee – engagement – 195, 198
Fayettesville, North Carolina - 321
Fifteenth Army Corps - Union - 244, 306, 318-319
Firey Gizzard Creek in Tennessee - 176
Fletcher's Ferry in Tennessee – 209
Flint River, Georgia – 197, 282, 286
Florence, Alabama – 214, 217
Floyd's Springs, Georgia - 244
Forsyth, Georgia - 305
Fort Donelson, Tennessee – 11, 90, 97
Fort McAllister, Georgia - 306
Fort Sumter – 8
Fosterville, Georgia - 281

Fourteenth Army Corps -
  Union - 165, 173
Franklin Pike - 97
Franklin, Tennessee – 118-121,
  123-126, 129, 132, 135-136,
  138-143, 146, 148, 150, 155
Freedom, Illinois - 1
Freeport, Illinois – 25
Friar's Island, Tennessee - 179

G
Gaylesville, Alabama - 294
Gettysburg, Pennsylvania – 167
Gideon's Ferry, Georgia - 242
Glasses Bridge in Georgia -
  275, 287
Goldsboro, North Carolina -
  323
Gordon's Gap, Georgia - 240
Great Pedee River near
  Cheraw, South Carolina –
  320
Greenville, Tennessee - 288
Griswoldville, Georgia - 305
Guy's Gap, Tennessee - 163

H
Hamsling, Kentucky - 93
Harpeth River in Tennessee -
  125
Harris Bridge on the Flint
  River in Georgia - 287

Harrison's Landing, Tennessee
  – 177-179, 183-184, 192
Hickman's Bridge on the
  Kentucky River – 69
Hill's Gap – skirmish - 195
Hog Jaw Valley - 204
Hospital – Lexington,
  Kentucky – 65-66
Hospital – Mount Sterling,
  Kentucky – 43
Hospital – Nashville,
  Tennessee – 79, 103, 109,
  153, 155, 164, 166-167, 169-
  171, 173, 267
Hospital – Triune, Tennessee -
  155, 162
Huntsville, Alabama – 199,
  202-206, 209, 212, 214, 217,
  229

I
Illinois - $8^{th}$ Illinois Cavalry -
  20
Illinois - $11^{th}$ Illinois
  Volunteers - 25
Illinois - $15^{th}$ Illinois Infantry -
  8, 11, 115, 117, 264, 270, 276,
  296
Illinois - $34^{th}$ Illinois Infantry -
  8, 84, 93, 104, 109, 230, 237-
  238, 264
Illinois - $92^{nd}$ Illinois Infantry -
  later became the $92^{nd}$ Illinois
  Mounted Infantry - 25, 30,

35-36, 39, 41, 43-44, 46-50, 58, 62-63, 65, 69, 74, 81, 83-85, 87, 90, 93-94, 97, 101, 107, 115, 117-118, 122, 124-125, 128-129, 132-133, 138, 147, 153, 155-156, 161, 163-165, 169-170, 173-174, 176-178, 182-185, 188-193, 195, 198-202, 204, 208-209, 216-218, 220, 229-231, 235, 237, 239-241, 244, 246, 248, 255, 257, 261, 264, 266, 268, 273, 275, 277, 281-282, 285-288, 290, 293-294, 296, 299, 301, 303, 305-308, 312, 314, 317-320, 322-323, 328, 330-331, 333-335, 337, 339, 343

Illinois - 96th Illinois Volunteers - 47, 115, 117, 135

Illinois - 98th Illinois Volunteers - 169, 177-178

Illinois - 115th Illinois Infantry - 115, 117

Illinois - 123rd Illinois Infantry - 198

Illinois - 146th Illinois Infantry - 290, 342

Indiana - 18th Indiana Battery - 177, 179, 181, 188, 195, 201

Indiana - 34th Indiana Infantry - 115

J

Jacksonboro, Georgia - 306

Janesville, Wisconsin – 38

Jasper, Tennessee – 183, 199

Johnson's Farm near Mount Sterling, Kentucky – 39

Johnson's Station near Augusta, Georgia - 318

Jonesboro, Tennessee – 281-282, 285-286, 288

K

Kenesaw Mountain, Georgia – 266

Kenosha, Wisconsin – 4-6, 15-17, 31, 34, 66, 276

Kentucky - 2nd Kentucky Cavalry, Confederate - 52

Kentucky - 3rd Kentucky Cavalry - 237, 244, 282

Kentucky - 5th Kentucky Cavalry - 237, 241, 244

Kingfisher, Oklahoma - 345

Kingston, Georgia – 244-245, 256-257, 261, 264, 266

Knob Creek, Tennessee - 173

L

Lafayette, Georgia – 185

Lanark, Illinois – 37, 111, 148, 327, 345

Lawrenceburg, Kentucky - 93

Lay's Ferry near Resaca, Georgia - 241-242, 244

Lebanon, Kentucky – 63, 91

Lebanon, Tennessee – 120
Lee and Gordon Mills, Georgia - 185, 189
Leet's Cross Roads, Georgia - 237
Lewisville Pike in Tennessee - 133
Lexington, Kentucky – 25, 39-40, 44-45, 65-66, 111
Lexington, South Carolina - 319
Liberty, Tennessee - 120
Lima, Illinois - 1
Lookout Mountain – 183-185
Louisville, Kentucky – 26, 46, 62, 90-91, 93-94, 97, 102, 107-108, 113, 181, 188
Lovejoy Station, Georgia – 282, 287-288, 293, 304-305

M
Macon, Georgia – 304-305
Marietta, Georgia – 257, 278, 293, 296, 299, 301, 307
Maysville, Alabama – 199, 201
McDonough, Georgia – 281-282
McMinnville, Tennessee – 120, 195
Memphis, Tennessee – 123, 131
Michigan - 9th Michigan - 334
Michigan - 19th Michigan - 129
Milledgeville, Georgia - 305
Milledgeville, Illinois – 84

Millen, Georgia - 305
Mirror - Mount Carroll Newspaper - 11, 49, 66, 270, 284
Missionary Ridge Road – 185
Missionary Ridge, Tennessee – 191-192, 202
Monroe's Crossroad in North Carolina – 320
Monticello, South Carolina - 319
Mount Carroll, Illinois – 1, 7, 9-11, 24, 28, 35, 52, 66, 84, 88, 104, 111, 125, 153, 172, 219, 233, 265, 267, 270, 290, 301, 324, 326, 331-332, 335, 342, 344-345
Mount Olive, North Carolina - 323
Mount Prospect, Illinois - 327
Mount Sterling, Kentucky – 39-40, 43-44, 46, 48, 111
Muldraugh Hill, Kentucky – 62
Munfordville, Kentucky – 62
Murfreesboro Pike in Tennessee - 79-80
Murfreesboro Road in Tennessee - 195
Murfreesboro, Tennessee – 70, 77, 102, 108, 120, 130, 155

N
Nashville, Tennessee – 52, 55, 79-80, 90, 94, 98-99, 101-105,

108-110, 112, 115, 119, 153, 155, 164-167, 169-171, 173-174, 176, 186, 199-201, 206, 216, 267
Nelson's Ferry, Tennessee – 195
Neuse River in North Carolina - 323
New Hope Church in Dallas, Georgia – 247
Newton Ferry, Georgia - 242
New York - 4-5, 306
Nicholasville, Kentucky – 39, 41-42
Nickajack Gap, Georgia - 232-234, 257, 327
Nickajack Trace, Georgia - 240
Normandy, Tennessee – 165
Noyes Creek, Georgia – 293

O
Ocmulgee River in Georgia – 305
Ogeechee River in Georgia - 307
Ogle County, Illinois – 25
Ohio - 9th Ohio Infantry - 115, 117
Ohio - 40th Ohio Infantry - 135
Oostenaula River, Georgia – 242, 245

P
Palestine, Texas - 344-345

Pea Vine Creek near Chickamauga River – 189
Peay's Ferry on the Catawba River in South Carolina – 319
Pegue's Ferry on the Great Pedee River – 320
Perryville, Kentucky – 46
Petersburg, Virginia - 276-277
Poe's Tavern in Tennessee – 177-178
Pond Springs – 185
Powder Springs, Georgia – 293
Preamble and Resolutions of the Second Brigade, General Baird's Division - 114-117
Proclamation of Amnesty and Reconstruction - 206
Prospect, Tennessee - 211
Pulaski, Tennessee – 209, 211
Pumpkin Vine Creek, Georgia - 247

R
Raccoon Valley, Tennessee – 183
Railroad - Atlanta - 257
Railroad – Atlanta & Macon – 278
Railroad – Atlanta to West Point - 277, 281, 285
Railroad - Chattanooga to Nashville - 300

Railroad – Louisville & Nashville – 62, 64
Railroad - Macon - 281, 304
Railroad – Memphis & Charleston – 197, 199
Railroad – North Carolina & Atlantic - 323
Railroad – Nashville & Decatur – 125
Railroad – South Carolina - 318
Railroad – Western & Atlantic - 293
Railroad – West Point – 288
Raleigh, North Carolina – 320, 323
Reed's Bridge on Chickamauga River – 189
Resaca, Georgia – 240-242, 244-245, 261, 268, 271, 293
Richland Creek in Tennessee – 211
Richmond, Virginia – 131, 253, 263, 266, 298, 329
Ringgold, Georgia – 184-185, 190, 203, 229, 231, 233, 235-238, 248, 252
Robertsville, South Carolina - 318
Rock Creek, Illinois – 1, 37, 84
Rock Springs, Illinois – 17
Rockford, Illinois – 21, 25, 28, 31-32, 36, 49, 58, 260

Rocky Mount Ferry in South Carolina - 319
Rome, Georgia – 244, 257
Rossville, Georgia – 185, 190

S

Salem, Illinois – 1, 2, 4, 33, 54, 60, 88, 108, 163, 221, 233, 260, 273, 308
Salkehatchie River near Barnwell, South Carolina – 318
Saluda River in South Carolina - 319
Sandtown, Georgia – 275, 277-278, 281
Savannah, Georgia – 196, 298, 301, 303, 306-309, 311-315, 317
Savannah, Illinois - 1
Savannah River between Georgia & South Carolina - 317
Sequatchie River in Tennessee - 177, 183, 198-199
Shelbyville, Tennessee – 120, 163-164, 173, 195
Shenandoah Valley, Virginia - 167
Sister's Ferry on the Savannah River - 317
Smithfield, North Carolina - 323

Smithfield Road in North Carolina - 322
Smith's Cross Roads near Resaca, Georgia – 241-242
Snake Creek Gap, Georgia – 240-241
Snake Creek in Georgia - 242
Snow's Hill, Tennessee - 155
Soldier's Aid Society - 107, 109
Solemn Grove, North Carolina – 320
Spottsylvania, Virginia – 253
Springfield, Illinois - 342-343
Springhill, Tennessee – 173
Squire Mitchell's near Crawfish Springs - 185
*Star of the West* - Federal Ship - 8
Stephenson County, Illinois – 25
Steven's Gap - 185
Stevenson, Alabama - 204
Stone Church, Georgia – 235
Stone's River in Murfreesboro, Tennessee – 70, 77, 79, 104, 120
Summertown, Tennessee – 183, 185
Sweetwater, Georgia – 217

T
*Tempest* - Packet Boat - 94-95, 97

Tennessee River in Alabama – 204, 218, 220
Tennessee River in Tennessee – 178-179, 195
Tennessee Valley – 177
Thatcher's Ford, Tennessee - 195
Therman's in the Sequatchie Valley, Tennessee – 177, 183
Thompson's Grove – 195
Tilton Road – 241
Tracy City, Tennessee - 177
Trenton, Georgia - 183
Triana, Alabama – 218, 220-223, 225, 230
Trickum, Georgia - 240
Triune, Tennessee – 153, 155, 162
Tullahoma, Tennessee - 120, 164-165, 173-174
Tunnel Hill, Georgia - 235, 240, 293
Twentieth Army Corps - Union - 188, 240, 318-319, 322

U
Unionville, Tennessee - 173
United States - 4$^{th}$ Cavalry - 80
University of the South, Tennessee - 176

V
Van Wert, Georgia – 293-294

Van Wert Road – 257
Vicksburg, Mississippi – 73, 76-77, 79, 89, 107-108, 113, 144, 146, 149, 156, 167
Villanow Cross Roads - 240
Villanow, Georgia – 240, 261, 293

**W**
Walden's Ridge, Tennessee - 177
Walnut Grove, Tennessee - 163
Wartrace, Tennessee – 120, 165, 169
Washington, D. C. - 330, 334
Washington, Illinois - 1
Wateree River, South Carolina - 319
Waynesboro, Georgia – 305-306, 316

Whippy Swamp in South Carolina - 318
White Side County, Illinois – 74
Widow's Creek – 203-204
Wilmington, North Carolina – 312
Winnebago, Minnesota – 7, 19-20, 31
Winnsboro, South Carolina - 319
Wisconsin - $1^{st}$ Wisconsin Cavalry - 16
Wisconsin - $22^{nd}$ Wisconsin - 129
Woodbury, Tennessee – 120
Woodland, Illinois - 1

**Y**
York, Illinois - 1, 8, 52, 108

The family genealogical histories as seen below are shown only to give the reader an idea of who the various people in the letters were and what their connections were within the family. They are not complete as there were many more children and descendants than are listed. People mentioned in the book are underlined.

Eugene Swaggart's paternal family[1]

## Swaggart Family

1 Hans Georg Schweigerth – changed later to George Sweigart, b. Germany, d. bef. April 23, 1806 in Earl Township, Lancaster Co., PA
   m. Elizabeth ?
  2 John Swaggart, b. PA, d. IL (based on will of John Swaggart, Jr. who mentions George as his brother).
     m. Elizabeth ?
    3 George Swaggart, b. Oct. 7, 1796 in PA, d. Nov. 18, 1857 in Carroll Co., IL
       m. 1st Elizabeth Brown on June 20, 1816 in St. Clair, IL
        4 Nelson Swaggart b. January 16, 1817 in St. Clair, IL, d. 1907 in OR
          m. Mary Adeline Harper
        4 Mary Ann Swaggart b. 1826 in St. Clair, IL, d. 1845 in Carroll Co, IL
          m. Clifton Lundy
          5 Leticia "Lettie" Lundy b. 1844, d.1861
       m. 2nd. Sally Stillwell on March 11, 1827 in St. Clair, IL
         no known children
       m. 3rd Magdolin Teeter on April 5, 1829 in St. Clair, IL
         no known children

---

[1] The genealogical history of the Swaggart family came from personal research and from information supplied by Lucille Bigelow, descendant of Nelson Swaggart and Richard Swaggart, descendant of Moses Swaggart, through his wife, Lynda Swaggart. Thomas Swaggart, descendant of Moses Swaggart, also sent some information.

m. 4th Sarah Whiteside/Reynolds on June 22, 1834 in Madison Co., IL. She d. Dec. 5, 1834 in Carroll Co., IL daughter of William Bolin Whiteside and Sarah Elizabeth Raine and divorced wife of Robert Reynolds, Jr.

m. 5th <u>Sarah Whiteside/Miller</u> in 1835, daughter of Uel Whiteside and Nancy Anne Raine. She was b. May 6, 1806 in Monroe Co., IL, d. June 7, 1872 in Carroll Co., IL. She had one son by her previous marriage to John Miller.

- <u>John Miller</u>, b. February 22, 1834 in Carroll Co., IL, d. bef. April 18, 1922 in OK.
  m. <u>Mary Ann ?</u>, b. 1839 in PA, d. in OK.

4 Uel Swaggart, b. 1836, d. 1840 in Lee Co., IL

4 <u>Moses "Mose" Swaggart,</u> b. November 12, 1837 in Carroll Co., IL, d. 1897 in Sumner Co., KS.
  m. <u>Amanda Ludisky "Dickie" VanAlstine</u>, b. April 16, 1837, d. March 14, 1895 in Sumner Co., KS.

  5 <u>Jennie "little Jennie" Swaggart</u>, b. 1858 in Carroll, Co., IL, d. 1920 in OK, buried in Sumner Co.,KS
     m. I. H. Fossitt

  5 <u>Frank "Frankie" Swaggart</u>, b. 1860 in Carroll Co., IL, d. 1918 in OK
     m. Bythia Davis

  5 <u>Frederick "Freddie" Swaggart</u>, b. 1863 in Carroll Co., IL, d. 1941 in OK

  5 Thomas Edwin Swaggart, b. 1867 in Carroll Co., IL d. 1940 in OK
     m. Verna S. Bennett

  5 Albert H. Swaggart, b. 1870 in Carroll Co., IL, d. 1942 in KS
     m. Lulu Bell Peyton

  5 Linneous Sylvester Swaggart, b.1872 on trail from IL to KS, d. 1943 in KS
     m. Pauline Shaw Lyles

4 Eugene McBride "Mack" Swaggart, b. October 22, 1841 in Carroll Co., IL, d. March 17, 1933 in OK
  m. Elvira "Vira" VanAlstine, b. June 15, 1840, d. August 10, 1908 in OK
    5 George "little Georgie" Swaggart, b. March 4, 1862 d. 1923 in AZ
      m. Olive "Olie" Medina Wright
    5 Nellie "the Baby" Eugenia Swaggart[2], b. November 25, 1864 in Carroll Co., IL, d. 1951 in TX
      m. Joseph Henry Briggs on June 18, 1885 in Caldwell, Sumner Co., KS
    5 Josephine Swaggart, b. October 15, 1869 in Mt. Carroll, IL, d. 1953 in OK
      m. Isaac Sylvanus Jones in 1895 in Sumner Co., KS
    5 Charles Swaggart, b. 1870 in Carroll Co., IL, d. 1907 in OK.
4 Anna "Annie" Swaggart, b. 1845 in Carroll Co., IL, d. 1922 in Carroll Co., IL
  m. Albert H. Nyman on November 22, 1866 in Carroll Co., IL
  no children

---

Eugene Swaggart's maternal family[3] - Whiteside

## Whiteside Family

1 William Whiteside, b. 1699 in North Ireland, d. 1777 in NC
  m. Elizabeth Stockton[4], b. 1700, d. 1795 in NC

---

[2] LeOla Äline Briggs Meredith (book dedication) was her daughter and her grandchildren were John Lee Meredith, Jr. (book dedication) and Betty E. More.
[3] The history of the Whiteside family came from William Whiteside, descendant of William Whiteside, and Bill Boulineau, who, along with Lucille Bigelow, put me in touch with him and forwarded information to me.

2 William Whiteside, b. 1747 in Albermarle Co., VA, d. 1815 in Monroe Co., IL.
   m. Mary Booth in 1774, b. 1748, d. 1825 in Monroe Co., IL
  3 William Bolin Whiteside, b. Dec. 23, 1777 in NC, d. 1833 in Madison Co., IL
    m. Sarah Elizabeth Raine, b. 1779, d. 1833 in Madison Co., IL
    They had ten children including:
    4 Sarah Whiteside, b. 1799 in Madison Co., IL, d. 1834 in Carroll Co., IL
      m. $1^{st}$ Robert Reynolds, Jr. in 1817, divorced.
      m. $2^{nd}$ George Swaggart, b. 1793, d. 1857
  3 Uel Whiteside, b. 1778 in NC, d. 1818 in Madison Co., IL
    m. Nancy Anne Raine (sister of Sarah Elizabeth (Raine)
    They had eight children including:
    4 Sarah Whiteside, b. 1806, d. 1872
      m. $1^{st}$ John Miller in 1832
      5 John Miller, b. 1834
        m. Mary Ann ?
        6 Lemuel Eugene Miller, b. 1858
        6 Samuel Miller, b. 1859
        6 Bertha Miller
        6 Evelyn Miller
        6 Harry Miller
        6 James A. Miller
        6 Mattie Miller
        6 Ninian E. Miller
        6 Genie Miller, b. bef. 1862
      m. $2^{nd}$. George Swaggart in 1835
      5 Uel Swaggart, b. 1836, d. 1840
      5 Moses "Mose" Swaggart
        m. Amanda Ludisky "Dickie"

---

[4] It is believed by this person that the person referred to as "Aunt Davis" in the book was a member of the Whiteside family as a number of the male children were named Davis after Davis Stockton, father of Elizabeth Stockton.

VanAlstine
See Swaggart family for descendants
5 Eugene McBride "Mack" Swaggart
   m. Elvira "Vira" VanAlstine
   See Swaggart family for descendants
5 Anna "Annie" Swaggart
   m. Albert Nyman

---

Elvira Van Alstine Swaggart's paternal family[5]

## Van Alstyne – Van Alstine Family

1 Martin Van Alstyne, b. abt. 1591 in the Netherlands
   m. Unknown
   2 Jan Martense Van Alstyne b. abt. 1623 in Meppel, Holland, d. 1698. Came to America in 1652.
      m. Dirckje Harmense, b. abt. 1625
      3 Lambert Janse Van Alstyne, b. 1652, Holland, d. 1703.
         m. Jannetje Mingael.
         4 Thomas Van Alstyne, bap. August 22, 1688 in Kinderhook, NY, d. August 1765.
            m. Maria Van Alen on December 12, 1718, b. 1695.
            5 Pieter Van Alstyne, b. May 16, 1736
               m. Marritje Conyn on September 17, 1760, b. abt. 1738
               6 Peter Van Alstine, b. August 16, 1776 in Athens, NY, d. in Salem, WI.
                  m. Jane Watson on October 2, 1803. She was

---

[5] All information concerning the earlier generations of the VanAlstine/VanAlstyne family came from Lester VanAlstine's book "VanAlstyne – Van Alstine Family History, Volume 3" and his daughter, Beverly Seitz. Later information concerning the immediate family of Elvira and her brother, Sylvester and sisters, Amanda Ludisky, Jennie and Marie came from family letters and photos handed down by my family as well as the family of Moses Swaggart and Amanda Ludisky VanAlstine Swaggart which were shared by Richard (a descendant) and Lynda Swaggart.

b. Oct. 17, 1785, d. December 9, 1848 in Salem, WI

7 Alonzo Van Alstine, b. August 17, 1804 in NY, d. March 13, 1840 in Cato, NY.
m. Emeline Surepto Dodge on June 25, 1827 in St. John's Day, NY. She was b. August 20, 1807 in NY, d. November 30, 1855 in Kenosha, WI.

   8 Lineas Van Alstine, b. April 1828, d. July, 1828 in NY

   8 Maria E. Van Alstine, b. abt. 1830 in NY, m. Andrew J. Guyon on October 15, 1858 in Carroll Co., IL

   8 Jennie "Jane" Van Alstine b. abt. 1832 in NY

   8 Sylvester "Vet" Brooken Van Alstine, b. 1835 in NY, d. 1912 in Beloit, WI.
m. Ellen Amanda Meyer, b. in Savannah, Carroll Co., IL

   8 Elvira Van Alstine, b. June 15, 1840 in Yorktown, NY, d. August 10, 1908 in OK
m. Eugene McBride "Mack" Swaggart on December 25, 1861, b. October 22, 1841 in Carroll Co., IL, d. March 17, 1933 in OK
(see Swaggart family for children)

   8 Amanda Ludisky "Dickie" Van Alstine, b. April 16, 1837 in NY, d. March 14, 1895 in Sumner Co., KS
m. Moses Swaggart on July 3, 1857, Whiteside Co., IL, b. November 12, 1837, Carroll Co., IL, d. 1897 in Sumner Co., KS.
see Swaggart family for children

Elvira Van Alstine's maternal family[6] - Dodge

## Dodge Family

1 John Dodge, b. England, d.1635 in Sometshire
   m. Margary ?
   2 Richard Dodge b. 1602 in England, d. 1671 in MA
      m. Edith ?
      3 Lt. John Dodge b. 1631 in England, d. 1711 in MA
         m. Sarah ?
         4  John Dodge b. 1662 in MA, d. 1704 in MA
            m. Martha Fiske b. 1667 in MA, d. 1697 in MA
            5 Amos Dodge b. 1690 in MA, d. 1765 in CT
               m. Mary Webb b. 1694 in MA
               6 John Dodge b. 1724 in CT, d. 1797 in MA
                  m. Sarah Morse b. 1732 in CT, d. 1795 in MA
                  7 Ozias Dodge b. 1763 in CT, d. 1818 in NY
                     m. Elizabeth Warrin b. 1764 in MA
                     8  John Dodge b. 1783 in MA, d. 1867 in Ozaukee Co., WI
                        m. Sarah (Sally) Bullen b.1787 in MA, d. 1861 in Kenosha, WI
                        9  Emeline Surepto Dodge b. 1807 in NY, d. 1855 in Kenosha, WI
                           m. Alonzo VanAlstine b. 1804, d. 1840
                           10 Lineas VanAlstine b. 1828
                           10 Maria E. VanAlstine b. 1830
                              m. Andrew J. Guyon
                           10 Jennie "Jane" VanAlstine b. 1832
                              m. John Merril (from a letter from Jennie Merril and photos of the

---

[6] Information concerning the Dodge family came first from Jerry Harris, descendant of Edward Judson Dodge, and was verified (the first generations) by the books "Genealogy of the Dodge Family, 1629 – 1898" by Joseph T. Dodge and "Genealogy of the Dodge Family, 1898 – 1998" by Robert Livingston Dodge. All of the siblings of Emeline Surepto Dodge and of her father, John Dodge were due to research done by Jerry Harris who kindly shared his information with me. Other information was verified through photos owned by Richard and Lynda Swaggart.

children and of John Merril in family records but no proof has been found of the marriage)
   10 <u>Elvira "Vira" VanAlstine</u> b. 1840, d. 1908
      m. <u>Eugene McBride "Mack" Swaggart</u>
   10 <u>Sylvester "Vet" Brooken VanAlstine</u>
      m. Ellen Amanda Meyer
   10 <u>Amanda Ludisky "Dickie" Van Alstine</u>
      m. <u>Moses "Mose" Swaggart</u>
9 <u>Permilia "Pamila" Dodge</u>
   m. <u>Orlando Foster</u>
9 <u>Leander (S) Whitman Dodge</u>
   m. <u>Martha</u> ?
9 <u>Philander W. Dodge</u>
9 Achsa Dodge
9 Edson Dodge
9 Edwin Dodge
9 <u>Lyman Dodge</u>
   m. <u>Lizzie</u> ?
9 <u>Susan Nehsuh Dodge</u>
   m. <u>David Crosit</u>
   10 <u>Mary Crosit</u>
9 Wallace Dodge
9 <u>Edward Judson Dodge</u>, b. 1822, d. 1910
   m. 1st Elizabeth Posson
   m. 2nd Elizabeth Jane Thornton Wells

www.ingramcontent.com/pod-product-compliance
Lightning Source LLC
Chambersburg PA
CBHW071436300426
44114CB00013B/1453